"Justice delayed is justice denied? Not in this case. At long last, and at the skillful hands of Dean Reuter, a particularly nasty Nazi has been brought before the bar of history for a lasting sort of justice—the measured but stern judgment of a meticulous historian."

—GEORGE F. WILL, Pulitzer Prize–winning columnist

"*The Hidden Nazi* is a revelation: a spellbinding, at times harrowing new history of an epoch we thought had been covered from every angle, trained on as ingenious and monstrous a villain as total, global war could produce—Hans Kammler. With the invaluable scholarship and perseverance of his colleagues Colm Lowery and Keith Chester, Dean Reuter delivers a riveting mix of first-person accounts and expert analysis, from the excruciating depths of the Nazi slave and death camps to the thrilling heights and annihilative aspirations of Nazi rocket science. And of course, the gripping, morally vexing mystery: to deal or not to deal with the devil who has something invaluable to trade?"

—ANDREW C. MCCARTHY, a former federal prosecutor honored with the Attorney General's Distinguished Service and Exceptional Service Awards and the bestselling author of *Willful Blindness* and *The Grand Jihad*

"Reuter, Lowery, and Chester probe one of the enduring mysteries of World War II, the extent to which the United States absorbed and sought to utilize Nazi scientists in the race to develop the atom bomb. This is a riveting look into the awful tradeoff between pragmatism and justice."

—AMITY SHLAES, bestselling author of *Germany: The Empire Within* and *The Forgotten Man*

"Werner von Braun called him 'the greatest rogue and adventurer I have ever seen.' Albert Speer damned him as 'one of Himmler's most brutal and most ruthless henchmen.' He engineered the Holocaust, built the concentration camps, and perfected the gas chambers and crematoria. He pioneered slave labor and masterminded rocket, fighter jet, and secret wonder-weapon production. And at the end of World War II he vanished without a trace. Enigmatic SS general Hans Kammler is the most diabolic Nazi you've never heard of. Dean Reuter takes readers on a gripping, exciting, and suspenseful hunt in search of the mysterious war criminal. *The Hidden Nazi* is a fascinating forensic detective story that reads like a great crime thriller. Did Kammler fake his death and survive the war? How did he escape justice? Did America strike a deal with the Devil in exchange for his secrets? Splendidly written with verve and expertise, *The Hidden Nazi* is storytelling at its best. Dean Reuter and his co-authors combine superb narrative history with a riveting personal memoir of the harrowing psychological journey into Hans Kammler's heart of darkness."

—JAMES L. SWANSON, Edgar Award–winning *New York Times*–bestselling author of *Manhunt: The 12 Day Chase for Lincoln's Killer*

"It's strange that no one has yet written a biography of SS general Hans Kammler, one of the brutal masterminds of the German military-industrial complex and the Holocaust. But when you read *The Hidden Nazi* you will realize that until now no one had the knowledge, persistence, and sheer nerve that the authors brought to the job of unlocking the multiple mysteries surrounding this evil genius of the Third Reich. It's a story where *Schindler's List* meets *Doctor Strangelove*. Read it, be amazed and shocked by what Kammler did, and outraged by how he escaped final justice; but above all read *The Hidden Nazi*."

—ARTHUR HERMAN, Pulitzer Prize finalist and author of *How the Scots Invented the Modern World* and *1917: Lenin, Wilson, and the Birth of the New World Disorder*

"*The Hidden Nazi* by Dean Reuter is a stunning achievement. This tightly drawn portrait of SS General Hans Kammler takes the reader from his personal life as recalled in interviews with his son through his notorious work supervising construction of underground factories like Mittelwerk-Dora, where Wernher von Braun's V-2 rockets were built, and at Auschwitz where this ruthless Nazi perfected the gas chambers. Throughout the book Reuter tells a riveting tale of horror, ending with Kammler's escape from justice. But where to? Finally, I must compliment the researchers Colm Lowery and Keith Chester for collecting a massive treasure trove of documents that made this excellent book possible."

—LINDA HUNT, Investigative Reporters and Editors Award–winning author of *Secret Agenda: The U.S. Government, Nazi Scientists and Project Paperclip, 1945 to 1991*

"Remarkable. For sheer, dogged persistence alone, the authors of this extraordinary investigation deserve widespread recognition. They have shone a powerful and bright light on what may prove to be one of the last great secrets of the war."

—NICK COOK, author of *The Hunt for Zero Point*

"*The Hidden Nazi* is a must-read, especially in this age of increasing Holocaust denial and minimization. The horrors of the Holocaust and their primary perpetrators must be documented so that future generations will have the evidence necessary to defend the truth."

—ALAN DERSHOWITZ, legal scholar, high-profile defense attorney, and author of *Defending Israel: The Story of My Relationship with My Most Challenging Client*

The Hidden Nazi

THE HIDDEN NAZI

The Untold Story of America's Deal with the Devil

DEAN REUTER,
Colm Lowery, and Keith Chester

REGNERY
HISTORY

RegneryHistory™ is a trademark of Salem Communications Holding Corporation
Regnery® is a registered trademark of Salem Communications Holding Corporation

Cataloging-in-Publication data on file with the Library of Congress

ISBN 978-1-62157-735-5
ebook ISBN 978-1-62157-896-3

Published in the United States by
Regnery History, an imprint of
Regnery Publishing
A Division of Salem Media Group
300 New Jersey Ave NW
Washington, DC 20001
www.RegneryHistory.com

Manufactured in the United States of America

10 9 8 7 6 5 4 3 2 1

Books are available in quantity for promotional or premium use. For information on discounts and terms, please visit our website: www.Regnery.com.

To my loving family, and to B2247, B2248, B2249. . . .
—Dean Reuter

To my loving wife, Angela, and my amazing children, Amy, Conor, Ryan, Owen, and Jack, without whose love and support I could not have accomplished such a monumental task. Thank you to my father, John, for introducing me to World War II history and to my dear mother, Mary, for introducing me to the library!
—Colm Lowery

To the late journalist and author, Tom Agoston, whose book Blunder! *ignited the trail*
—Keith Chester

CONTENTS

Incredible

What if one of the most secret, fantastic stories of World War II has not yet been told? The question nagged me as I set the cordless phone on my desk, having just concluded one of the more improbable conversations of my life. In this, our initial conversation on the topic of SS general Hans Kammler, Keith Chester had been talking about exposing a major "untold story" of the war. A tale about a superpowerful, supposedly-dead-but-still-alive Nazi officer, secret German weapons, German nuclear weapons, stolen treasure, missing documents, covert deals with high-ranking American officials—even a coverup that has lasted decades. Absolutely preposterous claims, I thought. The stuff of fiction. But Keith had assured me it was all true; he said he had the proof, or at least most of it. I was beyond incredulous, but mostly held my tongue while he talked. He had reached me at my northern Virginia home office from his house north of Baltimore, having already researched this project for years.

I knew my skepticism was well-placed. Although World War II is one of the most fascinating eras in history, it is also one of the most thoroughly researched and documented periods of human existence.

Countless books and multivolume sets have been written on every conceivable aspect of the epoch. Feature-length films, documentaries, articles, oral histories, university courses, diaries—even books of poetry. The war was the most massive undertaking in the history of man, perhaps second only to the endless attempts to research, define, document, and explain it. What could Keith possibly have discovered? How could he, not even a trained historian, have come up with anything of even remote significance almost seventy years after the war ended? How could he find something "mind-bending," to use his phrase? Nuclear weapons? Mythical surviving Nazis? Not a chance, I told myself.

Keith's claim that he had government documents did surprise me, but frankly I doubted his ability to interpret whatever records he had in his possession. There is no untold story of the war, I assured myself. Not in the broad sense my old college friend was urging. There cannot be. Certainly there are gaps in our knowledge and there are things left to be discussed. Important new information continues to trickle out, but it only changes bits and pieces of history—the edges, nothing fundamental. Nothing truly revelatory could remain unknown for decades. Not in this world.

But I didn't have to buy into his research at this point. Keith was a friend. All he was asking of me, as a lawyer, was help in drafting a contract between him and another researcher, Irish university professor Dr. Colm Lowery, as they were entering a joint phase of their research. Already having worked independently for years on this story, Keith and Colm had found each other when Colm made an anonymous posting on a World War II discussion forum. Keith, the snoop, managed to trace Colm through the Internet and cold-called him at his office across the Atlantic. Colm, taken aback, nevertheless took Keith's call, curious as to how he had been tracked down. There followed several exchanges; it was like two boxers circling in the ring, learning about each other, but trust was established fairly quickly. Each of them had been toiling alone, and each was looking for someone like himself nearly as much as he was hunting Kammler. Refreshed by finding a shared interest and the same obsession, the duo was a perfect pairing—Keith with unending drive and commitment, Colm with a base of knowledge about the war that allowed him to sort the wheat from the chaff; Keith with access to records and sources in the U.S., Colm the continental traveler and researcher. Little did they know that they would spend a combined thirty thousand hours strategizing, digging, reading, filing, and interviewing. Keith told me that Colm's documents and interviews, obtained mostly from European sources, perfectly feathered his own official records, filling in important voids in the Kammler story. He described Colm, a scientist, as a serious and very learned student of the war. I silently noted that Colm, certainly highly educated and no doubt an intelligent man, was not a trained historian either. And so that was their team. Two relative novices, one of whom I'd known for over thirty years. The other I had never met.

If Keith was the rocket-fueled energy of the team, then Colm was the careful voice of reason, seeing the possibilities but always cautious, questioning, never jumping to conclusions. I liked that immediately when we met by telephone later. I also enjoyed his accent and his affable wit. Colm has the rare art of finding humor, but never at someone else's expense. From his home in Northern Ireland he had traveled through Europe extensively, visiting battle sites and archives. He had purchased and restored a vintage World War II battle wagon, painstakingly collecting rare parts, turning it into a museum-quality piece of history. He had even held his bachelor party in Normandy, watching the sun come up over Omaha Beach with his "mates," as he would say, awed by the scene stretched out before him. The same sand, waves, and terrain the D-Day landing forces had braved. Now forty-five, he already had impressive credentials in his field; his work in biomedical sciences—including the development of rapid DNA methods and their application to bioterrorism—had landed him a Winston Churchill Fellowship and the opportunity to travel worldwide to attend conferences and deliver lectures. Colm became interested in astronomy and space travel as a young man. He developed a fascination with the weaponry of World War II—and ultimately with Germany's undisputed lead rocket scientist, Wernher von Braun, who after the war went to America to head the U.S. military missile project and its successful moon launch. Colm was eventually drawn to the story of the supervisor of the Nazi rocket project von Braun worked on and Germany's advanced weapons research: SS general Hans Kammler. I got the impression that all of Colm's spare time was spent on World War II research until I learned that he is also an accomplished guitar player. No matter what else is happening on any given day, he carves out time to play and practice. Colm grew up in the picturesque resort town of Newcastle, Ireland, with the Irish Sea as his front yard. Growing up he helped his father dig potatoes and worked with his uncles building houses, either the source or a symptom of his mechanical aptitude.

Keith was asking me to draft a formal agreement between himself and Colm, but I felt there was more behind his call. He was telling me more than necessary—the details of their project, their theories, hints at some of their findings. I felt like I was being sold something, but I didn't know what. Maybe my old friend was using me as a sounding board? I liked Keith and I would happily draft a contract for him, even at no charge, whether or not the project was on a solid historical footing. He didn't need to prove himself to me. Perhaps he sensed my skepticism and was trying to convince me that he and Colm were onto something real. I did wonder about his objectivity, even with Colm by his side. Keith seeks intrigue and pines for it. I worried that he might too easily see a conspiracy where none really existed—willing it into existence. Keith is a different animal from Colm. He's an excitable guy who loves to be thrilled, living life wide-eyed and full of wonder, full of energy, always smiling, a bit of mischief in his expression. These attributes, I knew, could color his analysis of the documents he had discovered—even if he had had the training to interpret them in the first place. He so much wanted this to be a big story—I could hear it in his voice. He wasn't just talking about a scholarly article. This hidden Nazi history, he insisted, must be told in a full-length book, perhaps more than one book. I suspected Keith even had ideas about which Hollywood heavyweights would play the key roles in the inevitable film adaptation. With some publishing experience, I had seen this before—talented, ambitious people moving from their story concept right to a book title, to detailed book cover art, to movie treatment, posters, fame, glory, flashbulbs, accolades, division of the spoils, even literary and film prizes—all before a single word had been written. But, I reflected, these same traits would cut in a useful direction, too. They would lead Keith to suspect things others failed to imagine. They would drive him to pursue the story beyond the point of exhaustion. A mere glimmer of success, and he would persist long after others would have given up. Like a hunting dog on a scent, he would single-mindedly run a trail no one else could even sense. And Keith was no fool. To the contrary, I knew him to be not just an indefatigable worker, but also resourceful and smart. If there was something to be found, he would find it. Though I was doubtful, I was putting nothing more than a bit of my time at risk.

As we ended this first call, I consigned Keith's wild claims to the back of my mind and concentrated on drafting the contract. My day job as general counsel and vice president of the Federalist Society kept me plenty busy. In my own personal time I had been involved in a couple of serious book projects: *Confronting Terror*, which examined legal issues in the War on Terror, and *Liberty's Nemesis*, a study of the unending growth of the administrative state in the U.S. On those projects I was privileged to work with contributors who included bestselling authors, former U.S. attorneys general, judges, elite law school professors and deans, elected and appointed officials, and practitioners—all heavyweights in the legal community. And even before finishing the second, I had begun planning the third. Along the way, I was appointed by the president and confirmed by the Senate to serve part-time as vice chairman on the board of directors of a federal grant-making agency. I was also trying to be a worthy husband and busily raising my two children—by far the most important work in my life. I also spent far too much time exercising, mostly running, usually putting in as much as thirty miles a week (at my pace that took some time). So I had plenty to keep me busy beyond Keith and Colm's project. But, oddly, as the days after our call turned into weeks, I realized Keith had managed to pull me in to some extent. I found myself intrigued by his claims, by the documents he mentioned. It was like magma bubbling just below the surface. I realized I was interested enough to stay close to the project as it unfolded and as Keith and Colm's research continued—just to see what happened. I caught myself replaying our conversation in my mind, dissecting it. What if? I kept asking. What if Germany had been working on a nuclear weapon and, after the war, the U.S. recruited the war-criminal commander of that secret project and conspired to keep his secrets safe, burying the story? What if Keith and Colm could prove it? That would be extraordinary.

If Keith had been trying to bait me into greater involvement in this project, he had done a masterful job. I've never asked him if that was his original aim—to give me enough information about the project he and Colm were embarking on to entice me to become the author of their book. Looking back now, I see I was an easy mark. Like every other American grade-schooler, I had learned about the critical moments and larger arcs of U.S. history. I got strong doses of the history of the founding of this country, the Revolutionary War, the Civil War, World War I, and World War II. And as a young adult I had a special interest in World War II. I was always spellbound by the overwhelming barbarity of the era. How did Hitler co-opt an entire nation, and how were the collaborators so thoroughly enlisted in his campaign of horror? How could so many be so vicious, especially off the battlefield? If I allowed myself to probe one layer deeper, I was disturbed by my own macabre fascination with the evil that pervaded World War II.

And I had one very personal connection to the war: although I wasn't even alive at the time, I felt some bizarre sense of responsibility and guilt for what the Germans did. You see, I was born on German soil in Heidelberg in 1960. And all my ancestors are German. My family names include Reuter, Klein, Hasselbeck, and Krubitzer—even though I am and always have been an American citizen. Both of my parents are Americans who were born in the United States. My father was a U.S. Army officer, and it was only happenstance that he was stationed in Germany at the time of my birth. My forbears, though from Germany, had immigrated to the United States long ago—before 1900. None of my family members fought for Germany in the Great War, much less World War II. On the contrary, they served proudly in the United States military as freedom-loving Americans. We were the Allies, the liberators, the good guys. Still, I had a nagging sense of responsibility and even shame for what the Germans had done. They were—in some remote, but traceable way—my kin. I shared at least some ancient DNA with the regime that prosecuted the war, causing an incomprehensible fifty-five million deaths. This, I think, drove me to learn more about what Keith had dangled in front of me during that first memorable call. So while I decided to help him and act as his attorney, I also began to do a little research of my own, at first online. Eventually, though, I would find myself reaching out to others, spending hours at the Holocaust Memorial Museum Library, and plowing through every World War II book I could find. Keith and Colm began to feed me documents selectively, keeping me interested. Before it was all done, I would go from contract-drafter of their joint venture to the primary author of this book—a book that answers Keith's provocative opening "what if" question in a shocking way. In the end, seeing their entire collection of documents and interviews, I would be transformed from skeptic to believer. I would willingly join the effort to rewrite the story of Germany's ambitious secret weapons programs—the story of the hideous man responsible for overseeing those super-secret projects, the scandalous details of America's dark courtship of him, and the subsequent coverup. It is a spectacular and almost unbelievable tale involving international intrigue at the highest levels, deceit, duplicity, unknown weapons programs, treasure, and the nearly complete shift in the post-war balance of world power. If I hadn't been part of this story, I'm not sure I would believe it myself.

CHAPTER ONE

"One of Himmler's Most Brutal and Most Ruthless Henchmen"

*"You said your father was morally compromised.
Where do you think he first went wrong?"*

"Impossible to say, don't you think?"

—*interview of Jörg Kammler*

"I 'm thrilled to report I met with Jörg," my email to Keith and Colm began. "I thought he was going to shut me out, but he didn't. We talked for over an hour. More to follow."

I was on the return train from Osnabrück, Germany, home of Jörg Kammler, son of SS general Hans Kammler—the man Nazi armaments minister Albert Speer had called a "most brutal and most ruthless henchman" to SS chief Heinrich Himmler.[1] I had just interviewed Jörg and was headed back to the Radisson Blu Hotel in Hamburg, my base of operations in Germany, which was two hours away. After sending the quick email to my colleagues, I began to furiously type a summary of the extraordinary encounter that had just concluded while all the details were still fresh in my mind. I would share my full notes with Keith Chester and Colm Lowery later. Before I could get three sentences into my summary, though, my computer chimed with an incoming email.

"Well done. You've played it just right, obviously. Can't wait for the details." It was Colm, emailing me from his home in Northern Ireland. Before I finished reading Colm's email, I heard another chime—this time an email from Keith: "OMG! You're killing it!" Then another insistent

1

chime, again from Keith, "TELL US!!" I spent the next two hours writing up the interview—after turning off the notifications on my laptop so I could work in peace.

That morning I had walked to the Hamburg train station, just steps from my hotel, to travel to Osnabrück, which is southwest of Bremen. After having purchased a round-trip ticket at the kiosk, I found myself alone on the platform. I had come to the station not knowing the schedule, and the next train was twenty-five minutes out. I waited. I admit to being on my heels. I hadn't been in Germany since I was a young child and it felt, well, foreign. I was also planning to show up at Jörg Kammler's home unannounced—an uncharacteristic move for me, as I tend to be risk-averse. This could be a giant waste of time, or even lead to some sort of ugly confrontation, walking in on the surviving child of a Nazi madman. I had just one shot at interviewing him, so I did everything I could to be prepared. It was nerve-racking carrying my own high expectations and the hopes of my colleagues with me.

Sitting on a bench on the platform, oblivious to those around me, I reviewed what I knew, switching back and forth between a fistful of papers and information logged on my laptop. I was relying on a combined thirty years of research handed over to me by my colleagues—with a couple years of my own spare time thrown in.

"Some of the most heroic and dastardly acts in human reckoning occurred during the war," Colm, our historian, had reminded me when I first got involved in this venture. "At its end, the geopolitical world had been reshaped, new superpowers had emerged, millions of people had perished, and tens of millions more people were maimed, or homeless, or refugees. Over the course of six years, almost everyone on the globe had their life changed, if not devastated, in some very personal and important way."

I have always been perplexed by it—the whole world turned upside down when one of the most highly civilized cultures known to man went screamingly off the rails. All of this is recorded by historians and widely understood. But within this colossal landscape, one man is largely unknown to history, despite his war crimes: SS general Hans Kammler, the target of our investigation. Kammler had avoided scrutiny, apparently because of his death at the end of the war. But we had turned up evidence that Kammler was alive after the date of his supposed suicide—and that American authorities were involved in the cover-up.

Kammler's character is as irresistible to me as it is loathsome. He became a remarkably powerful man in the Nazi hierarchy, playing a central role in some of the most violent and despicable parts of the Holocaust, ultimately ruling over Germany's slave labor trade and its ultra-secret weapons programs. Documents compiled by Keith and Colm tell tales of Kammler's deeds that are, frankly, so horrific that they are hard to absorb. Kammler's rank, Obergruppenführer, was the highest possible commissioned rank in the SS. From 1942 to 1944, an extremely select group of just seventy-five Nazis was elevated to that honor. And *one* man alone achieved that distinction in the final year of the war: Hans Kammler. To me, that was striking.

These were my thoughts on the platform, even as the crowd grew around me—a mixture of locals and tourists, I thought. Much of our information on Kammler's early years and career came from original documents, but some of it was from Kammler's descendants. Colm had been in touch with various Kammler family members and associates for years, and they had been able to provide useful information, helping paint a full picture of this mysterious man. As the primary author of our book project, I was eager to meet Jörg, Hans Kammler's son; I felt I had an obligation to hear his story before we published.

I was momentarily distracted as an eastbound train entered the station, idled for a moment, and then carried on, leaving the platform on the far side of the tracks empty of people. I had already been in touch with Jörg by email, introduced by Colm, but he had shown no interest in meeting me. So I had decided to roll the dice and show up unannounced. Jörg could provide a unique angle on his father, but I was also interested in his own story. I had read riveting accounts of the surviving children of infamous Nazis, always wondering how they dealt with the sins of their father, and I admit to some morbid curiosity: *What was it like to grow up with a surname like Eichmann, Höss, or Himmler?* I was lost in thought when my train pulled into the station. This was my point of no return, I thought, as I boarded and found a seat. It was only a two-hour ride, and I spent most of it with my head buried in documents, furiously scrawling questions I thought I should ask, organizing and reorganizing. I was sitting across the aisle from a young family who broke out an authentic German picnic of pickled fish, potato dishes, and some sort of slaw. The only difference from what I might have been expecting was that they weren't costumed in *Sound of Music* garb, but were dressed just like I was. They spoke quietly among themselves as I continued my work, the children well-behaved, smiling at me when I looked up. I felt a little "watched," or at least pegged as an outsider, and wondered what they were saying with their quiet voices. I wasn't quite myself; I knew that from the way I couldn't help asking myself questions about this innocent family. Every person I had met or even seen in Germany—from the hotel clerk, to the waiter, to the train staff and passengers—I had unfairly dropped into my war paradigm: *Who were they? Did their fathers fight in the war? Were their ancestors Nazis? SS? Are they sympathizers?* I was making everyone a suspect. Could it be that I was too far down the World War II rabbit hole? I needed to settle down.

Then, perhaps from nerves, I waffled a bit, changing plans midstream, using the train's Wi-Fi to send Jörg an email, though I had planned on arriving completely unannounced. Before I had more time to agonize, we pulled into the station. I exchanged pleasant nods with the German family as I disembarked. They were traveling on. I caught a cab outside the station, amazed to see so many Mercedes taxis. The driver wouldn't take U.S. dollars, but he would take a credit card. This was the point of no return, I thought, entering the cab—and realized that this was my second self-identified point of no return!

Without the constant distraction of my materials, which I had stowed away, I found myself getting ever more anxious in the cab as I made the final approach to the home of Kammler's son. This was becoming real:

the man I was going to accost was the offspring of a genuine Nazi sociopath. It would be an extraordinary opportunity to meet him, even a privilege to get that close to history. If I could.

Thinking I might have the door slammed in my face or that Jörg, who hadn't responded to my email, might not even be home, I asked the cab driver to wait. The house was a modest two-story in the inner suburbs on a lot that couldn't have been more than a quarter acre and was overgrown with bushes and foliage to the extent that I couldn't see the door from the curb. As I approached, I realized the address was one half of a small duplex. Coming up the walk, I saw a woman in the picture window, felt as if I was stepping out of civilization, and regretted not having left a trail of bread crumbs. I admit that I may have looked over my shoulder to confirm the cab was staying. I had a momentary concern that I might never be heard from again. *What was I thinking?*

I rang the bell on the side door, the main entrance, and waited for what seemed like too long. The woman I had seen in the window, in her sixties or seventies, answered the door, and I identified myself, telling her that I had been in touch with Jörg and had him sent an email that I was nearby and hoping to chat—trying to minimize the intrusion. She disappeared, closing the door firmly behind her. I waited on the doorstep. She returned and asked me for my name again, then disappeared again after holding up one finger—which could mean, *please wait one moment*, or possibly, *I only need one reason not to let you in*. She was gone a long time, and I realized she didn't even need the one reason not to let me in; she just didn't have to come back. But she did reappear, and cautiously bade me enter. I asked for one minute to dismiss the cab. Back at the curb, I paid the driver and got my overnight bag (I was prepared to spend the night locally, if need be). When I turned around, the woman was right behind me, giving me a start. Like a ghost.

"On second thought, my husband can't see you. He's ill. Too ill." Her English was good. Her thin arms crossed in front of her. "Too ill," she repeated. So this was Mrs. Kammler. "You must go."

"Can I just see him? Just a question or two? I've come all the way from the United States. Can I just say 'Hello'?" This was totally out of character for me. As a lawyer, I can be insistent on behalf of a client, to the point of being a perfect ass. Advocating for myself, I do less well.

But I suppose in this moment I thought of myself as representing Keith and Colm. I became insistent. "I've come a long way. Just a minute or two, a question or two," I repeated. Then I waited.

"For a minute or two," she relented, her arms still crossed.

We went back up the walk and then into the kitchen where, with a silent tilt of her head, without breaking stride or looking back at me, Mrs. Kammler indicated I could leave my bag. I confirmed that Jörg wasn't well when I saw him lying atop a hospital bed, side rails up, in the darkened parlor, which had been converted to an in-home hospital room. It was very warm and permeated with a heavy, sour odor I could not identify. Jörg had had a stroke, but he was able to sit up without raising the back of the bed, and to speak clearly—English with a heavy German accent.

I said I was sorry to disturb him and thanked him for seeing me, "especially after I had come so far," I emphasized. "I'm sorry you didn't see my email." Or I may have said "emails," making it sound as if I had given him multiple warnings of my arrival.

The house was simple but functional—austere, with the well-worn look of a lived-in home. Not a stick of new furniture in the place. When Colm told me, much later, that surviving Nazis had stashed stolen money and valuables away in preparation for a planned-for Fourth Reich, I recalled this scene and thought, *The hidden money didn't reach the second generation.*

Mrs. Kammler brought in a straight-back chair from the kitchen for me and positioned it at the foot of the bed, at an odd distance, too far away. I scooched a foot or two closer as I sat down. She may have noticed. She sat in an armchair, to my right, now further from Jörg than I was, a bit outside our conversation. After introductions, Jörg seemed much more at ease and open than his wife, who repeatedly interrupted his responses and once or twice spoke to him sharply in German. When I was sure Jörg was about to consent to recording our conversation, she quickly said, "No."

"No recording"—a short statement, punctuated by a single arched eyebrow. She repeatedly tried to call the interview to a close along the way. Again, it was unlike me, but I essentially subtly ignored her, asking "Just one more question" several times—moving forward in my chair as if I were about to rise, or just sitting mum for what seemed like too long (an old investigator's trick) until Jörg, unable to bear the prolonged silence, began speaking again. It was positively exhilarating, like back in my government days when I was interviewing someone suspected of embezzling or outright theft. Not that Jörg or his wife had done anything remotely improper, I just saw him as a challenge—quarry, even. I thought Mrs. Kammler might be trying to protect the reputation of Hans Kammler, the family patriarch, but then wondered whether Jörg might want to publish his own book, so that she didn't want him to share any of his exclusive information with me, at least not without something in return. In my summary later to Keith and Colm, I said, "I wonder whether his wife, and not Jörg, had been responding to all my emails over the past several months. Perhaps Jörg knew about me for the first time when I walked into his parlor. She was definitely the gatekeeper."

I had a long list of questions, carefully sequenced, that I had planned to put to Jörg. But given the tension his wife created, I decided to rely on my memory. I have done interviews of all sorts over my career, but this one was different—an absolute rush. It felt as if I were sitting with a living relic, a talking piece of history, a true unvarnished (if not unbiased) original source. It was as if I was able to reach out and touch history directly—like holding tattered, musty documents, but being able to pose questions and expect and receive answers. Oh, how I wished it were just the two of us in the room.

To begin, Jörg confirmed for me that his father, Hans Friedrich Karl Franz Kammler, was born the son of Franz and Marie Kammler on August 26, 1901, in Stettin, in what is now northwest Poland—less than a two-hour drive from Berlin. Stettin, more a city than a town, was a major seaport at the time of Kammler's birth with a population of just over two hundred thousand. All but a small handful of its citizens were Protestants, with fewer than 5 percent Catholics and Jews. Hans Kammler had the good fortune to be born into the majority.

"Your grandparents' choice of name for your father is interesting: Hans Friedrich Karl Franz Kammler. Franz obviously follows from your grandfather's name. Does the "Friedrich Karl" refer to Karl Friedrich Schinkel, the famous German architect?"

"No," Jörg said firmly and quickly, as if he had anticipated the question, "that is a mere coincidence." He seemed mildly offended by the question, though I don't know why. No one but Colm could have been so thoroughly immersed in our materials as to catch this possible Kammler-Schinkel connection. Schinkel's most noteworthy buildings, found in Berlin, were created in the early 1800s. He had also famously been commissioned by Frederick William III of Prussia to design the original Iron Cross—evoking the cross borne by the Teutonic Knights of the fourteenth century. Created in 1813, Schinkel's Iron Cross was adopted as the symbol of the German army from 1871 to early 1918, then reintroduced in 1939 with a Swastika in the center. Issued in two grades, First Class and Second Class, the Iron Cross was awarded for bravery in battle. Hans Kammler would distinguish himself by earning both.

"Your father's earliest years are something of a mystery to us," I said next, "a problem for us in our book."

"Unfortunately, I have no personal memories of my father." Jörg was himself born in February 1940, so he was just five years old when the war ended and his father vanished. "Times were certainly hard growing up without a father. The hardest part for the Kammler family," Jörg said, almost as if he weren't a member, "was not knowing whether or not your father was dead. It was truly a mystery. There were many rumors that the Americans had him, that the Russians had him." I knew Jörg was speaking of rumors of then, not now. For more than seventy years the world has believed that Kammler died at the end of the war.

"We constantly sought out soldiers and other people returning from America or Russia to get information. Other people came to us and said he was alive." It sounded to me as if the Kammler family had sought and received information on his fate well beyond the 1948 adjudication of his death—indicating that they thought him alive at least at that point, even though they had had him declared dead. That was fascinating. Although Jörg seemed to believe "the official story" was the correct story, that belief had been slow to congeal.

"Did your mother have favorite stories she would tell about your father when you were growing up?"

"Of course," Jörg said. Then there was a long pause, and no further information. I waited. Still nothing.

"What can you tell me about the stories?" I nudged, as if there hadn't been an awkward silence.

"They were intimate accounts," he said, waving his hand to indicate that that line of inquiry was finished. Too personal. Move on.

"What has become of your siblings, the other Kammler children?" "Two sisters and one brother are still alive." But, he added quickly, he was the only one, save a nephew of his, with interest in his father. I believed him, though I thought there was a bit of dual purpose here—he didn't want me to contact them. "The others are content to let it fade into the past."

We know for certain that Hans Kammler turned out wretchedly, but we do not know whether some childhood trauma is partially to blame. We do know he became the kind of person who would both follow and even initiate the most sinister orders, causing countless deaths. I wanted to ask Jörg, *What happened to your father that he and your mother would suffer the deaths of two young daughters and know what it was to be heartbroken parents, and yet he would build the gas chambers that murdered millions of people, thousands of them children clinging to their desperate mothers?* But that, I judged, would be too confrontational. I needed to hedge my feelings a bit, make this a productive interview, not a series of accusations. I didn't know how much filial affection

Jörg had for his father—he might well consider him a hero and a moral icon. I needed to stick to more factual questions, though in my own imagination I saw Hans Kammler returning home and settling in on any given evening with his family when Jörg was only an infant—after helping to engineer the deaths of dozens or even hundreds of people, including someone else's children. What was Kammler's response when his wife asked the inevitable question, "How was your day, dear?" Kammler must have been devoid of empathy, a ruthless, murderous psychopath who could only mimic the emotions of others—traits that served him well in the Nazi regime.

Colm had already been able to tell me Hans Kammler attended school as a youngster, beginning in 1908 in what is now Poland. Although complete school records are not available, there is nothing in the records that do exist to suggest he was either an outstanding or an especially poor pupil. Kammler passed his graduating examination (*Reifeprüfung*) at the Humanistic Städtisches Gymnasium in Danzig (now Gdańsk), the rough equivalent of a high school diploma in the United States, on schedule and without difficulty, but also without distinction.

Kammler's father, Franz, had been a Royal Prussian Army officer and, in the prescribed course for "Prussian nobility," Kammler honored his father's service and joined the cavalry as a young man. Hans's father was a close friend of General Erich Wilhelm Ludendorff, who led Germany's military along with German legend Paul von Hindenburg in World War I. Ludendorff was a hero during the war and a political activist afterward—blaming Germany's political leadership rather than the army for the loss of the war. The coffin of Hindenburg, who would die between the wars, will reappear near the end of our story in a scene reminiscent of a Steven Spielberg movie, with an added patina of horror. Unfortunately, I never got to ask whether Jörg heard his mother speak of Ludendorff.

Jörg seemed proud of his father's career, at least up to this point. In the depressed economy of the time, few courses were open to Kammler, a young man who didn't yet have an advanced education or helpful experience. He volunteered with storied Prussian cavalry regiment Leib-Husaren Regiment Königin Viktoria von Preussen Number 2, which could trace its roots to the 1740s and the Second Silesian War and its history through the Seven Years' War and the 1813–1814 War of Liberation, when the regiment triumphantly entered Paris after Napoleon's abdication. They wore crisp black uniforms with an unmistakable Totenkopf, or Death's Head, symbol emblazoned front-and-center on the shakos they donned with pride.[2] The Totenkopf had first been used as a military insignium by the cavalry of the Prussian army under Frederick the Great in the 1700s. It originally implied not cruelty and viciousness, but rather loyalty that would endure unto death. Not until it was appropriated by the SS did it carry the stain that has marked it ever since. Although this was the first time Kammler would wear a black uniform adorned with the Death's Head symbol, it would not be the last.

Kammler, also wearing the impatience of youth and anticipating his regiment's decommissioning, was quick to move on. Intent on doing something momentous, he left the army on April 10, 1919, and joined the Freikorps's Assault Division Grenzschutz-Ost (Eastern Border Defense). The Freikorps was a right-wing paramilitary organization that sprung up at the end of World War I after the November 1918 Armistice in opposition to left-leaning ad hoc groups of revolutionaries—early Communists. Though it would be formally dissolved in the early 1920s, the Freikorps is the closest thing there is to a predecessor of the SS. It had brigade-strength units, armored cars, and even artillery.[3]

"My father," Jörg began, the pride now coming through in his strong voice as he declaimed, rather than simply stated, "fought back the Russians and other communists." Kammler's alignment of himself against Communism is the first clear manifestation of his ideology—an ideology perfectly compatible with Hitler's, which was being formed around the same time. If Hitler despised anything as much as the Jewish people, it was Communism, and he was clear on this from the beginning. In fact, he often collapsed the two nemeses into a single group of conspirators—the

Judeo-Bolshevist menace. Kammler's battles against the Communists demonstrate an aversion to Bolshevism—and possibly a natural affinity for Nazi doctrine. According to other descendants, Kammler saw Hitler speak in Berlin in 1923—which would put him on the ground floor. They also claim that Kammler's father, Franz Kammler, would have been distraught at Hans Kammler's affiliation with the Nazis.[4]

I decided to challenge Jörg, asking, "Is your father a war hero?"

"No," was his short answer—but a reassuring one. I was relieved to learn that Jörg was no Holocaust denier. Not only that, but he readily accepted the fact that his father was a war criminal. I wouldn't be faced with a defense of his father's misdeeds.

Kammler completed his service in the Freikorps only a few short months later in July 1919 immediately after the signing of the Treaty of Versailles—the agreement ending World War I. Here Kammler's career parallels that of his future colleague Heinrich Himmler. Although Himmler would become something of a mentor to Kammler, Kammler would eclipse him in the final moments of war. A post–World War II report on Himmler could as easily be describing Kammler: "Like tens of thousands of demobilized German officers, whose appetite for war was still strong, who refused to acknowledge defeat, and who found themselves thrust out of their protective uniforms into a turbulent and precarious civilian existence, Himmler found his outlet in the activities of numerous 'free corps' or 'murder gangs' which flourished in post-Armistice Germany."[5]

At this point during the interview I fast-forwarded past much of the early Kammler bio we had already confirmed—a series of government and military positions. Upon leaving the Freikorps, Kammler began his studies in civil engineering at the Gdańsk University of Technology (Technische Hochschule der Freien Stadt Danzig and Munich) in August 1919, finishing in 1923.[6] Kammler's alma mater would have a troubled history leading up to World War II, adopting and espousing Nazi ideology, with uniformed Nazi officers in teaching positions.[7]

To this day, the ancient school building Kammler attended bears a Latin plaque on its wall attributing its architectural design to Karl

Friedrich Schinkel, the same man whom Kammler may have been named after. Could this connection—which his son denied—have helped decide Kammler's momentous career choice to enter the building industry—and eventually build slave labor camps? Here again, Jörg took issue with my linking his father to Schinkel.

With his engineering degree in hand, Hans Kammler embarked on a career trajectory whose details, frankly, I find difficult to follow. He was invited to take up a training post in structural engineering under Prussian government architect Professor Dr. -Ing. (Engineer) Paul Weber. The one-year apprenticeship was essentially a point of entry into the Prussian civil service, which allowed Kammler to obtain employment as a municipal building supervisor in Berlin from 1924 until 1925.

Meanwhile, Hitler was released from prison in December 1924 and resumed his attempts to consolidate his power in the Nazi Party and oust his rivals. The following year in 1925, Germany joined the League of Nations and began to agitate loudly for a return to equal treatment with other nations—including the right to rebuild its military forces. Memory, it seems, can be short. That same year Himmler joined the SS, having joined the Nazi Party two years before. Himmler—eventually rising to the level of Reichsführer-SS, head of the entire SS, from 1929 until 1945—would be "Hitler's main henchman."[8]

Civil service, though without the prospect of instant financial success possible in the private sector, was a prudent choice for Kammler at this time, perfectly in keeping with his utilitarian outlook. He intended to use government positions to gain experience and catapult himself into the more lucrative private side of business. But at this point he was thoroughly a creature of the state. In this position, Kammler developed his organizational and leadership skills by managing the design and construction of projects throughout the Berlin area. He quickly won a reputation as a skillful contract bidder managing massive building projects, including apartment and office complexes, schools, and movie theaters. All this at only 25 years of age—a testament to Hans Kammler's extraordinary ambition, engineering skills, and vision.

Kammler's career continued to thrive when he entered the Prussian Building and Finance Administration (Preussischen Bau-und Finanzdirektion) in Berlin, where he oversaw projects such as the police communications towers in Berlin's Adlershof neighborhood, police vehicle garages, a police driving school with repair facilities, and other large-scale government office complexes. His other projects included workshops, classrooms, and a test track for the Police Transportation Administration in Berlin. Working on police facilities would have put him in the same circles as Himmler, though we cannot confirm their paths crossed this early in their careers. Although these pragmatic projects were not the stylish architectural accomplishments of Schinkel, by now Kammler was heading the design and logistical aspects of important projects and overseeing their finances and all aspects of administration, gaining diverse practical experience.

On April 1, 1928, Kammler was appointed as a part-time scientific officer at the Reich Research Council for Construction and Housing Economics (Reichsarbeitsministerium-Reichsforschungsgesellschaft für Wirtschaftlichkeit im Bau-und Wohnungswesen) in the Ministry of Labor. As ambassador to Germany's private construction industry, he began rubbing shoulders with Germany's industrial elite—making connections he would prize later—and he lectured extensively at technical universities in Germany and abroad. He became an expert in streamlining construction to ease Germany's housing shortage. Efficiency and utility would be Kammler's calling cards—the best way to serve his masters. He was not only climbing the ranks professionally, but he also was making a reputation for himself in the halls of government and in private industry, as well.

Kammler continued to make important professional connections in these positions. He can be seen more as a highly efficient construction manager than as an architectural artist. His work was technical—all straight lines and right angles. Kammler would never design grand buildings, lasting monuments, or soaring bridges. He would be confined to the practical and functional. And to the horrific—housing Nazi soldiers, gassing Jewish prisoners, and burning their bodies. His legacy would be of ghastly rather than beautiful proportions.

With Jörg, I was ready to skip ahead to his parents' wedding, which took place even as the German economy was beginning a downward spiral.[9] Now twenty-nine and having achieved a remarkable degree of professional success, Kammler felt established enough to take a wife. On June 14, 1930, he married Jutta Carla Anna Horn of Naumburg, Germany, a small town of just over twenty thousand people some 250 miles south of Berlin. Compared to the spit-and-polish Hans, Jutta was only a country girl. Naumburg, the childhood home of philosopher Friedrich Nietzsche on Germany's Saale River, is known for its quaint annual Hussite Cherry Festival, dating back to the sixteenth century and celebrated each year in June as the region's cherries ripen. Jörg was not sure, but Jutta may have chosen June 14 as her wedding date with the ancient festival in mind—the best time of year in Naumburg. He mentioned family pictures, and I thought I might have the great fortune to see some, even to get permission to use them our book, but I sensed Mrs. Kammler scowling through the dim light, and I think Jörg did, too. He told me they were in a room upstairs, as if that were an ocean away. No photos were forthcoming.

The details of the Kammler wedding called to my mind Heinrich Himmler's Engagement and Marriage Order of 1931, which Hans Kammler would help enforce. The order asserted Himmler's power to determine the appropriateness of the proposed marriage of any of his troops in order to ensure continued racial purity in the SS stock. Though that order was still in the future, Himmler would have undoubtedly approved of Jutta's pedigree and of her political views. At twenty-two years of age, she was already a member of no fewer than three Nazi Party organizations. And while Hans wasn't yet an official Nazi Party member, he was a sympathizer who soon would be. With Jörg sitting before me in his hospital bed, the Nazi obsession with racial purity took on an even more surreal character. Whether he liked it or not, whether he owned it or not, Jörg was the biological product of the Nazi race project. He was a child of a Nazi-approved marriage between two members of the Nazi elite. That was horrifying. Not wanting to destroy the rapport I thought I was building with Jörg, I kept that thought to myself.

The month of the Kammler wedding also provided welcome news for Germany when the last Allied troops remaining from World War I finally left the homeland. As Hans and Jutta Kammler settled into their home, Germany was finally left to itself. Now married, Kammler did not relax, for idleness was not his nature. That was one point made by Jörg—his father was unceasingly on the move. In March 1931, he was promoted within the Labor Ministry and made Research Officer for the Foundation for Construction Research (Förderung von Bauforschungen) in Berlin. This was his most important position to date. Kammler was collecting titles like precious coins.

Jörg spoke with great warmth when I asked him about his mother, who had lived until 1996. As we talked about her he looked robust, animated, more like a man who happened to be wearing pajamas than someone convalescing. Jörg knew his mother, unlike his father, from his childhood and long into his own adulthood; she had even lived with him and his own wife. It was easy to picture her in a similar hospital bed in this same room twenty years before. Jörg was, to use the American idiom, something of a mama's boy, I thought. It seemed perfectly natural, given that he had grown up with only one parent.

"Did your mother ever re-marry after the war?"

"No," Jörg said flatly, a little sadness in his voice. He waited patiently for my next question as a thought tumbled through my head. If Kammler had cut a deal with the Americans and had been able to get word to Jutta but needed to remain hidden, this could account for her never seeking another husband—she was already married. Or perhaps she never remarried because she simply never truly believed Hans Kammler had died. Either way, she endured fifty years of "widowhood," the vast majority of her life spent without her husband.

Jutta had undoubtedly settled into married life intent on becoming a recipient of the Cross of Honor of the German Mother, a decoration conferred for exceptional merit in mothering at least four ethnically German offspring. Soon enough though tragedy befell the young Kammler family. Their first child, a daughter born in the spring of 1931, died "of infection," Jörg told me, leaving behind two grief-stricken parents. At the time, Jutta would just have learned she was expecting a second child. Though she didn't know it, it would be their second daughter. Then the Kammlers' third daughter, Gisele, born not long after the second, would live only days before her own untimely death in the spring of 1936.

"The second one [to die—that is, Gisele, the third daughter] was killed by the accident of a nurse, who forgot to close a bottle of chloroform and the fumes overcame the newborn. She was just four or five days old. That was in 1936. This was a terrible tragedy and still talked about when I was growing up." Another distressing, ironic coincidence: Kammler, who engineered the gassing of Jews, had a child who died accidentally of gas inhalation.

I was more or less thinking out loud when I said to Jörg, "Wouldn't losses so acute and personal give a greater sense of empathy to a man?" It was a statement more than a question. Of course, Hans Kammler's deeds answer this question powerfully in the negative. There is very little of Kammler that suggests leniency, compassion, or anything close to an understanding of fellow human beings. Apparently the deaths of his two children served only to embitter rather than humanize him. This must have been an extraordinary household after the war—sorting out the missing husband and father, both emotionally and legally; knowing of the two dead sisters, but wondering how to speak of them; everything simmering just beneath the surface. If the father had survived, the mother could never, never trust a child with that information.

On March 1, 1932, just weeks before the birth of the Kammlers' second daughter and with Hitler's Nazi Party showing increasing gains in the German Reichstag, Kammler took the momentous step of joining the Nazi Party (NSDAP).[10] His decision was likely a combination of ideological bent and career opportunism. He was choosing sides in a way he calculated would serve him in the long run, but it was also a choice he was eager to make, given his political leanings. Considering Kammler's despicable acts throughout the coming war, whether he was a hardened ideologue, deft careerist, or both becomes incidental.

An early photograph of Hans Kammler, taken in 1932 and found in his National Socialist German Workers Party (NSDAP) ID. U.S. National Archives Record and Administration

Eight months after joining the Nazi Party, Kammler capped his formal education with a doctorate in engineering from the Technical University of Hanover. I had already scanned the walls in this front room for a framed diploma, a photograph of which would have been a great prize. No luck.

Shortly thereafter on the afternoon of January 30, 1933, a frightening new chapter in German history began as Adolf Hitler emerged from Germany's presidential palace as chancellor of the German Nation. Jörg made it perfectly clear to me that he was no fan of Adolf Hitler; it seemed important to him that I know this. But for Hitler's admirers and followers at the time, it was jubilation. Kammler had backed the right horse, joining the party before Hitler's triumph. Recounting Hitler's crowning achievement, Joseph Goebbels, Hitler's propaganda minister, wrote in his diary, "It is almost like a dream—a fairytale. . . . The new Reich has been born. Fourteen years of work have been crowned with victory. The German revolution has begun!"[11]

Now chancellor, Hitler could make his ambitious plans real. *Mein Kampf*, Hitler's manifesto, was clear: he would restore Germany's rightful position in the world order by rebuilding its military might and then expanding its territories. He insisted on more land for his people as if it was their birthright. He openly wrote and spoke about the *"Lebensraum,"* a German word that translates as "living space," beyond any boundaries that had previously constrained the German people, which was required for the propagation and thriving of the German people—perhaps even for their very self-preservation. This was a matter of justice and national dignity for Hitler, and he made it a rallying point for the German people. And it was clear that Hitler would use force if necessary: "This soil [Eastern Europe] exists for the people which possess the force to take it."[12]

While all this was unfolding politically, Hitler continued what should have been seen as an alarming military buildup in stark violation of the Treaty of Versailles. In an act of tremendous and unanswered defiance, Hitler announced in 1934 that he was building an air force (the Luftwaffe), and shortly thereafter he instituted a peacetime draft, swelling the ranks of the Wehrmacht, the German army. The German army predated the Nazi Party and owed it little in terms of allegiance or loyalty. The Luftwaffe, in contrast, was created by the Nazi regime and so, Hitler believed, could be counted on to support the party.[13] No nation acted to stop Germany's military buildup. Appeasement—letting Hitler have at least some of what he wanted—was seen as the best option, though the reputations of the appeasers would be forever ruined. As with his policy of escalating discrimination against the Jews, Hitler's step-wise military buildup—totally eviscerating Versailles—went unanswered, if not unnoticed. Jörg confirmed his father's service in the Luftwaffe, something that would later work in his favor as Kammler came up through the only branch of the military Hitler trusted.

Kammler now formally abandoned his religion in preparation for one of the most defining moments of his life and career—induction into the SS.[14] Within the ranks of the SS, abandonment of Christianity was common, and understood to be an indicium of ardency and loyalty to

SS leaders.[15] And so it was with Kammler. He declared himself a Gott-gläubige, a non-believer in God. And on May 20, 1933, Kammler donned the uniform of Hitler's elite black order, complete with the Death's Head symbol and double lightning strikes. His SS number was 113 619. In the previous four years, under Himmler's leadership, the SS had grown from 280 to 50,000 members, with some estimates even higher.[16] This was but the beginning—its size and power would continue to increase.

Jörg's wife suggested, for perhaps the third time, that he was exhausted, that he should rest. "Yes," I conceded, rising, "You've been very generous with your time. Just one more question. You said your father was morally compromised. Where do you think he first went wrong?"

"Impossible to say, don't you think?" Jörg began his answer with a question, taking off from there. It was such an open-ended question, and an issue that obviously bothered Jörg personally, that he went on at length. I shifted from one foot to the other, standing while he talked, and then crept back down to the front edge of the seat, never breaking eye contact with Jörg—making believe, I suppose, that his wife wasn't even in the room. We talked for at least another half hour.

A new inductee into the SS, Kammler was assigned to the SS Cavalry Corps in Berlin (Reitersturm 1 of 7 SS-Reiter-Standarte). These equestrian units were founded specifically to attract members of the German upper class and nobility to the SS. When Kammler joined, the SS Cavalry Corps was considered a stepping stone into the armed branch of the SS, the Waffen-SS. But by 1941, the once-proud SS Cavalry Corps would be little more than a social club, most of its more able members having transferred to units in the Waffen-SS, the armed wing of the SS that served in battle, leaving behind those least fit for combat. The cream would be poured off. Kammler was fit for military service, but he was something of an in-between problem. He lacked enough military experience to be a combat officer, but he was far too valuable to ship off as cannon fodder. As an engineer with prized organiza-tional skills, he was never destined to become a foot soldier. His future would be behind the front lines, leading rather than following.

Kammler next finally seized the opportunity he longed for—to pursue a career in construction engineering as a figure of national importance for the Nazi government. Within a few short whirlwind months, Kammler had finished his Ph.D., joined the Nazi Party, and signed on with the SS just as a new German class system was calcifying. The boldest line of demarcation was between those who were Nazi Party members—and, even better, SS members—and those who were not. But within the party and the SS, there was another line—those who had become members early on, and those who had not. So important were the distinctions that they were marked on the uniforms. Clearly visible on the upper right arm of Kammler's uniform in several photographs is the 'V' shaped "Ehrenwinkel" (Old Campaigners' Chevron) worn only by SS men who joined the ranks of either the SS, NSDAP, or one of the Nazi Party–affiliated organizations before January 30, 1933—the day Hitler became chancellor. I had scrutinized this and other Kammler photos for hours, but not until days after my interview with Jörg did the pose catch my eye. I had seen Jörg, from the foot of his bed, sitting up just like Hans Kammler in this picture, legs bent, forearms propped on his knees. I was never good at seeing parents' faces in their children's, but Jörg did have the same general characteristics as his father—lean but not wiry, taking up enough of the length of his bed that I thought him above average height.

Hans Kammler. The "Ehrenwinkel" (Old Campaigners' Chevron) on the right sleeve of his uniform signifies that he had joined a Nazi-affiliated organization before January 30, 1933—the day Hitler became chancellor. Courtesy of Tilmann Kammler

Colm had explained to me that the earlier one joined the party, the more devout and less opportunistic one was perceived to be by the old hands. Could this be why Kammler, otherwise prim and proper, "always [wore] SS uniforms somewhat the worse for wear"[17]—to show without having to claim out loud that he was an old hand?

While joining the party before or after 1933 was a difference in degree, party membership versus membership in the SS was a difference in kind. Within the party, none were seen as more strident, and consequently more feared and favored, than the SS. I thought of the SS as representing the lowest, darkest, most wicked circle of Dante's Hell within the Nazi Party. Having joined the party and the SS, Kammler was now all in—his fortunes would rise and fall with the party generally, and with the SS in particular. I mark this as Kammler's own point of no return in terms of ideological formation. From the critical period of 1933 to 1936 as Hitler continued to grow in power, he was the head of the Housing and Settlements Division of the Agrarian Policy Department of the Greater Berlin National Socialist Regional Administration (Leiter Abteilung für Wohnungs-und Siedlungswesen der agrarpolitischen Abteilung der Gauleitung des Gaues Gross-Berlin der NSDAP). He also held a leadership position in the Reich Federation of Small Gardeners. Its oval membership badge, which Kammler would have worn at the time, bore the typical Nazi symbology: a silver eagle set against a deep green background, its wings spread, feathers straight down, its head in profile, and a Nazi swastika emblazoned on its chest. The ubiquitous Nazi eagle in profile always expressed to me more defiant arrogance than nobility.

During this period, the SS continued to consolidate its power. While Hermann Göring took over the existing police forces in Prussia in the north and formed the Geheime Staats Poliezei, the Gestapo, Himmler's SS took over police forces in Germany's other thirteen states.[18]

By 1936, Kammler had moved on to the RuSHA, the Race and Settlement Main Office (Rasse-und Siedlungshraptamt), the office charged with preserving the racial purity within the SS. It accomplished this by thoroughly vetting applicants, and in part through implementing the aforementioned Himmler marriage order. Kammler's role in this office is evidence of his support for the Nazis' unabashed pursuit of racial purity. Later in the war the office would be responsible for resettling Germans in captured eastern territories, and even taking children of Aryan appearance from the occupied territories. After the war, Kammler's colleagues in the RuSHA were tried on various charges, including "kidnapping the children of foreign nationals in order to select for Germanization those who were considered of 'racial value.'"[19] Himmler himself had laid the groundwork for this program, saying in 1943, "I think it is our duty to take their children (those of pure blood in occupied lands) with us, to remove them from their environment, if necessary by robbing or stealing them."[20] Until I got drawn into the Kammler investigation, I had never before heard of this practice—literally stealing children from their parents so they could be raised by German couples. Barbaric. As sometimes happened during my interview with Jörg, my mind wandered—perhaps one of Jörg's siblings, or even Jörg himself, had been a kidnapped child, taken from a conquered family of Aryan appearance to replace his deceased sisters. We knew the kidnappings happened, and within the perverted Nazi regime, who better than an up-and-coming SS officer who had lost two children of his own to be a beneficiary of this twisted program? Again, this was way too hot to raise with Jörg.

By this time, Hitler was not just chancellor; he had become Germany's president with virtually unlimited power. He led in a dictatorial fashion as Germany passed the infamous Nuremberg Laws in 1935, stripping German Jews of citizenship and the right to vote or hold a government job and forbidding marriage or sexual intercourse between Jews and Aryans.[21] This might be the time a bureaucrat or rising star within the regime, if he had a conscience, would lie low, minimizing his participation. Even as a Nazi, Kammler could have spent his career in relative obscurity, devoting more time to his family. But he did not anonymize himself in the bureaucracy that was carrying out these crimes against Jewish citizens. Instead, he sped his career forward and upward to the center of the burgeoning system of racial categorization and persecution.

Though the average German citizen did not personally rush headlong into the extirpation of the Jews, neither did he object. A crucial characteristic of the Nazi's program of discrimination was its incrementalism. Yet when it came to persecuting the Jews, the Nazi leadership did not have a completely free hand: the "Nazis proved successful in prosecuting only those policies that encountered no inveterate resistance in the population at large."[22] The Nuremburg Laws are indefensible. But the Nazi regime got what we might call "buy in" from the public in a clever way. You could complain loudly about the family three doors down being forcibly routed from the neighborhood—or your complaints might be less vocal if afterward you were able to purchase their larger, more luxurious house at a fire-sale price: an insanely small percentage of its actual value. You might protest bitterly if an acquaintance was forced by law to sell his business, but you might be mollified just a bit if he offered the business to you on extremely favorable terms on his way out of the country. And if you did not buy it, after all, someone else would. Maybe under these circumstances you were even doing your friend a favor?

Germany's racial policies took the international stage when the summer Olympics were hosted in Berlin in 1936. (Germany had been awarded the games in 1931—before Hitler and National Socialism formally came to power.) Other Kammler family members recently told us that Hans Kammler attended the baseball game—baseball was a demonstration sport at that year's games with just one game on August 12, 1936—joining ninety thousand other fans in Berlin's Olympic Stadium to watch two American teams face off.

Jörg confirmed for me generally that Kammler thereafter had a series of administrative positions of increasing consequence. Next, as a member of the board of directors of the Homeland Building and Housing Cooperative (Heimat Gemeinnützige Bau-und Siedlungs AG) in Berlin's southwest Steglitz-Zehlendorf borough, Kammler oversaw the management of residential and settlement planning within the agricultural policy branch. As a second lieutenant (SS-Untersturmführer), Kammler continued to rise through the ranks of the Nazi Party. He was appointed as a top government official within the Reich Air Ministry with responsibility for all construction, including large building projects, among them staff housing and personnel structures and a Luftwaffe air transport communications network. He also oversaw construction of other special projects, including medical facilities within the Air Ministry. He was gaining not only prestige, but also critical experience in a variety of undertakings. It was at this point in his career, while achieving dramatically in his professional life, that Kammler buried a second child, enduring tragedy at home.

By June 1, 1937, Kammler was promoted to first lieutenant and became Chief Government Surveyor at the Air Ministry. While Kammler was busy raising buildings and a family, Hitler continued feverishly raising the German military. And as it swelled, there was something of a scramble for materials. Navigating implacable internecine enmity between various branches of government and private industry over materials and labor, Kammler became an expert at working the system to procure what he needed, sharpening an administrative ruthlessness that would serve him throughout the war.

In 1938, Hitler secured the return to Germany of Austria—the latest in a series of Nazi moves explicitly prohibited by the Treaty of Versailles—and the latest instance in which the French, British, and Americans failed to enforce the treaty. Germany grew larger, and Hitler's popularity soared. Later that same year, Italy, Great Britain, and France actually signed an agreement allowing Germany to absorb Sudetenland, a wide swath of Czechoslovakia peopled largely by ethnic Germans. The Czech leaders were deliberately excluded from the discussion that led to the multinational agreement ceding a large part of their country. Soon thereafter, under the pretense of putting down civil unrest, Hitler's forces occupied the rest of Czechoslovakia. Not a single shot was fired. Hitler's plans to expand Germany's empire were coming to fruition as if by magic, and his popularity soared still higher. I had always been puzzled by this history. *How could so many people sit idly by while Germany, so recently the main belligerent in World War I, gained military and political momentum?*

It was in 1938 that Hans Kammler was first called upon to apply his craft to military objectives when, as Jörg confirmed, he planned and supervised the Luftwaffe's most ambitious construction projects as state director of construction and senior government councilor at the Reich Air Ministry. Everything Kammler had done up to this point—including some police buildings and related projects—had been civil, municipal, or for the party. Now with Germany actually contemplating war, his projects included construction of an air transport communications network, hangars, barracks, and military medical facilities, as well as other special projects in support of the Luftwaffe.

Meanwhile, Hitler was taking an increasingly strident stand against the Jews. On November 9–10, 1938, SS units were dispatched in what became known as Kristallnacht (the Night of Broken Glass), a campaign of outright terror. Nearly 100 people were murdered, 7,500 Jewish businesses were destroyed, and over 250 synagogues were burned in a night of unmitigated mayhem.[23]

"I assume, given your father's work load, he could not have been at home much," was my next prompting to Jörg—an inexcusably leading question in a court of law, but perfectly permissible in a living room.

"Yes. But he always made time." It was at that point that Jörg and I discussed the Lebenbücher, his father's "Life Books." Colm had prepped me on these: scrapbooks put together by Hans Kammler between 1932 and 1944 for his children. I was enormously curious about these books and hoped to see them, even to come away with something from them. Colm described them as filled with photos, notes, and personal messages Hans Kammler had compiled for each of his children. I imagined them as a father's wisdom memorialized and passed on to his children, and I was sure they would provide enormous insight into our subject.

"No," said Kammler's son, when I told him my thinking. He characterized the "Life Books" in a very different way: "They were a defense."

Jörg explained that the scrapbooks were not simply the delightful compendiums I had thought. They were also a description and defense of Kammler's "radicalization," to use Jörg's word—or, as a less invested commentator might describe it, his descent into fascism. When I asked if I might see one, Jörg hedged. He never told me "no" flat out. But he never got around to allowing it. I felt a bit like a child whose parent answers, "Not now," meaning, "Not ever." Jörg said the "Life Books" did also include "words of wisdom for each child about life, about politics, and other matters." Jörg must have found a certain sweetness in this legacy from his father, for on the heels of this claim, he volunteered that his father's "strong family ties" would have prevented him from making a deal with the Americans and abandoning his family. Jörg called Hans Kammler "a good father, a good husband."

Other family members have suggested that some pages of these "Life Books" could have been excised before they were passed to the children, raising questions about what might have been taken out.[24] In any case, the scrapbooks are evidence of Kammler's tender care for his family—if for no one else. As are his careful provisions for their safety. During the war, they were ensconced in a villa in a heavily wooded area thirty miles south of Berlin. Their home was hidden behind high mounds of earth to provide blast-protection. They would not end the war there, though.

Kammler's CV began to sparkle with a host of honorary awards and special committee titles. But there is a single especially prescient remark about Kammler from around this time that caught my eye as I was doing research. Albert Speer, Hitler's Minister of Armaments and War Production, who worked closely with Kammler throughout the war, described Kammler during this period as an "inconspicuous, sociable and [a] very hardworking official."[25] Speer went on to say, "Nobody would have dreamed that someday he would be one of Himmler's most brutal and most ruthless henchmen. It was simply inconceivable, and yet that was what happened."[26] Remembering that Himmler is among the most despicable characters of the war, in charge of the entire SS, this is a particularly noteworthy statement. Kammler's evil character shone through as he gained more and more power and freedom to act. Speer was not alone in his assessment of Kammler, who was "noted for his great energy and aggressiveness, and his brutality."[27]

Two key international diplomatic actions took place in 1939. First, on March 31, France and Great Britain agreed to defend Poland from any future attack by Germany. Second, on August 23, mortal ideological enemies Germany and Russia stunned the world, including most Germans and Russians, by signing a non-aggression agreement—the Molotov-Ribbentrop Pact. With this in hand, Hitler could attack Poland with no fear of drawing the Soviets into war as an enemy. Relying on counsel from his most trusted advisors that France and Great Britain would renege on their commitment to defend Poland, Hitler launched his invasion of Poland just over a week later on September 1, 1939. For Germany, the invasion was at once a great success and an unmitigated disaster. In a totally new style of highly mobilized warfare that the Germans called the *blitzkrieg*,[28] ("lightning war"—the modern equivalent being "shock and awe"). Germany swept into Poland and routed the enemy, gaining miles and miles of territory daily.[29] This innovation relied on recent technological developments and an altogether new concept: mobility on the ground supported by strong dive-bombing support in the air attacking enemy supply and communication lines. Within four weeks, Hitler, aided by a Russian invasion mounted from the eastern border of Poland, had scored his first complete military victory over another nation. Poland was finished.

Sitting beside Jörg Kammler's bed, I had the sudden thought that precisely when Germany was starting this fateful war with the invasion of Poland, Hans Kammler would have learned that his wife, Jutta, was expecting another child. The Kammlers wouldn't know the sex of that child until its birth several months later, but their fifth child would be a boy—Jörg. Coming upon this realization while sitting with Jörg brought the war home to me in a powerfully poignant way—with a bit of sadness and sympathy for him and the unfairness of the life he had been born into. Keith later found a Kammler file including a piece of paper perhaps five-by-seven inches, bearing Kammler's signature. It read, in part, "I hereby announce the birth of the fifth child, a son named Jörg." It was an official document for the RuSHA, the office charged with enforcing racial purity—not a birth announcement to family and friends. But I imagine Hans Kammler took some pride in affixing his signature. I wondered whether Jörg had ever seen it, and made a mental note to send him a copy when I got back to the United States. I noted something else in this same document. Jörg was fifth in the birth order. Two of his older sisters died before his birth. Kammler could have considered Jörg "the third" child, but in describing him as the fifth, he explicitly recognized his two departed daughters—one of the few humanizing moments I found in the life of Hans Kammler.

Hitler's decision to invade Poland was a disaster for Germany in at least one important sense. Hitler had no ideological quarrel with France, Great Britain, or any other country to his west, and he had no desire to be at war with them. Despite the reassurances of his key advisors, France and Great Britain honored their promises to Poland and declared war on Germany within forty-eight hours of the Nazi invasion.[30]

Hitler may not have wanted war with France, but he didn't hesitate to fight the French when he had to. When Germany next preemptively invaded France, the French, caught off guard, were fatally slow to respond to German movements.[31] It was all over before the French had the Germans figured out. The Germans would find conquering Great Britain an entirely different proposition—indeed impossible. The English Channel was as valuable a buffer against Germany as the British navy. Mark the fact that Hitler had forced himself into an unwanted conflict with more formidable, and now multiple, enemies. Every breath of effort, every man, every tank or piece of armor, every bullet, plane, or pilot deployed in the West was a distraction from Hitler's true aspiration— conquering the *lebensraum* that lay to the East. Hitler miscalculated badly when he virtually invited France and Great Britain as enemies.

Having tasted military success, Hitler invaded and quickly conquered Denmark and then Norway, followed by Luxembourg and the

Netherlands. By mid-1940, Hitler controlled much of Europe and was a national hero. Austria, Czechoslovakia, Poland, Denmark, Norway, Luxembourg, the Netherlands, and France were all in the bag. To the thinking of many Germans, he was bringing back the proper world order, all at incidental cost. Hitler had blossomed into a leader to be revered and followed, though the seeds of his defeat had already been sown. It was Germany's technological advances in weaponry and warfare that had allowed Hitler to reap huge early dividends, taking Germany further than it had ever advanced in World War I, and with greater ease than anyone anticipated. Hitler and the High Command should have known that even newer and better technology would be a necessary condition of continued successes. But Hitler's commitment to maintaining Germany's advantage in technology would be uneven—a costly mistake.

The Battle of Britain, Germany's failed attempt to demoralize the Brits and run them out of the war through the relentless bombing of London, followed in July to October of 1940. Then Hitler made what would be another fatal misstep—this time against the advice of his military strategists. In the summer of 1941, he broke his non-aggression pact and invaded Russia. As is clear from *Mein Kampf*, Hitler always saw Communism and the Russians as enemies. But the invasion of Russia at this time would become another disaster for Germany. The Germans might have been able to defeat Russia, but not while dividing their forces and leaving too much committed in the West after Britain refused to make peace. This new strategy conflicted with Hitler's own admonition against warring on two fronts. Why now, of all times, turn on his Russian ally and open an entirely new, massively long, battle front?[32] Hitler believed he was forced by the circumstances to act, fearing that delay would allow the Russians more time to build up their own forces and training.[33] "You have only to kick in the door and the whole rotten structure will come crashing down," Hitler said of Russia,[34] speaking of his plan to crush the Red Army in eight to twelve weeks, again using the Blitzkrieg. He threw 3.5 million men, 150 divisions, and 3,000 tanks into Operation Barbarossa. When Winston Churchill heard of the invasion, he reportedly remarked of the Germans, "It will bleed them white"—and how right he was.[35] After early success, tens of thousands of German soldiers perished in the record cold of the Russian winter— just as Napoleon's men had succumbed in the winter of 1812. Having expected victory before winter, the Germans were ill-equipped for such harsh conditions. Germany also fatally underestimated the Russians' resolve, fortified by fear of Germany's notorious Einsatzgruppen killing squads. Russian soldiers and officers thought twice about surrendering to an enemy that executed prisoners of war and citizens alike. Germany badly misplayed the opportunity to enter Russia as liberators rather than bloodthirsty conquerors.

As the war raged, Kammler's manic work rate and ability to complete seemingly superhuman tasks within the shortest timeframes caught the attention of others, including Heinrich Himmler, the head of the SS. In the spring of 1941, Himmler invited Kammler and his staff to transfer lock, stock, and barrel to the SS. This was the proverbial offer Kammler couldn't refuse—not that he was disinclined, in any case. Kammler was by now considered an old-time Nazi Party member and SS soldier. Coming from the ranks of the Luftwaffe, free of the taint of the German army, Kammler arrived in Himmler's inner circle with Göring's personal approval, well-positioned to enjoy the confidence of the Führer himself.[36]

Although Jörg and I never had the chance to discuss Himmler, the SS chief deserves our attention—especially his knack for expanding his domain, as he was doing in bringing Kammler into his orbit. This was a regular strategy of Himmler's when it came to potential rivals and rising stars. In May 1940, not long after the invasion of Poland, Himmler had awarded preeminent rocket scientist Wernher von Braun the rank of second lieutenant in the SS, bringing von Braun within his control. Six years before, he had done the same with Rudolph Höss, the commandant of Auschwitz. Both von Braun and Höss will figure prominently in our story, but I mention them here to demonstrate Himmler's repeated ploy to offer SS rank to an established or rising officer in order to gain control or influence over the officer and everything that officer controlled—then and in the future. Himmler seized whomever or whatever he wanted, acquiring new underlings and projects like new tools on a utility belt. By June 1941, Kammler was officially assisting Himmler in the construction of the "vast building projects envisioned for the German settlements in Poland and Russia"[37]—Hitler's *lebensraum*.

While initially absorbing Kammler's basic bio, I had said to Keith and Colm, "If Adolf Eichmann was the architect of the Holocaust, General Hans Kammler was its engineer." I put it in more gingerly terms to Jörg, sailing close to flattery: "Your father rose through the ranks of the SS with dizzying speed. I know of many examples of the 'battlefield promotion' phenomenon—but even in this context, wasn't his history of a different sort altogether? How do you account for it?"

"It's all too complicated," Mrs. Kammler said loudly from the shadows, trying to snap her husband back to the present moment before he revealed still more insight into his father. She wanted this to end half an hour ago. At this point, I perhaps lost my interviewer's bearings. I began divulging as much as I was getting—maybe to placate Mrs. Kammler, maybe to show Jörg we were serious, or maybe even to help with his project. I was becoming fond of Jörg, had some sympathy for him, and was in a state of mild euphoria, having decided I would escape this interview alive with lots of valuable information.

Jörg and I didn't dwell on the SS, which must be a delicate subject for the son of Hans Kammler. The notorious group of super-Nazis began as a small outfit to provide security to Nazi Party members. It grew out of the party's first paramilitary bodyguard force, the SA (better known as the Storm Detachment). Under Himmler's leadership the SS became home to the most rabid, most despised, feared, and faithful Nazis—the core of the dark heart of National Socialism.[38] When Himmler was appointed the head of the SS (Reichsführer-SS) in 1929, the organization had a membership of just several hundred. But by 1933, "Himmler was well on his way to creating a state within a state."[39] At its peak, it had nearly a million members. To enlarge and empower the SS, Himmler capitalized on Hitler's growing distrust of every institution he had inherited, including the SA, coupled with his desire to have a fanatically loyal band of elite troops headed by someone he trusted absolutely. Himmler used his clout to make the SS a lean and attractive organization, using the racial purity standards to make it exclusive, unlike the SA, which was open to all party members. The SS was populated with men like Hans Kammler, who pledged fealty to Hitler over the German constitution and the country itself. This "Hitler Oath" was resented and resisted, even perceived as illegal by traditional German military men, but embraced enthusiastically by the SS.

Although it survived, the SA lost enormous power in 1934 when Hitler ordered a purge—an orgy of political murders that decapitated the SA. In this "Night of the Long Knives," the SS killed an estimated six hundred people, mostly SA leadership and key members. The main beneficiaries were the perpetrators of the massacre—Hitler, Himmler, and the SS. The SS, which at this point included Kammler, was now an unrivaled independent entity that answered to no one but Hitler himself. On July 26, 1934, Hitler elevated the SS to the standing of an independent organization within the Nazi Party and it became his private enforcement regime. It was an element of the Nazi Party, not the German state. The SS motto was born in the violent showdown with the SA and thereafter etched into SS uniform belt buckles: "My honor is called loyalty (*Meine Ehre heißt Treue*)."[40] According to prosecutors after the war, "the SS was the very essence of Nazism. For the SS was the elite group of the Party, composed of the most thorough-going adherents of the Nazi cause, pledged to blind devotion to Nazi principles, and prepared to carry them out without any question and at any cost."[41]

The SS was so evil that after the war it was deemed a criminal organization; membership alone made one an automatic target for arrest. In the Nuremburg Military Tribunal, eighteen leaders of the WVHA, the Main Economic and Administrative Office of the SS, were charged with conspiracy to commit war crimes and crimes against humanity, as well as membership in a criminal organization—the SS.[42] But Hans Kammler, the head of Amstgruppe C, the Building and Works Division of the WVHA, was not indicted before the tribunal for reasons that we shall see. A German newsman explained how the SS leadership perceived itself: "The Germans are the elite of humanity, the SS is the elite of the German people, and whoever in this corps is called to be a leader, is logically the elite of the elite."[43] The SS was pervasive, ubiquitous, and massive. "The SS had grown into its own state and society within the National Socialist Third Reich, with its own police, the Gestapo, its own secret service, the SD, its own army, the 600,000 fighting troops of the Waffen-SS, its own doctors and 'racial scientists' and a successful economic empire that ruthlessly exploited the forced labor and slavery of 700,000 people in its 1,000 Konzentrationlagern (KZ, concentration camps) it ran."[44] Kammler, at Himmler's personal invitation, now found himself in the SS inner sanctum.[45] And within this central core of the SS leadership Kammler thrived.[46]

As Jörg and I continued our discussion, I was left wishing he had more personal recollections of his father. One thing he did remember—despite having initially told me that he had "no personal memories" of his father—was his father being forever at work, "almost always away from home during the war." Late in the war, Jörg said, Kammler made only two "visits" to the family—an interesting word choice I might use for a distant relative dropping in for the holidays, not for my own father when I was growing up. A father doesn't "visit" his wife and children, he lives with them. Hans Kammler's long absences from home, though, allowed him to earn a reputation as the ultimate micro-manager. He appeared regularly at his many project sites, demanding frequent production reports, holding his managers strictly accountable. He was extraordinarily efficient, feared, and respected by subordinates and colleagues alike. He had an enormous personal drive, and he could cite the greater good of the *volk* as he demanded more and more from his underlings. He enjoyed even greater effectiveness when dealing with those outside the SS, with Himmler and Hitler figuratively standing behind him. Kammler freely exploited this intimidation factor to bend people to his will. Kammler knew if you have the ear of your superiors and enjoy their favor, your peers never quite know whether they are speaking to you or to someone even higher up. Was he different at home? If pressed, would Jörg remember his father being overbearing, or did he treat his own children and his wife differently?

Kammler helpfully documented his ambitions, as well as the business side of the SS, in his thirty-six-page "Plan for the distribution of work of Amstgruppe C of the SS Main Economic and Administrative Office [WVHA]" on January 1, 1943. The document lists the wide-ranging offices and divisions of the Amstgruppe C group that Kammler ruled, including library projects, a legal office, a photostat shop, a division for construction of bureau buildings, police buildings, buildings of the general SS, special construction, arms and ammunition installations, hospitals, industrial buildings, and agricultural buildings. He was in charge of a section responsible for irrigation and drainage projects, one for engineering and electrical matters, and others for surveying, town construction and planning, land planning, home schools, national political institutes, budget, raw materials, transportation of building materials, interior decoration, and on and on.[47] "SS buildings supremo Hans Kammler"[48] was now in charge of building anything and everything within the territory of the Reich. No one could erect anything more permanent than a billeting tent without Kammler's say so. If you wanted something built, you had to ask him to build it. If you had something in the way of supplies or materials, they could be taken at will by Kammler for his priority construction projects.

I marveled that a mind so aberrational as Kammler's could succeed within an educational system, within a bureaucracy, within any organized society. There is a profound schizophrenia in Kammler that cannot really be explained, though the same bifurcated life can be seen in figures throughout history. At times, demons seem to be able to live among us within the rules and systems of life, racking up socially acceptable achievements while developing their dark art. In Kammler's case, it is not enough to point out that the systems in which he succeeded were themselves aberrational, as corrupt as they were corrupting. To thrive as he did, he had to be highly organized, attentive, perceptive, without seeming unbalanced or erratic—in other words, to have many of the skills needed by ordinary people to prosper in life. Although ruthlessness might have been encouraged in the Nazi world, unpredictable behavior was not.

Kammler lived within a system that most assuredly exacerbated whatever pathologies he exhibited. When meeting Kammler for the first time, Albert Speer noted Kammler's "objective coolness." As the Nazi architect would recall, "In many ways he was my mirror image. He too had gone through university, had been 'discovered' because of his work in construction, and had gone far and fast in fields in which he had not been trained."[49] But as Kammler's power base began to threaten Speer, he changed his tune, likening Kammler to Reinhard Heydrich, author of the Final Solution policy. In comparing Kammler with Heydrich, Speer was linking Kammler to one of the most notorious figures of the Holocaust.[50] "Both [Kammler and Heydrich]," Speer wrote, "were capable of unexpected decisions at any moment, and once they had arrived at them would carry them through with a rare obstinacy."[51] The word "obstinacy" stuck fast in my mind. Nearly everything Kammler would accomplish during the war, so much of it so horribly sinister, would require that he possess an unrelenting single-mindedness without the inconvenient moral qualms that define humanity. Others who knew him well agree that Kammler cut an impressive and even striking figure.[52] "He had the slim figure of a cavalryman, neither tall nor short...broad-shouldered and narrow in the hips, with bronzed, clear-cut features, a high forehead under dark hair slightly streaked with gray and brushed straight back...piercing and restless brown eyes, a lean, curved beak of a nose, and a strong mouth.... That mouth indicated brutality, derision, disdain, and overweening pride.... He looked like some hero of the Renaissance, a condottiere of the period of the civil wars in northern Italy. The mobile features were full of expression. But the hands were thick and soul-less, almost coarse.... He was simply incapable of listening."[53]

Photographs of Kammler are not exactly plentiful, but several survive. None were on display in Jörg's home. What strikes me first about Kammler in photos is his penetrating, humorless gaze and his sleekness. Unlike others whose portraits show them at three-quarters profile, staring into the distance, Kammler confronts the lens directly. His face is bony and close-shaven, his expression always oddly neutral, but conveying a self-assurance and sense of importance and confidence. He is slightly taller than the average man, and there is not an ounce of fat to be seen on his frame, but his leanness conveys strength rather than frailty. He displays the rock-rib stance of an officer, the uniform bolstering his posture. In posed photographs, his head often pitches slightly forward, so that he is eying the camera from beneath his prominent brow. There is nary a hint of a smile, not so much as a wry expression, even in shots in which he is ostensibly relaxing. He is unfailingly all business—intent, on the job, stern, and serious. In group or candid photos, he is often an observer, but always looks ready to spring into action, ready to step forward from the midst of a small group of officers to take an order, or to take charge. One seeks in vain for any warmth in his eyes. He is almost always in uniform, almost always leaning into the camera, into the war. It was this man who, a war crimes court judged, conveyed to the authorities at the concentration camps Himmler's order that "no living inmate was to be allowed to fall into the hands of the enemy."[54]

Personal accounts and descriptions of Kammler are fairly consistent. Oswald Pohl, his one-time superior, described Kammler in almost fawning terms in his testimony at the war crimes trial that led to his own execution. Pohl saw Kammler as "eternally strong," accomplishing tasks in an unknowable, almost mystical way, with an "agility which could not be explained."[55] Rudolf Höss, commandant of the Auschwitz concentration camp, writing after the war, described a split personality, stating that by nature Kammler was open-minded and overflowing with great ideas but that he "used up countless construction chiefs and co-workers. It wasn't easy to work for him. He demanded too much work from a man" though he also had a "talent" for assessing a person's suitability for a job.[56] That

struck me hard—the commandant of the Nazi's most notorious concentration camp where prisoners were worked to death describing Kammler as
demanding "too much work from a man."

Jörg is understandably more forgiving, depicting his father's position
as "a complicated situation. The SS had a very complex construction
program that relied on labor. He was responsible for meeting deadlines.
This is why he was involved in expanding Auschwitz." But Jörg is not a
complete apologist, reaching the bottom-line conclusion: "He knew them
to be slaves, and it was wrong."

German rocket scientist Wernher von Braun, himself no angel, is
another interesting source on Kammler. After the war he would describe
Kammler's dichotomous traits: "Kammler is in fact the greatest rogue
and adventurer that I have ever seen. Character acrobat, dynamic personality, actor, criminal, all in one person. A shining product of the
atmosphere in which he became 'great.'"[57] Frederick Ordway and Mitchell Sharpe's history of the German rocket team contains more information about von Braun's impressions of Kammler. Von Braun, who was a
consultant on their book, answered to Kammler from the time Kammler
was in charge of the German rocket program.[58] Ordway and Sharpe note
that von Braun "reviewed virtually the entire manuscript" of their book
and gave "untiring aid, encouragement, and guidance."[59] When they are
describing Kammler and not citing other sources, I believe they are relying on von Braun's otherwise unrecorded views of Kammler: "a small-
town architect" who "was a non-achiever in the SA and,
consequently...joined the SS...He was an extreme egomaniac, which
accounted for his rapid promotion."[60] Ultimately, Kammler became "one
of the fastest ascending stars in the SS power constellation."[61] They go
on to quote a Kammler underling, Colonel Herbert Axster, as telling
them Kammler was "the worst man I ever met in my life."[62] Still another
Kammler subordinate described him as "a very forceful personality"
who was 100 percent driven. I had to remind myself to read expressions
like "a very forceful personality" in the context of wartime, within the

ranks of the dreaded Nazis, within the SS leadership.[63] A "very forceful personality" within those circles was an extraordinary thing.

It was time for me to take my leave of Jörg, and I would I spend the entire taxi ride and then my train ride back to Hamburg excitedly rapping out the email summary to my boon companions, Keith and Colm—one of our many conference calls would have been even better, but my mobile never converted to international capacity, so it was as useful to me as a child's toy.

Leaving the Kammler house, I had been aware that I had been hoping all the while that Jörg would summon me close to his bedside, look around conspiratorially to make sure no one else was within earshot, and quietly confide, "He survived. My father survived. He surrendered. The Americans shipped him to South America, but we were forbidden to speak of it." That whispered message, however, would have to come from other sources, from documents we didn't have—yet.

CHAPTER TWO

Evil Deeds

"The Jews arrive in special trains toward evening and are driven on special tracks to areas of the camp specifically set aside for this purpose.... The unfit go to cellars in a large house which are entered from the outside.... The prisoners are told that they are to be cleansed and disinfected for their new assignments.... Then they pass through a small corridor and enter a large cellar room which resembles a shower bath. In this room are three large pillars, into which certain materials can be lowered from outside the cellar room. When three- to four-hundred people have been herded into this room, the doors are shut, and containers filled with the substances are dropped down into the pillars.... A few minutes later, the door opens on the other side, where the elevator is located.... Then the corpses are loaded into elevators and brought up to the first floor, where ten large crematoria are located...."

—*Report of SS-Sturmbannführer Franke-Gricksch*[1]

This chilling SS account from 1943 describes the process that ended the lives of over one million people at the Auschwitz concentration camp complex.[2] Those fit to serve the Nazis as slaves were spared immediate death. All others were gassed and cremated. "Children of tender years were invariably exterminated since by reason of their youth they were unable to work." Auschwitz commandant Rudolf Höss explained in placid language, "Very frequently women would hide their children under the clothes, but of course when we found them, we would send the children in to be exterminated."[3]

It was sickening details like these, impossible to ignore, that drew me into this project. One story I heard during an interview with a survivor is so inexplicable, and so disturbing, that I hesitate to recount it in these pages. Joseph Gringlas, whose ordeal I will tell in the pages of this chapter, told me this story, which I include as representative of the deeds of the Nazis—and specifically SS general Hans Kammler. Stories like these have to be heard or we will never understand the depths of their depravity.

Joe Gringlas's first stop after being forced from his home as a Polish Jew was the Ostrowice Ghetto—a bleak, fenced camp and one of several Nazi collection points for Jews in Poland. Rubble lay everywhere within the ghetto; refuse was not removed. Joe had been housed there for a few weeks when, one grey afternoon, standing in a food line outside a building in the ghetto, he noticed an unattended child nearby, perhaps two years old. Even for the ghetto, the child was unkempt, though not in any obvious distress. Joe looked about for a mother, a father, some caretaker. No one. Others in line saw the child, but no one stepped forward to claim it. "Nearby, close to a hill of garbage and debris, stood an SS man. He made with his hand that the child should come to him," Joe told me, in his imperfect English. I could see the scene before me as Joe spoke, the trusting child toddling toward the SS officer. I feared what was coming, and Joe dropped the next line like a cold stone, the emotion washed out of his voice: "He took out a gun and shot the child." Joe read my face for a reaction, waiting for me to say something. I thought of my daughter Hannah at that age because for some reason the child in Joe's tale, though he hadn't specified, was a little girl in my mind. Joe's story was so appalling, I had nothing to offer. *What do you say to that?* I wondered, but I never came up with a satisfactory answer.

Many of the Nazi war criminals were identified, tried after the war, and given long prison sentences—or, like Auschwitz commandant Höss, faced the gallows. A few, because they had something of inimitable value to offer the Allies, were shielded from justice. I understand the antiseptic calculation made in deciding who received a "get out of jail free" card after the war, but it is troubling, particularly as a husband and a father, to know that the murderers of millions of people—including children—went free because they had something valuable to trade. It troubles me that the most powerful Nazis, and the most clearly guilty, were in the positions that gave them the best chance to buy their freedom after the war.

Keith and Colm had been able to show me through the documents they had painstakingly searched out and collected that Kammler was among that group of the most powerful Nazis—those the most responsible for the Holocaust. Kammler was key in building and expanding the concentration camps, installing the gas chambers and crematoria, and working slave laborers to death, as we will show in this chapter. Any one of these three crimes against humanity would make Kammler a high-level war criminal. In combination, they are thoroughly damning.

Keith and Colm left it to me to put it all down on paper—an emotionally taxing exercise that required confronting mankind at its worst. It was grueling finding one damning fact after another, one more atrocity, and then another authored by Hans Kammler in a seemingly endless cascade. I found myself irresistibly drawn to one story after another—tales of terror I could not help but pursue. I did my level best to stay objective about Kammler, and was helped in that because I began with a load of skepticism that he could be anywhere near as evil as Keith and Colm claimed. They would prove me wrong.

Hans Kammler, Overseer of the Concentration Camps

Though it would become the archetypal killing and slave labor camp, the Auschwitz concentration camp complex was not originally built for industrial-scale murder. It was first a holding camp for a few thousand political prisoners. For its far more sinister purpose, it had to be dramatically enlarged, and the notorious instruments of the Holocaust—the customized gas chambers and the crematoria—had to be designed and installed. Kammler was in charge of building out the camp and installing the gas chambers and ovens. As to the first step, the written order to expand Auschwitz itself came down from Kammler, who on September 27, 1941, mandated the camp be increased in size five-fold.[4] With that same order, Kammler also mandated the expansion of another killing camp in Poland, Majdanek-Lublin. He was the overseer of construction at other camps as well, but Auschwitz is obviously the best known.

Hans Kammler (on left with hands on hips) in Russia, 1941. From this picture it is easy to see how Kammler earned the nickname Staubwolke (Dust Cloud). Also pictured is Volkmar Grosch (second from right), one of Kammler's most trusted aides. Courtesy of Tilmann Kammler

Kammler conversing with Himmler during a visit to Lublin, Poland, in July 1941. Courtesy of Max Williams

When Kammler ordered this initial Auschwitz expansion, it was to turn Auschwitz into a slave labor camp for the POWs that Germany anticipated capturing in its ongoing invasion of Russia. Germany was suffering a severe labor shortage, making healthy bodies a prized asset, so Himmler bartered with the German army to receive a hundred thousand Russian POWs. Kammler, "one of the closest associates of Himmler," shared his boss's goal of creating a larger camp network, beginning at Auschwitz, to stockpile slaves.[5]

Joseph Gringlas, whom we have already met, was one of those slaves. I got to meet Joe through a strange turn of events. I was at a conference on terrorism in Washington, sitting at lunch next to a gentleman named Joel Greenberg, and we began talking. Joel and I had never met, and we began discussing our respective backgrounds—a very Washington thing to do. It came out that Joel had worked in OSI, the Office of Special Investigations of the U.S. Department of Justice. This was an office with an extremely small staff, and the likelihood of running into someone with an OSI past, even in D.C., is staggeringly small. Yet here he was. I explained my interest in World War II and the book I was contemplating writing about an SS officer who was involved in the Holocaust and slave labor and then oversaw rocket production. I mentioned Auschwitz, and also an obscure camp, Dora-Nordhausen, which Kammler built near the end of the war to support the relocated German rocket facility. And then Joel said something that sent an absolute chill down my spine, stopping me in mid-bite: "My father-in-law is an Auschwitz and Dora survivor."

"You're kidding," was the only retort I could muster, food nearly dropping from my mouth, my eyes bugging wide, trying to keep my composure. Inside, I was nearly bursting with a mixture of elation and confusion. How could someone survive Auschwitz *and* Dora? Almost all Dora prisoners were either killed or shipped out by the Germans when the camp was liquidated. Many of those transported to other camps died along the way. The odds of finding a Dora survivor were infinitesimal, so small I hadn't even seriously considered a search. Yet now one had sprung up before me—and he had been at Auschwitz, too. "Synchronicity," as Keith would say whenever we found unanticipated connections.

I had to meet him. He had passed through the apparatus built by Kammler. But he was in Florida, and I'd have to wait to be introduced until he returned to his Philadelphia home in the spring. In the meantime, I would learn as much about Auschwitz and Dora as I possibly could, no matter the emotional toll. I spent hours and hours at the Holocaust Memorial Museum Library in Washington, poring over books and records, many unavailable anywhere else in the world. I had more than once toured the museum; now I was upstairs in the private library of the building reserved for serious researchers. Knowing I was going to meet a survivor, everything I learned about Kammler's role in the Holocaust took on a personal cast.

I already knew that Kammler, as head of Amstgruppe C, the Building and Works Division of the WVHA, was in charge of the design and construction of all buildings and infrastructure—including concentration camps—throughout the Reich. The Nuremberg war crimes trial testimony of Kammler's deputy, Franz Eirenschmalz, chief of Amstgruppe C's subsection VI, confirmed the sweeping authority of Kammler's department to include "the planning, maintenance, and construction of concentration camps in the Reich and in occupied territories."[6] But we wanted more proof of his involvement in the concentration camps. Keith next provided me with the September 27, 1941, order in which Kammler proclaimed that the main Auschwitz camp (also known as Auschwitz I) and one of its sub-camps, Birkenau (also known as Auschwitz II), would each be enlarged to hold fifty thousand additional prisoners.[7] Solid proof—a signed order to expand Auschwitz. But Kammler's initial thinking soon broadened dramatically, and the Auschwitz footprint would grow much larger. Eirenschmalz confirmed at Nuremberg that it was Kammler who "ordered the building of a huge new camp near the town of Auschwitz (Auschwitz II-Birkenau)," and who "chose the location" of the new subcamp.[8] Not only had Kammler overseen the Auschwitz build-out, but he also had chosen the location. The international war crimes tribunal at Nuremberg strengthened our case that Kammler was a major war criminal—even though he was not a defendant there. As Oswald Pohl, Kammler's superior as chief of the WVHA, the Main Economic and Administrative Office of the SS, testified, "Kammler was thoroughly aware of the conditions in the concentration camps, and of the atrocities, murders, and ill-treatment of the inmates."[9] But Kammler was not merely aware of these conditions; he created them. As Armaments and War Production Minister Albert Speer, also a member of Hitler's inner circle, was well-positioned to verify, Kammler "was busy constructing crematoriums" and also "expanding the concentration camps."[10]

This alone would have been enough to convict Kammler at Nuremburg, but Keith and Colm went on to assemble a mountain of evidence documenting nearly daily activity linking Kammler to the Auschwitz expansion. Four days after his original edict in September 1941, Kammler created a new architectural office at Auschwitz to execute his orders. And apparently he would only be satisfied with a man of his choice, directly accountable to him, heading it: SS sturmbannführer (major) Karl Bischoff. Kammler and Bischoff had met during their time in the Luftwaffe, and Kammler had seen to Bischoff's admission into the ranks of the elite SS.[11]

At Auschwitz as elsewhere, Kammler demanded unconditional obedience from his subordinates, insisting his orders be carried out with "prompt and exact execution."[12] On the very day Bischoff took office, Kammler laid down his exacting expectations. He "issued a standard plan for the housing of concentration camp inmates," deciding how many prisoners could be forced into each barrack.[13] Then in a series of twenty-five drawings, he provided the construction specifications for *every concentration camp throughout the Reich*. What Henry Ford did for assembly-line mass production of automobiles, Kammler did for Nazi concentration camps, demanding fixed processes and materials to achieve speed and efficiency of scale. For example, he overruled Bischoff's proposal for brick barracks, opting instead for prefabricated wooden horse stables.[14] Though they provided far less protection from the harsh weather, they could be produced cheaply by the hundreds. Soon enough, Joe Gringlas would be housed in one of Kammler's wooden horse barracks.

Then after Kammler made the 350-mile journey from his Berlin office for an onsite inspection at Auschwitz and reviewed the topography on October 9, 1941—not yet two weeks after his first order—Kammler mandated the plans be changed radically, redoubling the capacity of the camp to two hundred thousand prisoners.[15] This second written order, doubling the camp capacity in the fall of 1941, precedes the formal adoption of the Final Solution by fully two months; but by this point Himmler and Kammler were apparently already informed of and perhaps advocates for the Final Solution.

Kammler's work reflected his cold priorities: minimizing costs while maximizing the potential camp population, squeezing as many bodies as possible into the smallest spaces imaginable: "Disease and death were built into the plans...the surface space allocated to each prisoner was, appropriately enough, the same size as a coffin."[16] This shoe-horning of human beings was accomplished in one audacious revision without expanding the size or number of barracks from an earlier plan. The original capacity of "550" people per barrack (already too many) was written over by hand with "744."[17] It was easy to envision Joe Gringlas in a horribly cramped wooden barrack in the darkness of night, surrounded by the sounds of suffering, wondering how many of his fellow prisoners would be dead by the morning.

Kammler, the Gas Chambers, and the Crematoria

Kammler was moving forward on the means for corpse disposal at Auschwitz, signing a plan for a crematorium on November 20,[18] though it is not clear if this oven was a tool of the Holocaust, which had not yet formally begun—but it was coming. As winter advanced in the southwest Berlin suburb of Wannsee, a small group of Nazi leaders acting under

Hitler's orders gathered secretly to devise the industrial-scale murder of Jews that became the Holocaust. I was becoming familiar with Germany's geography and realized that the picturesque Wannsee was only five miles—a distance I routinely covered during jogs—from Kammler's old Zehlendorf office.

I already knew that Hitler had identified the "Jewish race" as an eternal enemy from the outset of his political career. In *Mein Kampf*, he claimed that "the Jew" had "sinned against the masses in the course of the centuries...[and] squeezed and sucked the blood again and again," and, consequently "the people gradually learned to hate him for this, and ended up by regarding his existence as nothing but punishment of Heaven for the other peoples." He elaborated, his acrid language designed to provoke an emotional response among followers: the "black-haired Jewish youth lies in wait for hours on end, satanically glaring at and spying on the unsuspicious girl whom he plans to seduce, adulterating her blood and removing her from the bosom of her own people."[19] Now on January 20, 1942, Hitler was finally demanding the explicit means to address the menace of the Jewish race, whose very existence he "regarded as an insufferable provocation."[20] The resulting Wannsee Protocol called for the "Final Solution," the complete destruction of the Jewish race—a program to be overseen by the SS and Reinhard Heydrich, Himmler's "faithful lieutenant"[21] and Kammler's colleague.

Still living peacefully with his family in Poland at this time, Joe Gringlas, sixteen years old, had no idea of the storm that was brewing. He recalls feeling the tension build, sensing something was amiss; friends and older relatives were whispering, but no one knew what was coming. No one could have imagined the barbaric chaos that would tear his life apart.

With the Final Solution came the need for the gas chambers—for truly efficient mass murder—and, even more, for larger ovens to dispose of more bodies more quickly. These dual technologies were the two sides of a grotesque equation: killing and disposal. Millions of people would

be murdered. None of the tried and true methods of killing—mass shootings, hangings, the mobile gassing trucks of the Einsatzgruppen, or
simply overworking and starving people to death—would suffice. All
would continue, but none killed enough Jews quickly enough.

On February 27, 1942, a scant month after the Final Solution had
been formalized, Kammler was on the scene at Auschwitz again,[22] now
turning his attention to the crematoria. He "ordered that the two ovens,
each with three retorts, planned for this facility, be increased to five
ovens, with a total of 15 retorts,"[23] describing five large ovens, each
with three doors, each of which would take one body at a time, to be
built at Auschwitz I, the main camp. With this new configuration,
fifteen bodies could be incinerated at once. Shortly thereafter, Kammler
again refined his plan. Auschwitz I would now become a work camp,
a slave labor camp. Auschwitz II-Birkenau, a mile away, would become
the killing camp in service of the Final Solution. The existing train
tracks ran to Birkenau, emptying onto broad ramps. In keeping with
Kammler's eye for efficiency, those to be employed as slaves could trek
to Auschwitz I from Birkenau under their own power, while those
selected for death—the youngest, the sickest, and the weakest—would
already be conveniently close to the newly placed ovens. Accordingly,
Kammler countermanded his own most recent order, now requiring
his five new ovens to be erected at Birkenau.[24]

I had spent the better part of a week's "vacation" at the Holocaust
Museum Library, and now at last it was time for me to meet Joe Gringlas. I made the three-hour drive to Philadelphia, having been introduced
long-distance to Joe by his son-in-law. What was I walking into? Would
Gringlas be an embittered, angry old man? I tried to stay optimistic,
but it was daunting to walk into the home of a man I thought might
well be—should be—a wrecked human being. But quite the contrary:
Joe Gringlas was a joy to meet. He and I sat at his kitchen counter and
he told me his remarkable life story in an unhurried, friendly way. He
is a slight man. Nothing about his appearance, other than the "B2247"
tattooed on his left forearm, would indicate he was a concentration

camp survivor. I didn't expect such vitality and vigor from an eighty-seven-year-old man, let alone someone who had narrowly escaped the Final Solution. He moves like a man half his age—I could easily picture him with a tennis racket in hand. Joe has a special liveliness about him and an occasional twinkle in his eyes that reminds me of my grandfather. His gravelly voice is soft, and his hands get busy when he is talking. He has a kind, broad smile, sometimes tinged with wryness. As we spoke, I noticed he studied my face for reactions to his story, making sure I understood. He was apologetic and a little embarrassed when he lacked answers to some of my questions. He clearly wanted to be helpful. "How could anyone not like this man?" I thought, as our conversation unfolded throughout the afternoon.

Born in Ostrowice, Poland, in May of 1926, Joe speaks with a heavy accent that was at times a challenge for my untrained ear. But he was exceedingly patient with me. He is a survivor of three work camps, one death camp, and much more. He began his story with the removal of the Jews from his hometown and his internment in the Ostrowice Ghetto, along with one of his brothers. His parents, sister, and four other brothers were shipped to the infamous Treblinka death camp and never heard from again. In the blink of an eye, all but he and that one brother were erased. Joe gestured with a shrug of his shoulders. With the passage of seventy years, he has somehow accepted his family's fate. He has no explanation for anything that transpired, for anything he suffered, including the murder of his family. As he would tell me later, "I don't know what got into so many thousands of people." There is no irony in his statement, no disgust. He speaks more out of wonder than judgment. There is tiredness, but no resignation.

It was because of his youth and fitness for work that Joe was spared at Ostrowice and allowed to work as a laborer in a metal-machining factory. The heavy, treacherously sharp pieces made for perilous work. One wagon after another, after another. Endlessly. But when death is the alternative, even this type of work is welcomed. The Ostrowice Ghetto was soon evacuated and Joe, now separated from his only remaining family member, was transported to Blizyn, Poland, another work camp. He contracted a fever and suffered for a week with typhus, a disease he recalls killed many other workers. Typhus and dysentery flourished in the Kammler-built camps where malnourished prisoners were housed in deliberately overcrowded and unsanitary conditions. Immediately after regaining his health, Joe was so hungry he ate a single stolen potato cooked by another slave laborer, merely trying to survive. Found out by the guards, Joe was called forward at that evening's assembly and beaten by the Jewish policemen recruited to guard their fellow prisoners. The Nazis never missed an opportunity to terrorize one worker to keep others in line. This was their method of discipline—it made the slave laborers more compliant, and therefore more productive.

Joe's job for the months he was at the Blizyn camp was breaking large stones into gravel with a sledgehammer for use in making roads. His weight dropped to what he estimates was a precarious eighty pounds. Blizyn was one of many camps in Kammler's remit, as is proven by his March 10, 1942, letter describing sixty-one major projects he headed—all executed by Kammler's "SS construction brigades."[25] Among the projects Kammler lists in his letter are extensions to the crematoria at Buchenwald concentration camp (central Germany) and Mauthausen-Gusen concentration camp (upper Austria), as well as work on what is referred to as a "dead-house" at Dachau (southern Germany), a building used to stage corpses before they could be buried or burned.[26] Other documents record Kammler's murderous efforts at Bełżec (south-central Poland), Majdanek-Lublin (southeast Poland), and elsewhere. The list of Holocaust projects in which Kammler was a key participant is dizzying.

On August 8, 1942, Kammler and Himmler visited the notorious Bełżec killing camp, also in current-day Poland. And a month later, Kammler "ordered the erection of [a] camp on the edge of Lublin (now in Poland), with a projected capacity of fifty thousand prisoners." Kammler's plans for this newest camp, known as Majdanek or Lublin, would quickly grow larger, just like Auschwitz, tripling to house an astounding one hundred and fifty thousand prisoners.[27]

In May 1942, Himmler "dispatched SS Construction Chief SS Brigadier General Hans Kammler to Auschwitz" where he "toured the site and ordered that a peasant cottage there be converted into a gas chamber."[28] No sooner had Kammler left Auschwitz to return to Berlin than he was informed of problems with the construction: cracks in the smokestacks. Kammler answered the May 30 trouble report with a June 2 telegram demanding immediate repairs. His involvement at Auschwitz was continuous.

By early June, Kammler ordered yet another change to the Auschwitz project: each Birkenau crematorium must include a basement gas chamber.[29] This modification also bears the Kammler signature of lethal efficiency: build the gas chambers as close as possible to the ovens to reduce the distance over which tens of thousands of dead bodies must be hauled before burning.[30] To further ease the logistics, basement gas chambers were connected to the crematoria above by elevators. Healthy prisoners were forced to carry the bodies of the dead to help with their disposal. I asked Joe about this. Instead of issuing a judgment—his hands flitted with agitation, but there was no harshness or even criticism in his statement—he simply said that he would rather have killed himself.

Kammler received weekly written progress reports on the installation of the gas chambers and ovens throughout their entire construction, sometimes demanding updates within twenty-four hours. Hans Kammler left an utterly damning paper trail.[31] By July 4, 1942, the first Jews from Slovakia arrived and were sorted at Auschwitz. Those who could work were admitted to the camp. Those who could not work were gassed in the peasant cottage Kammler had converted to a gas chamber.[32] One thinks of Auschwitz commandant Höss's sickening statement about prying mothers from their children for execution.

Detail of a photo taken during a visit to Auschwitz concentration camp in July 1942. (From right to left) Bischoff, Kammler, Höss (Kommandant at Auschwitz), Himmler, and Pieper. Courtesy of Max Williams

Höss described a visit by Himmler, Kammler, and their entourage to the Auschwitz camp again on July 17, "where Kammler, using maps, blueprints, and models explained the planned or already progressing construction."[33] That same month Kammler visited Debica, in southern Poland, home to a Nazi ghetto that shipped Jews to Auschwitz. In August, he was on to Roztov-on-Don in Russia, the site of the slaughter of twenty-seven thousand Jews and Russians by Einsatzgruppen D.[34] It seems clear that Kammler was not showing up coincidentally as horrors were being perpetrated; he was traveling to these sites specifically to review the then-current methods of SS mass killings and plan for greater efficiency in the future—a serial killer on the prowl.

Kammler very likely viewed his handiwork in action during his July Auschwitz visit. Höss gives a description of Himmler witnessing "the complete extermination process of a transport of Jews which had just arrived. He also looked on for a while during a selection of those who would work and those who would die without any complaint on his part."[35] Presumably Himmler's entire entourage, including Kammler, the second-highest-ranking official on the tour, was also looking on with approval and interest. While this inspection by Himmler has been reported before, Kammler's presence on the tour has gone largely unremarked. And given Kammler's obsessive hands-on management style, it is virtually certain that he personally reviewed the killing process at Auschwitz—as we know he later did at Bełżec. It seems highly unlikely he would spend the energy he had expended without seeing the results personally, without standing at Himmler's shoulder, gauging his boss's reaction and receiving his nod of approval.

Himmler now asked Kammler to advise him on how to increase the daily killing capacity at Auschwitz II-Birkenau even further. Himmler also wanted the Auschwitz camp slave labor section enlarged yet again so it could house still more slaves. Himmler and Kammler, it would appear, were in a bidding war to murder more and more Jews more and more quickly, raising and reraising one another on the logistical limits of death and destruction, gassing and incineration. On August 11, 1942, construction of yet another round of ovens at Auschwitz was begun.[36] Auschwitz architectural office head Bischoff sent an immediate telegraph to Kurt Prufer, the designer of J.A. Topf and Son's newest ovens, speeding this next project forward.[37] Topf and Sons had an edge on the other crematoria-building firms, given their ovens' unique design, which appealed to Kammler. The industry standard for cremations was one body per oven to provide a measure of dignity and privacy in the cremation process and to render identifiable ashes. As these niceties need not be observed at Auschwitz, Prufer proposed a new design that burned two bodies in one muffle, yet another way to save time and money.[38]

Later in August, Kammler spent two weeks touring Ukraine and Poland with Himmler. Kammler visited the Bełżec concentration camp, witnessing the gassing procedure there.[39] He noted the use of carbon monoxide at Treblinka, but after an experimental killing of 850 inmates at Auschwitz in September he favored the deadlier Zyklon B, a crystallized prussic acid pesticide. Auschwitz commandant Rudolf Höss would note that Zyklon B killed within three to fifteen minutes, which to me sounds excruciating. Timers were not needed to mark the completion of the process, Höss would testify at Nuremburg: "We knew when the people were dead because their screaming stopped." *Their screaming stopped.*

Höss seemed unashamed—even proud—of one particular innovation at Auschwitz. As you read his words, remember that the camp commandant is testifying at his own trial, and still can't seem to keep himself from boasting about his ability to kill people at the camp Kammler designed and built: "Still another improvement we made over Treblinka [another killing camp] was that at Treblinka the victims almost always knew that they were to be exterminated and at Auschwitz we endeavored to fool the victims into thinking that they were to go through a delousing process." Do not make the mistake of thinking that the Nazis were keeping the truth from their victims out of empathy. The deception was merely to ratchet up efficiency: When the victims "realized our true intentions…we sometimes had riots and difficulties due to that fact."[40]

The invaluable work of the International Military Tribunal at Nuremberg names Kammler for his role in killing Jews and burning their bodies. Brigadier General Telford Taylor, chief counsel in the war crimes trial of Oswald Pohl, SS Main Economic and Administrative Office (WVHA) chief, provided a description of Kammler's Amstgruppe C, which "was in charge of building and maintenance of barracks, camps, training grounds, field works, fortifications and road making, and also of construction work in concentration camps, such as gas chambers and crematoriums."[41] Sturmbannführer Wolfgang Grosch, employed in Amstgruppe C, provided step-by-step detail at the Pohl trial on how the department that Kammler ran accomplished its work. "Amstgruppe C," he stated in a sworn affidavit, "was responsible for the construction of gas chambers and crematories…Amt. C I drew up the building plans for those installations as far as the construction work was concerned and passed this on to Amt. C III, who worked on the engineering section of the construction, as e.g. the airing of gas chambers or the appliances for the gas to enter the chamber. Amt. C III then handed those plans to a private firm which was to supply the special machinery or the cremations furnaces."[42] But there is more, I learned. The tribunal itself cited the criminality of the WVHA and Amstgruppe C for "the existence of the gas chambers and the crematories, the use of slave labor, the treatment of concentration camp inmates."[43] As renowned World War II historian Martin Kitchen explains, Kammler clearly "had overall responsibility for the concentration camps, including the gas chambers and crematoria."[44] Jean Michel, one of very few survivors of the Dora-Nordhausen concentration camp, calls Kammler "an excellently-qualified representative of his Black Order," that is, the SS, and charges him with the "architectural marvels" that were Auschwitz and other concentration camps and, critically, for the "innovation of the gas chamber."[45] Even if Kammler didn't invent the gas chambers, he certainly perfected them, and he oversaw their installation—after traveling the Reich to review the alternative methods and rejecting them as insufficient in comparison.

Astonishingly, Kammler commissioned ovens to burn forty-four hundred bodies a day—enough to incinerate the entire Auschwitz population every three to four months, had there not been a constant influx of more unfortunate souls.[46] Yet even this pace was insufficient to meet the goals of the Final Solution. As we have seen, many other concentration camps were built or converted for the Nazi killing program, many to Kammler's specifications and under his diligent supervision.

Kammler was key in building and expanding concentration camps, and also in installing the gas chambers and ovens that made the Holocaust possible.

• • •

While Kammler was perfecting the killing machinery at Auschwitz, months passed for Joe Gringlas at the Blizyn slave labor camp. With the German invasion of Russia having failed and the Russians now advancing, he and the other workers were eventually forced onto a transport train of box cars. En route to its destination, the train was attacked by the Resistance. Joe and his fellow prisoners had momentary hopes of liberation. I imagined them huddled together in the dark interior of the box car, light weakly filtering in through cracks in the wooden siding, gunfire and disorganized shouting outside, the men in the railroad car urging on the Resistance. Their hopes rested on the gallantry of the men trying to liberate them. But it was not to be. "No. They [the Germans] hit them back. They used the machine guns." There would be no liberation yet. The train rolled on. Still not yet fully a man, Joe was headed on to his first death camp.

There was no food or water on the transport train. Joe was so parched with thirst that when the train stopped and he was let off at Auschwitz, he fell to the ground and greedily drank water that lay pooled in a nearby ditch, left over from the work of a brickmaker. The scene was easy for me to recreate in my mind's eye. I worked construction as a younger man. I have done tile, marble, and stone, all using a wet saw, which discharges filthy water laden with ground stone and marble. Before the milky discharge can eventually seep into the ground, it puddles in the nearest depression of earth, mixing in with the mud. I wouldn't let my dog drink it. For Joe Gringlas, it was salvation; he was "lucky" to have it, he said. This was Auschwitz.

As remarkable as his journey had been, the next turn of events would stun me. Having heard the stories of the disembarking trains at Auschwitz, I asked Joe if there was a sorting of prisoners. Unsurprisingly, there had been, and he had been through it: "First, they put us in a barrack.... Next day, somebody came, and put numbers on the arm." He showed me his number, B2247. It is grayish green, on his upper left forearm, running vertically. I had seen photos of Holocaust survivors' arms with tattooed numbers on them before, but never in person. It is jarring. The "B" begins about two thirds of the way up to the bend of his elbow. The numbers run crookedly from there. It is crude workmanship. The "B," he tells me, denotes a series. He is series B, number 2247.

Who is B2248? I wondered, keeping the thought to myself. *Where is B2248?*

Their clothes were taken, Joe told me, and they were kept in the barracks without food for days, joined by more prisoners as more trains arrived. (My mind flashed on the precise drawings I had seen of the Kammler barracks design.) Days later, they were all led outside and then into another barracks. They stood naked in a long line that extended the length of the building and out the door into the cold air. Menacing armed SS men stood guard along the line. Was this to be the end?

Joe drew me a sketch of the building to help me envision the layout. Inside, at the far end of the building, were bright lights. I imagined spotlights on stands. The rest of the room was in relative darkness, giving the lighted portion the air of a theater stage, ready for a play to begin. Joe cautiously craned his neck around the line to look. Behind a table, under the bright lights, sat a lone man in a white coat, backed by a cadre of SS men. Dr. Josef Mengele. *Dear God*, I thought to myself. My skin tingled, an autonomic response, my animal instincts warning me of danger.

As he approached Mengele, Joe, like all the other prisoners, was naked. Nakedness was a regular tactic of the Nazis, reducing prisoners to something less than human—humiliating them and making them vulnerable, compliant. Joe was made to model. Hands above his head, rotating slowly on his kitchen stool, Joe mimicked for me the motions he went through for the Angel of Death. This was a selection process that meant either immediate death or some hope of life, however fleeting. Joe was face to face with Mengele, as close as we two sat for our interview, he explained. I was speechless.

"How old are you?" Mengele asked Joe. Joe said it to me crisply, imitating Mengele.

"Eighteen," Joe lied. Eighteen, he told me, was more appealing to the Germans, better for working.

"Can you work?" Mengele barked.

"*Jawohl*," Joe responded. He passed. Had he said "seventeen," would he have been gassed? Unknowable. His eyes twinkled at me. Was it my imagination, or was Joe now sitting a little straighter, defiance in his gaze? He was clearly proud that he had encountered the infamous Mengele and lived to tell of it. He knew he was telling me something huge. Technically, he was still a child at the time. But he had saved his own life. When I was seventeen, I was doing well in high school but driving too fast. My biggest concern was a girlfriend who had moved far away, leaving me momentarily lovesick. Joe was outwitting evil personified, hoping for and winning at least a momentary reprieve.

Joe was held in Auschwitz for months on the work camp side, Auschwitz I, avoiding Kammler's gas chambers. It occurred to me perversely that Joe was saved from Kammler by Mengele. What a twisted mess! He was then taken to nearby Buna Monowitz, one of the largest factories in Poland, which made not only all manner of munitions, but also Zyklon B—the killing gas. Against impossible odds, Joe found his older brother Sol at Buna. He can't explain this chance reunion any more than he can explain the actions of millions of Nazis and collaborators. Joe observed more than once that atrocities followed acts of bravery and kindness, which were followed by more atrocities. Even having lived through it, he couldn't make any more sense of the Holocaust than anyone else. The reunion between brothers was joyful, but tempered by the reality of their situation. Surviving was a day-to-day challenge. Their job at Buna was moving monstrously heavy concrete pipes, and a single error, a single dropped pipe, would cost them their lives. Any injury could cost them their lives. Any illness could cost them their lives. But they survived.

● ● ●

Kammler's work at another concentration camp, Dachau, is especially interesting to me because of the camp's long history. In an interrogation after the war ended, camp commandant Martin Gottfried Weiss confirmed that the crematoria at Dachau were upgraded in November 1942.

The onsite work was supervised by the head of Building Inspection for the Weapons XX Police South, Obersturmbannführer (Lieutenant Colonel) Hubert Karl, who was "subordinate to Obergruppenführer Dr. Kammler."[47] Weiss was at the beginning a camp engineer, later an administrator, and still later the commandant.[48] While the point is contested, many historians contend that Dachau had no gas chambers. In their view it was a work camp, and those who perished there died under the Nazis' slave labor program instead of being gassed.[49] What is beyond debate is that a modern facility for burning and disposing of the bodies was constructed by Kammler and his engineers. With these ovens Kammler, at a minimum, erased the evidence of the deaths of tens of thousands of human beings who were worked to death—though not quite of all who perished there. One terribly moving photograph taken after liberation depicts Allied men near a pile of dead bodies stacked on the ground outside Kammler's crematorium at Dachau. A towering chimney is visible in the background. The pile of bodies appears to me to be about three feet high and thirty feet long in what had become an impromptu staging area for cremation. It is obvious from the photograph that the ovens had been overwhelmed by the death rate.

Dachau Concentration Camp, May 1945, photograph by Gilbert R. DiLoreto. Courtesy of the Jewish Virtual Library[50]

Corpses stacked at Dachau Concentration Camp, May 1945. Detail of photograph by Gilbert R. DiLoreto. Courtesy of the Jewish Virtual Library[51]

Kammler's significant role in the Holocaust has been largely over-looked by historians, so I was surprised to learn how well-known his crimes were to the Allies during and immediately after the war. United Nations War Crimes Commission (UNWCC) documents reveal the reach and variety of Kammler's criminal conduct, covering concentration camp construction, including of the gas chambers and ovens. Kammler was wanted by Belgium for torture and murder at Buchenwald and Mauthausen. He was accused of having "[d]irected the building of the Conc. Camp Auschwitz" in documents filed by Poland, with Czechoslovakia charging murder of its citizens at Auschwitz. A separate set of UNWCC documents filed by the Poles charged him with leveling the Warsaw Ghetto, an act that resulted in the termination of thousands of lives.[52] Also, France wanted Kammler for murder, torture, and abuse of French prisoners at the Dora-Mittelbau concentration camp.

To this day there is debate about the exact number of people killed by the Nazis in the concentration camp system, but most historians agree to a total of some two million people. It's important not to just glide over that number. Stop and think of the small handful of people in your life you love most dearly, the ones most essential to you—your spouse, your children, your parents, your siblings. Make it about them. Imagine all of them—all innocent—taken away and tortured, beaten, starved, made sick, marched through winter snow barefoot in threads of clothing, and in the end gassed and burned, their ashes tossed into an anonymous grave. Your loved ones. Your child. Then multiply that sick play by hundreds of thousands, millions. Only then can we even begin to appreciate the enormity of the Holocaust.

And so much of this barbarity was made possible by the ingenuity and wicked diligence of Hans Kammler, who made killing his vocation. Disturbing imagery from the Holocaust is seemingly endless. But no image is more universally recognized than Kammler's gas chambers and crematoria. Newsreels depict captive souls pressing against the perimeter fences of the concentration camps, trying to reach their liberators, and trying to put as much distance as possible between themselves and these implements of death. While there are hundreds, even thousands, of Nazis who share blame for the killing of the Holocaust, Kammler must be near the very top of the list.

Hans Kammler as the Key to the Nazi Slave Labor Program

Kammler was also deeply involved in establishing and running Germany's cruel slave labor program. He was a champion of slave labor from before its adoption until Germany was overrun by the Allies, when the slave laborers were abandoned by their Nazi captors, released, killed en masse, or force-marched into the interior. During the forced marches, stragglers were routinely shot along the road. My friend Joe Gringlas recounted seeing "perhaps a thousand dead on the roadside" during his forced march from Auschwitz to Gleiwitz, Poland, in the snow in late 1944. Then he spent two weeks on an open-car train, without food and with only falling snow for water en route to Dora.

Germany's use of slave labor, slow to be acknowledged after the war, is widely recognized today.[53] By 1944, almost eight million foreign workers and POWs were toiling away for Germany in a program that qualified as a war crime.[54] Slaves were used by both Germany's government and its industry, representing fully one-quarter of the country's total workforce.

I can't emphasize enough how much meeting Joe Gringlas meant in my evaluation of Kammler's role in the Nazi slave labor. It's one thing to read about it in the history books, or even in musty original documents. It's quite another to have it described to you by a man who endured it, gesturing with the hands that did the lifting.

There is no need to reproduce the work proving slave labor existed, but understanding Kammler's leadership role in persuading Germany to use POWs, and later Jews, as slaves is important. As Germany's military prospects began to decline in 1941, a tension began to arise within the Reich. One faction of leaders, those behind the Final Solution, were obsessed with the complete extermination of the Jews. Another powerful group remained committed to winning the war and saw advantage in using able-bodied Jews to replace the ever-waning ranks of German workers. The second group believed that the Holocaust distracted and detracted from the military campaign: it required essential human resources to locate, confine, transport, and then kill and dispose of Jews. It needed camps and ghettos as collection points, trains to transport them, and people to guard them. It demanded considerable staff to build and then operate the killing camps.

Adolf Eichmann, Reinhard Heydrich, and their ilk were immovable proponents of the Final Solution. They believed that leaving any Jews—particularly healthy Jews—alive was an invitation to their later resurgence as a stronger race. It was a typically craven Nazi interpretation of natural selection. Industry leaders and generally those charged with producing goods and materiel were in the other group, wanting to exploit the discounted Jewish labor to increase output and profits.

Kammler adroitly straddled the line between the two opposing camps. He smoothed the edges of these seemingly mismatched jigsaw puzzle pieces—these divergent goals of winning the war and exterminating the Jewish race. As we shall see, Hans Kammler was among those who first proposed the broad use of Jews as slave laborers, making it a goal to work all Jews fit for labor to death after murdering all others. Kammler, it seems, was eager to help create and then preside over a system explicitly designed to literally work its unwilling participants to death. In the process of eliminating even the healthiest Jews through "annihilation through labor," Kammler would extract every ounce of energy from his victims, aiding the German war effort in the process of ending the Jewish problem. As Rudolf Haunschmied and his coauthors explain in *St. Georgen-Gusen-Mauthausen: Concentration Camp Mauthausen Reconsidered*, "Murder would remain the shared ultimate goal of all segments of the SS,"[55] while it would freely exploit slaves to help win the war and to enrich and empower itself.

Kammler's thinking on efficiency at any cost, including the exploitation of slaves, was developed years before the Reich ever began its slave labor program—even years before the war began—as is documented in a 1934 treatise he coauthored.[56] He and his coauthor envisioned the use of concentration camp inmates in the SS construction corps. They managed to create a link between engineering, sound management, and Nazi ideology: "The policies of National Socialism are now dedicated to the firm connection of the man to the soil through hearth and home as the basic foundation of the people (*volk*) and the state."[57] The SS organization that Kammler eventually built purposely mirrored the railway network and tracked the slave labor camp locations, which Kammler "featured as labor depots."[58] While the Nazis often used euphemisms and indirect language to describe their killing, enslavement was more openly documented; it was as if Kammler and his SS colleagues saw no legal or moral infraction there. Hitler proclaimed a national policy of geographical expansion of Germanic culture and ideals in broad strokes, and Kammler filled it in with his blueprints, then brought it to life and made it a reality with slave labor.

Kammler's 1934 cogitations became national policy in the form of Germany's Overall Eastern Plan (Generalplan Ost), an elaborately developed scheme to create a Jew-free expanse of Nazi-ruled and Nazi-colonized lands in Eastern Europe, linking Germans to their God-given soil in the East. The explicit goal of the plan was to populate Russia and its "vassal border states"—Poland, the Baltic countries, the Ukraine, Crimea, and more—with ethnic Germans, killing, evicting, or ghettoizing the previous occupants—or converting them into slaves. Kammler's town of Auschwitz was to be among the first model communities, including ultra-modern infrastructure, new buildings, agricultural and industrial projects, new roads, parks, and schools for the German families Hitler would pay to resettle to replace the undesirable Poles and Jews. Tax incentives would be provided to German companies that agreed to open factories there.[59] This model was to be duplicated as Germany took more and more territory, ensuring German culture kept pace with the Reich's military victories.

Kammler's first practical iteration of the plan in January 1942 was budgeted to cost twenty to thirty billion Reichsmarks to implement and would consume the lives of 175,000 slave laborers.[60] Incredibly, Himmler's handwritten notes in the margins of this first iteration bade Kammler to plan on an even more expansive scale.[61] And Kammler was willing to think bigger: in his twenty-year forecast of Nazi conquest, twenty-nine million prisoners from occupied territories were to be made into slave laborers and worked to death in the construction of a vast SS empire.[62] There can be no more solid proof of Kammler's guilt for the murder of the Nazis' slave laborers. He literally made plans to kill tens of millions.

As Holocaust historian Robert Jan van Pelt demonstrates in "A Site in Search of a Mission," it was Kammler who saw the empty billets in the camp at Auschwitz, originally built for POWs, as a home for Jewish slaves and expanded it for that purpose. It was Kammler who fundamentally set a new course and "designated both Soviet prisoners of war and Jews as potential slave laborers for the building brigades."[63] And when the Overall Eastern Plan was put on hold, given the exigencies of war, it was Kammler who preserved the slave labor program. Kammler moved the Jews, like pieces on a chessboard, from enslavement under the plan to other purposes: enslavement for German industry, the

German government, and his SS construction brigades. Kammler not only exploited the Nazi's Jewish slave labor program—he invented it.

Kammler was fiercely loyal to the SS. He foresaw armaments facilities in Germany and the occupied territories—the Netherlands, Czechoslovakia, Scandinavia, and Germany itself, and as far off as the Urals and Baku on the Caspian Sea—producing weapons to be used by the SS's military arm rather than the German army. The Reich was a beneficiary under Kammler's plan, but the SS was its real winner.

In order for the SS to become truly dominant, it would have to achieve nothing short of independent sovereignty. This meant the SS needed to become financially and legally separate not only from the German army and the German government, but also from the Nazi Party itself. Kammler's plan was a state of total self-reliance for the SS, from which total autonomy, total power, and total self-governance would follow. To achieve this state, Kammler knew the SS needed its own generous and reliable source of income—slaves.

This revenue source flowed from a confluence of events Kammler helped create. First, the SS commanded the concentration camps, giving them control over the slaves. Second, the SS had responsibility for overseeing newly vanquished territories, where those to be newly enslaved resided.[64] Third, Kammler had sole authority for construction projects throughout the Reich—an ideal avenue for utilizing the slaves and turning a profit. Finally, Kammler enjoyed good relations with the giants of German industry, which was ever hungrier for manpower as more and more able-bodied German men were siphoned into military service.

Many German companies of all sizes, including some whose names are still familiar—Volkswagen, BMW, Daimler-Benz, Siemens, Messerschmitt, Blaupunkt, to name but a few—rented Jewish slave laborers from the SS, often for less than ten Reichsmarks (about sixty U.S. dollars today) for a twelve-hour day. The German government also rented Kammler's slaves, making direct payments to the SS. As an example, one Kammler chart shows a total of 90,785 slaves working within the aircraft industry in the month of January 1944 alone.[65] Kammler had claimed the slave laborers as an asset for himself and the SS and then leased them back to German industry and government, rechanneling money from the German war economy into SS coffers.[66]

Private industry within the Reich and much of the government and military were now dependent on the good graces of the powerful duo of Kammler and Himmler for the cheap labor of slaves like Joe Gringlas. At any given time Kammler had under his personal control as much as 40 percent of Germany's slave labor population. The Nuremburg Military Tribunal agreed he was its undisputed leader.[67] It described the WVHA as a sprawling commercial enterprise that generated hundreds of millions of Reichsmarks every year for the SS. The ultimate aim was to "make the SS economically independent, both from the State and from the Party. The SS was to become a 'state within a state' industrially and commercially, as well as politically and militarily." In the WVHA "fanatical Nazis turned into fanatical businessmen, and their business was profit for the SS state and for themselves through the fraudulent income of the SS industries."[68]

Proof abounds of Kammler's extensive criminal use of Jewish slaves. The Dora-Mittelbau concentration camp complex stands as a particularly compelling example of his guilt because Kammler was in charge of building Dora from the ground up, not just expanding it.[69] Since before the start of the war, the Germans had housed a top-secret rocket research and production facility at Peenemünde, on Germany's northern Baltic coast. Though the Allies were slow to catch on, they eventually discovered the site and its purpose, and so the Germans decided to relocate the rocket project. Kammler was integral in choosing Nordhausen as the new site in the German interior, out of range of Allied bombers. He personally signed the order on January 31, 1945, moving the rocket team to the new location.[70]

To ensure its secrecy, Kammler would build the entire Nordhausen facility underground, using massive slave labor to dig miles of tunnels. Dora was the name of the camp Kammler constructed to house the slaves as they built and operated the Nordhausen assembly plant for the V-1 unmanned bomb, the V-2 rocket, anti-aircraft missiles, the Heinkel He 162 jet fighter, and more. Construction of living quarters for the slaves would not even begin until the factory space had been dug out of Kohnstein Mountain in the Harz mountain range. Over months, Kammler's slaves excavated a network of colossal caverns using sheer human effort, primitive tools, and hazardous blasting. The result was the largest underground facility ever created—and the deaths of thousands of slaves. Lead German rocket scientist Wernher von Braun confirmed in post-war interrogation that Kammler was in charge at Dora-Nordhausen and readily used slaves. One must know about von Braun's extreme reluctance to ever refer to slave labor, much less to acknowledge having been close to it, in order to appreciate the significance of this admission.

Not only did Kammler use slaves, but he also used them ruthlessly. In selecting Kammler to lead the entire Dora-Nordhausen project, Himmler assured Albert Speer that he would be satisfied with the results,[71] and Kammler delivered the impressive facility with incredible speed. Albert Speer considered it an "astonishing performance." In a letter to Kammler, he noted that the feat "does not have any remotely similar example anywhere in Europe and is unsurpassable even by American standards!" The unprecedented undertaking was completed at a horrible cost to the slave laborers, whose conditions were deplorable. Kammler readily sacrificed basic living conditions in the interest of expediency. His orders to subordinates were clear: "No matter the number of human victims, the work must be executed and finished in the shortest possible time."[72]

The slaves were forced to live underground, never seeing the light of day, never drawing a breath of fresh air. When not working they tried desperately to sleep despite the tunnels' stale air, thick with dust, amid explosions and constant digging, as slaves worked in unending rotations.[73] Speer conceded the lack of oxygen in the tunnels made him dizzy, and the stench of human excrement was unbearable. His diary recounts a December 1943 inspection of Nordhausen by his entourage: "Some of the men were so affected that they had to be forcibly sent off on vacations to restore their nerves."[74] After a few minutes of exposure to the routine the Dora slaves endured around the clock, Speer's men apparently suffered the equivalent of battle fatigue or today's post-traumatic stress disorder. The International Military Tribunal's summary of the conditions at Dora was succinct and damning: "Clothing was insufficient, especially for cold weather; barracks were inadequate; the air was very bad from lack of ventilation. The inmates, approximately 1,500 to 2,000, were housed in the shafts of tunnels, which were 8 to twelve meters high. The inmates slept on bunks, four on top of each other, and had insufficient covers.... The food was insufficient.... Medical care was also insufficient."[75] Dora, referred to as "the dreaded Dora camp" in a U.S. Army report on Buchenwald, which had its own indefensible standards of mistreatment,[76] was known to be much worse than other camps. Stunningly, one internee who had arrived via the dreaded Auschwitz was heard to remark, "Compared to Dora, Auschwitz was easy."[77]

One inmate of Dora who survived described a particularly harrowing event: the execution of thirty slaves suspected of sabotaging the rockets they were forced to assemble. It was grizzly. Within the confines of the largest of the bleak Dora tunnels—wide enough to accommodate side-by-side railway cars with room to spare—the entire workforce was assembled to bear witness and to be taught a lesson. The victims' hands were bound closely behind their backs and thick wooden dowels were placed in their mouths like horse bits, secured tightly behind their heads with heavy-gauge wire. Ropes around their necks were fastened to the arm of a crane, which was raised at a torturously slow pace, strangling the victims in a miserable, protracted death. As if the message needed reinforcing, the victims' bodies were left hanging for hours afterward. Kammler would later boast in a business meeting that he had ordered the slaves hanged to ensure those remaining understood the imperative of following his orders.[78]

The death rate from overwork, mistreatment, and malnutrition—not including the very infirm and sick who were shipped out of Dora before they could expire there—was predictably abysmal. Inmates were so emaciated they could be mistaken for dead: "On one occasion a Dutch priest was carried away. He recovered consciousness later to find himself lying naked in a pile of corpses."[79] One account puts total deaths at thirty thousand.[80] For Kammler, the death of each slave was its own small victory.

A rare photograph of Hans Kammler, circa 1943. U.S. National Archives Record and Administration

Joe Gringlas's survival of Dora completes the story he told me in Philly. Joe left Auschwitz when it was liquidated in the depths of winter in mid-January 1945. He and his fellow prisoners were marched through the snow to Gleiwitz, Poland—a forced march of some forty miles. They wore no coats, just the flimsiest of clothes. Temperatures were unbearably frigid. No food was available. Stragglers—and there were many—were summarily shot. Joe saw the bodies left unceremoniously on the side of the road. Gleiwitz was a major collection point for workers coming from camps all over Poland heading west, always away from the advancing Russian army. From there, prisoners were loaded onto open train cars "like cattle." "*Open* train cars," he repeated slowly, making sure I understood. He gestured with his flat hand at his chest, and I pictured side walls on the cars as high as a man's chest. Joe told me that he and his brother Sol were among the first to get on their train car. That meant they were furthest from the doors, pressed against the far wall of the train.

"On top of each car were SS men, with machine guns," Joe said, indicating the front and backs of each car. They guarded against escape. Unknown to him, the train was bound for Dora-Nordhausen by way of Czechoslovakia. The meandering, tortuous trip, fully and constantly exposed to the winter weather, took two weeks with no food and no water. When I incredulously insisted that they must have gotten water from somewhere in order to survive, Joe said that they collected and ate snow that fell into the open cars. As he said this, he reflexively looked ceiling-ward, drawn into the moment from the past.

"I tell you what happened," Joe said, leaning forward on his kitchen stool with an eagerness that suggested he liked the next part of his story. Some common civilian workers in Czechoslovakia, understanding exactly what was going on as the train passed through their village, threw their lunches into the open cars. Alert SS guards responded swiftly with warning shots fired into the air, putting a quick end to the acts of compassion. Joe was careful to make certain that I understood the good-ness of these people. He found it remarkable that they would share their food, scarce even for the civilian population, while risking retribution from the SS men. He didn't focus on the behavior of the SS. Ever the optimist, I thought, always describing himself as lucky. But that is a good thing that in this story was probably necessary for bare survival.

The Dora-bound train rolled on to a disturbing incident. At one of its very frequent unscheduled stops without warning in Czechoslovakia, the SS "opened up the train. With the SS on top, they opened up the train. And they throw bread out onto the ground. So, all the people standing in the front of the train by the door run out, because they are hungry.... And they are all killed right away. 'Bop bop bop bop bop.' The machine gunners killed them.... Lucky thing I was inside [far from the door]—otherwise I wouldn't be here." I see in my mind a scene from a movie. Dark brown loaves hit bright white snow as the train creaks to a stop. Emaciated passengers push through opening doors in a growing frenzy. A few jump the sidewalls of the car, joining the melee, desperate for food. The guards, smiling to each other, watch the prisoners rush the bait, churning the snow in their urgency. There are whoops and cries of joy from the prisoners. The starvation is about to end. They have arrived who-knows-where, but here is bread. Suddenly, gunfire erupts. The snow is splattered with bright red blood. Fabric and skin tear. Bones crunch. Bodies fall. A lone prisoner, miraculously unharmed, breaks for the tree line. He is cruelly allowed to run for a bit, creating hope, but is then shot in the back—the last to fall. The guards exchange words in German as the muzzle smoke clears—crass jokes about marksmanship and hunting licenses.

This wasn't a movie, but real life. Joe estimates that two hundred people were murdered that day. "This was play for them," he observed of the Nazis. I just can't understand it. Days later, their interminable ride over, at Dora they were ordered to shower in cold water. It was the first time Joe had bathed in weeks. They were then made to walk, completely naked and barefoot, through the snow over a quarter mile to their barracks. I have heard and read of many, many people who wonder why the Jews didn't resist. How they could let themselves be walked into a gas chamber, thinly disguised as a delousing chamber or a shower? But sometimes, it seems, a shower is just a shower, as it was here for Joe and Sol. Had they resisted, perhaps they would have died then and there. Such was the life of the Kammler slaves.

Joe and his brother worked in one of Nordhausen's underground tunnels—not a main tunnel, but an isolated tunnel still being prepared as a production line. On one occasion a civilian field engineer in civilian clothes snuck Joe a piece of bread during the workday. Joe described it as an incredibly tense moment, with the scientist looking around furtively before slipping the morsel into his hand. I imagined the scene like two CIA agents passing a palmed note on a crowded rail station platform. This was another dangerous act of selflessness that Joe was careful to relate to me, gesturing toward my notepad, silently urging, *write it down.*

One of the things that amazed me about Joe was how, in what should have been a constant state of misery, he collected and remembered acts of human kindness like flowers pressed into the pages of a book or held close in his breast pocket. These memories are foremost in his mind. The evil is never forgotten, but it is carefully consigned to a remote, locked chamber of his mind he can access as needed. It is the sweeter memories that inform his life today.

At Dora-Nordhausen, Joe's health declined. A few weeks before liberation he was categorized as unfit for work. He felt certain he was slated for extermination, and to this day doesn't know how he survived. Joe remembers as if it were yesterday—April 11, 1945—when American tanks arrived at his part of Nordhausen. "They came in with a tumult." Sol was put on a medical stretcher car and Joe hopped a ride with him to avoid being separated yet again. They were put in a field hospital and gradually regained their health. The brothers left the area weeks later, making the long journey home to Poland in search of family, only to learn that no relatives remained and none would be returning. All had been murdered. They were the only survivors.

With Russia occupying Poland, they were forbidden by the Communists from leaving. But they were determined to not live under yet another oppressive regime, so they hatched a plan. Joe understandably has a soft spot in his heart for Czechs who had tossed food to his train as it was bound for Nordhausen. Now with the aid of a small handful of Czechs, Joe and Sol escaped Poland and traveled through Czechoslovakia back to Germany, where they were interned in Lundsberg under a special Allied program for displaced persons. Joe was trained in radio and television repair, which ultimately became his career, and he made his way to America. He met his wife, Reli, in Detroit in 1950. She herself was a hidden child during the war, and that also helps explain his fondness of Czechs—his wife is from Czechoslovakia and was sheltered throughout the war by the Czechs. Joe and his brother Sol had survived Kammler's system of death camps and work camps, as well as his credo: "No matter the number of human victims, the work must be executed and finished in the shortest possible time."[81]

After I interviewed Joe, I wanted to express my gratitude. He had begun by telling me it was difficult for him to relive these wicked memories. But as I began to thank him, he held up a hand, cutting me off, and *he* thanked *me*. What felt to me at the outset like a great way to help tell the Kammler story now took on the weight of an obligation. I was now Joe's messenger. And the messenger for B2248. And B2249. And all the others who perished in Kammler's camps.

● ● ●

While he was building Nordhausen and Dora, Kammler was also in charge of the construction at Ebensee, its nearby liquid oxygen factory, and the Messerschmitt 262 plant at St. Georgen—all the manpower for which was provided by slave laborers. Kammler headed up the Blizna V-2 firing ranges, as well. Himmler attributed the success of the build-out of all these missile and airplane factories to the "technical brilliance" of the SS which, of course, meant Kammler and the SS slave labor program.[82] According to a trial affidavit of Heinrich Courte, an engineer who worked for him within Amstgruppe C, Kammler was put in charge of construction of the Weimar-Buchenwald railroad in early 1943.[83] The eight-mile span was built entirely by forced labor using eight hundred slaves. As ever with Kammler, speed was of the essence and prisoner conditions were awful. "Twelve-hour night and day shifts," reads a prisoner report, "a regime of terrible beatings for all the prisoners, the use of a dog squad against them both during work and during their marches to and from the workplace." The report documents that these atrocities "took place in the presence of SS Brigadier General Dr. Kammler…and other Nazi bigwigs."[84]

A Kammler subordinate also documented Kammler's use of 2,518 slave laborers to work on fortifications and supply lines for V-1 and V-2 rockets. The report describes the conditions of the slaves' existence at four sites in northern France as "comparatively good and clean,"[85] so one might expect this particular cadre of slave laborers to have fared somewhat better than most. Yet in four months it experienced twenty-eight reported deaths—and that figure is incomplete. Adding to the admitted death toll of the prisoners transferred to Buchenwald, the "escaped" prisoners, the prisoners "shot while trying to escape," and the prisoners missing after bombing attacks renders a shocking 27 percent of prisoners annually dead or missing. And that is under conditions deemed "comparatively good and clean." Sadly, the report was accurate. Conditions and death rates were even worse elsewhere. In some of the worst cases, as many as 80 percent of a workforce died within three months of arrival at a slave labor camp.[86]

Kammler's guilt in the slave enterprises was again documented by his own hand in a letter he wrote to Richard Glücks, inspector of concentration camps: "In view of the increasing shortage of civilian workers the execution of the construction tasks devolving upon the SS Economic Administration Main Office in the third year of war, 1942, requires the employment of an increased number of prisoners, prisoners of war, and Jews."[87] This is not a request. It's Kammler telling Gluecks, ostensibly his peer, the way things will be. The tone reflected Kammler's momentum and future more than his position at the time. He enjoyed the confidence of both Himmler and Hitler, and he used that clout freely.

At Mauthausen-Gusen in Austria, Kammler's slave labor policy resulted in the deaths of over forty thousand human beings in construction of another underground factory, one for the Messerschmitt Me 262, the revolutionary German jet fighter. By the end of the war, over 320,000 slaves had died in the Mauthausen-Gusen concentration camp complex.

Oswald Pohl, the head of the WVHA, spotlighted the Kammler slave empire in his own post-war affidavit: "The most important employers of concentration camp prisoners in the order of the number of their employees were the following: a) my Office group (Amstgruppe) C 'construction,' head Obergruppenführer Dr. Kammler...."[88] The Nuremburg

Military Tribunal prosecutor, in agreement, said plainly of Amstgruppe C, which Kammler headed: "They were the greatest user of concentration camp labor in all of Germany...."[89]

At the end of his memoirs, Auschwitz commandant Rudolf Höss wrote about several seminal characters. In pronounced contrast to the contempt he showed for nearly every SS officer, SS chief Höss practically fawned over Kammler. He claimed that Kammler made strong and continued efforts to improve living conditions at Auschwitz and other labor camps. He also admitted, though seemingly without grasping that he was making a damning admission, that Kammler sought these improvements only so the slave laborers could be more productive. "Kammler knew quite well that only healthy prisoners would do well for the war factories." So even Höss's praise was an indictment.[90]

The callousness of the slave labor system is reflected in the words of an October 1943 speech by SS chief Himmler: "Whether or not 10,000 Russian women collapse from exhaustion while digging a tank ditch interests me only in so far as the tank ditch is completed for Germany."[91] Himmler then outdid that shocking statement: "Whether nations live in prosperity or starve to death interests me only insofar as we need them as slaves for our culture."[92] The notorious Heinrich Himmler was articulating the rationale for the Nazi war crimes, but the much less well-known Hans Kammler, another criminal of the first order, was carrying them out.

● ● ●

I wrote this chapter in my home office in bits and pieces over several weeks—drafting two or three pages and then escaping to fresh air and sunshine for mental breaks. I might have been better off speeding through as quickly as possible, writing it all, and then moving on. In retrospect, I was simply drawing out the mental torment of confronting this poisonous history. I am usually an expert at compartmentalizing—dealing with something and then walling it off in my mind, not letting it worry me.

This material, though, was having a cumulative corroding effect. The numbers of dead were hard to even contemplate. When falling asleep at night, I had visions of the concentration camp victims gathered silently at the perimeter fences from the newsreel footage. Sometimes I saw Joe Gringlas as a young man, a boy really, fending for himself in those horrific camps.

At the recent funeral of a close friend's mother, I could feel the healing that began during the service, and I couldn't help but wonder about all the Kammler victims who never had a funeral or proper burial; how many orphans he made, how many children he killed. Were Joe and Sol able to erect headstones for their lost family members? Do they still wonder whether one of their siblings might somehow still be alive? I felt an obligation, almost a mental compulsion, to keep the people of the war and the Holocaust front and center in my mind. There is an inhumane, barbaric cruelty I could never fully absorb without experiencing it firsthand, but I did not want to disrespect the victims' suffering by reviewing only moldy records antiseptically and then just moving on with my own comfortable life.

Sorting through all these documents should have been a thrill for me. With my fresh eyes, I made a couple of connections and important finds that Keith and Colm had overlooked. I should have come away with the satisfaction of solving a uniquely challenging puzzle one piece at a time. It was an exercise I would normally enjoy. I grew up loving history, craving knowledge. I had at my fingertips scads of official records, including documents that had been seen by fewer than a dozen people since they were filed away. I held truly rare papers with Kammler's signature and Franklin D. Roosevelt, Winston Churchill, Adolf Hitler, Dwight D. Eisenhower, Omar Bradley, and George S. Patton's names. I remember as a child learning that my father's lieutenant colonel oak leaves came directly from Patton, and I was in awe—Old Blood and Guts himself. I should have been elated by the work I was engaged in, but I was mortified, conflicted about turning the page to see what was next. It was heart-wrenching, exhausting.

We know Kammler was among the worst of the worst. And it is excruciating to realize, but the maniacal and ruthless drive that made Kammler such a successful Nazi war criminal also made him vital to America's post-war plans. Hans Kammler's high position in the Nazi war machine meant he deserved prosecution, conviction for war crimes, and the death penalty. But that same position meant that he had bargaining power. Power that may have been enough to make the Americans forget, if not forgive. Colm was our expert on Germany's rockets. It was up to him to convince me that the rockets Kammler ruled made him an attractive bargain for the Americans. That's where I turned next.

CHAPTER THREE

Vengeance

*"You must realize that the rocket is no longer
your private baby."*

—*Heinrich Himmler to Wernher von Braun*[1]

"**W**hat do you know about Germany's World War II rockets?"
I asked my son, Taylor, who was in high school at the time.
I hadn't discussed the war with him before, and having seen
his history text book, I assumed his study of the twentieth century in his
public school had been cursory, at best. But I knew Taylor was an avid
consumer of information—forever online, reading books, watching the
History and Discovery channels. "Where did you hear that?" I was
always asking him, about some esoterica he was spouting. His answer
was almost never "school," almost always some outside source. When I
asked about Germany's rockets, he said without hesitation, "The V-1
and V-2? Peenemünde? Von Braun?" He knew a lot, it turned out, even
beyond these key words. My father did as well, and so too did some of
the friends I asked. No one, though, had heard of Kammler. Even those
who considered themselves students of the era looked at me with blank
stares if I mentioned the name. And I kept coming back to the same
question: *Was German rocket and other secret weapons technology so
superior to that of the Allies that they would disregard Kammler's unbelievably long list of crimes and make a bargain with him?*

The value of the rockets is already proven by history—confirmed by the fact that we brought hundreds of German rocket scientists to the United States—including lead scientist Wernher von Braun—and employed them for decades. Somehow that was a sudden realization for me. The Russians had also frantically tried to recruit the same Nazi rocket team members in the aftermath of the war, offering to double any deal made by the Western Allies.[2] The rocket team members, as well as the hardware and the technology they controlled, were highly prized by all the Allies. "Even more so than you think, Dean," Colm told me. "Have you spoken to Keith today?"

"No. What's up?" I asked, my curiosity aroused.

"He sent me a doc late last night for my review. He thought he had something useful, but he wasn't sure. It's gold. Never been disclosed before." Keith and Colm often spoke together, reached tentative conclusions during their consultations, and only then brought me into the loop. This was my preferred method of operation. Frankly, I didn't have time for their detailed and seemingly endless cogitations. I was in "bottom line" mode. The bottom line on this particular document—a 1947 "Security Survey" from Fort Bliss in Texas[3]—was that it contained one of the single most interesting tidbits of information I learned during this project, and it went miles to prove the value of Germany's rocket technology.

"The Russians sent paratroopers to kidnap von Braun after he was in U.S. custody, attacking American troops in the process," Colm told me. "It was a military-style attack; an attempt to get von Braun for themselves, and Keith's doc proves it. The document speaks of 'the Russians [sic] strong desire to gain control or possession of Dr. von Braun.' Dean, the document reads, and I quote, 'When Dr. von Braun was taken by American troops in May 1945, a detachment of Russian soldiers attacked American troops holding Dr. von Braun, in an attempt to take him from American power,' close quote." Colm went on, "Historically, there have been friendly fire incidents, cases of mistaken identity, even a few skirmishes we've heard about," Colm said, "but this is an altogether different sort." Even in the frothing aftermath of World War II, with belligerents everywhere, this was an insanely dangerous Russian action, risking massive retaliation, and I couldn't believe I hadn't heard of it before. This operation took planning, on-the-ground intelligence, clearance at an undoubtedly high level, and resources. The mere fact that the Russians had attempted such an audacious, premeditated mission after the end of the war reveals the value of von Braun. I never ceased being amazed at the fabulous details and stories Keith and Colm were able to extract from records long untouched.

Enormous effort, time, money, and science went into developing Nazi Germany's rockets. And every single step and misstep in that elaborate process could be avoided by the Americans if they seized Kammler's rocket team. Taking advantage of the Germans' research, leapfrogging over all the steps they had already completed, would mean huge savings in money. And it would also save something vastly more valuable than money in the Cold War arms race with the Soviets—time.

● ● ●

I live well over an hour from my downtown Washington, D.C., office. My commute varies between a long, unpredictable drive, a trip on an unreliable metro system, or a ride on a commuter bus. If I drove, I was listening to books on tapes or Great Courses. When I took the bus, I was reviewing documents, even books on the war or on rocket science. Now for the second day in a row, Keith called my mobile while I was making the long slog home by car. The day before he had talked my ear off about the war, and I had been able to parry with some of the information I had been digesting. Today, he called again and kept me talking most of the way, asking me outright what more he and Colm could do to get me on board as the author of the book. Today his energy was coming out as mild frustration. I owed him an honest answer. I told him I had read all their documents, but remained undecided. I was reading other material for context, even doing research of my own. I wasn't stringing them along. I just truly believed they weren't quite there yet.

"You need to read more. Study more. It's all there," Keith, always congenial, could be insistent without being overbearing.

"I've read everything you've sent," I countered.

"I'm not sure you have," he challenged. There was an unfamiliar cleverness in his voice when he said this. What was this? Keith wasn't suggesting I was lying, but he was up to something, and he didn't usually play games. Then he abruptly said he had to head to dinner, saying goodbye before I was ready. That was odd, too. When we connected during my evening commute, we almost always talked until I reached home unless I had another business call to make.

Close to home now, I rounded the final corner puzzled by our exchange. I backed into my driveway. It was hot summer day so, as was my practice, I left the car in the driveway to cool before pulling it into the garage, which would otherwise get intolerably overheated. As I walked up my front steps, I saw a half dozen cardboard boxes stacked on the porch— a UPS delivery. Sender: Keith Chester. Six very heavy boxes, as it turned out. What the hell was this? I dragged them inside my front door, where my wife Lou Anne had been waiting for me—the boxes were too heavy for her to move easily, like they were filled with bricks or sand.

Right there in my foyer, I cracked open the first box, the flaps popping up themselves when I cut the clear tape, the box packed to overflowing. I pulled out a packet of several fourteen-inch manila folders, four inches thick, bound in layers of saran wrap to keep them together. I unspooled the wrap and could see these were Keith's personal files—one marked U.S. Naval Technical Mission, the next labeled CIOS, another BIOS, another Beasley. They were warm to the center, having spent the afternoon in a box outdoors in the sunlight. Beneath them were four books: *Blunder!* by Tom Agoston, *Crossbow and Overcast* by James McGovern, then *Science with a Vengeance*, then *The Nazi Rocketeers*. Then another batch of files, and more books, more files. The collection had the familiar musty smell of an old municipal library.

I cracked a second box, this one more folders than books, Keith's scrawl on the tabs giving some names that I knew, and some that I didn't—Bełżec, Treblinka, Fleming, Gutman. The third box I opened had been intended as the first, and on top inside was an envelope with my name on it. A handwritten note within, from Keith: "Everything we have…." was all it said, but that said it all. The contents were spreading throughout our ample foyer, some books stacked on the stairs heading to the second floor. The sheer volume was getting out of hand. After a questioning look from Lou Anne, I decided to stop opening boxes. I would move them into my office before making a bigger mess.

My life is full of before-and-after moments, significant and defining events. There is before my children were born, and after; before marriage, and after; before I went to law school, and after. For me and this book project, there is before that day Keith buried me in information, and after that day. Before that day I was dubious, unsure, and on the fence. After that day, after seeing so many files brimming with original material, I realized how serious this project was. Nearly every one of the folders I began examining—and there were hundreds of them—had an interesting angle, a nugget of useful information— Something I could write an interesting paragraph or two about, though I still wasn't sure I could stitch the various parts together into a narrative. I took what I knew and began field-testing our information. Through my job and previous writing, I had the good fortune to know some people, so I had meetings with bestselling authors, several literary agents, and—this was important—lots of academics, including a couple of chaired history professors. I wasn't yet convinced we could write a great book, but after bouncing some of our materials off this informal group of advisors, I was sure we could produce something new and compelling.

Keith's note—"Everything we have"—was, it turned out, not quite accurate. The next day, six more boxes arrived. And then two more. Then Colm began sending me books, many of them used, bought online, rare and out of print. These were the academic and foreign language materials, records from the other side of the Atlantic. Those two certainly kept me churning. I was happy to have a basement. And I needed to spend more time on the bus, time for uninterrupted reading. I would begin by learning more about the Nazi rocket program.

• • •

There were tens of thousands of people employed in the research and production of Germany's rockets, but our story involves three most intimately. In addition to Kammler, the central characters in the German rocket program were General Walter Dornberger and Dr. Wernher von Braun. Dornberger, who served in artillery in the German army during World War I, spent his entire adult life lobbing explosives as far and accurately as possible. In 1930—well before Hitler became a household name, even in German households—the aptly named German Army Weapons Office established a specialized unit charged with developing military applications for rockets. The unit was housed at an army facility in Kummersdorf, a small town about sixty miles south of Berlin. Dornberger, then thirty-five years old, was the military administrative head of the project from the outset and for its duration. He was to begin secret research on what most engineers were convinced was an unattainable objective—a liquid-fueled long-range military rocket. The V-2 would become the best-known of 138 rocket models developed by the Germans,[4] and the technology that powered it would ultimately lead to the American ICBM and the moon shot. It and the V-1 were "Vengeance" weapons produced and used in combat late in the war as revenge for the devastating Allied bombing of German cities.

After the war, Dornberger wrote a book, *V-2: The Nazi Rocket Weapon*, half autobiography and half hagiography of himself, which Keith had included in one of his gift boxes to me. The author stakes his ultimate claim to fame at the end of his forward: "We have led our generation to the threshold of space—the road to the stars is now open." He wanted his legacy to be a contribution to space exploration, not Nazi weapons, a desire shared by von Braun. Dornberger was smart in his field, but also wily. When he was interned after the war he never let on to the fact that he understood English. Thus during interrogation he heard each question first in English, then translated into German, giving him more time to formulate his response.[5] Of his experience with Kammler as his supervisor, Dornberger wrote, "The first two months after Kammler's appointment were hard and bitter ones. I had to endure a whole series of humiliations. I had to submit to a chaotic flood of ignorant, contradictory, irreconcilable orders from this man who was neither soldier nor technician." In a single day, Kammler sent 123 teletype orders to Dornberger, many of them contradictory, demonstrating his frenetic pace and his penchant for micro-managing. Kammler—no love lost— called Dornberger "a public danger" who "ought to be court-martialed."[6] I had to hand it to Keith—it was literally amazing to be reading Dornberger's own account of working under Hans Kammler.

Dornberger's first major move in 1930 as head of the nascent research unit would forever define his career—he recruited Wernher von Braun, perhaps the greatest rocket scientist the world has ever known,[7] a man who would be even more acclaimed for his American career than for his work for Germany. At least one record Colm discovered indicates that it was von Braun who most clearly saw the military applications of rockets and approached Dornberger.[8] But however it came about, von Braun was the wunderkind who was the Nazi V-2 rocket program.[9] And he went on to put the United States into space—and on the moon. Without him, it would have happened in time, but it's impossible to say exactly when.

The fact that both von Braun and Dornberger enjoyed successful post-war careers in America—and in von Braun's case, widespread acclaim, however disturbing it may be—supports the possibility that Kammler, too, could have been saved and then sheltered by the Americans. The convenient myth is that Wernher von Braun was just a scientist whose priority was always space exploration, never weaponry. The excuse for the lethal work he did for the Nazis is that von Braun failed to leave his mother country before matters got out of hand. Once Hitler and the Nazis revealed their true colors, von Braun could no longer easily leave. But that's the same reasoning that many collaborators and faithful Nazis offered after the war—and didn't get away with. Unless, perhaps, they had something really valuable to offer the United States. Like von Braun. And Kammler.

In one of the books Keith sent me, an historian refers glowingly to von Braun's "art," emphasizing the peace-time applications of rocket technology.[10] He recounts the story of an automobile accident near the end of the war on March 12, 1945, in which von Braun broke his arm: "Von Braun remembers shouldering open a door, pulling the unconscious driver away from the wreck just before its motor caught fire, and becoming aware of searing pain in his left arm, which was dangling below his knee."[11] The selfless, injured rescuer pulling the lowly soldier free of the wreckage just before the flames erupt was a well-worn cliché even in the 1940s. Wouldn't it be pleasant to think that the Nazi bigwig scientists we allowed to thrive in the United States because we needed their rocket-building expertise were all genuinely nice guys?

As Dornberger's team designed and built increasingly larger rockets with greater range, the rocket program outgrew Kummersdorf within five years and moved to Peenemünde—one of the Germans' most remote research facilities during the war, located in the furthest reaches of northern Germany, a peninsula on the coast of the Baltic Sea.[12] Peenemünde, code-named HAP, short for Heimat Artillerie Park,[13] was home to the entire research team by August 1939. From there test rockets could be launched over the open sea with little possibility of detection, falling harmlessly into the water, green dye left behind to gauge their accuracy. The peninsula was also perfect for keeping people out, and the closest foreign land was the southern tip of Sweden, some two hundred miles north over water.

The elaborate Peenemünde site was planned as one-stop shopping, including research, development, and production—though subassemblies and components would be brought to Peenemünde from plants elsewhere. Reading up on the rocket program, I learned that in this context "research" means the theoretical, chalk-board work; "development" is building and assembling prototype rockets or rocket motors; "production" means building rockets in numbers for battlefield launch. Peenemünde had a factory to produce its own liquid oxygen, which fueled the rockets; its own power-generating station; a wind tunnel that operated at Mach 4 (like none other—so valuable it ended up being disassembled, moved and reassembled by the Germans during the war, and again by the Allies after the war), allowing researchers to test aerodynamic properties that until that time were mere theories; rocket motor test stands; rocket launch areas; a Development Works that included eighty buildings; a six-hundred-thousand-square-foot-rocket assembly building; quarters for the scientists—and a slave labor camp, in plain view.[14]

The eastern side of Peenemünde was for the V-2, developed under the auspices of the German army until the project was seized by Kammler and Himmler. On the western side, the air force worked on the subsonic V-1 "flying bomb," also known as the buzz bomb, another project ultimately subsumed under Kammler's wingspan. Under the Versailles Treaty there was no bar to Germany developing rockets, which simply had not been foreseen when the treaty was executed, so the Germans had a free hand. Imagine if, at the conclusion of a war in 1970, the losing belligerent had signed a surrender agreeing to strict limits on a long list of weapons. Because cyberwarfare was unknown in 1970, it would not have been listed among the prohibitions, and the losing belligerent would technically be free to develop an aggressive program to study, develop, and refine cyberattacks. So it was with Germany and rocket warfare after World War I.

● ● ●

After learning a bit about the performance and potential of the V-2, I wasn't the least bit surprised that Kammler sought to rule the project. It was a bona fide engineering marvel. The challenges the Germans faced in producing a rocket of the size and speed and with the requisite accuracy to make a difference on the field of battle were mind-blowing. They needed to create a shell that would withstand supersonic speeds and exit from and reenter the earth's atmosphere. Almost every component utilized in the final product was developed by their team—from gyroscopic stabilization devices, to a revolutionary liquid-fuel motor with its own high-speed pressurizing pump to inject fuel into the burning chamber, to precisely timed, radio-controlled engine cut-off that ensured the rocket completed its designed arc of travel onto the target area, to internal rudders that would allow controlled vertical take-off, to an extremely sophisticated guidance system the likes of which had never before existed. In addition to creating hundreds of individual features, they had to make them all work together as one system—a truly breath-taking engineering feat. One adroit commentator has written that "the V-2 cannot be thought of as a single device, but as a complex weapons system that created an industry dispersed across Germany requiring long supply lines and constant communication between hundreds of groups responsible for production, testing, integration, and firing."[15] Albert Speer aptly wrote of the making of the V-2: "It was like the planning of a miracle."[16] As a testament to its intricacy, Dornberger and von Braun estimated that over sixty-five thousand modifications had been made to the design of the V-2 before it was ready for mass production.

One German rocket engineer in his post-war memoir quoted a "common saying" I found enlightening: "a rocket is a sustained explosion." With the great force exerted in take-off and during flight to attain supersonic speeds, the liquid fuel consumed in great gulps, and the blasting furnace of exhaust flames, the description is perfect.[17] The Americans would have to recreate every aspect of this daunting project if they didn't capture the rocket team that Kammler could deliver. Even in today's world of computerization, the task seems nigh impossible to me, and I can understand why the Americans would, if they could, take this off-the-shelf technology at the end of the war rather than begin from virtually nothing.

I was surprised when I first learned the dimensions of the V-2. I'm not sure what I expected—perhaps a rocket as tall as a man. The V-2, though, was a forty-six-feet-tall, twenty-three-ton beast of a rocket that would fly over 180 miles, powered by a precise mixture of liquid fuels with a level of accuracy that would challenge the bomber aircraft of the day—all without risking a plane or aircrew.

One early episode of rocket research deserves retelling, if for no other reason than it demonstrates how far Dornberger and von Braun, later with Kammler's oversight, would take the project. In one experiment von Braun attempted to ignite a much smaller prototype rocket motor fueled by common gasoline. For the lighting, von Braun used a twelve-foot pole. The rocket motor exploded in a fiery ball, sending shards of metal into nearby tree trunks, but missing von Braun.[18] Given this primitive beginning, it is an understatement to say the German rocket team achieved amazing things in a very short period of time.

The V-1, which looked a bit like an awkward airplane with no cockpit, was a different weapon entirely from the V-2. The V-1 travelled at a top speed of four hundred miles per hour and had a range of just over 150 miles, with a payload of just under one ton.[19] It required a separate boost of speed to get aloft—either a pre-built, fixed ski ramp–like apparatus with a boost, or later it was launched from the under wing of a modified bomber aircraft. Constructed from plywood and sheet steel and powered by a simple yet ingenious Argus pulse jet engine that ran on low grade petroleum, the V-1 proved to be a cost-effective means of delivering a one-ton warhead. It also had a proximity fuse, which meant it would, by design, detonate just before it struck the ground—creating a more destructive explosion and shock wave that was a devastating way to maximize the effect of the payload. The Allies feared that the V-1 would be paired with payloads of high explosives, incendiaries, toxic gas, or even "biological toxins" and launched on London.[20] But we did have some countermeasures against the V-1: knocking them out of the sky with anti-aircraft weapons or even airplanes, or deploying barrage balloons to run interference.[21]

Both the V-1 and V-2 had good accuracy, given their very long ranges. But because they flew such great distances, even a divergence of

1 percent meant the missiles could easily be a mile or more from the heart of the target area. So their tactical value was greatest against very large targets—large urban areas like London and Antwerp, where even a miss of a mile or two was a hit in the eyes of the German leadership.

Kammler wanted control of the V-1 because, on the battlefield, the buzz bomb proved to be a highly effective psychological weapon; the distinctive drone of its engine struck absolute terror in the public. It meant something terrible was coming on fast. If the V-1 was the Volkswagen Beetle of the era—reliable, inexpensive, and easy to mass produce—the V-2 was the most exotic sports car imaginable—sleek, fast, full of features never seen before, but also highly temperamental. The V-2, known during its development as the A4 (for Aggregat) or simply as "das Gerät" ("the device"), looked much like the rockets we know today.[22] It flew at unprecedented speeds of thirty-six hundred miles per hour, traveling nearly five times the speed of sound. Once it was launched, there were no defenses against it. In its travels to a distant target it reached a height of fifty-five miles, and when its motor burn ended it "coasted" down upon its target. The varying amounts of resistance created at the differing levels of the atmosphere had to be accounted for and calculated into the exact flight path and burn time for the motor. Both heat and vibration had to be mastered, as did the effect of electricity on the rocket's skin and the disturbance that torrents of jet wash caused in radio communication and guidance.

Each V-2 had two power centers. The first was a sophisticated diesel-powered turbo pump, itself an engineering marvel the Allies thought physically impossible. It produced steam, which turned a turbine, which force-fed the rocket fuel into the rocket's combustion chamber. Only by generating enormous horse power and pressure could the pump feed the liquid fuel quickly enough. But brute force was not enough—the fuel feed, a mixture of ethyl alcohol and liquid oxygen, had to be extremely finely calibrated to prevent a flame-out (not enough fuel) or explosion (too much fuel). The Allies thought it impossible to master the combined challenges of generating these levels of pressure with the required degree of precision within the snug confines of a rocket's housing. The jet combustion chamber itself was the other, primary power center, providing the thrust for the rocket's flight.

In tests when fired straight up, the V-2 reached 128 miles. That is a fantastic number, considering that the typical modern commercial airliner travels at an altitude of about six miles. The V-2 had a payload of 2,200 pounds. But even at its peak production of about 900 missiles a month, the Germans could launch only one one-hundredth of the bomb tonnage it was receiving in return. A great part of the value of the V-2 was drawing away the resources used for Britain's countermeasures. England used 36,795 aircraft on counterattacks and dropped 102,491 long tons of bombs on Vengeance Weapons production sites and supply lines, and deployed even more reconnaissance aircraft—a total of 280,000 man hours was consumed flying 4,000 sorties, 40 percent of all surveillance flights from the U.K. in the 23 months from May 1943 to April 1945.[23] That is a tremendous amount of manpower and resources, reflecting the Brits' fear of the Vengeance Weapons.

The V-2 did not just emerge on the battlefield fully dressed out; it took years in the making. By 1933, shortly after Hitler became chancellor, the team at Kummersdorf had produced the forerunner of the V-2— its first Aggregat rocket (the A1), a 330-pound "projectile" that failed to fly at all. "Aggregat" is an aptly chosen name that captures the complexity of the series of rockets the project would produce—in German "Aggregat" means a group of machines working together. The several machines that together made up the A1 just did not work as one quite yet. Years of trial-and-error experiments and refinements were made by the rocket team on the A1 and increasingly larger iterations—the A2 and A3. Experimenting on smaller models required fewer materials, less elaborate construction and testing facilities, fewer expenses, and far less time, yet still rendered valuable theoretical data needed to move up to the next level. The full-sized A4 would be rolled out only after many of the technological challenges had been mastered on a smaller, less expensive but still very expensive level.

The second prototype, the A2, built in 1934, flew to a height of seven thousand feet and included gyro-stabilizers designed to smooth and control the flight path. The gyro-stabilizers, which would continue to be perfected over the next decade, would provide information on the position of the rocket and coordinate finely tuned adjustments with the steering rudders. The A2 represented quite an advance in technology in a relatively short period of time. Even before the build-out of the rocket stands used to test the bare rocket motors, the rocket team used a small island off the coast to begin testing the A3 with a first launch on December 4, 1937. This was the same time von Braun joined the Nazi Party. He would claim that Dornberger told him that he had no choice if he wanted to continue at his life's work.

The A3 was twenty-two feet long and liquid-fueled and had one ton of thrust, but it didn't fly well. As a result, the rocket program experienced a period of disfavor from above during which it was a low priority for receiving supplies and manpower from the Reich. It was not until after the historic aerial Battle of Britain was abandoned as hopeless in the fall of 1940 and Britain had gained air superiority that Hitler would again make the rocket program a top priority. Germany did not need air superiority over England to launch V-2s at London from as much as two hundred miles away.

But the V-2 (called the A4 at this time) was not nearly ready to be deployed, so the Germans labored on, overcoming still more challenges. Two recurrent problems they faced related to the shape of a rocket. Long and thin, the rocket body is a master at slipping through the air as it provides next to no wind resistance. But that same shape made early versions difficult to control. The absence of wings meant that small steering rudders, mounted on the outside of the rocket's body, would provide the only steering. The air moving over the steering rudders gives the steering effect—the greater the speed at which the air moves, the greater the steering effect. But as with the body of a canoe working its way down rapids, forward movement through surrounding water or air is required. If a boat is moving at the same speed as the current, its rudder has no

effect. Likewise, rocket steering rudders have no effect during take-off because there is insufficient air coursing over them as the rocket initially creeps upward. For this reason, all functional rockets to this point in time required a launch tube or a ramp to enable steering while the rocket body gained speed. By the time the rocket reached the end of the ramp or tube and began to fly freely, there was enough air flowing over the steering rudders for control. In an innovation clever because of its simplicity, the Germans overcame this limitation and perfected the vertical launch. They placed highly heat-resistant molybdenum (and later carbon) rudders inside the rocket housing, just below the exhaust ports of the combustion chamber, and the powerful jet wash provided steering from the moment of ignition—even during initial launch when the rocket moved only a few feet per second. This allowed the first true vertical take-off, which would later confound British intelligence as it searched from the air for non-existent launch ramps and tubes.

The round shape of the rocket body also meant that it was inclined to spin on its long axis. Undue spin has a negative effect on control, and even the slightest spin could throw the V-2 off course. Spin also caused problems with the liquid fuel, which through centrifugal force was spun to the outer parts of the fuel tank, causing havoc with the precision flow of fuel into the combustion chamber. The seemingly bizarre black and white patterns painted on prototype rockets seen in films and photographs allowed observers to easily plot acceleration and track spin in the body of the prototype. Having mastered the vertical take-off, the Germans then learned to use gyro-stabilizers to control spin.

The technical challenges in making the V-2 fly were not limited to building the rocket. The rocket team had to make extraordinary advances on the ground, as well. In addition to designing and building the structures necessary to assemble the V-2 components and the V-2 itself, they had to design purpose-built equipment to transport fully assembled rockets and raise them into firing position. They had to design test facilities with complicated test beds that deflected the jet wash during tests. Test beds had to include specialized tubing that carried thousands of gallons of water per second to provide cooling. Launch-control buildings monitored every conceivable aspect of the rockets and their individual components. The Germans had to invent cutting-edge monitoring and analysis technology to measure the performance of every component of their revolutionary rocket technology, and they had to do it anew each time they began work on a larger model.

Static test facilities were used to run rocket motors (sometimes bare motors, sometimes motors built into entire rocket bodies) without any movement of the motors themselves—which were strapped down to the launch bed rigging. Test launches were altogether different; the goal being actual flight of a fully assembled rocket. Elaborate, custom-designed monitoring equipment to judge the performance of the overall rocket and many of its individual parts had to be invented and perfected.

Even with its priority treatment rescinded, by March 1942, only months after Germany declared war on the U.S., the fourth iteration rocket, the A4, was ready for field testing. Both the first and second launch were dismal failures. The first A4 blew up on the ground on June 13, 1942, never even getting airborne. The second prototype was prepped to fire, and then stood on the launch stand for over a month while the engineers made various modifications. Interestingly, Royal Air Force (RAF) reconnaissance planes coursed overhead snapping photographs, but given the vertical positioning of the A4, saw nothing that aroused suspicion. The second prototype, when launched, rose to a level of three miles, though with little control, and slipped into the sea—a disappointing bare mile from the launch pad.

It was not until October 3, 1942, that the rocket team met with unequivocal success, blasting an A4 (V-2 prototype) that flew beautifully. The success caught the attention of Speer, who convinced Hitler to sign an order for mass production. Von Braun, for his part, was awarded the War Service Cross, First Class, with Swords. Dornberger summarized the situation at this point succinctly: "Our most urgent task can only be the rapid perfecting of the rocket as a weapon."[24]

There would be an enormous difference between perfecting the V-2 for one successful test firing and mass production. Indeed, at this stage the V-2 was more "a complicated lab product"[25] than an item ready for mass production. And nearly as quickly as mass production plans were adopted, they were reversed. In March 1943, Speer reported to the rocket team that Hitler had dreamt the V-2 would fail, never striking England. The program's priority plunged as suddenly as earlier failed launches. To me this dream-tale is ludicrous, hearkening back more to Greek mythology than Germanic engineering rigor. Within a month, though, Hitler reversed himself yet again, restoring the rocket program's priority and approving a plan to begin construction of fixed bunkers in France from which to launch both the V-2 and the V-1. The rocket program was vexed by the ensuing debate over using these static, fixed, heavily fortified launch bunkers[26] or the Sonderwagen, a reusable "chassis and a cradle holding the rocket" which was a more nimble, hard-to-combat mobile launch vehicle.[27] Hitler's insistence on building no fewer than two or three colossal and almost absurdly-reinforced concrete bunkers along the coast of France, just across from England, swayed the debate.[28] The dizzying chaos in the Nazi leadership is starkly evident here, as both the fixed bunkers and the mobile launch Sonderwagon were developed, requiring enormous time and energy.

The seemingly endless changes in the V-2's priority as a German weapon are confusing. The project that Kammler would ultimately rule went from bottom of the barrel to the highest conceivable priority and back again.[29] In his position, I would have found this maddening. And these shifting priorities were just one example of Germany shooting itself in the foot, as it were.[30] Rocket team member Dieter Huzel described Germany's ridiculous misassignment of scientist and engineers as foot soldiers at the front, slowing all research efforts—a policy reversed only late in the war. Suddenly one day in the spring of 1943, as Germany's war future darkened, the decision to deploy highly skilled talent to the front lines was reversed: "Overnight, Ph.D.'s were liberated from KP duty, masters of science were recalled from orderly service, mathematicians were hauled out of bakeries, and precision mechanics ceased to be truck drivers."[31]

• • •

"How did you find all these files?" I asked Keith, having digested only part of the original materials he had given me. I had assumed it was a brute-force sort of exercise at National Archives—launching yourself at one box after another of records marked "WORLD WAR TWO." I was way off.

"I developed a battle plan," Keith explained, reverting to military jargon. "It wasn't random. Colm and I drew up lists of names, locations, operations, projects, and dates to target. National Archives has record groups, loose organization of files, and we had to target those. I learned those record groups and crossed them with the names and locations. At Archives, they'd bring me all related boxes, as many as twenty-four at a time. I learned along the way to plow through individual folders or boxes I could quickly tell weren't on point. I learned how to narrow searches, how to hone in."

"I also made written requests of other archives. Lots of military bases all over the country have various records. Lots of libraries have inherited records. Records are everywhere. Colm is doing the same in Europe, and he reads Ph.D. theses, German-language books, obscure books out of print, academic book chapters, archived CD ROM documents. He's written archives everywhere, embassies, government departments in Europe, North and South America, all sorts of stuff. Now, more and more archive material is available online."

For the first time, I began to understand the scale of the work put into this project. Keith and Colm had cast an unbelievably broad but fine net.

"There were also followup FOIA requests; dozens, even hundreds. And then challenges to FOIA denials." A lot of the boxes Keith was given to review had folders noted as "withheld." Those were files that might or might not be relevant, but Keith couldn't tell, so he had to use the special Freedom of Information Act (FOIA) procedures to try to access them. If denied, he could appeal. Every step required more paperwork, and often fees.

"There were also hundreds of interviews Colm and I divided up. Colm did most of those. People who fought in the war, government officials, people who studied and wrote about the war, journalists, research librarians around the world. Colm also went to a lot of these places." I was impressed.

"You can't believe the number of dead ends we ran into. We had to hound people sometimes to hear back. So many leads never panned out. But we have so much good stuff."

The value of Keith's gift to me was increasing by the minute.

● ● ●

We know that Kammler actually viewed a successful trial launch of the V-2 in August 1944 on the Baltic. He would have been positioned on a flatbed railway car that served as an observation post some five hundred yards from the launch site.[32] Bolted to the bed of the car was a metal observation platform with handrails, which stood approximately ten feet above the flatbed, linked by a metal ladder. The elevated platform was large enough to accommodate three or four men.

I pictured a clear, late summer night, a cool breeze blowing in from the Baltic. In my mind's eye Kammler watched the rocket troops as they hurried to prepare the V-2 for launch. The Technical Troops had fitted the live warhead and transferred the missile to the Firing Troop's Sonderwagen. Dornberger handed Kammler a clipboard of papers detailing the night launch exercise. Kammler officiously flicked through the documents and listened intently as Dornberger ticked through details.

A soldier signaled to Dornberger that the final launch procedure was about to begin, and Dornberger suggested to Kammler that they ascend to the observation platform. As Kammler climbed the steps of the ladder, he glanced up just as a shooting star streaked high across the heavens: "Just like a V-2," he smiled inwardly. Dornberger removed his wrist watch and handed it to a soldier standing on the platform below, telling the soldier to call out each passing second after launch so he and Kammler could calculate the speed and distance of the V-2 as it soared into the earth's upper atmosphere.

The launch team was now locked into a very precise and well-rehearsed firing procedure. They had already computed the missile's flight path and set the advanced gyroscopic system to direct the rocket towards the test target. Inside the dimly lit fire control vehicle the launch commander, the Feuerleitpanzer, watched the missile two hundred yards from him through the observation slit—a big cat ready to pounce. Hoar frost formed around the stern of the missile and white vapor plumed and wafted from its engine as the rocket stood in readiness. The launch commander glanced at his watch as he called out to the soldier seated at the fire control desk behind him: "Control Clear!" The command crackled through a loud speaker near Kammler and Dornberger's position.

"Control Clear!" a soldier responded almost mechanically.

The soldier scanned the instrument panel in front of him. "On firing, light clear," he said. He pressed a button, and immediately the rocket engine roared to life and rumbled violently under 2.5 tons of thrust. The huge twelve-and-a-half-ton missile began to tremble on its launch table, straining against invisible straps that tethered it to Earth. The commanding officer's final order could barely be heard over the rising pitch of the engine: "Main stage…ignite!"

The soldier pushed another button on the instrument panel to remotely engage the rocket's fuel and oxidizer pumps, and immediately the steam turbines began to scream. The jet wash flowed over the internal rudders even as the rocket began to creep upward, preventing the rocket from listing and allowing complete control.

Kammler reflexively pressed his hands over his ears and watched through darkened goggles as night exploded into day and the rocket motor powered up to its full twenty-five tons of thrust. You've never heard anything like it. The earth shook as Kammler watched the beast rise from its firing table and turn slowly on to the direction of the target.

The engine howled at full thrust as the rocket thundered overhead into the night sky. The sight was nothing short of exhilarating.

Dornberger and Kammler watched the flaming exhaust gases of the rocket through their binoculars. At twenty-five seconds the sonic boom of the missile rang back through the launch site, signaling the V-2 had accelerated through the sound barrier on its way towards Mach 5. The missile's on-board accelerometer clicked and whirred as it computed the speed and engine burn time. After the planned engine cut-off, the missile coasted silently at supersonic speed out over the top of its flight curve, and gravity did the rest. The missile ultimately splashed into the Baltic two hundred miles away. Success.

A V-2 launched from Test Stand VII, Peenemünde, in the summer of 1943. Bundesarchiv, Bild 141-1880/CC-BY-SA 3.0

• • •

In July 1943, Dornberger and von Braun flew to Hitler's Wolf's Lair headquarters in East Prussia. Part of their presentation to Hitler was the film of the recent successful launch. Students of the era called the film spectacular and awe-inspiring. The Führer was smitten, totally taken by the weapon's raw power and potential. Something that could fly so grandly, seemingly effortlessly once clear of the ground, and deliver a full one-ton payload on the far end of its calculated arc, striking at the enemy's heart, was a weapon for the ages. Hitler's new decree went further than requiring mass production, concluding: "The success of the war against England depends on peak A4 [V-2] missile output being attained as soon as possible."[33] Later Hitler would claim, "If we'd had these rockets in 1939 we'd never have had this war,"[34] meaning that the V-2 was so potentially powerful, frightening, and dissuasive that the Allies would never have dared to fight against a Germany armed with them. In putting Kammler in charge of the weapon's development, production, and deployment, Hitler was placing the future of the Third Reich in Kammler's hands.

Dornberger asserted that, but for a lack of alcohol, V-2 production could have been doubled.[35] But even if all landed on or near their targets, which is highly unlikely, a rather paltry twenty-five thousand tons of explosives would have hit England. By comparison, in 1944, the Allies dropped over nine hundred thousand tons of bombs. But without a meaningful air presence late in the war, the Germans were unable to drop conventional bombs en masse on England, so using missiles was their only long-range option. Missiles required no pilots and were far cheaper than German bombers or fighters that, though theoretically available for multiple sorties, were shot down in droves. In the end, Germany's V-Weapons research cost the equivalent of forty billion dollars (in 2015 dollars)—half of what was spent on the Manhattan Project.

● ● ●

Concerned about the potentially devastating effect of the V-2, the Brits decided to bomb Peenemünde in an awesome show of force, dispatching their entire strategic force of six hundred aircraft.[36] This all-out effort demonstrated the value the Brits placed on Germany's V-2 and the degree to which they feared it. While studying the Peenemünde raid I learned a great deal about World War II state-of-the-art bombing campaigns and their limitations. Three waves of bombers were used in the massive attack by the RAF, which began the evening of August 17, 1943, and continued through the next day. Only Peenemünde East, home of the V-2, was targeted.[37] The primary targets were the workshops, the Development Rocket Works, and the scientists' housing, with a third of the bombers out to destroy the brain trust. These were the same scientists who would be targeted by the Americans as the war closed—not by bombardiers, but by recruiters, in an altogether different sort of head-hunting. Tragically, the slave barracks were hit in the raid, resulting in hundreds of deaths.[38]

There is sharp disagreement about whether that night's mission was a success for the Allies.[39] An interrogation of a Peenemünde veteran claims that 70 percent of the facility was destroyed, large workshops were hit, and over 180 buildings were heavily damaged or destroyed outright. Craters were to be found throughout the facility, key scientists were killed, and that night and the next fires burned everywhere.[40] But in secretly recorded post-war conversations, Dornberger claimed that the bombing set back German rocket research by only two months.[41] In his book, he put the delay at four to six weeks,[42] while in a post-war interrogation he claimed that work at Peenemünde went on normally with no measurable setback,[43] an assertion also made by Nordhausen plant manager Georg Rickhey in his interrogation.[44]

I found statistics on World War II bomber accuracy surprising in today's age of pinpoint targeting of missiles launched from thousands of miles away—not simply into a particular building, but just the right quadrant of a building while real-time satellite imagery records the results. By today's standards, Allied bombers in World War II were wildly inaccurate, and it is against that performance Germany's rockets should be evaluated.

After the Peenemünde bombing, Hitler ordered "a long term effort
be made to manufacture the most sensitive products...in factories that
are totally under concrete protection."[45] Peenemünde had been home to
V-1 and V-2 research, production, and testing since 1937, but now virtually all weapons creation would be relocated, following Hitler's mandate,
and reflecting the growing understanding that the "shifting of the arms
factories to underground facilities was vital to victory, as the Allies bombing persisted."[46] Kammler was appointed by Himmler to replace Hermann Göring as Special Plenipotentiary of the Führer for Jet Aircraft
and the V-1 and V-2—making Kammler the complete ruler of the skies.
Himmler and Kammler together chose the new site for V-2 production—
Nordhausen. It was Kammler who gave the order to evacuate Peenemünde on January 31, 1945, according to Wernher von Braun.[47]

*V-1 cruise missile assembly line at the underground factory, Nordhausen. Bunde-
sarchiv, Bild 146-1991-076-02A/CC-BY-SA 3.0*

For the relocation, Nordhausen's lone cavern in the Harz mountains
was enlarged by Kammler's slaves by hand to create tunnels over forty
feet wide and thirty feet high. Each of nearly fifty cross-tunnels were 650
feet long, altogether an astounding thirty-five million cubic feet of space.
And the Nordhausen complex also included twenty-eight other tunnels

of various sizes in the surrounding mountains—an eight-hundred-acre compound for producing weapons or their components. Within the first three months, Kammler's slaves had readied one hundred thousand square meters of space. The genius of relocating the rocket production plant underground is revealed in the fact that the Nordhausen site was totally unknown to the Allies until August of 1944 and was unreachable until even later during the war.[48]

Von Braun would explain that the Nazis had evacuated "to get the Peenemünde material out of the way" of the Russians. This statement supports our theory that Kammler moved rocket research assets—equipment, documents, and experts—at least in part to preserve them for turnover to the United States. Kammler shipped an impressive "twelve thousand tons of material, instruments and equipment" out of Peenemünde by sea, but that did not include the "most important" items, which were sent by rail.[49] Dornberger recounted an important detail of the plan to move the scientists: Kammler had stated that if the scientists did not obey his evacuation order, "the SS would shoot them all."[50] Secrecy—something at which the SS excelled—was of paramount, almost obsessive concern. In the eternal quest for impregnable security, Kammler even prepared a feasibility study for building entire aircraft and missile factories beneath lake beds. In the end the Nazis, like subterranean gargoyles, slithered into a netherworld below ground.

The relocation of nearly all weapons production to Kammler-built underground facilities presented an important opportunity that Himmler and Kammler seized. The concentration of funding, brain power, and cutting-edge weapons in development was an irresistibly delicious prize. I could imagine the two of them literally licking their chops at the prospect of wielding still more power. With the rocket team labor requirements exploding, given Hitler's order to mass produce, and with the need for the secrecy that only the SS could provide, Himmler wedged his sinister organization into the ongoing administration of the rocket program more deeply, bringing Kammler with him.[51] After the Peenemünde bombing, Himmler convinced von Braun that only he, Himmler, could make the rocket program fly, bringing the material and personnel needed to ensure success: "I have access to Hitler…I am the right man to expedite" the rocket program.[52] Imagine Himmler circling, whispering in von Braun's ear, "I have an 'open door to the Führer any time.…'"[53] The smart (and safe) thing was obviously to believe Himmler and walk through that open door with a courteous nod of appreciation. Von Braun urged Dornberger to work with and "help Kammler" so that one day they "would have a place in the history of technology, and receive recognition from the world for their invention of the long-range rocket."[54] Although Dornberger and von Braun resented Kammler as a meddling overlord, they assented.[55] The SS and Kammler now controlled development of the rockets.[56]

While rocket production and assembly would be shifted underground to Nordhausen in central Germany, testing and rocket firing would be moved to a new range in Blizna, southern Poland, the site of a former SS Heidelager, or health camp. And rocket research would move underground to Friedrichshafen, Germany, and Ebensee, Austria. This fractured approach to rocket research, production, and assembly had costs in terms of efficiency, but it also had the benefit of dispersing and protecting this critical work. Friedrichshafen and Ebensee, code-named Zement (Cement), also built by Kammler's slaves, would be the site—chosen by Kammler and Speer—for continued development of the mysterious "Amerika Rocket," also known as the A-10, an intercontinental missile that was a scaled-up version of the V-2 designed to reach New York City, Washington, D.C., or any U.S. east coast city, traversing the Atlantic in forty minutes. Dornberger once claimed development of the Amerika Rocket had been completed,[57] but later contradicted himself in an interrogation[58] when he was trying to avoid prosecution by the Brits and find a home in America. At that point it served his interests to downplay a weapon designed to attack the U.S.

SS lieutenant colonel Otto Skorzeny (about whom we'll learn more later), who led a program to develop a piloted V-1 craft, was in touch with von Braun regularly after the war. In his post-war memoirs, Skorzeny boasted, "Included in the V weapons program was the construction of a rocket capable or bombarding New York or Moscow. This rocket was practically finished at the end of March 1945."[59] Among tens of thousands of pages of air force records, Keith found an interrogation report on Dr. Hermann Oberth, a name that would be lost on many but immediately stood out to Keith. (So much of the search for records was knowing targets, important names, places, weapons, operations, and other minutia so you could focus on the most relevant documents—Keith and Colm were both experts at this.) Oberth was a decorated founder of the German rocket movement, and he worked at Peenemünde with von Braun and later at NASA in the U.S. The interrogation report by Major P. M. Wilson was fabulously rich in detail, beginning with a helpfully descriptive title: "Plan for a Trans-Atlantic Rocket." A transatlantic rocket. It revealed that from their very first moments at Peenemünde the Germans had been designing a missile to attack the United States.[60] Knowing that from the early moments at Peenemünde the Amerika Rocket was not just on the drawing board,[61] but was also categorized as "high-priority,"[62] it is impossible to believe that no significant progress was made in ten years. Even after the Allied bombing of Peenemünde, the Amerika Rocket project remained a priority. Astounding—just like that, Keith had uncovered new proof about how close the Nazis got to being able to hit the United States.

Hans Kammler (center) and Oswald Pohl (left), head of the WVHA, during an official visit to Ebensee, Austria, in 1944. Following behind is Karl Fiebinger (dressed in civilian clothes). Courtesy of Tilmann Kammler

Colm made a point no one had written about. A careful reading of
Dornberger's memoirs reveals important details here. The Germans were
testing a medium-range rocket, the A-4b, in January 1945. Dornberger's
memoirs reveal that he viewed the A-4b as an upper stage component
for the A-10 "Amerika Rocket." The A-4b was actually the forward or
uppermost part of the A-10, designed to separate from the lower body
of the A-10 and continue in flight across the Atlantic, delivering the
payload. In other words, real testing on intercontinental rockets had
begun. In fact, Dornberger said that twenty-two hundred scientists were
on the A-4b project—an astounding dedication of resources.

Now atop the entire rocket program, Kammler imposed his SS brand
of security. Nordhausen included a perimeter extending over fifteen miles
around the production facility, a tank battalion and other patrols, closely
guarded entrance into the facility, and redundant security checkpoints
within.[63] At Blizna, a garrison of Kammler's SS troops secured the region
and an area of some eight square miles vanished overnight behind a veil
of absolute secrecy. A mock village with cottages and other buildings
was constructed to fool aerial reconnaissance. Residential fencing and
clotheslines were added. Mannequins stood around the village and the
land was cultivated. A dummy farmer sitting atop a tractor in a half-
ploughed field completed the illusion of an inhabited village. The Allies
would not become aware of the Blizna facility until April 27, 1944, or
of Ebensee until May 1944, so the moves did completely confound the
Allies.[64] Sadly, I realized, Kammler's use of slaves who could never escape
made the security iron-clad.[65] One post-war interrogation even reported
that workers were killed after a certain period of time "to guarantee
security."[66]

Remarkably, within four scant months of having seen the V-2, Himmler and Kammler had taken control of its production—a project that
had been ten years and hundreds of millions of Reichsmarks in the making.[67] Everything seems to happen faster in war, but this was a speedy
and decisive victory.[68] It was just five days after the Peenemünde bombing, on August 22, 1943, that Himmler and Hitler added to Kammler's

responsibilities, putting him in charge of "Special Staff Kammler" (Sonderstab Kammler), an independent body commissioned "to ensure the serial production of the A4 (V-2) rocket" and for "special tasks in connection with the war economy"—a vague charge that was intended to convey authority over construction of all weapons facilities, but would come to mean anything Kammler wished it to mean.[69] Champing at the bit, Kammler immediately transferred his "Special Staff" offices to an administrative building away from the WVHA and incorporated his WVHA staff into his Special Staff. The speed with which he moved told me that he and Himmler must have hatched their scheme days or weeks before so that Kammler was able to pull the trigger on his plans quickly. Kammler head-hunted additional Special Staff from the Luftwaffe, the Wehrmacht (army), and the Kriegsmarine (navy), drawing from the Himmler playbook, taking what he wanted in terms of people and power. And Speer was noticing—he had clearly grown wary of Kammler, whom he now described as "a cold, ruthless schemer, a fanatic in pursuit of a goal and as carefully calculating as he was unscrupulous."

Kammler, with total budgetary, labor, materials, and logistical control over all aspects of Nazi Germany's colossal construction projects, had slipped the yoke of WVHA oversight. The wartime economy was being run by the SS, and Kammler was now occupying a position that gave him free rein over all the resources of the Reich. An April 1945 document generated by the Ninth Air Force's Air Prisoner of War Interrogation Unit would reveal the incredible "spider's web" network command structure he built within Sonderstab Kammler. Eventually, Kammler would duplicate nearly the entire Armaments Ministry structure within the SS, running a parallel enterprise that siphoned power to Kammler as Speer lost his.[70]

Kammler was now running full speed ahead. Soon enough, he would have the V-2 ready for battle. With conventional air superiority slipping, Nazi Germany would again and again rely on the V-2. Would it perform so well, prove so valuable a weapon, that it would be an irresistible acquisition for the Americans?

CHAPTER FOUR

On the Battlefield

*"The Angel of Death is abroad in the land, only you
can't always hear the flutter of its wings."*

—Winston Churchill on January 15, 1945, referring to the V-2 rocket

"I 've read everything I can on the rockets," I began by telling Keith. I was on Bluetooth in my car, stuck in Washington's evening rush hour. "Gridlock" in Washington applies equally well to Congress or traffic. Unwisely, I live west of the city, so my morning and evening commutes are worse than most peoples'—directly into the rising and setting sun. But today there was a light rain, which was actually even worse than the regular "sunshine delay." I was crawling. The only thing worse, in terms of traffic debacles, was light snow, which led to bumper car conditions. The best use I can make during lost time when I drive is a business call or, as on this day, a "book call."

I went on: "The Vengeance Weapons, the V-1 and the V-2, once deployed in battle, were devastating but not decisive. Although they caused widespread terror, and attracted broad, sustained Allied bombing campaigns and countermeasures that could have been used elsewhere, by the time they were rolled out, there were too few missiles and Germany's strategic position was beyond repair."

"I agree, but you have to admit the V-1 and V-2 were revolutionary weapons, extraordinarily useful at crucial moments. Think about what they meant, the mere threat of them, in the build-up to D-Day, then the bombing of London."

"Yes. They also played a role in triggering the Allies' failed Operation Market Garden—I've read about that—and in the Battle of the Bulge with the bombing of Antwerp. And Colm has given me tons of good info on the V-2 and the felling of the Ludendorff Bridge at Remagen. But I think our best approach for the book is to emphasize the *potential* of the rockets, not what they were in 1945, but what they led to later. The ICBM. The moon landing. Winning the space race and the arms race. That's what Kammler was offering."

"It can be both, right?" Keith came back at me. "Why not show what the rockets actually did in battle, and what they were capable of in the future?"

● ● ●

Final victory for the Allies would depend on many things breaking their way. In the European Theater of World War II, perhaps none was more vital than the success of the D-Day landings in Normandy, France. Even if the Vengeance Weapons did not achieve a military victory on D-Day, their mere presence played a role, provoking untold anxiety and very nearly causing the invasion to be launched prematurely. During the Allied build-up for the landings, British general Bernard Montgomery made numerous arguments for beginning the invasion early—even ignoring adverse weather conditions in the English Channel—in part because British intelligence was receiving an alarming number of reports that the Germans were preparing to open their missile offensives against London. Though some elements within British intelligence were skeptical about whether a futuristic rocket-powered V-2 even existed, the conclusion finally reached in White Hall, the nerve center of Great Britain's intelligence operations, was that the Vengeance Weapons were real and attack was imminent. The RAF air raid on Peenemünde might have delayed German plans for the mass launch, but it did not shutter the program.[1] On November 13, 1943, only three months after that RAF bombing, Constance Babington Smith, a flight officer and photographic interpreter in the Central Interpretation Unit at RAF Medmenham in Buckinghamshire, England, was studying a series of high-altitude reconnaissance photographs taken over Peenemünde when she made a startling discovery. Using her stereoscope, she identified what she described as "a ramp holding a tiny cruciform shape on rails"—a V-1 flying bomb being prepared for launch from a ski ramp–shaped structure. Reexamination of many thousands of photographs identified approximately one hundred such structures in German-occupied territory between Dieppe and Calais along the extreme northern coast of France, a bare twenty miles from England on the thinnest expanse of the channel. Allied intelligence estimated each of these "ski ramps" was capable of launching twenty missiles over a twenty-four-hour period, meaning an overwhelming two thousand V-1 missiles each day. The damage and loss of life could be catastrophic, and the Brits were convinced they were facing a game of Russian roulette with a bullet in every chamber. Suddenly there was enormous pressure to neutralize the threat—not just for London's sake, but to keep safe the rallying point for the coming invasion forces.

In December 1943, swarms of Allied bombers were sent to destroy the V-1 launch ramps. But after a nearly month-long campaign—largely because of limitations in bombing accuracy—only seven had been destroyed. The Americans reluctantly agreed to commit a large portion of their own bomber force to the campaign, and by the end of May 1944, eighty-two launch sites were believed to have been destroyed—but only at the cost of heavy losses of Allied aircraft and crews.[2]

Now newer modified ski sites were built much more rapidly, some in as few as six days.[3] Also, the heavily fortified and more extensive sites, thought to be for larger rockets (that is, the V-2)—the fixed bunkers Hitler had insisted upon—were discovered on the French Channel Coast. The Allies' concerns were intensified by the possibility of chemical or biological payloads.

After numerous delays, on May 16, 1944, Hitler issued orders for the long-range bombardment of England to begin in the middle of June. On June 6, 1944, the Allies made the difficult landing at Normandy and set out across France to Germany. Then on June 13, anti-aircraft Regiment 155 under the command of Luftwaffe colonel Max Wachtel received the coded order "Polar Bear," and the very first German V-1 offensive commenced. Within hours the first salvo of V-1s was crossing the channel toward London. The relentless Robot Blitz had begun. For the British public the "quiet euphoria of the Allied invasion of D-Day was short lived and quickly gave way to a feeling of grim determination to withstand this latest manifestation of Nazi terror from the air."[4]

Colm assured me that if you did not live through this barrage, you really cannot understand the terror. Seventy-three V-1 missiles hit the greater London area on the first two days. Ecstatic, Hitler flew to northern France to personally congratulate the launch coordinator and ordered that the "Cherry Stones" (Hitler's nickname for the V-1, derived from the project's original code name, Kirschkern) were henceforth to be targeted against London exclusively. Hitler would try to bring the war home to Britain's citizenry, breaking their morale. Within three weeks, 370 V-1s struck London, killing twenty-five hundred people and immobilizing the city. Londoners were terrified. A critical part of the psychological terror inflicted by the V-1 was the droning noise of its engine overhead—people breathed a sigh of relief when it passed onward, because when its engine stopped overhead, the missile tumbled to earth. Picture the major city in which you live, or the one nearest to you, and then imagine fifteen to twenty bombs exploding every day—*every day*. Think about the calamity and strife caused in the U.S. on 9/11, or by the Las Vegas shootings, or the Boston Marathon bombs, and imagine a string of fifteen attacks like those every day in a loop carrying on for weeks with no end in sight.[5] This was precisely the terror Hitler had hoped to mete out to the Brits with his Vengeance Weapons.

At last, the Allies launched Operation Crossbow, which made Germany's rocket supply lines and launching sites the highest-priority targets of the combined bomber forces, except for those related to the ongoing trek of Allied forces across France. Here, though, the Allied response played into Hitler's hands. While Allied air forces were directed at Vengeance Weapons launch sites, known production sites, and transportation routes, other German weapons production sites and German cities enjoyed a respite. Also, thousands of Allied personnel were pulled from other assignments as the Brits painstakingly customized their defenses against the V-1 flying bomb, committing fighter planes to patrol the channel and a thick band of anti-aircraft guns along its own coast—all backstopped by a cordon of two thousand barrage balloons.

But meanwhile in the war of intelligence, the Allies seeded false accounts in London papers, manipulating the locations of British missile casualties, giving the Germans the impression they were overshooting London. In response, the Germans shortened their range, and for a long while many of the V-1s were off course.

● ● ●

While the V-1 wreaked havoc on London, Kammler's engineers working on the V-2 were trying desperately to overcome a nagging technical problem—a premature air burst that caused the V-2 to explode mid-flight. Kammler cajoled his rocket engineers day and night to fix the V-2's air burst problem. At one point they thought the problem was caused by excessive heat in the warhead. Later they came to suspect it was being caused by the rocket's fuel tank fracturing under extreme heat and vibration. The Nordhausen engineers strengthened the fuel tank area, riveting steel reinforcing sleeves around the fuel section. The fix worked and the V-2 was at last ready for battle.[6] In a resounding affirmative answer to my question about whether or not the V-2 was effective, I was interested to learn from Colm that the British intelligence service

MI6 was so concerned that it urged Churchill to nuke Berlin in answer to Germany's V-2 campaign.[7]

Meanwhile, a different sort of explosion rocked the Nazi hierarchy. The suitcase bomb of Wehrmacht officer Claus von Stauffenberg exploded in Hitler's Rastenburg headquarters on July 20, 1944. Operation Valkyrie, the failed assassination attempt on Hitler, presented a further opportunity for Kammler and Himmler. In the aftermath of the near miss a huge number of top officials—some five thousand alleged conspirators—were ousted and many of them were executed. Among the dismissed was General Friedrich Fromm, commander in chief of the Reserve Army (Ersatzheer).[8] Himmler—fully exploiting Hitler's long-festering suspicions of the Wehrmacht, the German army—succeeded Fromm, acquiring the title and trappings of the head of the Army Weapons Office.[9] Wasting no time, Himmler appointed Kammler, now a lieutenant-general in the SS, as his Special Commissioner for V-2 Operations with official responsibility for pressing the V-2 into immediate service. On August 8, 1944, Kammler was given the grandiose title, "Special Representative of Reichsmarschall Göring for Smashing the Allied Terror in the German Air Space."[10] Speer, his power in the Reich already waning, was defenseless against the coup.

By August 29, the German troops had mostly withdrawn east of the Seine and were making a run for the "Siegfried Line," the heavily-reinforced western border of the old German Empire.[11] The speed of the Allied advance had stretched its own supply lines almost to the breaking point. At a meeting with Eisenhower on August 23, Montgomery argued that it was no longer possible for the Allies to continue their advance on a broad front. Instead, the British general reasoned, a single northerly thrust would allow the Allies to cut off German troops along the French Coast and eliminate the scourge of V-1s launching out of northern France and western Holland.

As the Allies stretched their supply lines, Colonel Wachtel's V-1 regiment began to withdraw from its launching sites in France, and on September 1, after an eleven-week barrage of missiles, the last ground-launched

V-1 fell from the sky over London. But the Luftwaffe continued the V-1 assault on London, using modified Heinkel He-111 aircraft, a German medium-sized bomber, for midair launches of over eleven hundred additional V-1s. As the Germans retreated, bringing the V-2 to battle became ever more important for Germany; only it could traverse the greater distance now needed for the Germans to continue to strike England from the soil they still controlled.

The Heinkel He-111, a medium-range bomber, modified to support a V-1 buzz bomb under-wing. This configuration was used late in the war, as German-held territory contracted, to extend the range of the V-1. U.S. Air Force

Serial production of the V-2 became an imperative for Kammler. But this was precisely the time von Braun was finding important differences between—on the one hand—making a small number of prototype V-2 rockets at Peenemünde, test-firing them, and making some tinkering-type changes, and—on the other—mass-producing the missiles in an assembly line at Nordhausen. It was like moving from the laboratory to the factory, but not for a simple item that could be easily mass-produced—for a marvel of technology that contained thousands of parts, many of them representing completely new technology, many of them never before mass-produced. So the task at hand had the complexity of piling mass production upon mass production times a thousand. And that was not the only problem—often the scientists who knew about design knew little about production, and vice versa—something that caused its own legion of headaches.[12]

Pressed for a decision on who controlled the V-2 on the battlefield, Hitler placed Himmler in charge of V-2 deployment on August 31, 1944. And on that very day Himmler delegated this authority to Kammler. "In a few words Kammler had been given the powers that were absolutely necessary to carry the program from the development stage to actual operations," Dornberger complained bitterly.[13] The circle was complete— Kammler now had complete control of the V-2 program from research, to production, to testing, to battlefield deployment.

During this time Kammler and his construction brigades were constantly busy with migration to the underground everywhere in the Reich. It is important to understand the scale of this move. Think of the city or town in which you work and imagine slaves digging, by hand, tunnels to fit all its manufacturing plants and large offices. That process was repeated over and over throughout the German interior. Chalky-colored architectural plans depict excavation projects Kammler oversaw, each bearing a legend and project number. Drawn to scale, these plans show aerial views, as if one could peer through mountaintops to the webs of tunnels and caverns being built within, and reveal the geographical features, outbuildings, roadways, and railroads in the surrounding areas. Elevation depictions showed the tunnel mouths and approach roads *in situ*. Most of the plans bear Kammler's signature in the lower righthand corner. It was a white-knuckle experience to lay eyes on Kammler's actual working plans, to see his pen strokes on paper, his signature. I could see the slaves toiling, SS guards and attack dogs at the ready for anyone who dared to step out of line. Kammler was never shy about his inhumane recipe for success: "We run 72-hour shifts according to our characteristic methods without difficulty.... For all these projects I had to pump in an additional 50,000 political prisoners."[14]

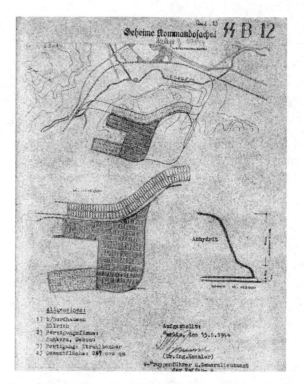

Underground map of tunnel system B12 Nordhausen, bearing the signature of Dr. Ing. Kammler and dated June 15, 1944. From the Samuel and Irene Goudsmit Collection, courtesy of the U.S. Holocaust Memorial Museum, Washington, D.C.

Kammler ordered the reorganization of rocket launching troops into what he called Group North and Group South. I was surprised at the number of troops involved: each Kammler group consisted of 5,306 personnel and 1,592 vehicles. By the end of October, Kammler would have twenty-four mobile launch tables ready for use for the V-2. He issued a stream of orders for rocket-launching batteries to be moved up, sites occupied, and supplies ensured. Railway cars carrying hundreds of heavily camouflaged rockets rumbled day and night through Germany to launch sites in Belgium and Holland. The wisdom of developing the mobile launch sites was now powerfully demonstrated, as without them the V-2 would never have been put into battle.

In ideal conditions, Antwerp, Belgium, was less than a two-hour drive from the German border. On September 3, 1944, Montgomery, who had been promoted to field marshall, ordered the British Second Army to take and hold the port of Antwerp. And the following day, meeting little resistance, they did. Holding the city, however, was never going to be enough because Antwerp was eighty miles from the open sea along the River Scheldt, and those eighty miles of river and estuary were still controlled by Germany. General Gustav-Adolf von Zangen's Fifteenth German Army (troops that had escaped from Normandy) had turned the area into a fortress, making it impossible for Allied supply ships to make the final approach into Antwerp from the open sea. It was like holding the port of Baltimore but not controlling the Chesapeake Bay to the open ocean.

Meanwhile, less than a hundred miles to the southeast, Kammler ordered the first V-2 readied for launch against Paris, a target selected by Hitler himself, from an area close to Malmedy, Belgium. Hitler's oddly-named Operation Penguin, the highly dreaded V-2 assault with Kammler at the helm, was at last ready to begin.

The morning of September 7, 1944, the first V-2 hit near Paris, killing six people and injuring thirty-six. Later that same day, the first V-2 rocket was launched against London from the Wassenaar area of Holland near The Hague, some eighty miles north of Antwerp. Minutes later, a huge explosion in Staveley Road, Chiswick, southwest London, reduced a row of houses to rubble, killing three people and seriously injuring seventeen others. The V-2's extended range and mobile launch platforms left the Allies guessing as to the location of the next launch and strike. A game of cat and mouse was underway with the Allies trying furiously to determine just what they were up against with some squads measuring impact craters and others trying to determine launch sites and calculate trajectories, flight speed, and more. Because design on both the V-1 and V-2 continued to evolve, the Allies were chasing facts and figures that constantly changed.[15]

• • •

As a young man, I had thoroughly enjoyed the film *A Bridge Too Far*, a Hollywood account of Operation Market Garden. I was about the same age as Joe Gringlas when his odyssey began, when he and his brother were forced from home and the rest of their family was murdered.

Colm, our European expert, gave me his readout: "Under Market Garden, Montgomery was to neutralize the V-2 launch sites around The Hague. His plan to thrust north, into Holland, would catch the German 15th Army between the inland city of Arnhem and the shores of the Ijsselmeer Bay, and eliminate the Vengeance Weapons bases that would be isolated in western Holland. This northward thrust would be a huge airborne drop, some of it deep behind enemy lines. In coming this far north, upstream, Montgomery could more easily cross the Rhine, eliminating the need to attack the more stoutly defended Rhine bridges or the Siegfried Line further south. It was the largest airborne operation in history, involving three Allied divisions and approximately 30,000 men."

Colm explained, "What has never really been examined is the role of the Vengeance Weapons. The V-1 and V-2 in large part triggered the whole Operation. Although Kammler's missiles continued to bombard England, they weren't targeting the Operation Market Garden troops themselves. In addition to circumventing the Rhine, the military objective was for the U.S. 82nd Airborne to seize bridges across the Maas and Waal Rivers, while the U.S. 101st Airborne landed at Eindhoven and captured the canal crossings at Veghel. At the northern end of this 60-mile corridor, later nicknamed 'Hell's Highway,' the British 1st Airborne and Polish 1st Airborne were to seize the bridge at Arnhem, sixty miles behind German lines, where they would await the arrival of reinforcements before pushing beyond Arnhem to the Ijsselmeer Bay. Part of the objective was to seize all the territory from which Vengeance Weapons could be launched on England."

While I had seen the film version, Colm had done me one better by visiting Arnhem after presenting a paper at a nearby international academic conference in 2004—a date that reminded me how long Colm and Keith had been chasing Kammler. Before his trip, Colm had assembled and studied maps and battle plans and memorized troop movements and street names. Once he arrived, he staked out the drop sites, the major points of battle, the bridgeheads, and every conceivable detail. He had collected hundreds of battle photos and stood in the precise spot a war photographer had stood decades before, capturing a sense of the "then and now of history," as he put it.

"Some of the U.S. Army forces trained on my local beach for the Normandy invasion," he said. "Other elite airborne units were encamped within a stone's throw of my home town." It never ceased to amaze me—almost everyone alive even today can find some sort of meaningful, personal connection to the war.

"The bridges at Nijmegen and Eindhoven in the south were seized, but heavy German resistance stopped the Allies at Arnhem. After eight days of bitter fighting, two thousand British soldiers slipped away to safety, with seventeen thousand dead or missing Allied soldiers."

Though a decided failure, the operation did temporarily displace the newly deployed V-2 launch troops.

Then Colm gave me a final nugget on this operation—a wrinkle in history that remained undiscovered until he and Keith began their investigation. Montgomery's men nearly bagged a handsome prize on September 17. German archive records and a 1950 U.S. assessment of the use of the V-2 show that Hans Kammler was very nearly captured by Allied troops who landed at Groesbeck and Grave, Holland, on that date.[16] His narrow escape meant that he would continue to bedevil the Allies with his V-2 rockets,[17] but it also meant that he would stay in position in the SS to order the final movement of Germany's rocket experts out of the path of the Russian advance and into the arms of the awaiting Americans.

Once Kammler learned the Allies had been checked at Arnhem, he ordered his launch troops forward again to The Hague to resume the V-2 attack on London. Londoners and Allied ground troops alike would pay dearly for the failure of Market Garden as the missile attacks continued. Colm discovered a personal memorandum dated January 22, 1945, through which SS Reichsführer Heinrich Himmler submitted a report detailing Kammler's actions during Market Garden:

> The A4 [V-2] rocket was first deployed under the most difficult of circumstances while our armies were disengaging from the West. It is only due to the tremendous drive and superior command of SS Gruppenführer and Waffen SS Lieutenant General Dr. Ing. Kammler that seemingly insurmountable obstacles were overcome, which enabled the deployment of this new and devastating weapon. For despite coming under heavy enemy artillery and relentless aircraft machine gun fire, the constant personal intervention and prudent leadership of Kammler allowed for the successful completion of the operation. Time and time again, in often seemingly hopeless situations, General Kammler managed to keep the long supply routes open through Holland, which enabled the launch of V-2 rockets from The Hague against England and other strategic targets.[18]

The report ends with a striking description of Kammler leading his men from the front. Himmler notes his "regular visits day and night to the most exposed and isolated fighting units proved crucial for spurring on the division, who were inspired by the personal charisma of their commander. All of the drive and enthusiasm are due solely to General Kammler's personal intervention." Dornberger, with nothing to gain by dramatizing Kammler's role, described him during this period as a "single berserk warrior" standing defiantly "against the menace advancing irresistibly from the west with a power beyond calculation." Dornberger also records with astonishment Kammler firing his Maschinenpistole 40, the rough equivalent of a Tommy gun, in the middle of the night to rouse his personal staff to action—if Kammler could not sleep, neither should his staff—and off they would speed to the next critical encounter.[19]

The concept of the mobile firing teams was ingenious, and a newly simplified launch table meant the V-2 could be quickly launched from any rural or urban terrain. Kammler's V-2 rocket troops would arrive in an area, set up, fuel the rocket, fire it less than two hours after arriving, and then speed off to another firing location. The Allies were left trying to interrupt transport and communications in and around the general launch areas. But on Kammler's orders, specialized Railroad Brigades[20]—not unlike his construction brigades—operating in groups of a thousand men strong[21] were deployed along bomb-damaged railways, communications, and supply lines.[22] Kammler made split-second decisions allocating precise quotas of personnel and materials to carry out speedy repairs. Kammler's authority gave him access to locomotives and supply trucks running in constant loops day and night between factory and launch troops. He even outfitted his troops with cutting-edge infrared technology that enabled them to see in the dark, so they never shut down their operations.[23]

For his actions during these opening months of the V-2 offensive, Kammler was awarded the German Cross in Gold on November 28, 1944, and the highly coveted Knight's Cross of the War Merit Cross with Swords on February 1, 1945. The Knight's Cross with Swords was truly exceptional (though a non-combat award); only 118 were awarded during the entire war. Kammler had already proved himself vicious and relentless as an administrator and fixer. It shouldn't surprise us that he would maintain those qualities in the face of fire on the field of battle, as well.

It is perhaps too much to say that Kammler and his V-2 played a major part in stymieing the Allies in Operation Market Garden, but I think it is fair to say that trying to displace the V-1 and V-2 launch sites was one of the objectives of the failed Operation.

• • •

By late 1944, victory on the Eastern Front was out of the question for Germany; the Russian army was simply too powerful against Germany's divided forces. The Germans had suffered devastating, unexpected defeats at Stalingrad and Kursk. On the Western Front, however, Hitler thought Market Garden highlighted the vulnerability of the Western Allies' overextended supply lines. Unbelievably, he thought one decisive German victory would force the Western Allies to negotiate a separate peace, one independent of the Soviet Union—the Yalta provision that the Allies stand and fight together notwithstanding. Germany could then concentrate its forces solely in the East—perhaps, Hitler hoped, as part of a new German–U.S.-Anglo alliance. The fact that Hitler planned his final major offensive in hopes of prompting such an alliance demonstrates just how bizarre his military and political judgment was.

SS-Brigadeführer und Generalmajor der Waffen-SS Hans Kammler. Under the War Merit Cross First Class with Swords, Kammler wears his Equestrian and German Red Cross badges, 1942. Courtesy of Tilmann Kammler

On September 16, 1944, at the Wolf's Lair, Hitler's East Prussian Headquarters, Colonel General Alfred Jodl, chief of the Operations Staff of the Armed Forces High Command, delivered a situation report on the

Western Front to the Führer. Germany's position was now desperate. The Germans were outnumbered two to one.

Jodl's blunt remarks were followed by a long, strained silence, after which Hitler precipitously announced, "I have just made a momentous decision. I shall go over to the counterattack, that is to say"—and he pointed to the over-sized map unrolled on the desk before him—"here, out of the Ardennes, with the objective—Antwerp." While his audience sat in stunned silence, none daring to object, the Führer began to outline his plan.[24]

The German High Command agreed that it would be a master stroke to deprive the Allies of supplies; that was axiomatic. Although the Allies had Antwerp, they had not yet secured the Scheldt estuary, but all sides knew they inevitably would unless Germany somehow turned the tables—quickly. If Germany's attack succeeded, four Allied armies would be trapped behind German lines. But Hitler's generals thought his plan to recapture the port was unattainable. The better course, they knew, was to wait at the Siegfried Line. But Hitler gave his orders and transferred his headquarters from the Wolf's Lair in the east to the Eagle's Lair near Bad Nauheim in the Rhineland to direct the battle personally. (I always thought the choice of the word "lair," which to me connoted a wild animal's den or a villain's refuge, was an ironically appropriate choice for Hitler's headquarters.) Operation Watch on the Rhine (Wacht am Rhein), later changed to Autumn Fog (Herbstnebel), was set for December 16 to allow the Germans time to assemble troops and equipment. By then, the Allies controlled the Scheldt and were using Antwerp as a fully functioning deep sea port. As prologue to the ground attack, Kammler received a coded order directly from Hitler—"*Anton!*"—signaling the full-out V-2 assault concentrated on London and Antwerp. Luftwaffe colonel Max Wachtel received similar orders to begin a coordinated V-1 offensive against the Antwerp region. Late in the evening of October 9, 1944, SS-Werfer-Abteilung 500, a motorized convoy of elite rocket troops under the immediate command of SS captain Johannes Miesel, crossed the German border into Holland to resume V-2 operations. The full weight of Germany's long-range missiles was brought to bear, inflicting profound misery on London and Antwerp alike. By November 20, 210 V-2s had been launched against England and 95 struck London, killing 450 and injuring hundreds more. In the same month, 126 V-2s and 94 V-1s exploded in Antwerp. By the end of November, special launch troops of the V-3 "super Gun" and the Rheinbote multi-stage missile had been absorbed into Kammler's command. The Rheinbote missile was a thirty-five-foot solid-fuel rocket with a range of one hundred miles. The missile reached an incredible speed of Mach 5.55 (over 4,200 mph), but with its small, ninety-pound warhead, with just twenty-five pounds of explosives,[25] it was considered by many to be a waste of valuable resources. But Hitler had ordered the missile into service, and that month Kammler fired 220 Rheinbote missiles at the port of Antwerp as a complement to the hundreds of other rockets he sent over.

Hitler's plan was to repeat the breakthrough of May 1940 in the Ardennes at the junction of the British and U.S. armies, but this time moving on Antwerp instead of careening through France. The Allied depots along the way would be a welcome reward, fueling and feeding the German army. It was such an audacious, improbable plan that the Allies were taken by complete surprise and retreated in disorder, leaving behind vast quantities of arms, ammunition, food, and fuel, as the Germans had hoped. On the first day of the offensive, a V-2 launched by Kammler's SS 500 hit the crowded Rex Cinema in Antwerp and killed 567 people. It was the largest loss of life from a single rocket attack. Over the next few months, the rockets and missiles continued to strike Antwerp with an increasing intensity and accuracy.[26]Against London and Antwerp, the V-2 was a devastatingly effective weapon of terror. And yet, as we shall see shortly, at the very same time that Kammler was sending his missiles into Antwerp and London, he was sending peace feelers to the Americans through Lisbon, Portugal.

The Germans managed to move forward through the Allied lines in the Ardennes, creating a fifty-to-sixty-mile westward bulge in the lines, giving the Battle of the Bulge its name. The U.S. lost over eighty thousand men to death, injury, or capture—the most of any battle in U.S. history, though German losses of men and heavy weapons, including six hundred tanks that could never be replaced, were even greater. The action kept Kammler close to the front, utilizing his special weapons unmercifully, inflicting heavy damage on military and civilian targets alike. The Vengeance Weapons offensive on Antwerp lasted nearly six months. During that time more than seventeen hundred V-2s and four thousand V-1s were launched on Antwerp, disrupting Allied supply columns, killing 1,736 people, and seriously injuring forty-five hundred others. Over six thousand buildings were completely destroyed and twenty-three thousand others were badly damaged. Seventeen ships in the harbor were damaged; supplies through Antwerp never came close to expected levels while the V-2 was operational. Almost every street was filled with piles of rubble.[27] A *Time* magazine article labelled Antwerp the "City of Sudden Death" where "people closed doors softly and talked in low voices. Hollow-eyed citizens, clinging to their homes, skulked through the ruined streets."[28] There was no sleep for the defenders and the city was on constant alert: "In Belgian cities along the V-bomb routes, sirens wailed frequently, as the noisy V-1s passed overhead. No sirens sounded in Antwerp, however, the bombs' principal target. In Antwerp men never left the ack-ack guns, the city's defense against the V-1s."[29]

I had the good fortune to meet Maurice Moortgat, who was born and raised in Belgium, one of eight children. He spent the war years in Willebroek, some fifteen miles south of Antwerp. His older sister worked for Bell Telephone in Antwerp. The Moortgats were among those who endured the V-2 assault. It was a straight line from the V-2 launch sites in Holland, through Antwerp, to Willebroek, so they suffered some over-shots, and Maurice knew all about the German rockets.

On one occasion Maurice and an older brother were scavenging for food in a farmyard greenhouse near Fort Breendonk, which guarded the approach to his small town, when they heard the "bad motorcycle muffler" sound of a V-1 overhead. The droning cut off suddenly, and they dove for cover under the greenhouse tables. They were unharmed by the explosion nearby, but people outside were cut by flying glass from the greenhouse. I asked Maurice if he and his brother went to see the impact crater. "No!" he exclaimed, "We ran home. We were safe!"

Maurice recalls another V-1 exploding in Willebroek's famous canal, which dates back to 1550. "The rocket killed only fish, which was a good thing, because many people ate the fish"—the only good I have ever heard coming from a German rocket attack.

Mercifully for the Allies and for Maurice, the German offensive in the Battle of the Bulge stalled, and on January 7, 1945, Hitler ordered the withdrawal of his forces.

● ● ●

Secretly recorded post-war conversations with Walter Dornberger, the military administrative head of the Germans' rocket project,[30] confirmed that as the Battle of the Bulge was being waged and lost, he and rocket scientist Wernher von Braun agreed that the larger war was lost. Therefore, they got in touch with the U.S. government and a prominent U.S. business through the German Embassy in Lisbon to broker a deal. Colm gave me this revelatory information while I was on a business trip. He thought he was catching me on a day off, but I was on a break from a Saturday meeting in a conference room on the fifty-third floor of a law firm in Manhattan with ninety or so other lawyers. I paced the wide room, now half empty, peering through the floor-to-ceiling windows at the city below, speaking softly to not disturb others, as Colm laid it all out for me. I had only a few minutes before my meeting resumed, so Colm came to the point quickly.

"According to Dornberger,"[31] Colm said, "he and von Braun made contact as early as December 1944"—but I couldn't hear the other details; the connection was spotty at that moment.

"Contacted who? Who did you say they contacted?" I asked Colm, a forefinger in my free ear, straining to hear. This seemed like really important information to me.

"The U.S. government, maybe the Army, maybe State Department. Frankly, we're not sure who they contacted. Or how."

"No, you said someone else. A private company? A business?" That didn't make sense, but that's what I thought Colm had said.

"Yes, a private business," Colm confirmed, "Dornberger and von Braun were in touch with G.E.... General Electric. The American company."[32]

My pacing stopped, and I looked out the big glass windows, and then quickly at the faces in the room with me. I had a momentary thought that I was being punked, made the butt of a joke, for squarely before me out the windows was the landmark General Electric Building, which has adorned the NYC skyline since 1931. An amazing coincidence, I thought. "Synchronicity"— Keith's voice rang in my head.

"We have no conclusive information as to how Dornberger and von Braun reached out to GE, but we're certain they did. We don't know whether it was in person or not, or whether the contact had been initiated the other way around. It's not clear whether von Braun and Dornberger traveled to Lisbon, or communicated by telex, diplomatic pouch, or even through an intermediary. But this has Kammler's fingerprints all over it," Colm assured me.[33]

Colm went on, "Camp 11, Latimer House, is a luxurious English country mansion in Buckinghamshire that became a hold for high-ranking German and Italian prisoners after the war. You remember Dornberger was held by the Brits for two years after the war? This is where they held him, at least for a time. And the entire facility, inside and out, was bugged with hidden microphones."

Colm could sense my uncertainty from across the Atlantic, and offered, "This is solid information, Dean—it comes from a secretly recorded conversation Dornberger had with another interned Nazi at Camp 11. It's recorded in a British interrogation center document. Let me read the relevant portion to you. Here's the whole quote: 'Dornberger, in conversation with Generalmajor Bassenge, made the following miscellaneous remarks dealing with the "V 2". He said that: Braun and Dornberger himself had realized at the end of December 1944 that things were going wrong and had consequently been in touch since that time with the General Electric Company through the German Embassy in Portugal, with a view to coming to some arrangement.'"[34]

That was pretty definitive; there certainly had been contact by von Braun and Dornberger, but it allowed room for interpretation. There had been an opportunity to make a deal, even an express willingness to make a deal—an arrangement—but there weren't a lot of details. Colm readily conceded the information was helpful, but limited. The exact timing, mode of contact, or even whether there had been intermediaries could not be determined from this language; we couldn't even tell which side initiated the contact, only that Dornberger *and* von Braun had "been in touch" with GE to come to some "arrangement." I flashed on the memory of Jörg telling me that his mother had always insisted that Kammler never approached the Americans to make a deal, but that they had approached him. Either way, I thought, this news was huge.

Colm quickly gave me his analysis of the new information, in light of our other known facts. He was certain Kammler would not have let von Braun out of the country (and I agreed), so if in-person contact had been made in Lisbon, it would have been through Dornberger. Colm said it was possible that Dornberger made the trip to Lisbon with Sigismund von Braun, Wernher's brother. "Sigismund was a German diplomat with great influence, and a Nazi. After the war he would become West Germany's Secretary of State, living to a ripe old age, until 1998. During the war he was a German representative to the Vatican. The Vatican," Colm continued, "was instrumental in other negotiations at the end of the war, and Sigismund is also known to have participated in other talks, so he might well have been involved here. He would certainly have an interest in helping his brother, and Wernher would have preferred having his own brother, his own flesh and blood, not just Dornberger, at the table on his behalf." That made sense to me, but there was even more to this thread. What has seemingly never before been discussed is Sigismund von Braun's role as an apparent SD agent within the Vatican—as indicated by a January 1945 document that Colm had uncovered, by the acting director of the Washington, D.C., office of the OSS, the precursor organization to the CIA.[35] The SD, or Sicherheitsdienst, headed first by Holocaust mastermind Reinhard Heydrich, was the intelligence arm of the Nazi Party, charged with rooting out enemies of the party—both externally and from within the ranks. Frankly, I wasn't sure if Sigismund as an agent of the SD would have been more or less likely to have facilitated the Lisbon contact, though these connections never ceased to amaze me.

We also have wartime intelligence records that connect Sigismund von Braun with Baron Ernst von Weizsäcker, the German ambassador to the Holy See and the father of noted German nuclear physicist Carl Friedrich Freiherr von Weizsäcker, in November 1944.[36] It would also have made sense for Dornberger to choose von Weizsäcker as a travel companion because von Weizsäcker's diplomatic status and likely frequent trips would have meant he could make the trip to Lisbon without raising an eyebrow. We can also tie von Weizsäcker's son's nuclear research to Kammler and von Braun.[37] Moreover, the senior von Weizsäcker was one of the perceived neutrals authorized by Hitler's foreign minister, Joachim von Ribbentrop (who himself had been authorized by Hitler), to make peace overtures to the Western Allies.[38] In the end, I decided it didn't really matter whether Dornberger went to Lisbon himself, with a fellow traveler, or at all. What was plain from this new record was that he and von Braun were in contact with GE.

"All good. But why meet with GE?" I asked Colm, still confused. I knew General Electric was big today, but I didn't know much about its history. Colm told me GE was a contractor.

"Contractor for who? For what?" still befuddled, not quite following.

"For the U.S. government; for Project Hermes," Colm said, pausing for my response. I could tell from the note of finality that this was supposed to mean something to me.

Project Hermes? That rang a faint bell, though at the moment my head was not in World War II but in my work world—where Hermes was an expensive neck tie, not some military op. I couldn't place it.

"Project Hermes was the General Electric project to develop a U.S. version of the V-2," Colm prompted.

"What the hell?" I said too loudly, turning the heads of a few colleagues. "That's unbelievable."

What did this mean? The contract putting GE in charge of the American V-2 project was let on November 20, 1944,[39] Colm told me. And before the ink was dry, GE was in contact with Dornberger and von Braun, Kammler's underlings? That was astounding. I noted that GE would never have contacted the Nazi rocket team without explicit authorization from the contractor, the United States government. So the contact must have been sanctioned at the highest levels of the American government.

And on the German side, Kammler had to have been involved. Von Braun and Dornberger had no authority or ability to manipulate events as the war wound down—but Kammler did. They could not order the cream of the German rocket team to evacuate Peenemünde for Nordhausen, and then evacuate Nordhausen for Oberammergau, ultimately to the waiting U.S. Army—but Kammler could.[40] (Von Braun himself told us it was Kammler who ordered the Peenemünde evacuation.)[41] Von Braun and Dornberger could not ensure that Hitler's orders to destroy the rocket facilities were ignored. And they could not disobey Hitler's orders to annihilate the entire German rocket team, specifically to prevent them from falling into the hands of Germany's enemies. But, as we shall see, Kammler could and did.

Naturally, Dornberger and von Braun would never have proposed such a plan to Kammler. It would have been treasonous. We are admittedly speculating here, but it is logical to conclude the entire affair had to be the brainchild of the superior—Kammler. Von Braun and Dornberger had to have made the contact not only with Kammler's permission, but under his orders and with his backing. While neither von Braun in his interrogation nor Dornberger in his book confirmed the role of their boss in the deal with the Americans, we have to conclude that Kammler used the pair as his emissaries to do his bidding. And the venture was successful. A deal was made.[42]

Naturally GE wanted everything it could get—every German scientist down to the electrician who designed the circuits for the switches in the launch sequence, every document and blueprint, every test launch result, all the plans for future revisions.[43] Dornberger and von Braun alone could never provide that complete package. Only as Kammler's emissary could they hope to satisfy the Americans.[44] Only Kammler himself could promise and deliver.

Wernher von Braun would become the leader of this key GE project, whose in-house director was Richard W. Porter. GE was so hungry to collect the Nazi rocket resources that at the end of the war Porter was flown to Europe to hand-pick German scientists and engineers most capable of helping. Porter would also helpfully identify essential rocket parts for shipment back to the U.S.,[45] all to the benefit of the U.S. and, of course, GE, his employer. Indeed, a post-war report by the U.S. Air Force claimed that using German scientists meant a savings of 40–50 percent on the overall Hermes contract.[46] GE was able to pick up where the Nazi rocket project had left off rather than reinventing the wheel (literally, reinventing the rocket).[47]

The timing of these seemingly unrelated events is the key to understanding them. The Hermes-GE contract was inked in November 1944. Dornberger and von Braun were in contact with GE in December 1944. In January 1945, von Braun held a "secret meeting" in Peenemünde with colleagues, including Dornberger's chief of staff, to discuss the "eventual feasibility of surrendering the development team intact."[48] The Kammler order to evacuate Peenemünde would come on January 31, 1945.[49] Thereafter, Kammler would move the rocket scientists into the waiting arms of the Americans in Oberammergau.

The tightly sequenced events tell a clear story: Kammler was behind a deal for U.S. forces to capture the Nazis' rocket program and give a new home to the Nazi rocket scientists—and perhaps to their boss, Hans Kammler himself. Kammler would preserve the rocket team, turn them over to the Americans, and in return hopefully save his own life.

A final piece of evidence in documents discovered by Keith struck me as powerful. Himmler, Kammler's mentor, was known to have reached out to the Americans himself. His earliest attempts to broker peace with the Western Allies were initiated in the safety of…the German Embassy in Lisbon. I couldn't help but smile—it looked like Kammler had followed in SS chief Himmler's footsteps once again, even when reaching out to make a deal to surrender to the Americans.

This had all the tells of an elaborate deal with all parties benefiting. On the one side, the Americans inherited priceless work product and brain power. On the other side, von Braun was guaranteed a post-war career that rose to the level of celebrity, while Dornberger also thrived in America, becoming vice president of Bell Aircraft, returning to his beloved Germany in his twilight years. But what of Kammler? Does his suicide argue against his spearheading or even being part of the deal? If Kammler was trying to save his own hide, he was taking a tremendous calculated gamble, putting himself in terrible peril. It was a high-wire act: he now had to do everything in his power to safeguard the rocket team, its hardware, and its records—but without overtly seeming to do so, without appearing to be a traitor.

● ● ●

On January 13, 1945, the very month after the Kammler team's Lisbon outreach to the Americans, Speer had issued a directive called "Opposing and Breaking the Enemy Air Terror" (Bekampfung und Brechung des Feindlichen Luft-Terrors), in which he said that it was "necessary to put effective weapons into development as quickly as possible." So Göring appointed Kammler as the descriptively titled Special Commissioner for Breaking the Air Terror Using Missiles. Kammler boldly wrote to Hitler and Göring in early February and outlined his understanding of his new responsibilities for the production and development not just of the V-1 and V-2, but also for more than twenty of Nazi Germany's most advanced rocket and missile systems.[50]

His empire spreading like bad news, Kammler spent more and more time frantically racing among his growing variety of operations in Germany, Austria, Poland, and Czechoslovakia—from test station to test station, factory to factory, launch site to launch site. His son Jörg recalled that Kammler's pace was so frenzied he was known to his staff as "Staubwolke"—Dust Cloud. As Martin Allen reports in *Himmler's Secret War*, "telegrams and briefs" from Kammler were crossing "Himmler's desk from all corners of the shrinking Reich, hinting at a frenetic, insomniac rush."[51]

Kammler had a fear of flying, so he was driven everywhere in his staff car. As Jörg explained, his father was also wary of enemy aircraft strafing his car, so he insisted that the convertible top be kept down at all times for an unobstructed view of the sky. He sat in the front passenger seat, his Maschinenpistole resting on his lap and his free hand on the door handle—ready to spring from the car at the sound of approaching aircraft. The near-fatal strafing of General Erwin Rommel in his staff car in July 1944 may have contributed to Kammler's apprehension, and late in the war he was right to be fearful. The Allies owned the skies and picked apart defenseless targets on the ground at will. A staff car meant an officer inside, a high priority target for the fearless airmen. Colm recalled for me his own experience when a World War II–era P-51 Mustang from a nearby air show made a strafing-style pass over his home. He described the screams and snarls of the engine as "truly demonic…terrifying." Like a freight train powering through your family room. The dishes rattled, and picture frames were atilt.

● ● ●

The V-2 would prove to be important on one final battlefield—at Remagen in the battle over the Ludendorff Bridge, a site Colm had personally explored. He made special note of the single white cross on the hilltop overlooking the scene, a memorial to those who lost their lives there.

At Remagen, for the first time, a Kammler rocket would be deployed against a relatively small fixed target—a wholly new challenge.[52] In March 1945, with spring weather in the offing, the U.S. First Army launched Operation Lumberjack to capture important German cities like Cologne and Bonn and give the Allies a foothold on Germany's western border, and hopefully a way across the Rhine—the last major geographic obstacle between the Western Allies and the Fatherland. Hitler, in desperation, ordered the destruction of every bridge spanning the Rhine, an order carried out imperfectly. A single bridge was left standing: the Ludendorff Bridge at Remagen that was 1,345 feet long and 28 feet wide.[53] The bridge, built by the Germans in WWI, bore the name of Erich Friedrich Wilhelm Ludendorff, a World War I hero and Kammler family friend.

On March 7, 1945, a small forward reconnaissance unit of just two Allied companies emerged quietly from the wooded hilltop overlooking Remagen. Peering through field binoculars, the unit's leader, Lieutenant Colonel Leonard E. Engeman, was dumbfounded as he surveyed the scene. Still standing in the valley below, spanning the Rhine, was the bridge—a hive of activity as German troops and machinery headed east. Engeman had received orders that could not have been clearer: capture the towns of Remagen and Kripp but do not to attempt a river crossing; instead keep moving south, hard and fast along its west bank until you link up with Patton's Third Army. Engeman's unit could seize Remagen, on the western bank of the Rhine, without crossing the river. Unknown to Engeman, in a telephone discussion that morning, Major General John Millikin had told Engeman's commanding officer, "You see that black line on the map?... If it is still there and you can seize that, then your name will go down in history." The black line Millikin was referring to was the Ludendorff Bridge at Remagen.

Engeman disobeyed orders and swiftly organized an assault on the bridge. Within minutes, four new Pershing M26 tanks were racing towards the bridge with supporting infantry. Four minutes after the assault began, the Americans had secured the bridge. Sergeant Alex Drabik of Toledo, Ohio, went down in history as the first enlisted man to set foot on the east side of the Rhine.

As a testament to its strategic value, General Eisenhower's chief of staff would later proclaim the bridge at Remagen was "worth its weight in gold."[54] Was this a rare moment of hyperbole for the Allied Supreme Commander? Hitler's response suggests otherwise. After hearing about the stunning Allied triumph, he flew into a rage and ordered courts martial, condemning to death the German officers responsible for not destroying the bridge.[55] Knowing that Allied troops and equipment would now begin pouring over the bridge, Hitler demanded its destruction by any means necessary, sparing no expense in men or equipment. Over the next ten days the Germans would throw everything they had at Remagen and the bridgehead the U.S. Army had established on German soil in a desperate attempt to stem the flow of Allied troops.

Americans were arriving in great numbers in preparation for what they knew would be a thoroughgoing, focused attack. They secured the bridgehead, placing five anti-aircraft battalions in and around the area. An American war correspondent described the firing of the U.S. anti-aircraft defenses when German planes arrived as so strong the ground shook, engulfing the entire Remagen valley in a cloud of dust and smoke in minutes. It was absolutely monstrous. Remagen ranks as the greatest anti-aircraft artillery battle in American history—an all-out war concentrated on one tiny patch of ground over ten days.

Germany's 9th and 11th Panzer Divisions were ordered forward as a string of German Ju-87 Stuka dive bombers and fighter aircraft bombed and strafed the bridge seemingly without pause. A steady stream of German heavy "destroyer" fighter aircraft and Heinkel He 110 bombers joined the onslaught. The Germans also had over one hundred heavy field guns trained on the bridgehead, including 105 mm and 150 mm guns and howitzers, and they timed their artillery fire to coincide with their air attacks. A German artillery observer sneaked forward, concealed himself, and from a hilltop directed artillery strikes that pounded the bridge and its approaches. A relentless barrage of German artillery shells screamed in high across Remagen valley and exploded in fiery geysers in and around town, some striking the bridge directly, sending pieces of its metal structure careening into the Rhine. The entire bridge groaned and shuddered under the sustained attack, but stood defiantly.

Göring ordered the formation of a special jet strike force of thirty Me 262A-2a fighter bombers and forty Arado 234 Blitz (Lightning) jet-powered bombers carrying 2,200-pound bombs to destroy the bridge. This was the first-ever jet powered bomber, produced in very limited numbers at the end of the war, and used primarily for reconnaissance. These would be the last Luftwaffe aircraft to fly over England in April 1945. Both aircraft types, with the speed to press home their attacks while evading the Allied anti-aircraft fire, were almost impossible to intercept, but they lacked the precision to score the knockout blow to fell the bridge.

German Heavy Artillery Battery 628, on its way toward the Vistula Front, was ordered to the Remagen area. Battery 628 was responsible for firing the huge siege howitzer "Karl"—the largest self-propelled weapon used in the war. At over 120 tons, this gun was so massive as to be unwieldy. For long-distance moves, it had to be dismantled and then reconstructed. Only seven were ever built. Karl had been deployed ruthlessly during the Warsaw Uprising. The German High Command war diary reported that Battery 628 fired a total of 14 rounds on Remagen— each around two feet in diameter and weighing over a ton.[56] Through the clouds of dust and smoke the bridge stood, surrounded by the detritus of war.

Hitler next turned to the head of his Special Operations Commando, Otto Skorzeny. Skorzeny's exploits had already won him an international reputation, James Bond style, as "the most dangerous man in Europe." He was a legend for having rescued deposed Italian dictator Benito Mussolini from the anti-fascist Italian government. At six feet four with a sabre-dueling scar running from his left ear to the center of his chin, he was an imposing figure; one observer described the indomitable warrior as looking like a "man-eating tiger on parole."[57] Skorzeny was training a team of demolition "frogmen" in Vienna when Hitler summoned him for the Remagen mission. When Skorzeny heard details of the plan to destroy the bridge, he doubted it could be done. Given the treacherous conditions of the Rhine and the impassable Allied defenses along the approach to the bridge, Skorzeny's concerns proved to be justified. His mission failed.

The bridge withstood every extraordinary measure tried by the Germans. So Hitler called on the one man he hoped could make the impossible happen, by now his number one trouble shooter. Kammler was ordered to attack the seemingly indestructible bridge using his V-2 rockets. This presented Kammler with an opportunity to demonstrate the V-2's unique powers against a discrete strategic military target. Destruction of the bridge, pushing the Allies back across the Rhine, could catapult Kammler to almost God-like status in Germany. And perhaps Kammler, an agreement with the Americans in his hip pocket, was trying to impress the Allies as much as Hitler with the value of the V-2.

A former motorcycle dispatch rider from Kammler's SS 500 V-2 firing team we spoke with was willing to recount the V-2 assault on Remagen. At his request, we have changed his name to preserve his privacy. "Gerhard Schmidt" was just seven years old when Hitler came to power, thirteen when the war broke out, and seventeen when he joined the Waffen SS in 1943 as an artillery gunner—too young to vote but not too young to fight. After being injured in combat he was assigned to SS 500 in the spring of 1944. His job was to courier messages between launch sites, supply, and command, on roadways heavily targeted by the Allies.

Early on the morning of March 17, 1945, Gerhard was busy running between various elements of the unit's Technical Troops and Fire Troops. He recalled being sent to the unit's stores to retrieve a replacement part—a solenoid—for one of the rockets destined for the bridge. The launch teams had been suffering from a severe shortage of both rockets and fuel for weeks, despite Kammler's success in keeping the supply lines open. There just wasn't enough of everything to go around at this point in the war.

Gerhard remembered the V-2 firing area and the highly choreographed activity there. NCOs bellowed orders and heavily camouflaged vehicles raced back and forth along the flat, narrow forest tracks around Hellendoorn. In the vicinity of the launch site soldiers were busy putting the final touches on a series of defensive emplacements to protect the rocket and the team before and during launch. The undergrowth bristled with anti-aircraft observer teams scanning the sky, searching for any signs of Allied planes.

Under the watchful eye of the unit's CO, SS-Hauptsturmführer Johannes Miesel, the rocket crew placed and then precisely levelled the V-2 launch table. The distinctive sound of a small Volkswagen "beetle" engine could be heard powering the hydraulic rams that inched the missile into its launch position. Engineers then hurried to remove the protective covering from the rocket engines and attach the steering rudders. Tanker trucks arrived and pumped eight tons of alcohol and liquid oxygen into the V-2's fuel tanks, white frost crystalizing on the hoses. The fueling complete, the support vehicles and crews withdrew to the protection of slit-trenches prepared the previous night. As Gerhard lay in the trench, he monitored his watch. He watched the V-2 sail away towards its target, and then at just over four minutes the rocket's warhead slammed into the ground at Remagen.

Dornberger described the force of a V-2 ploughing into the earth at three thousand miles per hour as equal to "50 locomotives impacting the ground at 60 mph." Then the one-ton warhead exploded. Unlike the V-1, the V-2 warhead did not have a proximity fuse, meaning that it didn't explode above ground but instead, given its high impact velocity and mass, penetrated to a depth of about ten feet before exploding, muffling the explosive effect in the earth and making the V-2 less than optimally effective.[58] Even so, the recent BBC television series *Blitz Street*, which studied the effect of World War II ordnance exploding in an urban area, determined that when the one-ton warhead erupted, it disgorged an incredible six million pounds of debris, blasting a crater sixty feet wide and twenty-five feet deep. Dual ground and air shock waves raced out from the point of impact, damaging buildings to a radius of a thousand yards. And displaced earth, concrete, and steel equal to the weight of over two thousand four-door automobiles rained down after being hurled into the air by the force of the explosion.

The plentiful anti-aircraft guns that had proved so confounding for Germany's bomber wings were useless against the V-2. Once the V-2 entered the field, all the Americans could do was dig in and hunker down. A double clap of thunder heralded the arrival of that first V-2 at Remagen as it struck less than three hundred yards from the bridge, destroying farm buildings and killing three American soldiers. The sound of the missile's approach was a low, shrill whistle rising to a deafening roar that gave way to the agonizing sound of twisting steel and falling debris. The earth shook and the sky darkened—it was as if hell itself had been unleashed. The V-2 rocket impacted at approximately four times the speed of sound. British Type 9 Mark V Radar had tracked the missile's approach from Hellendoorn, an impossible 130 miles north of Remagen. Time from launch to impact was four minutes and ten seconds. All the characteristics of this weapon—its speed, power, and complexity—suggested it did not belong on the battlefields of this war; it was like something from a future era, a weapon in kind and effect totally alien to the World War II battlefield. This was the first of eleven V-2s hurled at the bridge by the SS 500 under the direction of its commander—Hans Kammler.

Hours after the V-2s exploded, the mighty bridge creaked and groaned, twisted in slow motion, then reeled and plunged into the river below, killing twenty-eight engineers and wounding sixty-three others. The bridge had taken quite a pounding over the previous ten days from demolition charges, artillery strikes, aircraft bombing, and a persistent traffic jam of heavy armor and troops crossing over. But it was

Kammler's rocket attack that had delivered the final blows just before the bridge collapsed.[59]

Some historians have argued that at Remagen Kammler merely opened a stubborn jar of pickles whose lid had been loosened by other hands. But one entry in a U.S. War Department file Keith found, dated March 1945, notes "Kammler boasted openly that it was a V-2 rocket that caused Remagen Bridge to collapse."[60] And it was true, at least in the eyes of Adolf Hitler, as the Führer confirmed the following day when he sent Kammler a telegram congratulating him for destroying the bridge.[61]

Hitler had imagined Kammler launching a sustained rocket attack on Remagen over a two- or three-day period using fifty to a hundred V-2s to disrupt the entire area even after the bridge fell, driving the Allies back across the Rhine. But at that late stage of the war the rocket units were all but spent, and bringing down the bridge would have to suffice.

● ● ●

In late March 1945, Kammler ordered a last V-2 salvo launched at England, and one of the missiles impacted at Stepney, Hughes Mansions, flattening two London city blocks and killing 134. The following day the last V-2 of the war struck close to Antwerp as the continuing Allied advance finally forced Kammler's V-2 rocket troops to withdraw from Holland. But a new V-1 model of lighter construction and longer range enabled Kammler to open a new V-1 offensive against London. After firing 275 missiles, Colonel Wachtel, now Kammler's underling, was also forced to withdraw to Germany, putting London beyond range. Fortunately for the Allies, the German A-4b missile—which, with a range twice that of the V-2, could have reached Great Britain from within Germany's borders—was only tested in January 1945 and was never deployed in battle.

There is no consensus on whether the V-2 rockets were important
to the course of the war. But a U.S. Strategic Bombing Survey (USSBS)
report did note that the Vengeance Weapons and the Messerschmitt Me
262 jet fighter merited the underground protection of Nordhausen—
indicating at least a perceived importance. The USSBS also concluded
that had the V-2 been deployed in greater numbers at an earlier date, the
story of the war might have been quite different, since there were no
known countermeasures. Winston Churchill, not just a political leader
but also a great military historian, called the V-2 "an impressive technical
achievement."[62]

An illuminating, if anecdotal, comment comes from a B-24 gunner.
Bomber missions were fraught with danger, recording among the highest
casualty rates of all forms of service in the war. Over half of the RAF's
heavy bomber crews were lost. U.S. fliers, coming to the conflict later in
the war when Germany's defenses were less effective, had fatality rates
of over 25 percent, with another 20 percent taken prisoner. Yet this
bomber crew member said he would rather be aloft in a bomber than in
a V-2 target area: "I was more frightened in London during the V2 rocket
attacks than in the air on missions."[63] The strain of living under constant
attack in London or Antwerp was nerve-racking in the extreme.

● ● ●

The V-2 had proved itself in battle and, more importantly, had nearly
unlimited potential. With the V-2 technology alone Kammler had plenty
of value to trade, and he was in total control of it. Even von Braun, the
rocket genius, thought of himself and his colleagues as possessed by
Kammler, one of "Kammler's eggs."[64]

And Keith and Colm had evidence that Kammler had disobeyed
direct orders from Hitler to keep all those eggs in his basket—to keep
his end of the deal and deliver them to the Americans. On March 19,
1945, with failure on the Western Front assured, Hitler issued his infamous scorched-earth order from his Berlin bunker, ordering the total

destruction of German infrastructure to prevent its use by the conquering Allied armies. This so-called Demolitions on Reich Territory Order, more widely known as the Nero Decree, applied to all research facilities and their documentation, which were to be destroyed immediately, simply as the Allies got closer and closer, threatening to overtake each facility. Everything was to be destroyed immediately. This would have meant the loss of all records and equipment—V-1, V-2, Me 262 jets, and all other special weapons. I imagined Kammler must have been thrown into an absolute panic—Hitler was pulling the rug out from under him, ordering him to destroy the research he was counting on trading to the Americans. Both Albert Speer and Kammler defied the Nero Decree.[65] Instead of Hitler's scorched-earth policy, Speer implemented a policy of "paralysis"—retreat without destruction[66]—a "quiet surrender" of Europe's priceless architectural and artistic treasures to the Allies. Likewise, in direct violation of Hitler's Nero Decree, Kammler worked hard to preserve the Reich's technological treasures—the men, materials, and facilities. Kammler was unable to move weapons factories at this point to deliver them to the Americans—they were simply too large. The best he could do, Keith and Colm told me, was to preserve the facilities in defiance of the Nero Decree, move the scientists and some of their working documents, and disclose the various facilities' locations to the Americans and hope they got there before the Russians.

The Bergkristall plant at the Mauthausen concentration camp and manufacturing complex is an apt case study. In early May 1945, Mauthausen commandant Franz Ziereis received an order from Hitler via SS chief Himmler to use explosives to destroy the facility, the slave laborers, and even the local population. The plan was to lure the locals and the slaves into the tunnel with a false air raid. Machine gunners posted at the entrance would prevent any from leaving. The tunnel was to be pre-wired with explosives. Fortunately, the murderous demolition never took place. After the war, Bergkristall plant manager Paul Wolfram, the only explosives expert on site, took credit for preventing the execution of the plan, invoking Kammler: "Kammler would never give approval to destroy these important production facilities."[67] Note that Wolfram was more willing to disobey a direct order from Hitler and Himmler than go against even the perceived wishes of Kammler.

CHAPTER FIVE

Saving the Technology for the Americans

"He was the worst man I ever met in my life...I have no words. He was arrogant. What he said was as if God would have said it."

—Dr. Herbert Axster, describing Hans Kammler[1]

With most of the rocket team in Nordhausen, central Germany, in the Kammler-built underground facility to which they had moved after abandoning Peenemünde, the military map was changing yet again as the Germans' position continued to degrade. On April 3, 1945, Kammler ordered the rocket team's final move, further south and west, from Nordhausen to Oberammergau in south-central Germany—significantly, from territory that would be occupied by the Russians after the war directly into the path of the advancing Americans, who arrived the following week.[2] The final transfer, organized in three days, was more flight than relocation, a six-day trip aboard Kammler's personal train, *The Vengeance Express*, on a perilous, winding journey high into the Bavarian Alps. While ordering this movement, Kammler was discharging other duties elsewhere, launching the last V-2 of the war.[3] With the final collapse of Germany imminent, large movements like this were especially dangerous, so Kammler's order has special weight as evidence of his intentions—and of his deal. Important rocket records were buried in central Germany before the trek; there was no sure way to transport them over the five-hundred-mile journey without

putting too many assets on one vulnerable train. And so a small town
an hour's drive from Kammler's Ilfeld headquarters near Nordhausen
became the hiding place of fourteen tons of research documents and
blueprints, stashed in numbered boxes.[4] On April 1, Easter Sunday,
1945, rocket team member Dieter Huzel received the order from von
Braun to collect and then hide these most valuable documents, which
had not been centralized and organized since the move from Peenemünde. Various departments and staff were still scattered throughout
the region in small clusters, each with their own files. Huzel described
the near-panic pace at which he and a small crew of men headed up the
collection and consolidation. They located the perfect mine and stored
the documents before fleeing to Oberammergau. The mission was
accomplished with a handful of men shuttered in the backs of enclosed
cargo trucks so that only two others, "Kammler's lorry drivers,"[5] knew
the location of the fourteen-ton stash.[6] In Huzel's words, "these documents were of inestimable value.... a treasure trove...a cache of scientific information unlike any before in history.... Whoever inherited them
would be able to start rocketry at that point at which we had left off."[7]

As Huzel returned from burying the documents at Goslar, he made
a circuitous trip via Berlin to pick up his fiancée. Along the way, as he
would explain in his memoirs *From Peenemünde to Canaveral*, he was
to take one truck to "pick up some of the professor's stuff." Unfortunately, Huzel did not elaborate further, and we are left to wonder whether
he was hauling valuable rocket research or von Braun's furniture.[8] This
is one of those dead ends that Keith warned me about: a tantalizing nugget of information—and then the trail simply goes cold, with no
resolution.

Weeks later at Oberammergau in the south, Huzel was approached
by Dornberger, who said together they might take a trip to the north "in
connection with the classified material you have hidden in the Harz
Mountains."[9] The two of them never made that trip, but the statement
shows that Dornberger knew of the stash. Huzel also noted that he had
"disclosed the hiding place to Wernher von Braun and Karl Otto

Fleischer, as instructed, right after that mission had been completed." Others agree von Braun knew the location of these stashed documents,[10] as did Dornberger.[11] The documents that Huzel buried at Goslar comprise the single largest cache of hidden documents from the Nazi rocket program. It infuriated me to learn that neither von Braun nor Dornberger—both of whom were supposedly cooperating with the Allies after the war—disclosed the existence of these Peenemünde documents to the Americans. They did not so much as lift a finger to make certain the United States, the country for which they aspired to work, got to the documents before the Soviet Union did.

● ● ●

Even with the stashing of documents and the running of *The Vengeance Express*, the evacuation of Nordhausen was not quite complete. Under Kammler's orders, some scientists stayed behind and the plant remained intact and operational until April 10, 1945. The very next day, the spearhead of the advancing American troops, Combat Command B (CCB) of the 3rd Armored Division, took full advantage of Kammler's generosity in preserving the facility. The Americans, arriving first, would scour it for weeks—even longer than anticipated, when the deadline for handover to the Soviets was twice extended.

Faced with the opportunity to take Berlin or direct his forces to the south and west to take Nordhausen, Eisenhower had given up on Germany's capital and instead headed to the Nordhausen rocket facility. Taking either objective would cost the Western Allies unavoidable casualties to take territory that they had committed to turning over to Russia after the war, at the Yalta Conference in February 1945, where the Allies had agreed to post-war occupation boundaries regardless of where the respective armies were positioned when the war ended.[12] Despite that agreement, every Ally wanted its own morale-building victories, rewarding conquests for troops, to score political points at home and points of pride in being the liberators of Paris, Rome, and Sicily, as well as the first to enter the great German cities. Perhaps even more, they wanted the technological spoils—the factories, engineers, scientists, and documents—to improve their own technologies, both military and civil.

In what was the clearest overt signal possible to the Western Allies that Berlin was open to them and Germany would rather have Berlin fall to them than to the Russians, German general Wenck's Twelfth Army, which was the western defense of Berlin, was withdrawn and pivoted east against the Soviets, allowing Eisenhower an essentially unfettered path to Berlin. So why didn't Eisenhower rush in? In the capture of Berlin, he still saw a long haul that would cost him hundreds if not thousands of men, only to have the territory revert to the Soviets after the war. Turning toward Nordhausen, Eisenhower made the choice to forego Berlin for rocket science.[13]

Colm told me about the American–Great Britain rift on this point. Churchill wanted Eisenhower in Berlin—the Yalta agreement be damned. He saw Berlin as a political center, with its occupier enjoying strategic and psychological dominance throughout post-war Europe. Churchill leaned hard on Truman, the new American president: "We should march as Far East into Germany as possible, and…should Berlin be in our grasp we should certainly take it." But on March 28, 1945, when Montgomery acted alone to begin an assault toward Berlin, he was relieved of his command of the Ninth Army by Eisenhower.

I understood that, given their proximity, the Brits had a much greater and more immediate concern about limiting the extent of Russia's geographical post-war reach than did the Americans. Great Britain would be more threatened by a Soviet-occupied Berlin than was the United States. But even so, I was surprised by the profound differences between Churchill and Montgomery on the one hand and Truman and Eisenhower on the other. Why would the Americans be so reluctant to take the advantage here? Then Colm reminded me that Patton had come into some key intelligence—one of Kammler's men captured in central Germany informed Patton that the road to Prague was wide open; there was no Alpine Redoubt, no amassed German forces for a last stand.[14] Perhaps

Patton's approach reflected nothing more complicated than the path of least resistance. Or maybe Truman and Ike were simply more interested in moving toward other, secret targets. Could it be that, looking forward to the coming stand-off with the Russians, they saw the technological battlefield as even more important than the geographical one?

It was at this point that Keith began to drop hints about a super-secret Kammler-run think tank, something he called Working Staff Kammler, in Czechoslovakia, even further south and east than Nordhausen. He and Colm were sure Eisenhower had left Berlin to the Russians not only to get to Nordhausen, but also to claim the Skoda Werke Armament Factory in western Czechoslovakia, though nothing in the records proves this. Skoda was among the largest munitions factories in the world, and capturing it would be a major prize.

Keith could make a convincing argument that Allen Dulles of the OSS (later the CIA) played a role in turning Eisenhower's amassed forces south; but again, this was just his gut instinct. Though he had no proof, it was an interesting thought experiment. Was Dulles pushing Eisenhower toward the V-2 scientists? Might Dulles have played a role in the Kammler Deal? Was Dulles urging Eisenhower beyond Nordhausen to Prague? And if so, why? Keith argued that weaponry made in Czechoslovakia was the reason.

Once the Americans secured Nordhausen, Colonel Holger Toftoy, Chief of Army Ordinance Technical Intelligence stationed in Paris, knew they had hit the big time. Toftoy immediately dispatched Major James Hamill to investigate and oversee "Special Mission V-2." Finding the main V-2 assembly plant intact was a gift—though its's not clear Toftoy knew it was a gift from Kammler, who should have leveled it.

Toftoy authorized the immediate evacuation of one hundred complete V-2s to Antwerp, and from there to the U.S. Up to that point the U.S. had captured just nine complete V-2s, kept seven for their own purposes, and allocated two to the Brits.[15] Because the Americans would have Nordhausen for only a limited period—Yalta having assigned it to the Russians—the work there was a race against time with experts, rockets, parts, and diagrams sent this way and that over rails and roads, often the same stretches the Germans had used to move live missiles forward to launch areas.

Colonel Peter Beasley of the U.S. Strategic Bombing Survey, Aircraft Division, was in charge on site. I was not surprised to learn that he chose to set up his field headquarters at the site of Kammler's former HQ in Ilfeld, less than five minutes north of Nordhausen. The space ideal for Kammler to oversee Nordhausen from was the same space from which Beasley could manage its exploitation. Beasley was a "Michigan man, about sixty years old. He was a very rich and important man, a former president of Lockheed with many other industrial concerns." He was to get into the facility first and determine everything built there during the war, then assemble a detailed picture of how it functioned. The task required a full audit of the management and production records, including minutes of management and factory meetings and even records of sabotage and disciplinary measures. Every document Beasley's team could locate was scrutinized for information on how the plant functioned.

Responsibility for hardware and manpower was divided. As Beasley worked frantically to package and export as much hardware as possible, a young Army Ordnance officer, Major Robert Staver, was put in charge of identifying and rounding up the rocket scientists and engineers remaining in the area—those who had not made the trip to Oberammergau on Kammler's train. Access to key personnel was critical, not only for their own knowledge but also for anything they could reveal about documents that were missing or hidden.

Major Staver fought tooth and nail to bring von Braun, who had surrendered in the south, back to Nordhausen to identify and coax the hold-out experts to move west to avoid capture by the Russians. Accompanying von Braun to Nordhausen for this critical task was Dr. Richard Porter of GE—the same Porter who would head GE's Project Hermes,[16] the Americans' effort to reproduce their own V-2. While cooperating with U.S. Army officers roving the countryside, von Braun had numerous opportunities to mention and even lead the Americans to the fourteen-ton cache of rocket documents hidden by Huzel, but he chose not to do so. And there were yet other secret buried documents von Braun failed to disclose, even as he was driven past them by his American chauffeurs.[17] What must he have been thinking?

Also working closely with Major Staver to find scientists was engineer Ed Hull, yet another GE official. Nordhausen was filling up with American industrialists. The fact the Americans had GE personnel in place at Nordhausen indicates they had been tipped off in advance to its purpose and location—by Kammler's emissaries, is my guess. Porter and Hull may even have been at the German embassy in Lisbon in December 1944 to make the contact with Dornberger and von Braun, though we can't prove this.

The Americans had three main tasks at Nordhausen, each of great importance: First, collect as much hardware as possible, whether complete missiles or components, and destroy anything they could not take with them.[18] Second, collect the scientists, denying them to the Russians, and pump them for information. Third, collect documents that described or explained the missile production and technology—including accurate, if complicated, records of trials and errors and blueprints for assembly—for the Americans' information, but equally important, to deny them to the Russians. Unlike the scientists, the documents wouldn't lie.

Finding and then swaying the scientists was not easy; they could be temperamental and non-cooperative. These were the experts who had either been left behind or refused to make the trip to Oberammergau because they had wanted to surrender.

Colonel Beasley managed to befriend the most prominent member of Kammler's staff at Nordhausen—Georg Rickhey, Kammler's chief deputy and Nordhausen's general manager. Beasley actually moved in with Rickhey and ultimately sent him to Wright Airfield, Ohio, with forty-two boxes of recovered rocket records, likely making Rickhey the first German shipped to the United States after the war—not to face trial, but to enjoy a long, profitable career. These forty-two boxes of documents were but a small fraction of the rocket team's records and were separated from the fourteen tons buried by Huzel. Rickhey had personally accompanied the truck that took the forty-two boxes of records to be buried, and "he changed drivers three times; and...subsequently, all three drivers were liquidated"[19]—a horrifying detail that Beasley reported but otherwise overlooked. Beasley's report describes these hidden documents as "a complete set dealing with the manufacture and development of all rocket weapons in the development stage or being produced at Mittelwerke," and also details Rickhey's extreme nervousness on arriving at the cave where the forty-two boxes were hidden, over the possibility the documents had already been removed.[20] Rickhey and the documents were out of Germany within forty-eight hours. Remarkably, while later working at Wright Field for the U.S. government, Rickhey's name was prominently displayed on U.S. Army war crimes lists, wanted for murder. Ironically, Rickhey was paid handsomely to translate the documents shipped from Nordhausen—which American prosecutors sought to use as evidence of his war crimes.

On May 18, the big gun, Dr. Howard P. Robertson—Eisenhower's scientific adviser—arrived in Nordhausen. Robertson, a Princeton mathematical physicist, was attached to the Office of Scientific Research and Development (OSRD) London Mission. He was also Chief of the Supreme Headquarters Allied Expeditionary Force's Scientific Intelligence Advisory Section (SIAS) and Chief of the Field Information Agency, Technical (FIAT), the U.S. agency that investigated and captured German technology. After the war, Robertson would take a professorship at CalTech, but he would also be employed by the CIA. Only something of dire importance could bring General Eisenhower's top scientific advisor to Nordhausen. For a great while Robertson had been toggling between the U.S. and Europe, reporting to the Crossbow Committee, which was responsible during the war for destroying Germany's secret weapons. He approved the use of GE specialists for high-tech interrogations even before the war ended.[21] When Robertson met Staver at Nordhausen, he initially told Staver he was there only to pick up two German scientists to fly them to the Allied interrogation center at Garmisch-Partenkirchen. This was a lie, or at best a half-truth, for we now know the two scientists Roberston wanted were Rees and Fleischer—two of only three men (the other being Wernher von Braun) who knew the story of the buried fourteen tons of missing documents. Robertson's true mission was to find those documents, and he needed Rees and Fleischer to lead him to them. Though Staver would be just as keen as Robertson to get as much intelligence in whatever form as possible, Staver objected to Rees and Fleischer being released to Robertson. Robertson wasn't expecting such stiff resistance from Staver,[22] and he decided to confide in Staver and showed him a note from Major Hans-Friedrich von Ploetz, Kammler's intelligence chief, which said that Kammler had revealed that documents had been hidden near Nordhausen. (In his 1946 report on Nordhausen, Staver would say that he had never even heard of von Ploetz or Kammler until this point in time, so we know that all his information on von Ploetz and Kammler and the hidden documents was coming to him from Robertson.)

The next day, Staver told Rees and Fleischer that he knew they could locate hidden documents and that Kammler himself had said it was okay for them now to reveal where they were secreted. Staver would later say that this was a ruse to get the two men to reveal where the documents were buried. Rees and Fleischer were forced to either disclose the location or risk disobeying what they were told were the wishes of Kammler. And it worked. With the help of Rees and Fleischer, the fourteen tons of documents were recovered by Staver and the Americans on May 21, 1945.

That's the official historical account. But perhaps Staver's play was no ruse at all. What if it was a genuine Kammler directive? Kammler might well have told von Ploetz, his director of intelligence, to direct Rees and Fleischer to cooperate with the Americans. Doing so fits the Kammler pattern, established at Ebensee and Ohrdruf, of preserving documents and sites for the Americans, even leaving his key staff behind to guide them. I had to wonder, was Kammler pulling the strings, either from beyond the grave—or from the shadows?

CHAPTER SIX

The Reveal

"In peace, sons bury their fathers. In war, fathers bury their sons."

—Herodotus

We aren't the only ones who think Kammler survived," Keith began. "From the beginning, at least Speer believed he lived on. In his interrogation just after the war, Speer pointed the Allies to Kammler, telling them that Kammler had more information on rockets and underground facilities than he, Speer, had."

"Right," I said, "one report, from one fellow Nazi."

We had agreed it was time for another conference call. Since the time Keith had given me his entire collection of books, and many of his files, I had committed to writing this story. Now we needed an honest inventory because I thought we were still coming up short, and I was beginning to get concerned. This was a possible turning point for our team.

Colm chimed in next with a bit of a summary: "We know about the Lisbon contact. Dornberger, or even von Braun, couldn't have done that without Kammler. So, we know he had contact with the U.S., through emissaries. And Jutta"—Kammler's wife—"told Jörg the Americans reached out to Kammler, not the reverse."

"We just don't have the documents proving the deal, proving Kammler surrendered," Keith noted, trying to be helpful.

"That's my point," I said, "too much of what we have is circumstantial. Interesting. Exciting even, but circumstantial. This is a great character in history. We've proven he was an evil bastard, and that alone is a great story, but we haven't really nailed him to the wall. We can't yet *prove* he did a deal."

"Well, we're not making a case in court," Colm said, a bit defensively. We'd had this discussion before, about my levels of required proof being impossibly high. Colm switched to another tack: "We know the rocket team went to America after the war. Who else could have made that happen? It had to be Kammler."

That was common knowledge—that the German scientists ended up in the United States. But we needed evidence that Kammler delivered the rocket scientists—beyond the argument that he was the only one capable of doing so. I wanted affirmative proof. Still in recap mode, I tried to find something we could hang our hat on: "We have the hidden documents, we have all the GE people at Nordhausen, we have Kammler ignoring the scorched earth policy." Don't get me wrong, I was pleased that our team was finding indications and hints, like Speer's statement at his interrogation, that Kammler had survived the war. And I was excited about the abundance of new details we had uncovered about Kammler's "death" that didn't hang together. But I wasn't sure we had a definitive case.

"Well, we're not done yet," Colm resolved, rallying. We knew a lot more now than when the project began. We agreed that I would go back to the Holocaust Museum Library, Keith would return to National Archives as well as scour the past Freedom of Information Act (FOIA) responses to work up possible appeals and new requests, and Colm would take another look at our mass of material with fresh eyes—all in light of the new information we had. That had always been their recipe for success—more work. Thankfully, Keith and Colm would soon bolster our case definitively.

● ● ●

Keith always memorialized his research in regular field reports, memos written to me and Colm, describing his searches and findings, attaching choice documents he had uncovered. Having encountered the frustratingly disorganized halls of the National Archives, he was determined to create a sensible, searchable record of his own work. He wrote his reports in classic military style, giving all three of us ranks, characterizing his trips to National Archives as missions or forays, calling his interviews with various authors and retired military "contacts," trying to keep our work fun. On any given day, Keith might send me something marginally useful—a two-hundred-page thesis that could be helpful on background, some general war statistics, details on the SS—or something that amounted to a quantum leap forward.

On this day, just days after our conference call, I knew Keith was sending me something momentous because his email was preceded by a near panicked voice mail message. I'm not sure how I missed his call, but his message was clear: "Sending you an email. Priority one"— something he described as "the mother lode." He was hyper-excited about getting my reaction, no doubt turbo-charged on caffeine. I have already mentioned Keith's energy, his unapologetic, infectious enthusiasm. I could often picture him smiling widely on the phone. He goes through life like a half-mad football fan in the final two minutes of a tie game. Edge of the seat, top of the roller coaster. Today, even though he was trying hard to restrain himself, it sounded like he was bouncing on the balls of his feet. I took "mother lode" with a grain of salt, though, thinking Keith was probably overstating. It turns out he was dead on.

I will never forget where I was—my home office in northern Virginia on an otherwise quiet Saturday afternoon. My office had everything I needed—broadband internet, state-of-the-art computer with all the right software, oversized monitor to blow up grainy documents, speaker phone, and perhaps most importantly, the kitchen close by. I had cleared off about forty-five feet of bookshelf space, which quickly filled with

World War II tomes and materials and, with Keith's shipments, overflowed to the basement. A double window looked onto the serenity of my suburban backyard, framing a willow tree that had grown faster than my kids, and like them was in constant motion. There was a Bradford pear inconveniently close to that overwhelming willow, and on the pear tree's lowest branch a weathered wooden birdhouse that Taylor and I had made for my wife, Lou Anne, one Mother's Day years before. When working on the book and losing myself in thought, my eyes would stray to the bird house—on the best days a small, feathered head peeking out of the hole we had drilled, no bigger than a half dollar, or the mama bird resting on the dowel peg just below.

In retrospect I realize that, more than a way to reflect, this was a way to extract myself from information too intense—stories involving murdered children, persecuted masses, starving people, stacked bodies. In the course of my research I once came upon a photograph of a victim of the Gardelegen Massacre in northern Germany. At the very end of the war four thousand prisoners were being transported from a shuttered slave labor camp, and then time ran out. The SS in charge of the transport took the sickest, over a thousand people, and herded them into a barn. The doors were bolted, and the barn was set ablaze.[1] A horror. The photograph I saw, taken from outside the barn, showed a man who had tried to squeeze under the wooden planks of the barn wall, frantically digging away the earth beneath. Only his head, one shoulder and arm had made it. The flesh of his face was leathery, charred, fixed in horror. It was beyond grotesque. That was the one life this young man had on earth, I thought, ended in agony in this remote spot. The *one* life. What was the sense of all this...? That train transport originated at Dora, Kammler's custom-built slave labor camp, and the evacuation order came from Kammler. For some reason, or "no reason at all," as he might say, Joe Gringlas had not been forced to board that train. Those were the moments my eyes sought the birdhouse in my back yard.

Anxiously, I opened Keith's email and attachment. The first thing I saw was his field report, formatted as usual. I began reading, scanning really, and quickly surmised Keith had gotten his hands on a Third Army Wanted List. These were monthly documents put together by U.S. Army intelligence after the war that listed "high-value personality targets"—wanted Germans and collaborators. Keith's report noted that the wanted list included an entry for Kammler. I couldn't wade through the rest of the several pages of Keith's writings. Instead I cheated, scrolled down, and opened the attachment, the original document. Now I was on the edge of *my* seat.

I dialed Keith's number. He answered immediately, and I put him on speaker. "Hold on."

My monitor showed me the photograph of a grey-white, eight-and-a-half-by-eleven-inch paper framed within the back of a manila folder, as if it had been photographed from above inside an opened file folder—page one of the wanted list. The parts of the page that should have been white paper were various shades of grey to almost black, making the type difficult to read, typical of World War II documents, like trying to see the picture on an old, staticky television. The top line header screamed a warning: "S E C R E T." Below that: "Headquarters, Third United States Army." Despite the graininess, the date of the wanted list leapt off the page at me—April 20, 1946. *1946?* Whoa—a year after the war ended. And Keith's field report said Kammler was on the list, a wanted list?

"How was a dead man a 'high-value personality target?'" I said out loud.

The first name on the top of page one of the wanted list was "Absalon, Gunther" followed by cursory bio information; then "Ackermann, Warner." Then "Ahrens, Oberst." My eyes flitted. Bottom of page one was "Baranski, Nieszystan." This first page had fifteen or so names, I quickly surmised, with various amounts of bio information for each, to facilitate identification and capture. I didn't recognize any of the names, though I wasn't so much trying to read each name individually as determine that none of them was Kammler. I scrolled on and on, through the following pages, impatiently, amazed at the number of people on the list. Top of page eight, "Heubner, Rudolf." Getting close. My eyes scanned down, through the I's and J's to the K's. There it was—"KAMMLER (FNU) [First Name Unknown], SS General."

"Kammler," I said out loud. Again, Keith just waited for me to read on. He already knew what was coming. Seeing Kammler's name caused a tingle along the back of my neck and shoulders, literally a primeval hair-raising experience. Not fear, but intense excitement. His name was clear on the page, though the m's in the middle were slightly faded. Finding the name was itself extraordinary—Kammler seems never to have existed when it comes to official records anywhere. Finding him on a wanted list was a heart-stopping piece of evidence that he had lived into 1946. I read the bio information: "In charge of rocket operations in the West; Head of Amstgruppe 'C' of SS Wirtschafts and Verwalterngshauptamt Sonderbehollmachtigter 2; commanded Army Corp XV...." I reread the description, letting it sink in. There was no doubt about it.

"This is our Kammler. The bio info, even without a first name; it's a perfect match."

"It is," Keith responded, "Kammler was alive in 1946! Unbelievable!" Keith was practically exploding through the telephone. There was more in the Kammler entry, so I read on, my heart stepping up its pace, feeding off Keith's energy, my mind buzzing: "last reported being captured by the Ninth US Army; wanted by Theater PM. Apprehend." I had to read that two or three times, leaning in close to the monitor, the document enlarged to ridiculous proportions. One word filled most of the screen: "captured."

"What the hell!? He was captured??"

I replay this scene over and over, seeing myself gazing into my computer screen. Captured by the Ninth U.S. Army? *Captured by the Ninth U.S. Army*?? Not only was Kammler still alive in 1946, but the Americans had had him before that!

"I know! I know!" was all Keith could say over and over again. "I KNOW!!" Then he was laughing.

"This is huge! This is it. This is what we need!" I congratulated Keith on his find, and we shared a few minutes of unmitigated joy as I confirmed for him that I read the document the same way he did. Long-distance high fives and more laughter. Kammler had indeed survived the war—the "official" account of his death, and all other accounts, were untrue. He was still alive as late as April 1946, long after the war ended, long after the May 1945 date of his officially adjudicated death. And now we held the evidence to prove it. We did not celebrate long, though, as Keith was itching to phone Colm, in Ireland, before it got too late. We wanted him to share this spectacular moment he had helped create. That conference call had a much different tone than the previous one.

When we adjourned, though, and I was left to myself, my elation abated and doubts did begin to trickle in. That's my nature and my legal training. I could still too easily pick this record apart. Maybe Kammler's name and info on the list were clerical mistakes. Did his name appear on the previous and subsequent month's Wanted Lists? Why did the Theater Provost Marshal (PM) want Kammler? If he had already been captured, as the document said, why was the action requested "Apprehend"? Finally, there was no date of capture specified, which was troubling—could this capture be consistent with a later suicide? As always, I knew our team needed more. Now it was Colm's turn.

● ● ●

Colm was the "junior" member of our trio, not yet fifty years old, but he also had the most experience studying the war and the most hands-on experience researching sites in person. He had also been on Kammler's trail for some twenty years, and he brought to our team a number of personal relationships with scholars and historians, having conducted countless interviews that had led to more and more data points. Among his more significant interviewees was Professor Gerald Fleming, retired from Surrey University, whose life work was documenting Nazi atrocities—especially through Russian archives and refuting Holocaust deniers.

"He is *the* expert on Kammler in Europe," Colm had said to me, hitting the word 'the' hard.

"Originally, years ago now, I phoned Fleming at his London address," Colm explained. "After gaining his confidence, Fleming said, 'I can prove Kammler survived the war and made a deal with the Americans.' I was astounded, as this was the very first suggestion that Kammler lived on, and this is what really triggered my hunt for Kammler. But, like most researchers, Fleming was slow to share his proof with me." I could hear mild frustration in Colm's voice as he described himself in the same position as—I thought, with some amusement—Colm had put me in later when I was recruited into this project: confronted with someone making fantastic, mostly unbelievable claims, dangling the proof just out of sight.

"Fleming dropped details to me over the years—'Kammler didn't die.' Then 'Kammler surrendered.' 'To the U.S. Army.' 'To the 4th Armored.' Then the date of surrender, May 6, 1945. Greater and greater specificity in drips and drops. Fleming claimed he had a document to prove all this."

Colm recounted for me one particular conversation he had had with Fleming. Colm had taken this call one morning while walking his Doberman, Max, on the blustery beach near his home. Max was roaming freely in the sand, hunting for interesting tidbits delivered personally to him by the previous high tide. Colm wore a thin windbreaker, not quite enough, and hoped the wind on his end of the phone didn't give Fleming a background roar.

"I always assumed Kammler surrendered in Czechoslovakia," Fleming had begun, "Then I was told [by a Czech archivist] he surrendered at a U.S. Army checkpoint near Prague. So much of my hunt was centered there. I approached the Czech government in the 1970s and they stonewalled me. But I never gave up. I hounded them for a great while, seeking information on Kammler. I was merciless. I thought they would be a great source, the Czechs, maybe opening up a bit." Colm was accustomed to taking himself back in time to the 1940s. Now Fleming was asking him to recall 1970s Czechoslovakia. Under a Communist government after World War II, war-era documents had been even less available in

Czecholslovakia than in other countries. But Fleming had thought that with the passage of time he could pry something loose. "By the 1970s, who is left to protect?"

But Colm knew there were plenty of people—and institutions—still left to protect.

"I was told they had his personal papers, his medals, his diary," Fleming told him.

"Told by who? Who had them?" Colm questioned, pointedly.

"The government. The Czech government. They said Kammler had surrendered nearby, at an Army checkpoint. They said they had Kammler's papers. And Kammler's diary. Very clear." Though the transcript of the conversation seems inexact, Colm knows from context that Fleming had been dealing with official archivists in Czechoslovakia and the office of the Czech Minister of the Interior; they were the ones insisting they had Kammler's papers in their archives, and that Kammler surrendered at an army checkpoint—an American army checkpoint.

Before Colm could get too excited, before he could begin laying a strategy to get a copy of the diary, Fleming dropped the other shoe. "When I tried to get access, they denied. Poof! They said they no longer had it. Later they said they *never* had it. Then they said if he had surrendered at a checkpoint, the Americans would have everything, they were operating in the area then. How can you believe this, this changing story?" Again, Colm notes from the context that by "they," Fleming was referring to government archivists in Prague.

"That's unbelievable," Colm said.

"Yes. Unbelievable. A good word."

"Did you ever get it sorted?"

"Never."

The excitement building in Colm evaporated into nothingness. It was another one of the many dead ends our team confronted. Colm called the Czech archives himself, and they told him with certainty: "We have no current or past knowledge approving or disproving speculations about Kammler's supposed suicide committed in Czechoslovakia in May 1945

nor of his capture by the Americans." Both the archives and the Czech
Minister of the Interior did confirm that Fleming had been in touch with
them in the 1970s.

As Colm related these tales of woe in dealing with Fleming, I began
to think he had been led down the garden path. The story Fleming told
was interesting, but essentially useless without confirmation—
"speculations," as the Czechs had called it.

Colm had to have been the most patient fisherman ever, waiting
months for these nibbles, unsubstantiated but always enticing. Frankly,
I think I would have cut bait, though Colm had other hooks in the
water at the same time. Finally after more months of cat and mouse,
Colm had worn Fleming down and received something our team now
calls "the Fleming document." It is, in a word, spectacular. Just a single
page—it is short, but explosive. Within its four corners it has everything
Fleming claimed and more. The header labels the document "Top
Secret." It is dated May 7, 1945. The letterhead was redacted, as was
the signature line, as well as parts of the body of the report. It says a
lot that the identity of the person and entity conducting the interrogation was obliterated. We can tell, because the document notes it, that
it traveled "By Diplomatic Pouch." The relevant portion of the single
page is below:

The subject line read, *"Interrogation Report [redacted] HANS
KAMMLER"*.

That in and of itself was astonishing. Kammler interrogated?

And then an identifier: *"General der S.S. KAMMLER (chief of all
V-Weapons production) office at Taunusstrasse, Berlin— Grunewald."*
Correct name, rank, office address. This was Kammler being ques-
tioned—just two days before his reported suicide.

The body of the document was three paragraphs. The most important text read:

> *Dr. Ing. KAMMLER is a trained architect by profession and
> was head of all secret projects including the V-1 and V-2. He*

further claims to have been head of [redacted] project based at the [redacted]. CIC Officer is in possession of documents from KAMMLER which may prove to be of considerable value.

Dr. KAMMLER surrendered 6 May with other named persons attached. Dressed in Heer uniform he later identified himself to an officer of [redacted]. By way of special order KAMMLER is to be transferred immediately to KOHNSTEIN, Germany for purposes of detailed interrogation and evaluation of underground weapons research and production facilities.

At the suggestion of the investigating officers Kammler is preparing a detailed report (in German). This is to include the following:
Secret weapons development
[redacted]
Underground research and production facilities
Security measures concerning the above

The report ends there.

So much jumps off the page. Astoundingly, we now had a second document that proved Kammler had surrendered. Colm's contribution here was tremendous—straight corroboration that Kammler had surrendered. Of course, I also took this as compelling evidence that Kammler had not committed suicide. His being in U.S. custody on May 6 and 7, with orders that he be sent to central Germany, was impossible to square with the official German court finding that Kammler died by suicide near Prague just two days later on May 9.

Colm also noted the "special order" that Kammler be moved to Kohnstein, Germany, meaning Kammler was headed to Nordhausen, V-2 rocket central, where Beasley, Robertson, Staver, Hull, and all the other Americans were scrambling to find rocket hardware, remaining scientists, and documents. Also at Nordhausen at that very moment was Wernher von Braun, along with the U.S. Ninth Army.

7 May 1945

BY DIPLOMATIC POUCH

SUBJECT: Interrogation Report ████ HANS KAMMLER.

General der S.S. KAMMLER (chief of all V-weapons production)
office at 7, Taunusstrasse, Berlin - Grunewald.

Age: 43 and party member since 1932. Dr. Ing. KAMMLER is a
trained architect by profession and was head of all secret
weapons projects including the V-1 and V-2. He further claims
to have been head of ████████████ project based at the
████████████ ████ officer is in possession of documents
████████ ████ ████ may prove to be of considerable value.

Dr. KAMMLER surrendered 6 May with other named persons
attached. Dressed in Heer uniform he later identified himself
to an officer of ████████████████ by way of special
order KAMMLER is ████████████ ████iately to KOHNSTEIN,
Germany, for purpose of detailed interrogation and evaluation
of underground weapons research and production facilities.

DETAILED REPORT: At the suggestion of the investigating
officers KAMMLER is preparing a detailed report (in German)
This is to include the following:

        Secret weapons developments
        ████████████████████
        ████████████ ████ and production facilities
        Security measures concerning the above

*The "TOP SECRET" May 7, 1945, "Interrogation Report" for Hans Kammler,
"chief of all V-weapons production," showing that Kammler was apprehended and
in U.S. custody on May 6, 1945, days before his driver—whose dubious testimony
of Kammler's supposed suicide was accepted by German courts as sufficient evidence to declare Kammler dead—testified that he was still at large. This is what
Colm, Keith, and I called "the Fleming document," after retired Surrey University
professor Gerald Fleming, who provided it to us.*

And Colm noticed something more. "Remember Speer. Remember Speer's book." The reference was too vague for me to follow. Speer had more than one book. I found them all useful, though I was always suspicious of Speer's motives in penning his accounts after the war. Nazi books, by self-described former Nazis. *"Is there any such thing as a former Nazi?"* I always wondered.

Colm explained: "Speer wrote about the last meeting he had with Kammler. April 3, 1945. Speer says Kammler told him he was going to give the Americans 'the entire technology for the jet planes, as well as the V-2 rockets and other important developments, including the transcontinental rocket.' He told Speer he was going to trade the technology and the rocket team for his freedom."

"I do remember that." I hadn't focused on it because the guys had presented it to me as proof that Kammler had more to offer beyond the rockets. That was always a Step 2 proposition for me, to be considered only after we proved Step 1—that Kammler had survived.

"It verifies that Kammler was dealing with the Americans," Keith interjected. Keith was right. It was a verification, in real-time, of the Kammler Deal. Kammler had told Speer exactly what he was doing—dealing with the Americans.

"The date," Colm said, "the date is the key. The date Kammler told Speer about the deal with the Americans. The same day, Dean, *the same day*, Kammler ordered the rocket team to move down to the Americans—April 3." The date Kammler talked to Speer about a deal with the Americans was the very date Kammler had ordered the rocket team to leave Nordhausen to get them out of the way of the Russians and over to the Americans. I actually got chills. It was like hearing the final tumbler falling into place, a final "click" as my mind processed the information. This recollection by Speer, along with the two documents we now possessed—documents with separate sources—made for a pretty tight case. But the team was not near finished.

• • •

We had really turned a corner now—and then Keith received an unexpected package in the mail from the U.S. Department of the Army. He found the document jammed into his mail box like an unwanted catalogue after returning home from a quick dinner out with his wife, Nancy. They lived north of Baltimore in a comfortable rancher big enough for them, but not quite large enough for the pair of Rottweilers they owned. The dogs were boisterously friendly with absolutely no sense of their own size or strength. I have known Nancy even longer than Keith, having met her at the beginning of college. She and Keith met there, fell in love, and got married on Halloween—one more clue to the quirky mind of Keith Chester.

Today's package from the army was a surprise because it was in response to a FOIA request that Keith submitted not to the army, but to the FBI, asking for all the information the bureau possessed on Kammler. The FBI was an avenue Keith hadn't pursued before because, after all, it was a domestic criminal law enforcement agency. And he had received so many dead-end responses from so many government agencies to so many FOIA requests.

But this response was different. It was a package, not the standard white business envelope used for a short letter. It was a nine-by-twelve-inch manila envelope, and he realized it had to contain more than just a boilerplate response claiming the FBI had no responsive documents. Given its heft, he knew right away it could be important. As he held it in his hands, standing in his driveway, he was startled by a buzz on his phone—a text from Colm, who, of course, had no way of knowing that Keith was holding a new packet of documents. "Can you talk?" was all the text said. "In a minute," was his hasty reply, the package tucked under one arm as he thumbed away at his phone.

The coincidence of the text and the unexpected vibration of the phone jolted him; Keith loved the coincidences: need I say it, "synchronicity." He pocketed his phone and tore the envelope open even before he got inside. A close inspection would reveal that the response totaled only eighteen pages, but each of the several documents those pages contained was dynamite. The documents had come from the army, to which the FBI had forwarded his request. It was odd, Keith thought: he had already peppered the army with direct requests, and there should by now be nothing more the army could provide him. He skimmed, expecting duplicates of papers he had already received from the army. But the documents looked new to his eyes, and promising. He texted another quick note to Colm: "Stand by."

Nancy looked on with amusement as her husband multitasked, standing in the driveway, turning from texting, to the document, and back again, excitement in his face. He absentmindedly handed her his phone after the second text, and then she became invisible to him.

The first document Keith saw was a file on Kammler, but not just any file. This was *the* file. It was the official dossier compiled by the CIC, Counter-Intelligence Corps. U.S. Army intelligence. "Oh my God!" Keith said out loud. Keith knew that the CIC, born out of the Corps of Intelligence Police, a World War I organization, had swept along with U.S. combat troops in World War II through North Africa, Sicily, Italy, France, Belgium, and into Germany, making both paratrooper and amphibious landings. Its members were front and center in the fighting on D-Day. After territory was secured, it fell to CIC to provide for the security of the troops on the ground. When the Allies had really begun to turn the tide against the Nazis, CIC focused on tactical intelligence.[2] It was charged with rooting out enemy spies, saboteurs, collaborators left behind by retreating forces, and the border crossers the Germans tried to reinsert into areas recently taken by the Allies, "sown like dandelion seeds in the hope that at least a few might get through and produce results."[3] The CIC—a force approaching five thousand souls—was a highly select group of soldiers with exceedingly high IQs and language and investigatory skills. Even lower-ranked officers in CIC often had graduate degrees from Ivy League institutions. Independent thinking and initiative were encouraged. It made sense for the CIC to have assembled a dossier on Hans Kammler. And if CIC played a role in making the deal with Kammler, its agents would have a very good reason to bury the file, and the classified records of the FBI would be the perfect place.

● ● ●

But now Keith had the CIC dossier on Kammler. The man who had been a collection of apparitions, wisps, and traces, had an official identity in U.S. records—File # D-6797. And the file had been active up to July *1949.*

Some of the pages Keith held were stamped with a researcher's worst nightmare: "Best Copy Available." This was the archives' way of saying, "Don't call us because you can't read this miserable document, it's the best we can find." Often documents with that denotation were completely illegible. On others you could read perhaps 20 percent of the words. Sometimes I would spend more than an hour gazing at a single page, straining to see every third word, trying to discern others from context. Despite that level of intense effort, when I returned to them hours or days or weeks later, I often saw something completely new. The CIC Kammler dossier was of uneven quality, but mercifully readable in most places.

Keith shuffled across his driveway, up the walk, and into his house, head buried in the pages he held, mesmerized, leaving his bemused wife behind in the fading sunlight. I knew the feeling—it was like opening the best Christmas gift ever as a child when everything around you just falls away.

The first page was a photocopied five-by-seven-inch index card giving birthdate, title, citizenship, and "Case History: Kammler headed the Amstgruppe C of the WVHA one of the main branches of the SS…Kammler was working on 'V' weapons." Then there was a confounding statement: "It has been reported that KAMMLER is a prisoner of the Russians and is working for them in the Russian zone. No confirmation of this has been obtained." This document was undated, so Keith had no context to evaluate the possibility that Kammler was at some point in the hands of the Russians. The assertion, though, as I would later discover, is duplicated in a November 10, 1946, USFET (United States Forces European Theater) document I found at the Holocaust Museum Library in Washington, D.C., which contains this statement: "It has been reported unofficially that KAMMLER is a Prisoner of the Russians and is working for them in the Russian Zone. No confirmation of this has been obtained."[4] But both references carried unusual qualifiers: "it has been reported," "No confirmation," "reported unofficially."

Keith was by now at his kitchen table, though later he would not recall how he got inside. The next page was a routing slip dated July 28, *1949.* More than four years *after* the war ended, Kammler's CIC dossier was being circulated, combed through, and summarized by the Headquarters of the European Command, returned to the CIC Central Registry by Lieutenant Colonel Richard E. Rudisill of CIC Region VIII.[5] Why was Kammler's file still under review at that late date, particularly if Kammler was over four years dead? That was the official story, but of course we already knew he was not—he had been captured or had surrendered. We speculate that in 1949 the lid on the Kammler coverup was about to blow, and American officials were reviewing files and doing damage control. Keith perused the next document hungrily, his sense of expectation now nearly boundless. It was a form dated February 26, 1946, from the Deputy Theater Judge Advocate's Office, War Crimes Branch. It was addressed to army intelligence and requested a status report on "current location of subject [Kammler]."[6] This document confirmed what we already knew from the Interrogation Report we had obtained from Professor Fleming—that Kammler had "surrendered to US Army May 1945" and was "reported in US hands." But this new document also had new and intriguing information. It showed that Kammler had stayed in custody for a significant length of time; he was still "in US hands" as of February 26, 1946. Our case was now irrefutable. Kammler couldn't have committed suicide in May 1945 if he was "in US hands" in February 1946. When it rains, it pours, as they say. Keith was torn between phoning Colm and me with these details and continuing his race through the docs.

When Keith later forwarded this batch of documents to me, I noted the origin of the February 26, 1946, request for Kammler's location. It had come from the office "assigned the duty of developing the evidence in war crimes cases and the trial thereof."[7] At the time of this inquiry, the International Military Tribunal was in the middle of the single largest war crimes trial of major civilian and military leaders—the famous Nuremburg Trials.[8] This was fascinating—the war crimes investigators knew that Kammler had surrendered and was in U.S. custody, and they wanted him for at least one war crimes investigation—as a suspect, or a witness, or both. That was stunning. In early 1946, long after the war was over, long after Kammler's reported death, one part of the American machine had Kammler and another was looking for him, his presence required for the trial of the century.

The following page repeated that Kammler could be in Russian custody, but again noted the assertion was unofficial and unconfirmed. These were the only times in thousands of pages of original records that I noticed qualifiers like these. It felt to me as if someone was trying hard to make a false suggestion that Kammler might be with the Russians, but did not want to be on the record as having made this assertion unequivocally.

This same document also says, with no such qualification, that Kammler "[s]urrendered to the 9th Army (May 45)". The dam had truly broken. This undated document went on: "wanted by Office of U.S. Chief Counsel (for the Prosecution of Axis Criminality)." And then yet another mammoth surprise: "Reason wanted: As a defendant in the War Crimes Trial." This beggared belief. Not only were officials looking for Kammler, but war crimes prosecutors were pursuing him, hot on the trail, *as a defendant* to stand trial for war crimes—not just as a witness. Kammler surely deserved defendant status, but in a flash our team had gone from proving Kammler surrendered and survived to proving he was hunted as a war criminal. So how did this war criminal who was already in U.S. custody elude the hunters and escape prosecution? Only one explanation met all the facts we know: this Nazi slavemaster must have been sheltered by someone in the U.S. government. This was the stuff of novels, not non-fiction!

The seemingly contradictory "unconfirmed" report of Kammler working for the Russians suddenly made sense. The War Crimes Branch wanted Kammler to stand trial and couldn't be moved off that position. The first line of defense for whoever in the U.S. infrastructure had Kammler was to claim he had gone to the Russians—but they didn't want to be held responsible for making that false claim directly, so it was couched in the form of unofficial, unconfirmed suggestions. Our multiple documents from different sources saying that Kammler had surrendered to and was held by the U.S. were more convincing than the fewer, qualified statements that Kammler was "reported" to be working in Russia.

Since we know Kammler was at one and the same time 1) in U.S. custody and 2) being sought by our War Crimes Branch as a wanted war criminal, his custody had to have been a high-level secret—secret and with enough clout to defy the War Crimes Branch, and indirectly the president of the United States, who had made war crimes prosecution a priority.[9] Everything American officials did from that point forward to help Kammler was aiding and abetting a wanted war criminal, which would have put his custodians in serious legal jeopardy. *Wow*!

If that weren't enough, at the bottom of the War Crimes Branch form requesting from Army CIC Central Registry the present location of Kammler was typed: "A request has been made by the British Gov. for the extradition of subject. Do you object to his being extradited?" When Colm learned this detail, he pointed out that it betrayed the fact that the British government knew that the U.S. had Kammler in custody—otherwise, the Brits' extradition request made no sense. What I couldn't figure out was why in one and the same document the War Crimes Branch was seeking Kammler as a defendant and asking Army Intelligence—CIC—if it had any objection to Kammler's extradition. I wondered, *Was this the Brits putting out a feeler for a possible trade,*

Dornberger for Kammler? We know the Brits had held Dornberger for two years, and then the Americans got him. *Was the idea for the Brits to trade Dornberger for Kammler, who bore more direct responsibility for the bombing of Britain's citizenry, and the Americans to get Dornberger, after they had thoroughly interrogated Kammler and exhausted his knowledge of special weapons, underground facilities, and more?* That made a lot of sense, particularly in hindsight, since we know Dornberger came to America and thrived professionally.

There was still more, though, in Keith's newest batch of documents. The answer to the proposed British extradition came from the Chief of CIC, Lieutenant Colonel Dale M. Garvey, just nine days later on March 7, 1946: "Subject has been cleared through all interested sections of G-2 [intelligence] division, and this Headquarters has no further interest nor objections to extradition."[10] G-2, the intelligence division, had been hurriedly consulted and had cleared the extradition. This exchange proves that Kammler was in U.S. custody until at least March 1946. Astonishing.

We assume the extradition never took place because there is no further record of what would have been a heavily papered transaction and there is no indication of Kammler being tried by the Brits in what would have been a well-publicized and documented public event. It is possible, but extremely unlikely, that the extradition did come through, and Kammler was treated quietly by the Brits. Again, though, this scenario assumes far too much. More plausibly, some other part of the U.S. military or government may have objected to Kammler's extradition. The Brits may have withdrawn the request in a document now lost. Or, as we shall soon see happened in the parallel case of Klaus Barbie, the "Butcher of Lyon," more nefarious reasons may have been at work keeping Kammler out of the hands of the Brits.

The final piece of the new Kammler materials was a hand-written note on that same document stating that Kammler was being processed by the Americans through something called the "Rogues Gallery." This record was dated March 14, 1946. That was more than ten months after

DATE 26 Feb 46

TO: Central Registry, Counter-Intelligence Branch, G-2 Division, U S
Forces, European Theater, APO 757. U S A rmy.

W.C.B. CASE NO. 008-5 US - British Misc.

[X] REQUEST PRESENT LOCATION OF SUBJECT
[ ] REQUEST APPREHENSION OF SUBJECT
[ ] REQUEST ANY AVAILABLE INFORMATION CONCERNING SUBJECT
[ ] REQUEST NOTIFICATION OF SUBJECT'S APPREHENSION
[ ] REQUEST INVESTIGATION OF MEANS AS INDICATED
[ ] REQUEST INFORMATION AS TO WHERE, WHEN AND BY WHOM SUBJECT WAS
    ARRESTED

NAME (WITH ALIASES) KAMMLER, Hans, Dr., Obergruppenführer   SEX M

NATIONALITY _____ AGE _____ SINGLE _____ MARRIED _____

FORMER ADDRESS _____ OCCUPATION _____

DESCRIPTION: DATE OF BIRTH _____ PLACE OF BIRTH _____

   HEIGHT _____ WEIGHT _____ EYES _____ HAIR _____ BUILD _____

DISTINGUISHING CHARACTERISTICS _____

_____

LAST KNOWN ADDRESS OR POSSIBLE WHEREABOUTS _____

_____

REASON WANTED: In connection with war crimes.

PREVIOUS HISTORY AND OTHER DATA According (regimering to CRX (B) files, sur-

rendered to US army May 45. Reported in U S hands SHAEF sent SchG3/A.

_____

WIFE OR HUSBAND _____ NATIONALITY _____ AGE _____

   ADDRESS _____

CHILDREN _____

FATHER _____ ADDRESS _____

MOTHER _____ ADDRESS _____

A request has b en made by the British Gov   C. B. Mickelwait,
for the extradition of subject. Do you object   C. B. MICKELWAIT
to his being extradited?   Colonel   JAGD

WCB Form #21   Acting Theater Judge Advocate
(Summary of Information Form)
340-46

This February 26, 1946, War Crimes Branch document says that Kammler "surrendered to US Army May 45," is "reported in US hands," and has been requested to be extradited by the British.

Basic : Summary of Information re ̶K̶a̶m̶m̶l̶e̶r̶,̶ ̶H̶a̶n̶s̶ ̶D̶r̶.̶

File : D- .(CIC/S-5/CH)   1st Ind

Headquarters, Counter Intelligence Corps, United States Forces European Theater (Main), APO 757, U.S. Army, ̶7̶ ̶M̶a̶r̶c̶h̶ ̶1̶9̶4̶6̶

TO : War Crimes Branch, APO 633, U.S. Army.

1. Subject has been cleared through all interested sections of G-2 Division, and this Headquarters has no further interest nor objections to extradition.

For the Chief, CIC :

DALE X. GARVEY
Lt. Col., Inf.
S-3

Central Registry : _____

Case Review   : _____

Interrogation   : _____

Intelligence Branch : _____

A March 7, 1946, "Summary of Information re KAMMLER" from the U.S. Army Counter-Intelligence Corps showing that CIC had no objections to the British extradition request for Kammler. It should be noted that Lieutenant Colonel Dale Garvey, the officer who signed this document, was a CIC official known to be associated with other verified Nazis who escaped, including Klaus Barbie, the notorious "Butcher of Lyon." We suspect Garvey was the point man handling Kammler's disappearance.

Kammler had been reported dead. This meant that Kammler not only survived the war—that he never committed suicide at the war's end—but rather that he was snugly in U.S. custody for at least ten months *after* the war!

Keith had by now stopped muttering to himself in his kitchen. Nancy handed back his phone and he texted Colm the good news: "New batch of FOIA documents looks great. Confirms Kammler surrender. Need a call with Dean!"

The FOIA response was less than twenty pages, but it was an avalanche of information, and Keith couldn't help himself, regardless of the hour.

● ● ●

By this point in the investigation, we were all becoming accustomed to the fact that every question we answered led to more new questions—like the mythical Lernaean Hydra. Our next question was what American officials did with Kammler during those months of captivity and, even more important, what they did with him afterwards. *Did America continue to hold Kammler after March 1946? Release him? Did they help him escape to points unknown?*

● ● ●

Back in the darkened parlor in Osnabrück, Germany, Jörg Kammler had told me that the entire family believed the official story of Kammler's death. His mother had had his father's death confirmed by a German court, after all, in 1948, when Jörg was still very young. If Hans Kammler had lived on, then he had abandoned his family. Jörg had also claimed that his mother had insisted until her death in the late 1990s that Kammler had never approached the Allies to make a deal, but that the Allies had approached her husband—"It was the Allies who showed interest."[11] I made a careful note on that: Jutta Kammler, asserting that

Kammler had been approached by the Allies to make a deal, though apparently she never told her son any details or terms. She clearly believed there had been contact between her husband and the Americans.

There were interesting parallels, one from halfway around the globe. Our research led us to the case of Harumi Ishii, director of Japan's diabolical biowarfare research project run through "Unit 731." His son also claimed that the Americans had approached *his* father to instigate a deal. Apparently both Kammler and Harumi had been sought out by the United States to trade their respective caches of information for some sort of immunity or special consideration. Interestingly, Harumi's case also involved a massive coverup by the Americans—but his was a tale that had already been documented.

If, as Jutta had claimed, the Americans went after Kammler, we needed more information on how they might have made an overture. We had evidence about the contact in Lisbon and good reason to believe Kammler was involved, but we all felt we needed more information. One obvious avenue to explore was the Combined Intelligence Objectives Subcommittee (CIOS), created by the Western Allies late in the war to scour German-occupied territory as it was retaken by the Allies. CIOS was charged with finding all manner of technology—and its creators— that had been left behind by the Germans. CIOS collated information from all intelligence sources and fed it to the various Allied teams racing to capture designated targets, collecting all documents, equipment, and employees. FIAT (Field Information Agency, Technical), the American successor to CIOS, received information from CIOS, and coordinated American collection efforts. BIOS (British Intelligence Objectives Subcommittee) was the British version. CIOS would be a perfect point of contact with the Americans for Kammler.

In a June 1945 meeting, high-level CIOS players discussed Albert Speer, then being held at the Allied detention center Camp DUSTBIN at Kransberg Castle near Frankfurt. Speer, as Hitler's Armaments minister, was a big fish and the focus of the CIOS meeting was his knowledge of weapons in development. "[E]xtensive rather than intensive," was the consensus, meaning Speer had big-picture information but lacked details. The meeting turned to the regrettable lack of information on Vengeance Weapons, questions "which could not be answered by Speer himself." Then a list of names of Speer's associates was read aloud in the meeting. The hope was one or more of them could provide more information on the Vengeance Weapons. A question was called: Would anyone object to rounding up those named and bringing them in for interrogation? Though the meeting memorandum does not record the names read aloud, Kammler was surely among them—we already knew that Speer had personally named Kammler as more informed than himself on these points. Our trove of documents proved not only that Kammler was alive, but that he was in U.S. custody and headed to Kohnstein-Nordhausen. And here we had an indication he might be headed to DUSTBIN, the Allied interrogation center, after Kohnstein.

Interestingly, the notes of this CIOS meeting were signed by "P.M. Wilson," a G-2 (Intelligence) major, the gatekeeper at DUSTBIN.[12] We have already heard from Wilson, whose report on the interrogation of Hermann Oberth revealed the Nazis' plans for a transatlantic missile that could attack the United States—and he will resurface again. Wilson was attached to Brigadier General R. J. Maunsell, Chief of Special Sections in the Office of the Assistant Chief of Staff, G-2, Supreme Headquarters Allied Expeditionary Force (SHAEF),[13] and to FIAT's Enemy Personnel Exploitation Section. Wilson, as the DUSTBIN gatekeeper with a foot in CIOS and FIAT, was in a uniquely powerful position. He was also supervisor of one Edmund Tilley,[14] a major and co-leader of a CIOS team, at the time working for the Brits.[15] Tilley spoke fluent German and was later the Chief Interrogator of FIAT. Tilley's name showed up in some of the Kammler documents discussed above, and he figured prominently in interrogations of von Braun conducted years after the war ended—which uncovered embarrassing, perhaps criminal information.

Maunsell was acting chairman of the Working Group that sorted the lists of German scientists to be detained, the camps at which they should be detained, and more. Under the mandate of this group, Counter Intelligence attached to SHAEF had authority to detain and exploit—meaning hold over a barrel and interrogate, or shelter from prosecution and investigation—with "absolute priority," any "individual scientist, industrial technologist or industrialist considered to be a potential danger to the Allied Nations," even where such a person was in "a mandatory arrest category."[16] The significance of this must not be lost—Wilson had the authority to pluck wanted war criminals like Kammler virtually from the gallows and drop them into the DUSTBIN center for interrogation, sheltering them from prosecution so they could be questioned and exploited for technical knowledge. Kammler could have been among those pulled to avoid prosecution. P. M. Wilson or some other American official might have shielded Kammler from prosecution on the grounds that he had invaluable intelligence. Something very much like that had happened in other cases, such as that of Harumi Ishii. But to confirm—if it was even possible to confirm—that it had happened in Kammler's case, we needed to reconstruct Kammler's movements in the last days of the war, and even thereafter. I asked the guys to give me everything they had on Kammler's final movements as the war ended.

● ● ●

We know Kammler was in Naumburg, two hours south of Berlin, on April 12 or 13, 1945, seeing his brother-in-law. He had most likely come there from Oberammergau, having just held his final meeting with von Braun, at the Haus Jesu Christi Hotel. We know that meeting with von Braun happened in April, but we don't know the precise date. Von Braun recounted the meeting as full of tension and uncertainty, with Kammler's adjutant, SS major Starck, in attendance, his weapon always within reach. Curiously, von Braun reported overhearing, before their meeting began, Kammler discussing the possibility of evading capture by taking refuge in the Ettal Abbey, established in the fifteenth century and famous for the Chartreuse-type Ettal liqueur made by the monks.

There is no evidence Kammler joined the monks—a proposition that became even more improbable once we had learned Kammler was in U.S. custody.

By April 13, Kammler was in Berlin, meeting with Speer.[17] On April 15, 1945, we know he traveled to the Tyrol region of Austria,[18] where his wife and family were ensconced in the home of famous Belgian chemist and industrialist Ernest Solvay. We have a second document saying that his wife, Jutta, was in the area of Salzburg, just east of Tyrol.[19] It was interesting to learn that the Allies were collecting information not just on Kammler's movements but on those of his wife, as well. Also of interest, the report states that in Salzburg Jutta had joined the wives of Himmler and Göring. Recall the Lebenbücher, "Life Books"—as much as eight hundred pages of photos, notes, and personal messages that Kammler's son Jörg possessed. On April 16, 1945, in Tyrol, Kammler presented his children with their last Lebenbücher, and then he was gone from their lives, but for a final radio message the family received a week later. That incoherent signal offered no clues as to his whereabouts or intentions and was cut short, ending with the words "constantly on the move...."

The next day, April 17, General Karl Wolff flew to southern Berlin for a meeting with Hitler, who had been holed up in his Berlin bunker since mid-January. But a week on, that route would be nearly impassable, so we know even the most essential travel was perilous at this point. We know from Kammler family friend and researcher Kristian Knaack that Kammler planned to meet with his wife and children later in Tyrol and from there escape to the south, but the family never made it to the rendezvous point. Knaack was one of the many assets developed by Colm, who had courted him for years after reading his German-language book on Nazi treasure.

"If Kammler had arranged a deal with the Americans, why wouldn't he personally oversee the surrender of his rocket team to the U.S., what we knew to be a key component of his bargain?" I asked, knowing Kammler had gone elsewhere.

"Perhaps," Colm suggested, "delivery of the rocket team was not enough to ensure Kammler's life would be spared. Rocket technology was the easy number one priority, but why shouldn't the Americans get more if Kammler had more? Why wouldn't Kammler sweeten the deal if he could?" Keith and Colm had always insisted that stolen treasure might be another part of the Kammler Deal, though I had always believed this to be a weak part of our case. I felt we had a history-changing tale already.

"Yes, we're rewriting history already," Keith allowed, and I could nearly see him waving a single finger in the air. "But what if Kammler had piles of stolen artwork, gold? What if he had treasure no one knows about?" At moments like this, I looked to Colm to slow down the freight train that was Keith. At this juncture I needed Colm to be the voice of reason, the cool-headed one, to step up and agree with me, to say, let's stick with what we know. Colm, always a man of few words, gave me just two: "What if?"

● ● ●

Though the value of what Germany stole from its enemies is staggering, and even though we know not all of it has been recovered, I have always been reluctant to delve into the world of treasure. As recently as 2013, German authorities discovered a stash of over one thousand pieces of art stolen by the Nazis with a value over one billion dollars.[20] I couldn't ignore that Kammler, given his authority and access to all forms of transportation and hiding places, could have moved plundered treasure, some of it with vast cultural and even political value. The Americans surely would have counted its recovery on the positive side of the Kammler ledger. Full disclosure: we have no absolute proof, but the circumstantial case is pretty good. Kammler himself had asserted that he had authority for the "[a]cquisition of artistic object cultivation of art and reproduction."[21] And I had to concede that the more Kammler could deliver, the more attractive he was as a bargaining partner. Then as I began to learn more about the "Nazi treasure" angle of the Kammler case, I began to see that the issue had intriguing implications for the motives and plans of Kammler and his fellow Nazis as they faced defeat.

At this point, Keith and Colm coughed up something they called the "Laudenberger document," which I later figured out they had been holding back, waiting until they thought I was ready for it—meaning I wouldn't reject it out of hand. Understandably, they wanted to make sure I was committed to our joint venture before they showed me something so utterly fantastic. Werner Laudenberger is a German lawyer with whom Colm had exchanged telephone calls and eventually documents years before. The lawyer had conducted a far-reaching investigation into "the Fourth Reich"— the Nazi leaders' plans for another run at world domination. Laudenberger shared his investigation report with Colm. According to Laudenberger, the Nazi plan was to preserve as much German technology and treasure as possible, both inside and outside Germany, controlled by a small cadre of the most faithful Nazis. Hatched at a secret meeting of Nazi hierarchy at the Maison Rouge Hotel in Strasbourg, France, on August 10, 1944, including S.S. Obergruppenführer (general) Dr. Scheid and representatives from Siemens, VW, Krupp, Bosch, Farben, and others—a Who's Who of German industrialists—the plot sounded like a spy novel. At the meeting, the SS ordered the business leaders to offshore as much gold and cash as possible. The German government was to do the same.

Much of this treasure had been stolen by the Nazis in the first place. As conclusive evidence of the illicit seizures of gold by Germany, it is known that by 1943 "Germany had already sold more gold than she had possessed in 1939."[22] The math is conclusive—Germany was stealing gold. In 1946, a special Tripartite Commission was established after the war to collect Nazi gold for return to claimant countries. It ultimately recovered over 742,000 pounds of gold, with a 2017 market value of nearly fifteen billion dollars. Even this staggering quantity amounted to less than two-thirds of the claims filed by aggrieved countries,[23] to say nothing of individual claims. Records were so tangled the commission did not complete its work for fifty years.

Moving assets out of the country during a war is nothing out of the ordinary—the Brits had sent massive amounts of their own gold to Canada as war approached. The evidence of this meeting indicates they planned to export it to establish a Fourth Reich. But note that some historians are skeptical that this meeting took place or, alternatively, that those attending it were in position to bring any such plan to fruition. But the U.S. Central Intelligence Agency certainly believed in the plan. A CIA report eight years after the war states flatly, "Preparations for the future resurgence of Nazism were made before defeat of the German armies was certain."[24]

Faithful Nazi leaders and industrialists hoped the coming surrender would be only a setback, followed by military rebuilding funded with the stolen treasure, backed by the hidden technology. They had, after all, all lived through the rebirth of Germany after World War I.

Unfortunately, the Laudenberger document, though it has mounds of interesting information about planning meetings, missing treasure, and secret Swiss bank accounts, provided no conclusive proof. Instead, it contained mysterious references to "the Kreuzer Aramis." Suddenly, I found myself in Da Vinci Code territory, where one mysterious piece of information is just an arrow pointing to the next. A "Kreuzer" is an ancient German coin. I knew "Aramis" only as the Alexander Dumas character in *The Three Musketeers*. "Kreuzer Aramis" meant nothing to me until I remembered that Aramis was an alias for the Dumas character when he was in hiding. So, Kreuzer Aramis means German coins of someone in hiding. Clever.

Laudenberger told Colm that the Nazi plan centered on a collection of discrete documents parceled out to various people by none other than Hans Kammler—"maps, trading cards, security codes"—so that Kammler was at the hub of a many-spoked wheel. Individually the documents were indecipherable, so individual recipients knew nothing; together, they were a roadmap to the secret Nazi bank account, today worth over one hundred billion dollars. Kreuzer Aramis was that collection of records, reunited and bound together in one document, which was the

Holy Grail for Nazi treasure hunters. And Laudenberger claimed to have it. We don't, but we do have his detailed thirty-four-page report, which he had eventually revealed to Colm. According to Laudenberger, he contacted the Swiss bank that held the illicit funds, and they set a meeting with him, meaning they found him credible. But shortly after telling Colm of the meeting, Laudenberger went radio silent and has not reemerged. Colm is understandably frustrated by his breaking off, and I'm left wondering whether Laudenberger was a just a fraud who ran out of running room with Colm.

Yet, it makes sense that Germany's disillusioned military and political leaders would try to preserve themselves and their ideology. Certainly there were Nazis who did this on an individual basis—readying false papers and uniforms to go into disguise, planning escape routes. Toward the end of the war the smart Nazis were already—in today's vernacular—plotting their exit strategies. All Laudenberger was alleging was a more coordinated effort. I'm certain the continuation of National Socialism was intended by the Nazis. The question is, how far beyond planning did they get?

We know the Strasbourg meeting, superintended by the SS, did take place; it has been confirmed by famed Nazi hunter Simon Wiesenthal and documented in the *New York Times*.[25] And a post-war U.S. Department of Treasury investigation confirmed that Nazi Germany did establish several hundred companies abroad.[26] The day after the meeting, Strasbourg, which had no discernible military importance, was thoroughly bombed by the Allies in a strike that Laudenberger postulates was meant for the meeting attendees. Laudenberger's report is accurate in the many verifiable facts it presents, but it relies on other documents we have never seen, and it is a bit inconsistent.[27]

We do know that Kammler, alleged by Laudenberger to be the center of the hub in this scheme, was in charge of other Nazi bank accounts, including an account with eighty million Reichsmarks in Austria—the rough equivalent of $275 million today. Also, at the end of April 1945, a series of trains laden with treasures plundered by the Germans began arriving in Prague, the same time (as we shall see momentarily) that Kammler himself arrived there. Two trains in particular, bearing the code names Adler (Eagle) and Dohle (Jackdaw), are known to have departed Berlin with Reichsbank gold reserves and headed south. The cargo was unloaded at various points along the way including Pilsen, Munich, and Bavaria, and despite protracted post-war searches by the Allies much of the precious hoard has never been recovered.

Furthermore, Kammler's disobedience against Hitler's "Nero Decree," the Nazi dictator's scorched-earth policy, preserved German assets for later, which was tantalizingly consistent with a Fourth Reich. Kammler's staged death, which we have verified as faked—something Laudenberger did not even know about, but which bolsters his theory—makes even more sense if it was intended that Kammler play a role in carrying the Fourth Reich forward years later. We also know that Kammler used relay-style messengers and partial, divided messages as a security measure in his underground facilities.[28] That's the same pattern as Laudenberger claims was used in "the Kreuzer Aramis."

There is one macabre thing yet to be discussed when it comes to treasure and Kammler: the strange case of Operation Bodysnatch, which if nothing else proves the Americans would make extraordinary efforts to seize and control artifacts and relics. On April 27, 1945, as Kammler was meeting in Salzburg and then racing to procure the release of Dornberger from house arrest imposed by Himmler, the Americans were discovering a treasure that may well have been hidden by Kammler's men. The Bernterode salt mine is in the Nordhausen district in central Germany, squarely within Kammler's realm. When the Americans found it, it contained four hundred thousand tons of ammunition within fifteen miles of tunnels. A masonry wall built into the side of the main gallery concealed a padlocked metal door, which itself concealed a bizarre site— a chamber-shrine with hundreds of colorful Prussian army standards— battle banners, some on staffs, others hanging from the ceiling, all precisely arranged. And four decorated coffins. The Americans had uncovered the temporary resting place of Field Marshall von Hindenburg and his wife, Frederick Wilhelm I, and Frederick the Great himself—Germany's most prominent historical figures. Nazi leaders would have taken any measures necessary to ensure the safety of these relics. Tellingly, unlike buried research documents, these were not booby-trapped, as the Nazis did not want to risk their accidental destruction.

While Toftoy and others removed V-2 missiles from nearby Nordhausen, another team of Americans toiled to remove the coffins and other artifacts, "[b]eating the Russians out of the historical remains of Germany's former leaders"[29]—a political coup. The extraction required eight trucks and two jeeps to move the relics to the distant American collection point. The coffins, one of which weighed twelve hundred pounds, had only recently been deposited in the mine by the Germans, the von Hindenburgs' bodies coming from East Prussia by way of Berlin, and Frederick the Great's from Potsdam, near Berlin.

But Kammler family friend Kristian Knaack claims to have found more detail in his research: religious icons being shipped with the coffins by the Nazis had been en route to the Americans as inducements to make peace, in a deal authorized by President Roosevelt himself. Half of those icons were delivered to the Americans, and only Roosevelt's untimely death, Knaack says, prevented the culmination of the deal. According to Knaack, the coffins were secreted by Kammler in the Bernterode salt mine to be used as a rallying cry for the Fourth Reich. Knaack offers no documentary proof for the delivery of the icons or the Roosevelt deal, but the Americans' discovery of the coffins is consistent with Knaack's claim.

Kammler certainly could have been in charge of moving the coffins and related relics. We know the coffins were moved very late in the war, and I'm not sure who else had the wherewithal to accomplish the move then. It would fit with the Kammler Deal we have laid out—Kammler delivering value to the Americans to save his own life. He wouldn't have been the only Nazi to offer the Americans treasure as an inducement for a deal—as we will see later, in the case of Karl Wolff, a Nazi who negotiated with Allen Dulles.

The Nazis undoubtedly stole an enormous amount of gold and treasure from other countries and individuals throughout the war. In the mad scramble at the war's end, that treasure was being moved hither and yon. And of all German entities, the SS alone had the resources to move it; within the SS, no one had situated himself better than Kammler. He was already identified as a "trouble-shooter" for the German Ministry of Transport,[30] with access to fleets of trucks, and even the power to summon up transportation to ship hundreds of rocket scientists from central Germany to Oberammergau in defiance of Hitler's orders. He had the ruthlessness to ensure Germany's plundered treasures would be moved to safety[31] in anticipation of a future Fourth Reich, or given to the Americans in a deal for his own benefit. Finally, Kammler alone knew the location of every secret underground Nazi facility, so he had hundreds of potential hiding places. He had built them all.

CHAPTER SEVEN

The Final Days

"Better to fight for something than live for nothing."

—*George S. Patton*

Colm tossed me another nugget of bizarre information about Kammler's movements at the end of the war. On April 17, 1945, Kammler sent a telegram to Heinrich Himmler in which Kammler refused to allow Himmler use of a "Junkers truck." But why on earth would SS leader Himmler be requesting a single truck from Kammler? More implausible still, why would Kammler refuse it? One logical explanation, particularly given Kammler's "trouble-shooting" role in transportation, is that Kammler was refusing Himmler the use of a Junkers *plane*—perhaps even the enormous Junkers 390 heavy-lift ultra-long-range aircraft capable of transatlantic flight. This bird was as exotic as it was large, capable of transporting an enormous cargo. For that reason the Luftwaffe often referred to the Ju 390 as a "truck"—the very language used in Himmler's request. Allied intelligence described the Ju 390 as "a very large six-engined aircraft with a span of 163-165 feet.... Six BMW 801 engines are fitted and the all-up weight should approach 40 tons.... An exceptionally long range [over 6,000 miles] is claimed."[1] Now in charge of the Nazi air forces, Kammler would control access to this mammoth plane.

To this day, the story of the Ju 390 is shrouded in mystery. Some claim only one, or perhaps two of the planes, were produced during the war.[2] Everyone seems to agree that one Ju 390 was stripped of parts and then destroyed near Dessau as the American troops approached. Consensus breaks down as to whether there were two or even more of the massive birds. If there was another of these planes, and if it wasn't destroyed, then any one of a number of Nazi brass could have faked his death, taken tremendous amounts of booty, and made it to South America without refueling. There were unconfirmed reported sightings of a Ju 390 in Uruguay, including claims it was dismantled at a private airfield on a remote ranch owned by a German national.[3]

But I'm not aware of anyone claiming the Ju 390s were ever produced in greater numbers—except for us. Colm uncovered a document squarely contradicting what the historians "know." An April 26, 1945, intelligence report based on the interrogation of four Junkers plant officials, including the Chief of Design and Construction, catalogues plant production at Dessau, where all agree at least the lone confirmed Ju 390 was built. But the report discovered by Colm, under the category Ju 390, says, "After the fifteenth machine had left the plant…it was decided to abandon the project."[4] So our new information indicates that the missing Ju 390s are a much bigger mystery than has ever been realized: *fifteen* of them, not a mere pair, rolled off production lines. If they were flown out of the Reich, who and what was on them? What were their destinations? And what ultimately became of their cargo and passengers?

But Himmler may have been requesting one of the more common long-range Junkers, the Ju 290 transport plane with a range of almost four thousand miles—enough to fly Colm from Ireland to my back yard. In either event, this Himmler-Kammler exchange is significant for two reasons. First, Kammler was asserting authority even against SS chief Himmler, itself an extraordinary fact that shows Kammler's true power at this final stage of the war. Second, perhaps Kammler was keeping a long-range transport plane for himself. He could well have packed it to the brim with stolen treasure or documents and hardware, destination unknown. But we know that Kammler was in U.S. custody for at least ten months after the war; so, though he may have shipped something on the massive Ju 390, he was not a passenger.

● ● ●

There is one additional intriguing fact about the balance of power within the Nazi hierarchy. On April 23, having received accounts of the situation in the Führerbunker in Berlin degrading precipitously, Hermann Göring sent a telegram to Hitler declaring that he would assume power later that day if he did not receive contrary orders from Hitler. Hitler perceived this act as treasonous and ordered Göring arrested, opening up the chain of succession to Himmler. So just as Himmler was assuming the position of second in command to Hitler, Kammler was in a battle royal with him, denying him the use of the Junkers aircraft.

Colm also has an email from Tilmann Kammler, Kammler's grandson, claiming that he has a letter from Kammler to Jutta telling her that Himmler three times tried to have Kammler assassinated at this late stage in the war. We have not seen the letter, but this is consistent with the power struggle between the pair. It would also help explain why Kammler was always on the road—presenting a moving target to Himmler rather than a sitting duck. Whether or not the assassination story is true, we know Kammler was in a contest for power with the number two man in the Reich, with Hitler himself approaching suicide.

Colm now hit me with a handful of additional prize documents. First, he had found a wartime diary that noted the April 22, 1945, arrival of Kammler and a staff of some six hundred in Oberammergau. Nobody else seemed to have this information, or anything firm about Kammler's whereabouts after April 17. Next Colm produced a telex sent the following day by Kammler.[5] In this odd communique of April 23, the very same day Göring ran afoul of Hitler—Kammler ordered one of his most trusted aides, SS major Grosch, based in Prague, to give a very peculiar order to SS lieutenant Schürmann of the elite SS-600 paratrooper battalion in

Berlin (under the command of SS colonel Otto Skorzeny, the singular SS officer): to destroy a "V-1 device" in Berlin, and to report immediately to a command center in Munich. Keith then produced a newly discovered U.S. Army report[6] that placed Kammler in Berlin on April 23 or 24, which means Kammler almost certainly phoned Grosch in Prague from Berlin to order Schürmann to destroy a V-1 housed in Berlin. At that point, Operation Clausewitz, Germany's planned "last stand" for Berlin, was under way,[7] so it was clear to every German in Berlin at that point, including Kammler, that Berlin would fall.

So, we see that Kammler left Tyrol on April 17, 1945, and went by way of Oberammergau to Berlin, arriving on April 23 or 24. But why was he ordering a V-1 destroyed? The "V-1 device" was not described in his telex to Grosch, but it could not have been a conventional V-1 buzz bomb. V-1s had been dropped by the thousands on Allied territory, and many had fallen into Allied hands. Others had been seized intact by the Allies. There would be no point in destroying an ordinary V-1 buzz bomb now. This would be akin to Kammler sending orders to destroy a conventional tank or anti-aircraft gun.

But Colm had material on a planned version of the V-1 that is little known to history, perhaps because it was never deployed. It was to be piloted by German fliers in a suicide squadron, equipped with either a chemical or a biological weapon, or even a dirty nuclear bomb. The ubiquitous Otto Skorzeny was involved in this plan, using famed test pilot Hanna Reistch in what became code named Project Reichenberg.[8] This fits with information that Hitler's own adjutant reported Germany had a pumpkin-sized nuclear weapon prototype, a perfect size for a V-1 and a potential game-changer in the war.[9] Just as interesting, we are able to link Nazi nuclear scientist Baron Manfred von Ardenne to the development of the V-1 buzz bomb.[10]

This information also fits with Hitler's 1944 threat to lay a curtain of poisonous gas along his Eastern Front.[11] Speer reported that, in the "early weeks of April…fanatics…argued for chemical warfare."[12] We know the Allies found stockpiles of Germany's deadly nerve gas agents at the end of the war. The planned use of a dirty bomb or chemical or biological weapons on American troops or British citizens might be one thing the Americans were unwilling to forgive of Kammler, so he would certainly want to erase evidence of them to prevent the Kammler Deal from becoming No Deal.

An alternate explanation for Kammler's order to destroy "a V-1 device" is possible. Colm told me the Germans used the term "V-1" not just for the V-1 buzz bomb, but generically to refer to "Version One" of many weapon prototypes. So Kammler may have been ordering the destruction of the "V-1" version of some unknown secret weapon in Berlin. That seems appealing and logical, though we do not have any documents on that point beyond what we've already presented.

Kammler's April 23 telex puts him in the capital as the Battle of Berlin raged until just before the Soviets completely encircled the city on April 25. But we also know that Kammler made it out of Berlin, for Keith's next unique find on the unstoppable Hans Kammler was his surfacing in Salzburg, Austria, on April 26 at a conference with SS armaments directors.[13] Given Kammler's known fear of flying, he most likely was driven by car out of Berlin. We know the last highway was sealed on April 24,[14] the same day Speer departed the *Führerbunker*,[15] so Kammler's margin for escaping the falling German capital city was razor-thin. Fortunately for him, he was able to take advantage of his position as supreme commander of secret weapons—one of which was an infrared night driving aid, a first-generation device "by which an auto-driver can see the road on a converter screen from infrared reflections, thus enabling him to drive at high speed along pitch dark roads,"[16] the same technology Kammler had deployed to keep his Railroad Brigades working around the clock.

Keith and Colm's talent for finding just the right document seemed almost magical, but I knew everything they had uncovered came not from luck but from dogged determination and a unique understanding of the records that allowed them to pluck the needle from an endless field of haystacks. The topic of discussion of the April 26 conference was Germany's tanks, but Salzburg was also an epicenter of research and production of exotic weapons, including guided missiles and infrared targeting devices—all under the supervision of Hans Kammler. Kammler may well have been in Salzburg to secure more secret weapons research documents.

Next, documents from a private Luftwaffe archive indicate that on April 28, 1945, Kammler issued a torrent of directives to Jagdverband 44 (JV 44), the acclaimed Me 262 fighter wing under the command of General Adolf Galland, which had been formed in the last months of the war by special order of Hitler. JV 44 was perhaps the most successful fighter wing of the war on any side. Its ranks were so thick with German aces that the running joke was the much-coveted Knight's Cross award was part of JV 44's standard uniform. The JV 44 pilots flew the Me 262, the first deployed jet fighter aircraft—extremely fast and heavily armed, and among the most effective fighters in the history of aviation, with an astonishing four to one kill ratio. On April 28, Kammler ordered them to relocate to a base close to Prague, Czechoslovakia, still in German hands. Though other Me 262s made it to the Prague area, JV 44 did not, as its unit commander, General Adolf Galland, was a strident anti-communist and feared his unit would end in Russian captivity. With or without JV 44, though, the Germans could not hold Prague for long, and they might have been put to better use elsewhere. So Kammler's order makes little sense unless he had some specific use for JV 44 in Czecho-slovakia providing protection for his upcoming sojourn to Prague.

Powered by two Junkers Jumo 004 B turbojet engines, the Me 262 surpassed the performance of every other fighter aircraft in World War II. The Me 262, pictured here in April 1945, was the world's first operational jet fighter. Bundesarchiv, Bild 141-2497/CC-BY-SA 3.0

After the war, Dornberger claimed that some time on or shortly after April 27 Himmler had him arrested and Kammler sprung him—after which he and Kammler drove to Garmisch,[17] in southernmost Germany, on the border near Innsbruck. This trek of Dornberger and Kammler syncs with the known surrender location of Dornberger: Garmisch Partenkirchen, May 2, 1945.[18] It is also consistent with Himmler ordering Kammler's assassination. It gives us yet another marker on Kammler's whereabouts, but is also another difficult-to-explain Kammler challenge of Himmler's authority.

Kammler would have learned of Hitler's death directly or through a series of May 1 radio announcements on BBC, Hamburg radio, Czech radio, and others. Kammler adjutant Heinz Schürmann places Kammler in Ebensee, Austria, an hour east of Salzburg, on May 3–5, 1945. Ebensee was a Kammler-built underground factory for the V-2 and Me 262. We had also confirmed—remember Keith's air force document—that Ebensee was where the even longer-range Amerika Rocket was being constructed.

Before Kammler left Ebensee, he cryptically whispered to Schürmann, "if they say I am dead, Little Hans is dead, but Hans will not be for a long time!"[19] We take this odd statement as a reference to an old German folk song and children's story about a boy called Little Hans, who ventures into the world on his own but ultimately returns to the safety of his family. Kammler then ordered everyone but Schürmann on to Prague. He ordered Schürmann to remain behind to complete the handover of the Ebensee facility to the Americans, whose forward reconnaissance units were by then already operating in the area. The Ebensee factory, with its information on the Amerika Rocket, would alone be a fine prize for the arriving troops. Ebensee is also the site where researchers have recently found evidence of nuclear research. Again, note Kammler's continuing defiance of the standing Nero Decree that all German assets be destroyed.[20] Kammler was again serving the Americans, openly flouting the authority of Himmler and Hitler, and delivering the goods.

Kurt Preuk, one of Kammler's drivers, reports that from Ebensee Kammler traveled back to Tyrol to meet Jutta and the family at Gries am Brenner Pass, which fits with information received from the family—though Preuk may have been the source of the family's information, too. This is evidence that the whole Kammler family intended to escape to the south along the monastery route—which, as we shall see, became the Ratline, a secret escape route that survived the war. But the Kammler family had been misdirected; the area had already been overrun by the Allied advance, making Kammler's rendezvous with his family impossible.

The Nazis controlled the southern half of Germany, much of Yugoslavia, western Czechoslovakia, and parts of Austria, but the German realm was constantly shrinking. Now with the Russians approaching from the northeast, the Americans closing from the west, and partisans roiling within the city, Prague was up for grabs. The Americans were between Kammler and Prague, perhaps necessitating a rare Kammler plane trip in order to reach the city. Indeed, one account has Kammler arriving in Prague by plane.[21] Several accounts have Kammler in Prague in May, just before the date we know he surrendered—May 7. But I was beginning to worry about possible contradictions in the evidence we had, and I posed the direct question to Colm: "One, we know Kammler surrendered to the U.S. Army, though we don't know exactly where. Two, we know Kammler went to Prague before he surrendered. Three, we know the Soviets occupied Prague. How could Kammler have surrendered to the U.S. if Kammler was in Prague, and the Russians ended up controlling Prague?"

"There are a couple answers to that question, Dean. Prague was to become the final battleground of the war in Europe," Colm began ominously, "Cut off, it was still home to thousands of German soldiers and families, desperate to escape the Russians, and equally eager to avoid the retribution of the Czech partisans. The city quickly devolved into mayhem and bloodletting as Czech insurgents rose in anticipation of their liberation, joined by eighteen thousand soldiers from Russian Army Cossack units that switched back to the Russian side. Seeing impending disaster, in a bold move, German Field Marshall 'Bloody' Ferdinand Schörner ordered his battle-hardened SS 'Der Führer' Regiment of the 2nd SS-Panzer Division Das Reich to enter the city, quash the insurgents, and open the road west from Prague at all costs—establishing the vital escape route for the stranded Germans, which likely included Kammler. It was a last-ditch all-out rescue attempt. With Schörner's Regiment threatening to overwhelm the partisans, German General Rudolf Toussaint, the last Nazi commander of Prague, was able to negotiate an armistice, allowing the evacuation of the Germans. So, on May 8, the SS 'Der Führer' Regiment, in full battle order, swept through the Prague outskirts and opened the road. A Czech officer stood on the running board of the lead vehicle to guide the way, and Czech sentries at each dismantled roadblock saluted as Schörner's SS columns passed on the way to the city center, within two hours leading the exodus." Colm had a way of relating this story that made it easy to visualize. "By the morning of May 9, the masses of German troops and citizens made it out of Prague and surrendered to the U.S. 2nd Infantry Division on the road to Pilsen, west of Prague. Kammler could easily have been within that evacuation."

I agreed.

The story becomes even more exotic, though, as Her Highness Ingeborg Alix, Princess Stephanie of Schaumburg-Lippe, enters the picture. When Colm first mentioned Princess Stephanie, my crap detector spiked yet again. Keith and Colm had convinced me of many things, but as a born and bred American, royalty was for fairy tales, Disneyworld. Of course, it turns out she was very real. And she was a bad princess, not a good princess, as sometimes happens in children's stories. She was the unrepentant leader of an SS Women's Auxiliary Corps in Germany, and for decades after the war she worked diligently in support of Nazi welfare organizations and causes, even aiding Nazis on the lam. It appears that the princess's contacts evolved into a SS post-war network, transferring millions of Deutschemarks to Argentina where, under Juan Perón, the U.S. could not freeze the money.[22] Keith found a document showing that the princess's husband was the highest-ranking Nazi official on Argentine soil. In Prague in May 1945, the princess was charged with organizing the civilian side of the Schörner-led evacuation we just learned about, so she was the hub for information.

A private letter from the princess to Kammler's wife, Jutta, written years after the war—a copy of which is now in Colm's possession—states that Kammler was in Prague with her until May 8, 1945, when they joined that heavily guarded German convoy heading out of the capital.[23] By the princess's account, Kammler and his right-hand man, Oberführer Erich Purucker, rode near her car, but the cars were soon separated in the confusion. When she next saw Kammler's vehicle, he was gone—reported dead, though without a reported cause of death. The princess added that among Kammler's final words to her had been a defiant claim that he would never work for the enemy, without specifying which of Germany's many enemies he meant. Given his long-standing anti-Communism, I believe he could only have meant the Russians.

Contradicting the princess and complicating the story, another source claims that Purucker was with Dr. Wilhelm Voss, director of Skoda Armaments Works, about whom we will learn more shortly. And discrediting the princess's claims is her assertion that Kammler was on his way to Berlin to be by the Führer's side—at a time when Kammler and everyone else knew Hitler was dead. In her account of the evacuation, she also put Kammler in the back seat of the car, when we know that because of his fear of being attacked from the air he always rode in the front seat with the top down. Given these problems with the princess's story, I tend to discount it as a fairy tale—either an attempt to provide cover for a Kammler she knew to still be alive, or simply a well-intended attempt to console his "widow." Clearly, her report of his death is inconsistent with the surrender documents we have, and the documents that show Kammler in U.S. custody until at least March 1946.

Unbelievably, the story of Kammler's final days becomes yet more involved, and even more interesting, from here. The account of Kammler's driver, Kurt Preuk, has become the most widely accepted version of Kammler's death, endorsed by the German courts after the war.[24] But it is problematic, to say the least. Preuk claims he and Kammler were headed southeast from Prague on May 9 to a thirty-minute meeting with Baron Hans von Ringhoffer, a partner in Skoda Werke, the armament manufacturer, at Ringhoffer's Štiřín Castle. Afterward, they headed toward the Czech town Jílové u Prahy, stopping at a wooded intersection twelve miles south of Prague to meet with the SS supreme commander of Prague, Ober-gruppenführer Carl Friedrich von Pückler-Burghauss. Driver Preuk said he could hear Pückler and Kammler arguing, without hearing details. After General Pückler left, Kammler ventured a short distance into the woods, purportedly to relieve himself. When Kammler failed to reappear, Preuk followed his path and found Kammler dead by suicide, a gunshot wound to the head. He dug a shallow grave and buried the body—which despite sophisticated modern-era searches, has never been found.[25] In fact, no one has ever made a claim to have found Kammler's body. Years later, Preuk undermined his own story by bungling the details, stating he didn't know the cause of Kammler's death and equivocating on the date of death. His story was further compromised by another Kammler driver, Heinz Zeuner, who also claimed to be present but reported Kammler' death in a different location, a different day (May 7), a different time of day, by a different means—self-ingestion of cyanide.[26]

Starck, the SS major who was present at the final meeting between Kammler and von Braun in Bavaria, claims Kammler died in Prague in a hail of gunfire.[27] Yet another account has Starck shooting Kammler in the back of the head during a firefight to prevent Kammler from falling into enemy hands—also in Prague.[28]

Kristian Knaack claims to have encountered thirteen different versions of Kammler's death. Could all these differences be attributable to failed memories? Or perhaps rather to a failure to coordinate fake stories among multiple parties? Given that we know Kammler survived, we can only conclude the latter.

Colm decided to take a road trip, traveling to the Czech Republic in winter to survey Kammler's official death site—the one adjudicated by the German courts. Knowing that most lies contain a kernel of truth, we had begun to think that although Kammler certainly did not die near Prague, he had traveled to and surrendered near Prague. This trip was part of Colm's eyes-on method of research. Colm's guide was Jaro Svěcený, a legendary treasure hunter who claimed to have inside information. Jaro was a native of Czechoslovakia who had escaped its communist regime in

1972 and spent much of his spare time since chasing Nazi treasure, working with Holocaust survivors, ex-KGB and Nazis alike, using documentary films to record adventures and findings. His remarkable finds included part of Göring's missing sculpture collection, the stolen coffins of Italian archduchess Maria Francesca de Tuscany and her husband, a cache of German rifles, machine guns and grenades, and a Jewish medallion with Swiss bank account numbers etched into its rim recovered from a Nazi officer's briefcase. Colm told me later the charismatic Jaro reminded him, at least in appearance, of Rolling Stone guitarist Ron Wood, which ruined my vision of him in an Indiana Jones–style hat, bull whip on his hip, dashing through underground tombs netted with cobwebs.

"Jaro smoked cigarettes like he was in a contest," Colm told us later. Jaro claimed he had new information from Kammler's driver, Kurt Preuk. Acting on Preuk's sworn statement, on which the German court's adjudication of Kammler's death had relied, Colm and Jaro took the journey that Kammler had reportedly taken on the morning of his death, to the exact spot. It was only a short drive from Prague.

The landscape had not changed in sixty years, Jaro told him, gesturing through the windshield as their car pulled up to the bucolic site and rolled to a stop in the gravel alongside the roadway. Colm got the feeling that Jaro had made this trip many times before, but he didn't press.

It could have been any intersection in nearly any flat, wooded area of any country in Europe, Colm reflected as he exited the vehicle. The leafless trees were plentiful, but appeared lifeless as corpses, pale silver ghosts crowding the narrow roads on all sides.

The afternoon sky visible between the trees was grey and cold, the clouds looming low, skating just above the reach of the uppermost branches. Bits of new snow were cupped in the dry, curled leaves on the otherwise dim forest floor, a mantle of evergreens keeping the light on the ground low. Colm's breath clouded before him as the shriek of a lone bird assaulted his ear. In answer to the bird, the car creaked and ticked, the metal settling into place as the engine cooled. The icy, bitter air seemed to rise up from the crusted earth. Colm's senses were in acute overdrive.

Then everything grew still. No cars could be heard. No other wildlife stirred. Infused with a penetrating sense of foreboding, Colm drew his coat closer around him, shrunk his neck into his collar, dug his fists into his pockets, and gazed around—not quite sure what to look at, what to look for. Jaro Svěcený stood passively by, giving him room, spouting smoke. Colm faced the scene.

Nothing jumped out at him. Nothing. There was no "Ah-ha!" moment here, no epiphany. No visual clue at all as to what had transpired at this spot so long ago. Had he hoped to find Kammler's bones? An earthen mound? A sunken trough, perhaps, earth collapsed in on his decomposed body? Kammler's skeletal hand reaching skyward from the grave? Some other remnant? Nothing was evident.

Still, the place had an unnerving, eerie feel. A bit on edge, Colm ambled about, taking a turn around the intersection, peering into the wood, Jaro following at an interval like an adjutant trailing an officer at a respectful distance. Colm became chilled and wondered if it was from the wintry air or from the legend of the place itself.

The location of Kammler's alleged "official" suicide in May 1945. The forest crossroads area is close to the village of Jílové u Prahy in the Czech Republic. Courtesy of Colm Lowery

He imagined a despondent Kammler wandering a short way into the woods and shooting himself, as Preuk had sworn so long ago. Was it true? Given the scrupulously made plans Kammler had for his survival after the war, that had never made a moment's sense to any of us.

Warding off disappointment, Colm remembered that he hadn't come here hoping to find conclusive evidence either way, had he? We weren't really expecting him to find the final piece of the puzzle that we were working. Rather, he came here looking for insight. We wanted him to see through Kammler's eyes, walk Kammler's path, get into Kammler's head—we wanted the feel of the whole scene, the *gestalt*, to borrow the German word.

Colm reset himself as Jaro ground a cigarette butt into the pavement while lighting another Marlboro Red, sucking down a lungful of smoke. Colm wondered momentarily about Jaro's one-room flat, stuffed to the gills with bookshelves of documents, books, tapes of his adventures. *It's a wonder he hasn't burned himself up,* he thought.

Then Jaro became very serious, beckoning Colm to the side of the road, inviting him to picture the scene. Jaro was doing a lot of talking and gesturing, producing documents and maps showing the location: "The Red Army was approaching rapidly from the east, driving tens of thousands of refugees westward; the German population of Prague was preparing to evacuate. Meanwhile, Patton's Third Army was probing the SS's defenses from the opposite direction. Patton knew that under an agreement forged between Roosevelt and Stalin, U.S. troops weren't meant to be in Czechoslovakia at all, yet he begged that Eisenhower allow him to take Prague before the Soviets. Just three days of war left to run in Europe, with Kammler—Hitler's plenipotentiary for all Germany's secret weapons—in a Mercedes escorted by two Kubelwagens leaving for a rendezvous at this very spot with Count Pückler, the SS commandant of Prague."

A shaft of sunlight broke through the clouds and raced across the ground that Preuk had allegedly crossed to reach Kammler's dead body. When Kammler had been here long ago—if he had been here, Colm reminded himself—buds were sprouting on the trees. The air was warming day by day. In the cycle of the seasons, life was springing forth—hope on Nature's lips. But for the Third Reich, the end was at hand. Roads throughout Eastern Europe were clotted with tens of thousands of battered refugees pushing west, trying to get to the American lines and escape the advancing Communists. The Germans had lost Berlin after a long, bloody battle with the Russians. Hitler was dead in his bunker, and the thousand-year Reich was in its final spasms. For Kammler, too, the end was supposedly at hand. The ultimate end.

Had Kammler really died? Right here—in this remote spot, just as his driver Preuk had claimed? And so the story ends here? Was there no covert deal with the Americans? Are we misreading our documents? These thoughts were coursing through Colm's mind when, without warning, Jaro made a bewildering admission:

"Two weeks ago, at this very spot, Preuk, Kammler's driver, broke down and confessed to me that his testimony about Kammler's death was a lie. He told me so himself, right here. He lied."

Still more confirmation that the whole story of Kammler's suicide was a hoax! This final unraveling, though, was coming from the sole proprietor of the original claim—the original and only eyewitness to the court-approved version of history. Colm was floored but exhilarated at the same time. Preuk, the driver, the loyal Kammler aide, had perjured himself, likely to ensure a clean get away for his commander. That made sense to Colm—much more sense than Kammler having killed himself.

What next? Colm was left wondering, as he felt the thrill of yet another piece of evidence vindicating his long-held belief that Kammler had lived on after the war—mixed with consternation as this astonishing story took yet another turn. At this point, one electrifying revelation after another, nothing seemed impossible. This was no death scene, after all. Just a common intersection in the country—not even a metaphorical crossroads. Colm smiled briefly at that thought, his good humor and resolution returning, but he knew we still didn't have enough. A secondhand account of recanted testimony was more clue than solid proof, more indication than verification. But we also had the surrender documents.

Colm was cheered. He had, after all, been handed another piece of the puzzle on this trip. Kammler hadn't died. Not then. Not there.

"I think we're done," he said plainly, mostly to himself, moving toward the car, more determined than ever to sort everything out.

● ● ●

Colm made an excited call to Keith, recounting the event and adding his analysis. "It never made sense. If Preuk had time to dig even a shallow grave, he had time to grab Kammler's identity disk, his personal ID papers and awards, and his sidearm. That was standard military protocol—the collection and surrender of these items to the nearest military unit, Red Cross station, or POW camp as proof of death. It was the same procedure on all sides, always observed, never abandoned with a high-ranking officer, an SS General for goodness sake. But those items never surfaced. There is something very wrong here. This would be the same as Patton dying in the field—same rank—and his body being abandoned in a ditch or shallow grave with nothing collected as proof of death. NO WAY!"

By now Keith had conferenced me in. I was in the middle of a run but took the call anyhow. Once again, Colm had framed the issue perfectly. The thought of Patton being left in a shallow grave, even after dying during a hurried evacuation, was preposterous. I shifted gears: "We know the court action to declare Kammler dead was undertaken by Jutta, with driver Preuk as the star witness. Why do that?" I was thinking out loud.

"Smokescreen," was Keith's answer. He was right. An undeniable result of that court ruling was a complete lack of searches for Kammler by outside pursuers like the Wiesenthal Center, the Mossad, and the U.S. Department of Justice Office of Special Investigations forever after. We had proved that. When we contacted Wiesenthal and OSI during our research, they acknowledged they had never gone after Kammler, believing him dead.

Unfortunately, of the many records we have noting Kammler's surrender, none gives a precise location. So the puzzle had to be worked backward, from Kammler's surrender opportunities. We know Kammler was in Prague, and we know he surrendered to the U.S. Army. There were only a couple of options: the army went to Kammler in or near Prague, or Kammler went to the U.S. Army west of Prague, or perhaps even elsewhere. It's quite possible, we believe, that Kammler joined the evacuation out of Prague and then met up with American forces. But Keith and Colm proved to me U.S. forces made it much closer to, even into and beyond, Prague than most acknowledge, so a link-up in Prague is possible. Keith relayed this new information: "Czechoslovakia had been penetrated by U.S. intelligence, the OSS, even before troops arrived en masse at the scene in 1945. OSS inserted an asset, a Major Charles Katek, into Czechoslovakia, behind the lines. Katek ran intelligence networks in Prague and Pilsen, and would have made an excellent contact point for Kammler's surrender.[29] Katek was a fixed figure, and could be found."

"Although historians generally agree Patton's Army came no further than Pilsen, an hour west of Prague,"[30] Colm took the baton, "some say sizeable advance forces ventured into Prague. Katek or any of these advance elements could have offered Kammler his surrender chance. Patton's orders, holding at the border of what would be the post-war Russian Zone of Occupation, officially stopped him some 55 miles short of Prague, at Pilsen, along a 110-mile front line, roughly north to south, between the towns of Karlovy, Pilsen, and Budejovice. Allied forces routinely penetrated further than the big brass authorized, or desired. Often, if they could take territory, an on-the-ground decision to do so was made. One excursion we know of went 60 miles behind the lines."[31]

As Colm went on, I pulled up a map on my phone screen, trying to follow. My run had turned into a walk, but Colm was racing: "Our archive documents show the OSS had other assets in Prague, too, having parachuted German-speaking troops wearing German Army uniforms into

Prague months prior.[32] I was interested to learn one of the OSS men was none other than Eugene Fodor, of travel guide fame, his name discovered on a hand-written list of personnel.[33] I walked those towns, interviewed people there." As Colm spoke, my phone chimed. He had sent me photographs and I spooled through them, Keith and Colm now on my speaker phone, their enthusiasm bleeding out onto the jogging path. One picture was a granite obelisk monument in Pilsen, the American eagle embossed in gold, beneath it, "Thank You America!"

"Some people in Prague remember U.S. forces there, in small numbers, but definitely there. One former U.S. soldier, Gaston Gee, clearly remembers his reconnaissance unit, of the 4th Armored Division, 51st Armored Infantry Battalion, made it to the western outskirts of Prague. Finally, there is solid evidence of a lone armored column penetrating as much as eighty miles east of Prague, in an unsuccessful attempt to negotiate a surrender with German Field Marshall Ferdinand Schörner."[34]

"After Berlin fell, Oslo and Prague were the only European capitals left on the board." Colm again. "Many U.S. leaders felt it critical for the Americans to occupy Prague, which as a military matter they could have done with little risk, in order to bolster Czechoslovakia as a post-war democracy. A small OSS ground team that we know penetrated Prague returned to Patton's stop line with leaders of the Czech resistance, imploring American military leaders to enter the city before the Russians, who were still 200 miles to the east. Given his orders, Patton was unable to openly aid the resistance. But he did send small numbers forward. Any of those could have been Kammler's surrender contact."

"We also know elements of the German 2nd SS Panzer Division surrendered some 15 kilometers east of Pilsen, meaning beyond Pilsen, to the 2nd U.S. Infantry Division," Keith jumped in, "east of the official stop line, closer to Prague, so U.S. forces were certainly in that locale to accept their surrender. Kammler could have surrendered there."

The Patton "stop line," it turns out, was ill-defined, even porous, giving Kammler several different surrender opportunities. So Kammler had the opportunity to surrender to the U.S. Army near or even in Prague, since we know both he and the American military were in that location at the time of his surrender. My mind fairly reeled, and then settled on one interesting observation. If Kammler did surrender to U.S. elements in Prague, unknown to his staff and the princess, then that would have been the last they had seen of him. With Prague eventually falling to the Russians, could the mere fact that his last known location alive was to become Russian territory have been the start of the rumors that Kammler was working for the Russians after the war? And could the lies about his death while fleeing Prague have been nothing more than an uninformed attempt to preserve his legacy to save history from recording that Hans Kammler had gone over to the dreaded Soviets?

"But," I said, still collecting my thoughts, "we already think the Princess was lying in her account. Too many things in her story don't add up."

"Right," Colm said encouragingly.

"And we know Preuk was lying about Kammler's suicide. Because we know Kammler surrendered. Preuk was lying to cover up Kammler surviving the war, right? So why are we so sure Kammler made it to Prague at all? Maybe both the Princess and Preuk were lying about Kammler even coming to Prague? Maybe after he missed the rendezvous with Jutta he turned toward the Ettal Abbey, or just surrendered to the U.S. Army along the way?"

"That's a good point," Keith said, but the questioning note in his voice was asking Colm for his thoughts.

"Too many other things point to Prague," Colm weighed in. "That's the one thing all these stories have in common—Kammler in Prague. We think that part was true, though the suicide was nonsense. Kammler had another dire reason to get to Prague once he missed the meet-up with his family. *Kammler's Think Tank.*" I let that last remark hang in the air like a dirigible.

● ● ●

From Kammler's detention by the Americans, his movements become a bit more certain. After his surrender in May 1945, thanks to the FOIA request document Keith obtained, we know orders were to take Kammler to Kohnstein Mountain in Nordhausen, central Germany. We also confirmed this through the Fleming document. Kammler was desperately needed there to identify scientists and help American forces understand the rocket facility. Nordhausen was scoured by the Allies until mid-July, when it was turned over to the Russians.

Colm produced another document—this one with implications that were nearly inconceivable. He sent me an atypically excited email, asking if we could speak later, politely suggesting a call on my drive home from work, though it would be late his time. I had agreed, but once in my car regretted it. It was darkening, and rainy. Highway traffic was heavy, my windshield a smear of red brake lights. I needed to pay strict attention to my driving. When my phone rang, I begged Colm's indulgence until I could pull over, and soon found myself in the parking lot of a shopping center in Fairfax, Virginia. We spoke at length, my wipers slapping the windshield in the unceasing rain, shopping center customers skipping back and forth in the deluge, lightning in the near distance.

"It's dynamite. A Kammler interrogation report," Colm said excitedly. As he detailed his find, I realized that it was even better than that. Colm had uncovered an official U.S. government report confirming that Kammler had been in American custody being interrogated by American officials. Up until that point, our only evidence for that fact was the Fleming document, a memo that appeared to be an official U.S. report of his interrogation, but whose origin and authenticity we could not prove.

As he spoke, I could picture him in the kitchen of his seaside home in Ireland, wife and kids already snugly in bed, Max curled at his feet, thinking his master should already be sleeping, wondering why the late-night activity, the house dark but for a single small lamp atop the kitchen table. I hoped unlimited international calling was part of Colm's mobile phone plan because he had been racking up some serious international minutes.

"Not only is this more confirmation Kammler survived his 'death,' it shows he was in Army CIC custody, being questioned." I could hear

Colm's air-quotes around the word 'death' across the ocean. This connection was good, despite the increasing rain and wind. It was now completely dark, rain pooling in the parking lot. Customers had given up going back and forth, staying put wherever they happened to be, waiting for the storm to pass.

"That makes perfect sense—the Army Counter-Intelligence Corps would be the right entity to have a turn at Kammler once he had surrendered." My car was rocking, now, buffeted by the storm's high winds, the sky completely black. I felt like I was in a small boat at sea. I nearly jumped out of my skin when a crack of lightning, which must have been within fifty yards, exploded all around me. The sound was hellacious, the light blinding. I actually ducked. Washington has regular summer thunderstorms, dangerous winds, ground lightning strikes, power outages, the whole lot. This one had to be directly overhead.

"What was that?" Colm asked, followed by something else I couldn't hear.

I took a minute—"Just the storm. Lightning. Go ahead." The connection was faltering now with the weather.

"Not a double-strike, I hope, like the Nazi Death Head symbology…. Anyhow, this new document also shows serious Allied concern for missing SS funds and other money. Kammler was suspected of burrowing funds. Burrowing, that is, not *borrowing*—stashing funds away. That's not all," Colm said in agitation, "among other things, it shows that, and I'm quoting from the document here, 'shortly *after the occupation*' Kammler appeared before the CIC in Gmunden, Upper *Austria*, to answer questions about *bank accounts* controlled by him or other elements of the SS."

The rain was now pelting my car, a dull roar on the roof, and I was hoping it wouldn't turn to hail stones. Hail isn't terribly common in D.C., but it could cover your car with dents in seconds. I asked Colm to repeat what he'd said. He managed to emphasize the words 'after the occupation,' and 'Austria,' and 'bank accounts,' and 'missing money,' roadmapping for me. Wow!

Ebensee and about S 2,400,000 were authorized for payment
to creditors. Payment, however, was stopped and this accounts
for the large balance. Had this sum been paid the balance
would have been 1,100,000. On the other hand some additional 3,000,000 was forwarded to this account by the
Reichsbank in München but the sum was not credited to the
account because it was stopped by the Military authorities
before it left München.

Shortly after the occupation, Hans Kammler appeared
before the CIC in Gmünden and made a detailed statement on
the operations and activities of the Baustelle Ebensee, as
well as on the account, and his own authority and authority
of Karl Englehardt. None of the present American Officers
at the CIC, Gmünden, is familiar with his statement but it
should be in the files there. Mr. Morrison of the CIC, Gmünden
was requested by the team to send a copy of this statement
to Mr. Loehr.

CONCLUSIONS :

1. Sammelkonto was established by the Financial Division
of the Military Government on 31 July 1945.

2. Sammelkonto received monies belonging to the German
Wehrmacht and its affiliated organizations.

3. The details of the account show that some of the
funds could not be classified as direct Wehrmacht funds without
a more thorough investigation. There could be other funds which
were erroneously classified as Wehrmacht funds.

~~4. Although the subsidiary organizations such as~~

This page from a July 15, 1949, memorandum by Louis D. Caplane and William G.
Magee on the "Source of certain funds held for Sammelkonto Accounts by the Austrian
National Bank at Linz, Upper Austria" includes the most significant and verifiable
official evidence indicating that Kammler was in Gmunden, Germany, "shortly after
the occupation," being interrogated by the Army CIC (Counter-Intelligence Corps).

This was extraordinary. I sat back and thought this through as the storm raged all around. An inside-out umbrella blew across my headlights and wedged under a car. Keith and Colm had already put so much on the table in terms of Kammler records, and now this single document could be the bow that tied together the entire Kammler Deal. Not only did Kammler survive, not only did he surrender, but he was involved in missing funds, in control of missing funds—the mystical Fourth Reich! This meant that by late May 1945 and likely even earlier, CIC knew that not only was missing cash an issue, but that Kammler was involved, perhaps even one of the masterminds. It also proves CIC knew Kammler was alive, CIC was able to question him, and he was in Gmunden, Austria, near Ebensee, for that questioning.[35] I rang off with Colm and got back on the highway as the rain began to abate. This was a truly fantastic find, but I had more questions coursing through my mind: *What else did CIC ask Kammler about? Who at CIC was doing the questioning, and who was behind it? Was this before or after Kammler was taken to Nordhausen? Were the missing funds ever found; had they been set aside for the so-called Fourth Reich?* One thing Colm made certain I remembered was that Ebensee, where the CIC questioning was taking place, was not just the site of the bank account in question, but also the site of the long-range Amerika Rocket facility.

My garage saved me a walk through the remnants of the storm when I got home. Thankfully, our power was still on, but dinner would have to wait. I grabbed a handful of files in my office and began poring over them. More archive documents. More Amerika Rocket. More Fourth Reich. It was going to be a late night for me, but a good night.

● ● ●

Other details on what happened to Kammler after the war soon became clear. On May 21, 1945, the Twelfth Army Group sent to G-2, the Third Army, the Seventh Army, the Ninth Army, and the Fifteenth Army a request for "complete rosters of captured enemy V-2 personnel" of German Armee Korps ZV, commanded by Kammler, as well as others under Dornberger and von Braun.[36]

Our next data point is June 23, 1945, over a month later, when CIC Third Army responded to the Twelfth Army Group, reporting that the "exact whereabouts" of Kammler "in Third Army area is unknown."[37] CIC goes on to state that its intelligence files note Kammler was seen at Oberjoch in the end of April 1945—the area where the rocket scientists surrendered, which comports with our other information. It adds detail, though: shortly before the arrival of U.S. troops, Kammler was seen in the company of physician Franz Gerl.[38] We have not yet been able to run down the Gerl connection, which might lead nowhere, but might be a profitable next step in our hunt. Interestingly, CIC failed to disclose to the Twelfth Army that Kammler had appeared before the CIC in Gmunden, Austria. We believe that at this time Kammler was toggling between Nordhausen and Oberjoch, in U.S. Army custody, but helping locate missing documents and German scientists and being interrogated to exploit his other knowledge, upholding his part of the Kammler Deal.

On July 3, 1945, C. M. Warburton of CIOS wrote to FIAT (Field Information Agency, Technical), noting that CIOS had requested that Kammler be located and taken into custody for interrogation. Recall that CIOS was a combined effort of the Western Allies. And by this point in time CIOS was morphing into its separate U.S. and British components: FIAT run primarily by the Americans, and BIOS (British Intelligence Objectives Sub-committee). So the July 3 request was directed to the Americans from the joint commission in its waning days. All indications are that this official request was promptly ignored. The Americans had Kammler in custody, but they were clearly icing out the Brits.

A second, lengthier request, "Subject: Exploitation of S.S. General Kammler," was sent to FIAT by Warburton of CIOS eleven days later, on July 14, 1945, stating more urgently that Kammler "is required for interrogation." The letter from CIOS assumed Kammler was in custody. The letter includes a lengthy quote from a CAFT (Consolidated Advanced Field Team) assessor, adding some muscle: "Kammler was last known to be in the Zorge/Harz or in Bad Sachsa near Ilfeld-Niedersachswer-fen....” These were locations in and around Nordhausen and Kohnstein, confirming that Kammler was there as late as mid-July, which jives with our other information. The CIOS letter continued, “Kammler would know about all underground sites in Germany...I have a feeling that Colonel Beasley of USSBS team stationed at Ilfeld knows Kammler’s whereabouts. Beasley would not let on where. Kammler is a man who ought to be shot.” We have already encountered Beasley, the unusual officer who bunked with Nordhausen plant manager Georg Rickhey and then shipped Rickhey and his documents stateside, while Rickhey was wanted for murder. So, we know Beasley had a tendency to take matters into his own hands—to put it mildly.

This second request from Warburton generated a series of handwrit-ten notes within FIAT, including one from Major P. M. Wilson of FIAT’s Enemy Personnel Exploitation Section, the prominent figure at DUST-BIN, the FIAT Allied detention and interrogation center.[39] On July 17, Wilson wrote to Captain Schaverien, his underling in FIAT, at least paying lip service to the CIOS request: “What have we got on Kammler’s whereabouts? Please ask USSBS if they can help.” Do not overlook the use of Kammler’s last name as the sole identifier, rather than “SS General Hans Kammler.” That indicates familiarity with Kammler within the halls of FIAT. Schaverien’s response came three days later, on the same small scrap of paper, miraculously preserved in National Archives: “No indication here of Kammler’s whereabouts. Letter sent to USSBS.” The same day, Wilson directed Schaverien to “Put on [illegible].” The heading of the scrap of paper included the notation “Pending reply from USSBS.” That was the U.S. Strategic Bombing Survey, Beasley’s outfit.

Ten days later, on July 30, Captain May of FIAT, again in a hand-written note, wrote to Major Wilson, “The hunt for Kammler is PWOR [proceeding without results]. G2 CI ask is still op [operational]—having been made by me personally again only yesterday.” So, the “hunt” for Kammler was continuing, but results were sparse, at least as far as FIAT was concerned.

COMBINED INTELLIGENCE OBJECTIVES SUB-COMMITTEE
32, Bryanston Square, W.1.

CIOS/113/6E/S   14 July 1945

SUBJECT: Exploitation of S.S. General KAMMLER

TO   :   G-2 FIAT,
          Enemy Personnel Exploitation Section,
          SHAEF Main.

        1. With reference to S.S. General KAMMLER who is required
for interrogation by Group 7, the following note written by a
CAFT 7 assessor was passed to 12 Army Group on 2 June, 1945:-

        "General Dr. Ing. KAMMLER was last known to be
        in ZORGE/Harz or in BAD SACHSA near ILFELD-NIEDER-
        SACHSWERFEN. He is neither place now. Accord-
        ing to Bernard Zaenker, ILFELD, who was accountant-
        inspector of OKG at Mittelwerke, Niedersachswerfen
        (V-1 and V-2) Kammler was head of the Einsatzgruppen
        Nord and Sued which supplied works like the under-
        ground Mittelwerke with foreign workers and PW's.

        Kammler would know about all underground sites in
        Germany. He was a member of the Beirat of Mittelwerke.
        ZAENKER knew that Kammler moved between offices in Bad
        Sachsa and ZORGE until 8-9 April 45. I have a feeling
        that Colonel Beasley of USSBB team stationed at ILFELD
        knows Kammler's whereabouts, Beasley would not let on
        where. Kammler is a man who ought to be shot. He
        is hated by all the DP's. He was SS Gruppenfuehrer
        member of the Reichsfuehrung SS, and a Lt.Gen. in the
        Waffen SS. "

        2. It is requested that Colonel Beasley of USSBS shall be
contacted for any information he may have on KAMMLER and that
steps shall be taken to locate him. Please inform the Secretariat
of the results of your enquiries so that, if necessary, arrangements may be made to send an escort to take him to DUSTBIN.

                        For the Combined Secretariat.

                                    C.M. WARBURTON
                                        S.T.A.

Copy To:-
        Major R. Pickering,
        E.A.B. 3, Foreign Office,
        Lansdowne House,
        Berkley Square, W.1.

This July 14, 1945, memo by C. M. Warburton of CIOS (the Combined Intelligence Objectives Sub-Committee) is the first document that indicates a mistrust between agencies regarding Kammler. Warburton quotes these telling words of "a CAFT [Consolidated Advanced Field Team] 7 assessor": "I have a feeling that Colonel Beasley of USSBS team [the United State Strategic Bombing Survey] stationed at ILFELD knows Kammler's whereabouts, Beasley would not let on where. Kammler is a man who ought to be shot."

Meanwhile on July 21, P. M. Wilson had, true to his word, pinged USSBS, writing on behalf of the Director of Intelligence: "We are anxious to locate S.S. General Kammler in order to bring him to DUSTBIN. It is understood that Colonel Beasley of the USSBS team at ILFELD may have knowledge of his whereabouts. Could Colonel Beasley please be contacted for any information he may have on Kammler?" The request to get Kammler to DUSTBIN jives with our assumption that Kammler would have been among the names of Speer associates read aloud at the June 1945 CIOS meeting. Tellingly, the subject line of the July 21 memo was "Location of General Kammler," not "Apprehend General Kammler," or "Status of General Kammler." Kammler was known to be in custody, but his precise location was unknown to FIAT's enemy exploitation section. This was now an absolute dog fight.

The USSBS sent a curt reply just six days later on July 27: "This organization has no information on the whereabouts of General Kammler." Pouring salt in the wound, the note added, "Colonel Beasley has returned to the Zone of the Interior." The missive was a clear rejection of the request, and a strong warning not to inquire further.

This classic tug of war for Kammler shows the rivalries and competing goals and needs of various parts of the military, but it also demonstrates that this entire group of actors—CIOS, FIAT, BIOS, and USSBS—knew General Hans Kammler still to be alive in July of 1945.

"Was Beasley remaining mum about Kammler on his own and, if so, why?" I asked Keith and Colm on a conference call.

Keith was first out of the gate, "More likely, he was ordered to discourage or even shut down all inquiries about Kammler. Beasley was shipped out to avoid pointed questions about Kammler." That made sense.

Colm added, "Covering up the deal with Kammler, and his post-war location, would take a lot of nerve, and authority. Of course, so too would making the Kammler Deal in the first place. This had to have gone higher even than Beasley." Another point I found hard to refute. We knew Beasley's boss, USSBS chief Paul Nitze, personally led the hunt for Speer, and got him on May 15, weeks before he was sent to DUSTBIN.

Speer, recall, was telling Nitze that Kammler was the best source for V Weapons information.

A July 21, 1945, memo from Major P. M. Wilson of FIAT (Field Intelligence Agency—Technical), also suggesting that Beasley knew where Kammler was. Note that the memo's subject line is "Location of General Kammler," not "Apprehend General Kammler." It's clear that Kammler was already in custody—and the subject of a dog fight between rival Allied authorities.

"I have to think Garvey was involved. CIC is everywhere on our paperwork, always with Garvey mentioned," I offered.

"I agree," Colm allowed. CIC chief Lieutenant Dale Garvey was in it. On October 26, 1945, six months after the end of hostilities in Europe, Army CIC, the Army Counter-Intelligence Corps, issued a Request for Apprehension/Request Notification of Apprehension/ Request Investigation of Kammler. This document recites Kammler's last known location as Oberammergau in April 1945[40]—the area of the rocket team's surrender, though we know that he was in

Nordhausen, still in U.S. custody much later than that date. Just four days later Garvey sent a request to CIC in Dahmen, north of Berlin, that it provide information on Kammler, along with fourteen others, mostly wanted SS criminals.[41] Because we know with certainty that Kammler was in Gmunden and Nordhausen after the date Garvey gave, the CIC chief must have been deliberately obfuscating—for reasons that will become clear. We also know that either the Kammler interrogation report, showing that CIC had questioned him at Gmunden, never made it into Kammler's CIC dossier, or else it was removed, because it was not among the official files Keith had received as the Kammler dossier in response to his FOIA requests to the FBI.

In 1949, Oskar Packe, a special investigator, stumbled upon the Gmunden document as well and wrote about it in a report on Kammler. Is it possible the Gmunden document was deleted at that time from what became the official Kammler file? We simply don't know.

CIC was integral in what became the best-known ventures to transplant Germans to America after the war, and I thought the deal with Kammler might have been a forerunner to Operation Overcast, a story told by other authors but never linked to Kammler. Overcast, a project to bring hundreds of German scientists to the United States, was later renamed Operation Paperclip when the camp where the families of the recruited scientists were ensconced was given the name Camp Overcast,[42] blowing the code name for the overall operation. The entire purpose of Overcast-Paperclip was to exploit Nazi research and Nazi personnel for American technological advantage, and the existence of the program proves that the United States was willing to harbor high-ranking Nazis to do so. Those facts made it more likely that Kammler had received secret help from the U.S. to get out of Germany. Originally the program operated without explicit approval, without public acknowledgement, and with doctored German personnel records to allow ineligible persons to enter the U.S. Was the Kammler Deal a forerunner of Overcast-Paperclip? Could it even have been the original blueprint for the larger operation? Most historians believe that Paperclip began in July 1945, but we think we can trace its roots to the early summer of 1944. The

Kammler Deal would have been a one-off at the time, but something that would have had to be authorized at the highest level—so it could have blazed a trail.

The U.S. Strategic Bombing Survey's Beasley, with his expertise on bombing, was in a unique position to understand the value of the German catalogue of rockets. Surely he would have given his right arm for Kammler. As the man who had run the Nazi rocket program, he was far more valuable than his underling Rickhey—who had already earned a Beasley get-out-of-jail-free card and a trip to the U.S. But as a colonel, Beasley wouldn't have had the chops to arrange the Kammler Deal. Rickhey was a mere plant manager; Kammler was among the highest-ranking generals in the SS.

Colm tried to give us a concise summary: "We know Kammler was in custody as the war ended, having surrendered to the Ninth Army. We know Beasley was operating in the same area as the Ninth. We know Major P. M. Wilson, who was responsible for collecting Nazi talent and moving it to DUSTBIN, thought Beasley had Kammler; and we know Beasley, a U.S. Army Colonel, subsequently vanished. We surmise someone above Beasley put up a smokescreen to frustrate everyone else searching for Kammler. As we know, when we look at other documented deals, the first instinct of the country making the deal, even within its own ranks, is to deny and cover."

Keith added, "A concerted coverup, at the highest level, all sounds a bit fantastic to you, Dean, I know. But consider one more critical fact—the surrender of Kammler, a notorious SS general (the only such man to achieve that rank during the final year of the war) has remained undiscovered for seventy-four years! Seventy-four years they've been saying he's dead, and he wasn't. We already know that. Only *we* know that!"

Documents uncovered by Keith nailed Kammler's next steps, and they implicated the U.S. Army Air Forces (AAF), the precursor to the U.S. Air Force, always high on Keith's list of candidates for the entity that had arranged the Kammler Deal. Following his hunch that AAF was naturally interested in offensive military missiles like the V-2, Keith

had been in touch with archivists at Wright-Patterson and Maxwell Air
Force Bases, both repositories of wartime AAF records. Three documents
he received from them now were enlightening, to say the least. The first
was an August 29, 1945, report on "German Underground Structures,"
from Brigadier General George C. McDonald.[43] A brigadier general is
certainly higher than Colonel Beasley, I reflected silently. McDonald had
heft; he was a powerful military figure; all air intelligence gathering missions were directed from his office—on German missiles, jets, installations, the whole gamut, in all theaters. McDonald created or had access
to all personnel, material, documents, and facilities with any connection
to air warfare or aeronautics. Kammler would have been on McDonald's
target list, near the top, if not heading it up. McDonald's August 1945
report covers six German underground facilities he visited, which he
noted with concern were well constructed, permanent, and would be
"available for bombproof housings of important industries in any future
war." He called for their destruction by engineers with "practical experience in underground construction."[44] McDonald was eying the facilities
for their possible misuse by a resurgent Germany or—in the cases of
facilities in the Russian Zone—by a belligerent Soviet Union, but he was
also trying to learn more about the methods of their construction.
McDonald knew America would need not only missile silos, but also
subterranean command sites and even fallout shelters impervious to
nuclear attack. Kammler was the key to understanding both how to
destroy the facilities that might fall into unfriendly hands and how to
build similar structures in the U.S. This report highlights yet another
way—a way wholly independent of his unique knowledge about the
German rocket team and rocket science—in which Kammler would have
been useful to the U.S.

Keith's packet contained a second memo by General McDonald, this
one written on November 2, 1945. The subject was "German Underground Installations," and it mentioned Kammler directly.[45] In this one-
pager McDonald asked his underling Major Ernst Englander to
"personally interrogate Speer, Kammler and Sauer and report your

findings to me as soon as possible." McDonald made note that it was of "the highest priority that we obtain all the benefit of the experience of German industry regarding use of such facilities" for "future planning." This memo is suggestive, though not conclusive, on the question of Kammler's whereabouts in November 1945. Speer was being held at Nuremburg at the time, and the grouping of his and Sauer's names with Kammler's suggests that Kammler may also have been at Nuremberg.

The possibility that Hans Kammler may actually have been at Nuremberg in November 1945 is jaw-dropping. The implication is that the Nazi slave master was actually on the site of the war crimes investigations and future trials, being interrogated by multiple agencies, including the Nuremberg prosecutors—but got away scot-free. We have several documents proving Kammler was actually wanted as a defendant in the war crimes trial, yet he was never charged or tried. The Kammler Deal was no low-level operation. Someone extremely high on the food chain had to intervene to permit him to walk away from the Nuremberg docks.

One final nugget came out of this batch of materials. General McDonald's bio had him working not just for AAF, but for OSS, the intelligence agency that was the precursor to the CIA, and home to the ubiquitous Allen Dulles.

● ● ●

We have shown that Kammler surrendered to the U.S. Army and he survived the war. And remember the document that Keith had provided showing that Robertson, Eisenhower's scientific advisor, had authorized G.E.'s experts—not just American military men—to conduct the interrogations of Kammler's rocket experts. We had also been able to document a great many of Kammler's movements before his surrender—Tyrol, Berlin, Garmisch, Ebensee, back to Tyrol, and finally Prague.

"All this activity is not random. Look at the bigger picture." Colm directed. "I believe what we are seeing here is Kammler securing his nest eggs, at one place and then the next."

HEADQUARTERS
UNITED STATES AIR FORCES IN EUROPE
Office of Asst. Chief of Staff A-2
APO 633

AAF Station 179
2 November 1945.

SUBJECT: German Underground Installations.

TO: Major ERNST ENGLANDER, A.C., Headquarters USAFE, APO 633.

1. I have been instructed by the AC of S A-2, Headquarters Army Air Forces, Washington, D. C., to furnish detailed information from many aspects on enemy underground installations, technique, etc.

2. In view of recent scientific developments, it is considered of the utmost importance for future planning and of the highest priority that we obtain all the benefit of the experience of German industry regarding the use of such facilities.

3. To implement the required study, you are directed to make the necessary arrangements to personally interrogate Speer, Kammler and Sauer and report your findings to me as soon as possible.

GEORGE C. McDONALD,
Brigadier General, U.S.A.
Asst. Chief of Staff A-2.

A November 2, 1945, memo from the Army Air Force Assistant Chief of Staff A-2 (Air Intelligence) General George McDonald orders, "You are directed to make the necessary arrangements to personally interrogate Speer, Kammler, and Sauer and report your findings to me as soon as possible." Since Albert Speer and Karl-Otto Sauer are known to have been in U.S. custody at the time at Nuremberg, this is evidence not only that Kammler was still held by the Americans in November 1945, but most likely being held at Nuremberg.

"In Berlin, he was making sure Grosch and Schürmann destroyed the modified V-1," Keith picked up where Colm let off. "He'd already been to Nordhausen to secure all the paperwork there. He'd checked in with his family and made arrangements for the final rendezvous. Then we see him at Ebensee, another major site, for the Amerika Rocket, to make certain Schürmann understands he is to destroy *nothing*; despite any conflicting orders from Hitler, he's to turn everything over to the Americans. Kammler's definitely preserving everything he promised the Americans."

"If you understand this," Colm resumed, "Kammler's next step makes perfect sense." Keith and Colm were tag-teaming me, and I got the sense their presentation had been rehearsed in a pre-call without me.

Keith carried on: "From Tyrol, on May 5, 1945, after he missed the meet up with his family, Kammler made for Prague, likely by plane.[46] All the stories of Kammler's death agree he was in Prague, and his presence there is confirmed by Speer's assistant in a 1948 interrogation report,[47] and plenty of other documents we have."

"Why? Why would Kammler go to Prague, of all places?" Colm asked me, I thought rhetorically. That was a question I had been asking myself; Kammler could have stayed in Tyrol and surrendered there to the Americans. After the slightest pause to allow me to venture a guess, which I didn't, Colm answered his own question: "To lock down Arbeitsstab Kammler, meaning Working Staff Kammler, a Kammler-run think tank. Kammler was trying to make sure the Americans got the research documents from his Working Staff Kammler, in Prague, another deliverable under the Kammler Deal."

Keith and Colm had for some time been mentioning this "Working Staff Kammler," a super-secret Kammler-run weapons project. As with their mentions of treasure, I had always expressed interest and allowed for possibilities, but hadn't jumped on board. Now it was coming up again. I remained to be convinced of the existence of "Working Staff Kammler," though admittedly there would have had to be something very important in Prague to draw Kammler to the madness going on there in the final days of the war—especially when he could have stayed in the Tyrol and looked for his family instead.

"Dean, we know all hell had broken loose between the Germans and the Russians, fighting northeast of Prague. The Russian columns were approaching in formation, with long lines of men, artillery, mechanized equipment. Refugees were fleeing to the west. The Germans threw everything they had at the Russians, including all remaining aircraft, like the Me 262, outfitted with R4M Orkan rockets that made it a turkey shoot. This was happening with Kammler at the helm, directing traffic, dispersing airplanes and rockets he had put into the field in the first place. He had even personally authorized the Orkan rockets for the Me 262, so again we see Kammler developing weapons and then on the battlefield using them."

"Why, was he stalling for time? Hoping the Americans got to him?"

"Keith and I think that is exactly what was going on. Kammler was waging a hellacious, final pitched battle to let Patton and his boys save Prague, save Czechoslovakia, while he took care of the research records he had in and around Prague." Records, Keith and Colm were telling me, that haven't been disclosed publicly to this day. This new vein of information was just overwhelming. I had to adjourn our call, pledging we would revisit this the following day.

CHAPTER EIGHT

Nuclear Secrets

"I do not know with what weapons World War III will be fought, but World War IV will be fought with sticks and stones."

—*Albert Einstein*

"I'm on," I said, indicating that I had joined the latest conference call. I was hoping this was to be a celebratory Sunday morning (afternoon for Colm) call, with mutual congratulations for establishing the Kammler Deal, documenting the United States had held the Nazi war criminal, and proving the Americans had covered up his survival. "You guys have done outstanding work. I think we've done it. We have our book," I said, beginning the call with a conclusion.

"Yes," Colm said, and I immediately detected hesitation in his voice, "Before we get to that, there's another matter we should discuss."

I suddenly had the feeling that I was joining a call not just moments old, but one that had been going on for several minutes, with Keith and Colm strategizing. I was right.

"We can mention lost treasure," I conceded, thinking they were out to convince me of that angle.

"It's not treasure, Dean, it's Working Staff Kammler, it's nuclear weapons," Colm said.

Good grief, I thought, *how many frickin' limbs are they going to ask me to climb out on? And how far?* But what I said was, "We can't just offer up some inane theory that Kammler's Think Tank, Working Staff Kammler, even if it existed, was working on nuclear weapons. We need proof. I'm going to need a lot of convincing." I was making no attempt to disguise the consternation I was feeling.

"We're used to that," Keith replied, beaming through the phone. "We love a challenge."

Nuclear weaponry was Colm's realm, and he started in with a long lecture. In 1938, Germany jumped to the early lead in a contest the world didn't know had even begun—the nuclear arms race—when German chemist Otto Hahn discovered nuclear fission. But the military implications were not as immediately obvious as we might think today; the truly devastating power of a nuclear explosion was not fully understood at the time, and it would be seven years until an atomic bomb was dropped.

There is no doubt that Germany planned from early in the war to create a nuclear weapon.[1] But the history books tell us that in 1942 Hitler decided a bomb project could not be completed before he won his war, so he shut down nuclear weapons research—as distinct from nuclear power research, work toward a reactor or "engine" that could provide electricity or perhaps even drive a submarine.

"History also insists Germany made no significant progress.[2] But we think history is wrong," Colm said through my speaker phone, pausing for my reaction. I had heard this before, and so remained silent. I was at home. In my office. I realized I was gritting my teeth, like a petulant child being fed his least favorite vegetable. I even had my arms crossed as I listened, feet on my desk.

Colm continued. Germany's atomic research efforts were reportedly splintered, less than ideally coordinated,[3] and reportedly not very informed, according to historians who have evaluated secret recordings of German scientists at the Farm Hall detention center near Cambridge after the war. Their conversations include instances when members of the German nuclear research teams are each learning, for the first time, only after the war, key details of each other's research, demonstrating a lack of coordination.

Colm insisted that he and Keith had documents that contradicted this "known" history. And I had some reason to believe them. After all, I had originally been put off by their claims that Kammler was as evil as they said (though he was), accomplished as much as they said (though he did), and survived the war (though he did). But wasn't this too much?

"Germany closer to a nuke than anyone thought?" I challenged, "Too many historians and scholars have studied this, Colm. I'm sure they've been in every archive of the world, all the documents, reading between lines. This is something lots of people, serious people, have been out to prove since the war ended. With Kammler, we were pursuing someone ignored by historians. Germany's nuclear history is totally different—that's well-trodden territory."

Colm quickly conceded the point, and I sensed that tact was something that he and Keith had agreed to before I joined the call.

"There's really no down side, though," Keith parried. "You're writing the book. You're on board. Just take a look." They were right, of course. I was fully along for the ride. I could at least review their documents with an open mind. And Colm, trained as a scientist, had credibility on this issue—he should be able to sort out the finer points of any technical documents they had discovered. And he and Keith had even consulted nuclear scientists to review some of their documents. Of course, they thought Kammler had played a secret role, heading a special project.

● ● ●

Hamburg physicist Paul Harteck headed a project for Germany's Wehrmacht, the German army. He was a superior scientist, very quick to recognize and document the explosive potential of a theoretical nuclear weapon, "many orders of magnitude more effective" than conventional explosives.[4] He was also central in the development of the ultracentrifuge,[5] an apparatus used to enrich uranium.

Baron Manfred von Ardenne obtained research funding through—of all things—the Reich Postal Ministry, the German Post Office, which, as strange as it may seem, has been described by some as the German equivalent of America's Bell Laboratory, headed by Dr. Wilhelm Ohnesorge, an early Hitler adherent with access to unusually large amounts of funding.[6] Von Ardenne was born in Hamburg and lived until 1997, with six hundred patents to his credit. His wartime projects included work on electro-magnetic isotope separation—the complex, labor- and time-intensive process of teasing out fissionable U235 from raw uranium ore. His work was a possible shortcut to making fissionable material that could be used in a bomb. In 1941, working for von Ardenne, Fritz Houtermans advanced thinking about plutonium as a fissionable material and made the first-ever, all-important calculations for the critical mass of U235[7]—that is, the amount of material needed for a chain reaction and violent explosion. Hitler himself, the enduring and unwavering espouser of a final German Wonder Weapon that would win the war, was a repeat visitor to von Ardenne's lab—a confirmation of its importance.[8]

Hitler's adjutant Julius Schaub reported that a German uranium bomb the size of a small pumpkin had reached a prototype stage under von Ardenne's supervision, ready for mass production at an underground SS factory in Harz, near Nordhausen.[9] Curiously, when the source for this information, *Hitler's Table Talk*, a German language book, was translated into English by British intelligence officer Hugh Trevor-Roper, all references to Germany's nuclear research were deleted.[10]

After the war von Ardenne would head his own Russian research institute—and the West would exert great efforts to monitor his work there.[11] In 1953, he was awarded the Stalin Prize for making a Soviet bomb a reality.

Walther Bothe carried out work in Heidelberg under the auspices of the German army. He was also instrumental in bringing a functioning cyclotron online.[12] But Bothe also arguably contributed to a crippling error in Germany's research. Based on the erroneous results of one poorly run Bothe experiment with unpurified graphite, the Germans unwisely eliminated it as a moderator. In the Manhattan Project graphite would prove to be a reliable moderator, and it was readily available. Heavy water was also effective, but the Germans had only one ready source, which was attacked by the Allies, and German research suffered from its scarcity.

Carl Friedrich von Weizsacker had quite a colorful life, a nobleman and a son of German diplomat Ernst von Weizsacker, whom we have already encountered. He was also the brother of Richard von Weizsacker, who as president of West Germany from 1984 to 1990 oversaw the reunification of Germany and became its president until 1994. Weizesacker lived in Germany after the war long enough to see the debut of the iPhone. He was involved in German research from the beginning, attending the seminal meeting of the German nuclear weapons project in September 1939.

Professor Erich Schumann led yet another major research wing of the German nuclear project with Kurt Diebner in the Gottow lab near Berlin that specialized in "atom smashing" research.[13] Schumann and Diebner were both ardent Nazis, joining the party early and never disclaiming their allegiance, even after the war.[14] Their party credentials gave them a leg up when it came to earning the trust of Kammler and Himmler and in gaining access to scarce research materials. Their level of expertise has been under-appreciated in history—overshadowed by Hahn and Heisenberg, perhaps because of their Nazi connections.

Schumann, the head of Germany's Institute for Physics of Explosives,[15] was an important administrative official in German nuclear research.[16] Diebner was a specialist in hollow charge explosives, or shaped charges, which concentrate the explosive energy of a conventional explosive into a single point. The shaped charge was first weaponized by the Germans in 1942, in the form of the *panzerfaust* ("tank fist"), the first disposable anti-tank weapon operated by a single soldier. The shaped charge warhead of the *panzerfaust* was ingenious: impacting at a little over the speed of a baseball, it could penetrate every armored fighting vehicle of the era, killing all crew members inside.

Throughout 1944, Schumann and Diebner and a small team of explosive experts embarked on a series of experiments to develop an atomic weapon. These experiments have gone unreported in the history of nuclear weapons, largely because Schumann and Diebner were not trying to build an atomic bomb based on the science of enriched uranium, but instead were exploring an alternative pathway toward development of an atomic bomb. They were working with the science of thermonuclear fusion: Schumann and Diebner's team was trying to build the world's first hydrogen bomb. By 1944, ten years had passed since German physicists had first recognized that the fusion of two heavy-hydrogen atoms produced helium and liberated large pulses of energy. In 1934, scientists Mark Oliphant, Paul Harteck, and Ernest Rutherford demonstrated experimentally this thermonuclear fusion process, which is the basis of the modern hydrogen bomb.

In a gross over-simplification of the science, for thermonuclear fusion reactions to occur—for two hydrogen atoms to become "fused" together to make a single helium atom—the hydrogen needs to be exposed to extremely high temperatures and pressures. In addition to producing helium, another product of a thermonuclear fusion reaction is the creation of a large pulse of energy—the same energy that drives the stars, including our sun.

Schumann and Diebner thought that heavy water would be a suitable fuel to supply the hydrogen atoms in a thermonuclear fusion reaction. They understood that for nuclear fusion to occur, the hydrogen atoms must overcome the repulsion forces (the Coulomb Barrier) to get close enough for the attractive nuclear forces to take over. They reasoned that an array of shaped charges exploding simultaneously around a central core of heavy water hydrogen would be sufficient to overcome the Coulomb Barrier and create a high number of thermonuclear fusion reactions in the heavy water fuel—an atomic explosion.

Based on what we know to be the rudimentary design of their early field experiments, they were doomed to failure, though Schumann and Diebner were certainly on the right path to developing the world's first thermonuclear fusion weapon—a hydrogen bomb.

In contrast to most of the other Nazi physicists, Diebner was an experimentalist, willing to get his hands dirty. We don't know how advanced his and Schumann's experiments were by the war's end; we simply don't have the documentation. But Colm was able to tell me that heavy water, which requires copious amounts of energy to initiate an explosive reaction, was far from the ideal fuel. In fact the temperature and pressure necessary for a modern thermonuclear weapon—a hydrogen bomb—are so great that they are often supplied by exploding a small fission weapon.

Interestingly, the same early experimental methods employed by Schumann and Diebner during World War II would ultimately lead to the development of today's small tactical nuclear weapons (of a size that might have fit in a German rocket). Their experiments may have been responsible for the small tactical nuclear explosions rumored to have happened in central Germany near the end of the war. And Diebner and Schumann did not operate in complete isolation. Their work was significant enough to merit a conference in Berlin in June 1944, at which Walter Schellenberg, Otto Skorzeny, and many Nazi scientists were present.[17]

The post-war narrative spun by the German nuclear scientists stressed that their work was not linked to Nazi ideology—in their telling of the story, it was about the search for functional nuclear power, not about weapons. You are correct if this tale sounds familiar. Substitute "space exploration" for "functional nuclear power"—in contrast with weapons research—and you have the same tired argument that von Braun, Dornberger, and the rest of Kammler's rocket scientists offered in defense of their research for the Nazis. Unsurprisingly, there is plenty of evidence that the goals of the German scientists were not that narrowly defined. In fact there may have been an agreement among the German scientists—crafted by Weizsacker—to claim they had purposely tried not to develop a nuclear bomb for the Nazis. The agreement was known as "die Lesart"—the Version.[18] And in spite of any such agreement, and in spite of the fact that the German scientists suspected that there were microphones at Farm Hall recording their conversations, they did make admissions that they had worked toward an atomic bomb—"war work."[19] Note also that not all the German scientists were interned at Farm Hall, so this cannot be seen as a complete record.

Moreover, what explains the archive document that claims theoretical if not practical success by Schumann and Diebner? In the last year of the war, "Professor Schumman declared that the problem of the uranium bomb had been solved...."[20] In late 1944, over two years after Germany's nuclear research was supposedly limited to energy production, the OSS reported that von Ardenne "claims he is inventing a super weapon,"[21] a confounding claim from someone whose work was supposedly limited to nuclear energy and propulsion.

But even if they were pursuing the atom bomb, just how close did the German scientists get? Comments of Nobel prize–winning physicist Werner Heisenberg at Farm Hall—overestimating the amount of fissile material needed for a bomb—were interpreted by the Allies to betray the German scientists' fundamental lack of understanding of the atomic bomb and are supposed to prove that the German effort was never close to a positive result.[22] But Paul Harteck, another German scientist also recorded at Farm Hall, made calculations just days later that are correct, indicating a greater understanding by the Germans.[23] There are also reports that early in the war Heisenberg accurately said that a nuclear bomb payload could be reduced to the size of a pineapple.

As we have seen, the Germans' research was hampered by a lack of coordination. Although each project made its own sort of progress, findings were not always shared and critical resources like heavy water and uranium were hoarded, stunting optimal progress. It was Heisenberg, against Diebner and Schumann, against the German Post Office, against Harteck in Cella, against Weizsacker, against the SS, which had its own department for nuclear research: the Waffenaut, headed by SS general Professor Schwab.[24] Furthermore, Keith and Colm thought that Kammler may have had his own operation churning out secret nuclear weapons research.

There is evidence of collaboration, though, such as the February 1942 meeting of nearly every principal German researcher, convened to discuss uranium.[25] But there was not enough real guidance from the top to ensure that future work followed the most promising present work.

• • •

When German scientist Otto Hahn bombarded an atom of uranium with slow neutrons (as opposed to fast neutrons), he had expected the bombarding neutrons to be absorbed by the uranium, changing the chemistry of the uranium and producing another element close to uranium on the periodic table. Instead he was left with something similar to barium, less than half the nuclear weight of uranium. Through the bombardment, the uranium atom had split into two parts, the resulting two weights not quite equaling the total weight of the original uranium. The missing matter in the equation had gone somewhere, as Einstein showed it must: it had been converted to pure energy. So not only was atomic fission possible, but it was a source of energy.

If, once the fissioning process was triggered by bombardment of neutrons, additional neutrons from the fissioning uranium were emitted in quantities sufficient to cause other surrounding uranium atoms to fission, a chain reaction would ensue. With enough fissionable material, extraordinary amounts of energy would be produced. A controlled chain reaction could produce energy to drive a nuclear power plant or nuclear submarine. An uncontrolled, robust chain reaction could cause an explosion unlike any ever witnessed.

Early experiments showed that each neutron absorbed during a uranium fissioning experiment caused 2.4 neutrons to be shed, making a chain reaction theoretically possible. But some of those liberated neutrons would leak out of the experiment, flying off into the surrounding space, not available to trigger continuing fission. Many of those wayward neutrons, though, could be kept in the fissioning process with a "tamper"—material that would reflect the escaping neutrons back into the reaction. German scientist Walther Bothe made the most significant progress in developing a functioning tamper, keeping the liberated neutrons in the fissioning material, ensuring a continuing reaction rather than a "fizzle." "Critical mass" is that amount of fissionable material required to ensure that enough neutrons are liberated to continue the chain reaction, even with tamper material in place. Critical mass is about 2.2 pounds of fissionable uranium, which would produce energy equal to some ten thousand tons of TNT.

The rest of the science is essentially about fine-tuning. The challenge is to get the correct type of fissionable material, in the correct amount, bombarded by the correctly moving neutrons. The element uranium, like all other elements, comes in various forms, depending on how many neutron isotopes it contains. All uranium has 92 protons, but U235, for example, has 143 neutrons, while U238 has 146 neutrons. Within a nucleus, protons typically bind together in pairs, as do neutrons. When there are an odd number of protons or neutrons, the nucleus is less tightly bound and more easily fissioned. So U235, with an odd number of neutrons (143), is an ideal material for splitting, or fissioning, because it is less tightly bound, while U238 (with 146 neutrons) will not split easily. The problem is finding sufficient quantities of U235. Uranium is scarce, and it is almost all U238. U235 is extremely rare—just one in 139 natural uranium nuclei are U235; all the rest are U238. The problem of isolating the U235 was solved through a process of isotope separation—an extraordinarily intensive process that leads to "enriched uranium," essentially increasing the ratio of U235 to U238. (The remaining U238 is considered "depleted uranium" and has other applications.) Isotope separation can be accomplished through a variety of means, including use of a cyclotron or centrifuge.[26] In 1938, the U.S. had nine cyclotrons, with twenty-seven under construction. Germany had at least four and had commissioned others.[27] Electro-magnetic separation, another method, uses huge magnets powered by massive amounts of electricity to separate by magnetic force. Isotope separation can also be accomplished by diffusion, forcing the gaseous products through a series of thousands of membranes that separate them. These technologies are large and complex enough to cost billions of dollars, and they are extremely time- and labor-intensive. Even today, a developed country's ability to produce U235 is measured in months and years, not days.

This knowledge, which we take for granted today, was all being discovered largely by trial and error, a fraction of a step at a time.

Harteck's team of just eight physicists, using an ultra-centrifuge or double-centrifuge method that exchanged separating gases back and forth between two connected centrifuges, was able to enrich as much as fifty grams of uranium a day from its natural state of 0.007 percent (1 in 139 nuclei) to 15 percent, according to the Allies' analysis[28]—not enough for a reaction, but sufficient over time for a dirty bomb.

Another practical difficulty: once a chain reaction begins, the critical mass of U235 instantly superheats and turns into gas, expanding as it does so, spreading out the molecules. As the distance between its gaseous molecules increases, the distance the liberated neutrons need to travel to impact another atom to sustain the fissioning process increases, and if it increases too much, the reaction shuts down. This complication was not completely surmounted even by the Manhattan Project before the U.S. bombs fell on Japan—the first bomb caused fission in only some two percent of its fissionable U235.

Neutrons come in slow and fast varieties. Fast neutrons must be available to sustain a chain reaction as the superheated uranium turns to gas and expands as the reaction begins. Thus a "moderator" is used to slow down the fast neutrons as they enter the reaction in the first instance. Moderators are especially important in slowing or controlling a chain reaction for use in a power-generating reactor. Moderators can be hydro-carbon-based materials such as graphite, paraffin, or heavy water, or even dry ice, all of which slow down the fast neutrons without absorbing them.

● ● ●

We do not claim that Germany made a bomb, or was even close. But the Germans were heavily engaged in nuclear weapons research, they thought they were further along than the Allies, and the German hierarchy considered using a nuclear weapon. And Hans Kammler was involved.

The American research effort, the Manhattan Project, was a huge undertaking with thousands working in concert to crack the problem of an atomic bomb. But, as Colm informed me, that is not necessarily the only approach that could have worked. Even without an operational nuclear bomb, the Germans might have gotten impressive results with a dirty bomb—radioactive material coupled with an explosive to poison the air, soil, and buildings of an urban center. Such a bomb, which could easily have been delivered by a German rocket, would have undermined Britain's economy and terrorized its citizens. It could even have stopped the D-Day invasion force in its tracks.

And there is further evidence that Germany had a viable nuclear weapons research program. Eight months after the war, the Allied Joint Intelligence Committee, with all the best information, came to the alarming conclusion that unless the Western Allies intervened to staunch the flow of German scientists into the Soviet Union, "the Soviets within a relatively short time may equal U.S. developments in the fields of atomic research and guided missiles."[29] And in fact the Russian project, with the help of these Germans, was quickly successful, with its first known detonation in Kazakhstan in August 1949. And if the Germans' research was half-baked, what could be made of the December 1945 U.S. government memo, quoting a French political report: "industrial production of the German atomic bomb was possible in six months' time"?[30] And how to account for the October 12, 1945, U.S. Army Corps of Engineers memo discussing Chinese, Russian, and French demands for the German "secrets of the atomic bomb," and Russian demands to force Czech general Bocek, their military liaison to the Allies, "to turn over German wartime plans, models, formulas, parts pertaining to atom bombs, new rockets and weapons, etc."[31] We also have a July 1944 report—note that this is just one month after D-Day—based on amassed intelligence, that Germany had been working steadily and successfully toward nuclear weaponization, along with a doomsday scenario under which Germany could be producing one nuclear device every month.[32]

In another document provided to the authors in response to a FOIA request, a May 1944 meeting with the deputy commissioner of the United States Strategic Air Force Operations (USSTAF) and others, including Vyacheslav Molotov, is recounted. At the meeting, just before D-Day, consideration was given to dropping Allied investigatory teams behind lines immediately after the war was over to ferret out nuclear research unknown to the Allies—on account of "concern that the Germans had an atomic bomb in development."[33]

High-level Russian army officers believed the Germans had actually tested nuclear weapons. Consider a compelling report in which the head of the Chief Intelligence Department of the Red Army, Lieutenant General Iliychev, informed the head of the Army's General Headquarters, General Antonov, that on March 23, 1945, a small "atomic bomb" had been detonated at Ohrdruf in central Germany, the site of the first Nazi concentration camp liberated by the Americans.[34] Ohrdruf was also the site of S-III, the final, uncompleted underground Hitler headquarters. Naturally, Kammler was in charge of its construction.[35] Because the area fell to the Russians, no Western Ally testing for radioactivity at the site of the alleged explosion was done after the war. Testing decades later was negative,[36] but would the radioactive signature of a small nuclear device be measurable so many years later, presumably after clean-up, at a time when Hiroshima was a teeming, reborn metropolis? Interestingly, during a 1962 tribunal in Arnstadt, only ten miles from Ohrdruf as the crow flies, local residents confirmed having witnessed a small atomic test in March 1945.[37] Speer was also questioned on Germany's atomic research at Nuremberg,[38] and Patton's intelligence man reported on POW accounts of the same.[39] Adding to the intrigue, we know Kammler and Himmler together rented a hunting lodge in the area in February 1945.[40]

There is also the fascinating case of the U-234, a Type XB, at 2,710 tons, the largest of Germany's many underwater ships, that departed the German-controlled port in Norway on March 25, 1945, and surrendered to the Americans off the Newfoundland coast in May 1945—just after Germany's capitulation. She was reportedly bound for Japan in a last-gasp effort to fortify Japan with German technology and make sure the German tech did not die with the Third Reich. The *New York Times* reported a spectacular claim that the sub carried exotic cargo, including some twelve hundred pounds of uranium oxide.[41] A contemporary memorandum cataloguing the cargo prepared for the Joint Chiefs of Staff includes "over 1,000 pounds of uranium oxide,"[42] reportedly sealed in cylinders "lined with gold," a device near perfect for containing enriched uranium but an incomprehensibly extravagant waste to contain nearly any other material.[43]

Carter Plymton Hydrick convincingly argues in a well-documented book that even after victory in Europe, America's atomic bomb needed to be completed hurriedly and dropped before the Russians could invade Japan and take Asian territory for their own. Hydrick extensively documents the story of the U-234 and claims that the U.S. bombs dropped on Japan were made possible only by the German materials aboard the U-234 (the enriched uranium for the first bomb, a uranium bomb) and German technology (the elaborately timed trigger mechanism in the second bomb, a plutonium bomb, requiring the detonation of sixty-four switches within 1/50,000th of a second). The first half of this claim is supported by Lieutenant Colonel John Landsdale Jr., a security official of the Manhattan Project, who asserted that the German uranium went into the mix of materials for the first atom bomb: "It went to the Manhattan District," meaning the Manhattan Project.[44] In its transatlantic journey, the U-234, supposedly bound for Japan with its technological treasures and materials, meandered inexplicably, was allowed to pass unmolested by more than one patrol of U.S. warplanes, and ultimately was detected by the Canadians in their waters, but insisted on surrendering to the U.S.[45] We do not need to accept Hydrick's final conclusions to acknowledge the strength of his argument that there was a substantial, successful uranium enrichment program in Germany[46] and plenty of fissile material—and yet conventional history knows nothing of either one. It is well-known that from very early in the war the Germans controlled Europe's most productive uranium mine in Czechoslovakia.[47]

One implication of the U-234 story did not become apparent until late in our research. Astonishingly, Colm had learned of a direct Kammler connection to the U-234: the husband of Jutta's lifelong friend was on that U-boat, an odd coincidence that made the U-234's trip worth another hard look. If a Kammler family friend was aboard, might Kammler have had something to do with the U-234, perhaps always bound for the U.S., rather than Japan? Colm made a new sweep through the U-234 material and sent me an early morning email about the results of his all-nighter: "The U-234 manifest included not only uranium, we knew that, but also Junkers aircraft plans, Junkers engines, three complete Messerschmitts (including a dismantled, crated Me 262, the jet, and the Me 163), BMW designs, 30 tons of mercury for extremely high-speed switches needed for an implosion-type nuclear weapon, V-1 and V-2 plans, aircraft factory plans, plans for several different U-boats and surface ships, bombsights, radar, and an Hs 293, one of Kammler's pet projects." The Hs 293 was a radio-controlled Henschel-guided missile dispatched successfully, sinking many Allied ships.

"Interesting," I wrote back, in the midst of my morning routine, getting ready to leave for work. "But what does that mean to us?" I had no idea where he was heading with this.

"Dean, the manifest looks like the U-boat was packed *personally* by Kammler. Virtually everything on the list is something that Kammler was working on, or something he oversaw. Virtually everything. The cargo document reads like he was filling a Christmas list the American military brass put together. I think the U-234 was part of the Kammler Deal, Dean."

Well, that was new, I thought. "Can we prove it?"

Colm sent another missive, our emails crossing in the ether: "The 293 was invented by Herbert A. Wagner. He was a Kammler man." Colm provided a few links to materials on Wagner. He was one of Kammler's Nordhausen rocket scientists, an expert on guided missiles and radio control and the inventor of the Hs 293. Another strong link between the U-234 and Kammler. Wagner's value was high enough that he had a seat on Kammler's *Vengeance Express* to Oberammergau. He wasn't on the U-boat, but his work was, and, according to a recent book on Operation Paperclip, Wagner was among the first scientists to come to the U.S. under that program, arriving at Fort Detrick, in Frederick, Maryland— the center of American biological weapons research—the very month the war concluded. Wagner traveled covertly in a "military aircraft with the windows blackened to keep anyone from seeing who was inside."[48]

"Hmm," I wrote back, fumbling for a tie in the morning darkness, my face illuminated by my iPhone, with Mia, my dog, urging me downstairs for her breakfast while Colm urged me to take a new step in our journey. I had actually spent my high school years in Frederick, Maryland, because my father was stationed at Fort Detrick—so that was interesting.

"Everyone has assumed the U-234 was always bound for Japan, to bolster the fight against mutual enemies, that Germany was basically tagging out, turning everything over to Japan. But the transport of every one of these items works even better as part of the Kammler Deal!" Colm's rare use of the exclamation point did not go unnoticed.

"You think Kammler sent the sub to the U.S.?"

"I can't say that for sure. But think about it. Hydrick catalogues its route. Given the date it put out, she should have been well south of the U.S. by the time the war ended, but she basically wandered across the North Atlantic. Not only that, she surfaced more than once, was sighted by U.S. planes, and was allowed to proceed unmolested. I think the U-boat was just waiting for the right moment to give up. The Americans knew it was on the way. Its crew was held in secret, and the list of cargo was embargoed for the entire cold war." I'd never heard of a German U-boat being given safe passage.

"This is major," Keith weighed in. Obviously, he had been lurking in the background of our email chat. He took his turn at bat: "Colm's right. I don't know how we missed it before. Only Kammler could have authorized this. And the Jutta connection is solid." Keith meant the officer on board, the husband of Jutta's "best girlfriend," Carmen von Sandrat. Jutta and Carmen had known each other since childhood and stayed in touch throughout their lives long after the war.

"So, both the contents and the personnel on board point to Kammler's involvement. With the uranium aboard, it provides another link between Kammler and nuclear research," Colm stated flatly.

I mulled. The timing of the U-234 voyage was interesting, I thought. How long would it take for Kammler to gather all this cargo? A week? Two weeks? I quickly checked the departure of the U-boat against other known dates and found what I thought was a perfect "match." The U-234 slipped out of the Norway port, laden with its technological treasures, less than a week after the pronouncement of Hitler's scorched earth policy, the "Nero Decree," which called for the destruction of all Germany's resources and technology—the order Kammler had to ignore to make the Kammler Deal work. If Kammler was going to ignore that order—and we have proved that he did—the perfect first step would be to secretly ship as much technology as possible beyond Hitler's control. It seemed pretty likely that Kammler had engineered the U-234's journey.

"I'm convinced," I wrote to Colm and Keith before I slipped off to work.

● ● ●

It was easy to believe that when Germany unexpectedly found itself in a protracted war, Hitler's earlier decision to curtail nuclear weapons research was revisited. Kammler had such broad authority and power it was precisely the type of project he could have initiated on his own, with bountiful SS resources and with SS security layered on top to ensure its secrecy. As plenipotentiary for rocket and jet-powered weapons research, Kammler could easily have been involved in the work of various teams known to have been working toward an atom bomb, or even headed an entirely unknown and insulated team also pursuing nuclear weapons. After all, research on biological warfare continued under Himmler, despite a 1942 Hitler order banning it.[49]

"What about ALSOS?" I asked Colm. ALSOS was the Allied intelligence mission that reviewed German research facilities as they were captured, charged with finding any and all nuclear research.

"Great question," Colm conceded. "The Farm Hill transcripts, along with the ALSOS findings, are probably the two most significant points people make when concluding the Germans had no viable nuclear research project."

"Agreed."

"You've already undermined the Farm Hill transcripts. Take a look at ALSOS and all the rest of it, like the lawyer you are, and make the best case against it."

That was challenge I couldn't resist, and Colm knew it. So I spent days and countless hours studying the records of the Allied pursuit of German technology. And in those records I came across numerous indications that the Germans were working toward a nuclear bomb, or at least a dirty bomb.

First, Allied personnel were enormously worried about ongoing German nuclear weapons research. That might reflect judicious caution, or might indicate Allied knowledge of German activity never publicly disclosed. Second, the Allied search for German nuclear research efforts during and after the war was severely flawed, and its conclusions are hard to accept without reservations. Third, the Japanese managed to conduct a broad bioweapons research program that went completely undetected by the Allies until after the war, and the Americans tried to conceal it when they finally discovered it. Germany itself had very large facilities of various types completely unknown to the Allies during the war. Fourth, a single German research program, or even a series of research efforts, might easily have been discovered after the war and not been disclosed by the Western Allies, or might have been covered up and exploited by the Soviets if discovered in the Russian Zone of Occupation.

Fifth, we have a collection of miscellaneous statements and activities that support the thesis that the Germans were working toward nuclear weapons. Finally, and definitively, Keith and Colm unearthed documents that actually describe a Nazi nuclear weapons research program overseen by Kammler.

First, the Allies acted during the war as if Germany might have a nuclear weapon, or at least a dirty bomb. Fear that the Germans might unleash a radioactive attack against troops storming the Normandy beaches went all the way to the top, to the commanding officers with the greatest access to intelligence reports and insights into Germany's weapons programs. General Eisenhower himself issued a memo calling for reports of blackening of photographic or x-ray film at the beach landing sites on D-Day. Geiger counters and fifteen hundred film packs were used to monitor radioactivity during the landing.

On the home front, when the first V-1s began raining down on London, scientists were rushed to the impact craters with Geiger counters to satisfy Churchill and the War Cabinet that the flying bombs did not carry radioactive elements. General Leslie Groves—the director of the Manhattan Project, no less—said then what is well-known today: "Radioactive materials are extremely effective contaminating agents." And he explained that those materials "are known to the Germans; can be produced by them, and could be employed by them as a military weapon."[50] The Brits even invented a radioactivity-sensing device and placed it in the nose cone of low-flying aircraft to sweep through Germany-controlled territory to locate nuclear research sites. Were these measures, taken by the men with the greatest insider knowledge, all extravagant excesses?

At the Norsk Hydroelectric plant in Norway the Germans produced heavy water for their nuclear research.[51] This is a fact. And the Allies went to extraordinary lengths to destroy Germany's supply. They bombed the Norsk plant in 1943 after a team of commandos on the ground failed to destroy it. Later in February 1944, when it was discovered that a large cache of heavy water still existed and was being shipped into Germany, the Allies worked with resistance fighters to sink the ferry used for one leg of the journey in one of Europe's deepest lakes, further squeezing the supply.[52] These were very dangerous steps for the Allies to have taken if they did not believe the Germans were actively engaged in nuclear weapons research.

● ● ●

Second, the search for nuclear research facilities as the Allies retook territory, and even after the war, was severely flawed in multiple ways, and we can completely demolish the findings, which are the foundation for the consensus that German nuclear research did not make much progress during the war. ALSOS was essentially handed the impossible task of proving a negative. I believe this intelligence mission underperformed and overstated results.

In *The ALSOS Mission*, Colonel Boris T. Pash described in detail the work of ALSOS, the code-name mission he led uncovering German nuclear research installations throughout the Reich and determining what progress they had made. ALSOS's work was bold, daring, and dangerous. They not only seized documents and research equipment, but also captured key German nuclear scientists—including Otto Hahn, Kurt Diebner, and Werner Heisenberg.[53] As the leader of an earlier stateside investigation into leaks of the Manhattan Project, Pash understood the stakes. But having been so intimately involved with the gigantic Manhattan Project, Pash was understandably looking for something similarly large in Germany.

Pash's work on ALSOS began in Italy, followed the advancing Allied forces north to Rome, and then jumped into France and Germany,[54] where he headed a number of investigative teams. He proudly recounted that his jeep was the second Allied vehicle to break through to Paris, following the lead tank. The ALSOS effort was certainly serious and a high priority. But Pash inexplicably reports that his Strasbourg team, on France's eastern border with Germany "exploded the super-weapon myth that had so alarmed Allied leaders,"[55]—by which he meant that it was in Strasbourg that he concluded Germany was never a nuclear threat.[56]Apparently Pash's team found no significant nuclear technology or research in Strasbourg, but it is difficult to understand how Pash could reach such a sweeping negative conclusion about the entire Nazi nuclear program before he had even set foot in Germany. Unfortunately, all ALSOS work from this point forward was done with a bias toward confirming the premature, unqualified conclusions of Pash's team. One ALSOS report, for example, concluded incorrectly that only German projects connected with the Kaiser Wilhelm Institute were working on the "uranium problem."[57]

Following behind the battle lines as closely as possible, Pash's men swept into known and suspected research sites, hoping to take control before retreating Germans could move or destroy records and instrumentation, and before Allied soldiers began looting and souvenir-taking. Still, we know the Germans did manage to remove key information and equipment, even entire factories.[58] A nuclear weapons research project could have been evacuated with all its equipment and papers before Pash arrived. In many cases, ALSOS team members complained that they had arrived at a site only to find severe bombing damage or cabinets of empty files—evacuated[59] or destroyed by the Nazis[60] or pilfered by early-arriving Allied forces.[61] Some German scientists admitted to destroying their scientific records on orders that had gone out to all researchers.[62]

Pash's lead technical assistant in ALSOS was Samuel Goudsmit, who was, remarkably, not a nuclear physicist.[63] In one memorandum, Goudsmit, venting his frustration at not finding relevant information, noted that the only way to find "the real secret progress reports" of Germany's nuclear weapons research would be in "a rapid surprise move" forward before the secret facilities could be destroyed or evacuated.[64] As there never was a "rapid surprise move" forward, I am left thinking that the chief technical advisor of the mission was never satisfied that ALSOS had examined all the relevant information.

It is also quite likely the ALSOS team overlooked sites. Its mission was so secret that even CIOS documents of the era only vaguely, even mysteriously, call it the "Special Section set up for investigating German secret processes."[65] Consequently it is unclear that other Allied forces would have known to funnel any information on nuclear research that they happened to discover and recognize to ALSOS.

In addition, when the earliest stages of the ALSOS mission reported little evidence of a successful German nuclear research program, the scope of the mission was expanded and consequently diluted.[66] ALSOS was thereafter charged with ferreting out scientific research in fields including bacteriological warfare, aeronautical research, proximity fuses, guided missiles, chemical and metallurgical research, and even shale oil research. In any case, even before Goudsmit came on board as chief scientific advisor, ALSOS's mandate had been changed to include only "problems of research and early development," as opposed to projects up and running.[67] Consequently, not only was there no unified Allied mission searching exclusively for German nuclear research, but no one— no one—was tasked with finding developed nuclear research. In other words, ALSOS's remit was a mile wide and an inch deep with a team barely exceeding one hundred men at its peak.[68] Even by Goudsmit's own account, the "amount of material, such as documents, personnel and laboratories, encountered during operations was so overwhelming that no intelligence agency of reasonable size could handle it all."[69] That statement by a lead official of the mission is mind-boggling, particularly given its sweeping and unqualified conclusions.

In addition to mission creep, ALSOS suffered poor communication once team members were deployed to individual and dispersed sites. This meant those teams made decisions on site without coordination. A final but jarring methodological flaw was ALSOS's exclusive reliance on pre-war information to identify targets to be investigated: "It must be noted that no information on scientific targets was made available through intelligence channels, and that all information was, therefore, based upon pre-war knowledge."[70] That is, ALSOS targets were identified only by information from the late 1930s. Having admitted this in his report, Goudsmit went on to describe some up-to-date intelligence information that ALSOS did receive as helpful, but fragmentary. The war had begun only months after German chemist Otto Hahn reported his seminal nuclear discovery, and Germany's nuclear program began only later. Would a fractured, roving intelligence commission trying to unearth evidence of an American nuclear program by examining only pre-war research and pre-war sites even have found the Manhattan Project?

In his report judging that the Germans made practically no progress in the nuclear field, Goudsmit makes a categorical assertion of a sort virtually never seen in government intelligence documents—a claim of complete finality: "It is certain that complete research data and all key scientists fell into the hands of the Alsos Mission."[71] That claim is even more jaw-droppingly astonishing given Goudsmit's completely contradictory characterization of the project as "so overwhelming that no intelligence agency of reasonable size could handle it all." Goudsmit knew that ALSOS was trying to collect information from an enemy that had multiple unconnected and uncoordinated veins of research—"parallel developments"[72] that could be confusing or misleading. How could he claim with such certainty that ALSOS had uncovered every parallel stream of research?

Perhaps more frankly, another ALSOS team member, Gerard Kuiper, wrote in March 1945 in a private correspondence, "One is again surprised to see quotations from U.S. senators who think that the war will be over 'within a few days.' It would be wiser to worry about the chance we still have of losing if certain high explosives are developed in time. This possibility may, incidentally, be one reason the Germans are not giving in."[73]

In addition, a lengthy U.S. Army report written decades after the war notes offhandedly that ALSOS never ventured into territory that would end up in the Russian Zone and was slow to explore the territory to be ceded to other Allies—terrain the report identified as singularly important, home to most of Germany's nuclear research. "Data uncovered in

Heidelberg also further substantiated earlier evidence that most of the other important German atomic scientists and their research installations were in the region south and east of Stuttgart. But ALSOS penetration of this area posed a problem because of the decision by the Allied leaders in early 1945 that it fell within the French zone of operations."[74] In the end, ALSOS made a mad dash into that area just before the French took over—only to hastily verify the conclusion they had already reached at Strasbourg.

In summary, I have no confidence in a search for German nuclear weapons research by an entity that was searching for scientific research projects of virtually every sort and which had often been plundered or evacuated, that suffered from poor communication, that complained it was understaffed, that based its search for cutting edge technology on information more than five years old, that covered only parts of the territory where the targeted research could have been conducted, and that purported to reach a starkly definitive conclusion in a search it said no intelligence agency could handle. But of course, this does not prove Germany *did* make progress; it just proves the infirmity of America's claim it did not.

Is it possible that Pash actually did make positive findings about Nazi nuclear research, findings that were never widely publicized but instead followed him quietly into his subsequent career with the CIA, the agency Allen Dulles would lead? It seems possible and defensible that an intelligence agency careerist could be ordered to suppress information about German progress on an atomic bomb for legitimate national security reasons, such as keeping valuable information out of the hands of the Soviets.[75] That makes more sense than the muddle I found in ALSOS's own reports and the memoirs of its leaders.

● ● ●

Third, consider the World War II–era research of Japan into chemical and biological weapons. It was barbaric. The Japanese bioweapons program run by "Unit 731" used human subjects—including captured Allied servicemen—as guinea pigs in experiments designed to test the effects of lethal diseases and poisons on the human body in a search for the deadliest chemicals and organisms. The program included uncontrolled field tests that intentionally exposed enemy civilians and prisoners to virulent biological agents. The research was widespread, conducted in occupied portions of Manchuria, China, and other countries. It was systematic and prolonged, having persisted for several years, with regular reports to and with the consent of Japan's central government. And it was completely and utterly unknown to the Allies during the war. This cuts in favor of the possibility that Germany could have operated a nuclear weapons research program unknown to the Allies.

Disturbingly, all information about the Japanese biological weapons program was kept in U.S. intelligence files and never presented in war crimes files or trials. The researchers were granted immunity by the U.S.—a fact that militates in favor of the conclusion that the Americans could have seen their way clear to giving Kammler immunity. After all, as we have demonstrated, Kammler was also handled through intelligence channels and kept out of the hands of the war crimes prosecutors.

● ● ●

Fourth, it is possible a German nuclear weapons research program was discovered by the Allies, but concealed. When Japan's biowarfare experiments eventually became known to the Americans, the Americans worked hard to conceal them because they wanted the research results and to incorporate all that knowledge into their own bio and chemical weapons programs. And if word of Japan's experiments on human subjects had surfaced, either through leaks or in public war crimes trials, the data could have been ruled off-limits. So the Americans deep-sixed every shred of evidence they gathered about Japan's program in U.S. intelligence files, where it would never be available to war crimes investigators or prosecutors. The official report of the special working group convened to analyze the pros and cons of prosecuting the Japanese scientists involved in these horrific experiments concluded, "The value to the U.S. of Japanese BW [biological warfare] data is of such importance to national security as to far outweigh the value accruing from 'war crimes' prosecutions." And as if we needed more evidence of America's readiness to conceal secret Axis research, even when it came to experiments on its own captured men, a March 1947 order from the U.S. Joint Chiefs of Staff said of the Japanese biological experiments, "The utmost secrecy is essential in order to protect the interests of the United States and to guard against embarrassment."[76]

A December 12, 1947, memo written by the Chief of Basic Sciences at Fort Detrick's biological warfare research facility in Maryland betrays America's position: "Evidence gathered in this investigation has greatly supplemented and amplified previous aspects of this field. It represents data, which have been obtained by Japanese scientists at the expenditure of many millions of dollars and years of work. Information has accrued with respect to human susceptibility to those diseases as indicated by specific infectious doses of bacteria."[77] Then comes a statement that explicitly recognized the illegitimacy of the methods used in the original experiments: "Such information could not be obtained in our own laboratories because of scruples attached to human experimentation."[78]

American officials were also worried that "public disclosure" of the Japanese biological weapons research could "assist the Soviet BW program"[79]—something that would have been equally true of any German nuclear research discovered by the Western Allies. So there would have been a double motive for keeping it secret: the Americans' desire to exploit the information for their own, coupled with the need to prevent its disclosure to the Soviets. Similarly, suppressing any information the United States had on a viable Nazi atomic weapons program would have been deemed in the country's national security interest.

• • •

Fifth, in addition to those already quoted above, many other war-era statements and activities suggest that a German weapons program existed. Krafft Ehricke, a Peenemünde rocket scientist, quoted Heisenberg as saying flatly, "Of course one could build an atomic bomb."[80] When General Karl Wolff and General Joachim von Ribbentrop met with Himmler on February 6, 1945, urging a negotiated peace with the Western Allies, "Hitler hinted at a weapon of extermination so appalling in its results that it would only be used in the worst emergencies."[81] This was after the V-1 and V-2 missiles had been revealed in battle, so Hitler could not have been referring to them. The existence of a spectacular secret weapon could help explain Germany's tenacity—some would say obstinacy—in the final stages of the war. As U.S. brigadier general Oscar W. Koch, the Third Army's intelligence officer, would write after the war, "Why did Hitler keep going? Did he plan to hold the Siegfried line at all costs? Was he trading space for time to develop a secret weapon to supplant the Luftwaffe, to no practical intent?"[82]

Dornberger stated in a post-war interview with U.S. military officials that just before Germany's final collapse nuclear scientist Heisenberg was supposed to make a report to him of his most recent progress—a report that never came. (Do note yet another link between the nuclear research and the rocket program, but set that aside for now.) Dornberger also said that "11 war technical projects in Germany were kept secret and very little information was exchanged between the various groups" and concluded, "It is considered improbable that anyone should know of any further work accomplished unless it was in his specifically assigned duties."[83] Dornberger was describing a widely dispersed program of research, compartmentalized and organized on a need-to-know basis. Such a program could have produced jumps forward in nuclear research each of which, in isolation from the others, seemed insignificant. Real progress, the full accounting of the success of the overall project, would be known only to those at the top, who could see the progress made by

every one of those eleven groups. This is precisely the kind of structure
Pash and his ALSOS team, looking for something like the massive, centralized Manhattan Project, would have overlooked. It was also precisely
the arrangement used by I. G. Farben in its secret development of poison
gases, for so long unknown to the Allies.[84]

We know there were large Kammler-built underground German
installations that were completely unknown to the Allies until they
stumbled upon them after the war.[85] Could one or more of them have
been a nuclear site? Remember that Nordhausen was ultimately discovered by the Allies only via aerial reconnaissance—not human intelligence. The SS controlled the land on all sides of its research facilities for
miles and constantly policed access, limiting access through a number
of mountain passes, even using a marauding platoon of tanks. Still more
layers of security within the factory were provided by the Gestapo, and
the even more dreaded Ober-Gestapo or SD (Sicherheitsdienst), with its
covert man in every department and a "secret manager" providing intelligence security. Kammler even had his own personal security forces,
which he deployed strategically at his most important and hyper-secure
sites. Speer remarked that Kammler had frightening powers through this
security department: "Kammler could order the arrest of any person
who, in his opinion, interfered unwarrantedly with the measures he
ordered. Since he made absolute ruthless use of this power, even against
SS officers, there was no way that people or agencies could interfere with
the most important aspect of Kammler's duties."[86]

Even the building phases of SS projects Kammler headed were locked
down. Designs for new SS construction sites were distributed in four
parts, by relay teams: "Each part was wholly unintelligible without the
other three parts."[87] Couriers would take plans only a portion of the way
from their point of origin to the ultimate facility site, turning them over
to a second courier. The first did not know the ultimate destination,
while the second did not know the point of origin. A Kammler-run
nuclear research program that remained secret throughout the war is by
no means implausible.

There was nothing fanciful about making an atomic weapon a reality. It was not easy, to be sure, but it was theoretically possible and would in fact be achieved. Colm assured me that quite a small team could have built a German atomic weapon, or at least a dirty bomb. Paul Harteck, the Hamburg physicist, commented after the war that radioactive isotopes he had developed via his ultracentrifuge could have devastated London, discussing the possibility of a dirty bomb.[88]

One must allow for the possibility that somewhere, in some corner of the Reich, a small handful of Kammler-led "mad scientists" were working off the grid toward a bomb. Even if Hitler thought a nuclear weapon could not be completed before the end of the war, someone of Kammler's character would rather have one than not.

● ● ●

In a call with Colm one evening when Keith must have been unavailable, I asked a straightforward question: "Can we link these contemplated German nuclear bombs or dirty bombs to Germany's rockets?"

"Well," Colm began his wind-up, "within a month after the end of the war,[89] U.S. bombing specialist Colonel Peter Beasley, a name I know rings a bell with you, said of the future of the V-2, 'It will have heat-seeking or other homing devices which will enable it to crash an atomic warhead into a city continents away—a few minutes after takeoff.'[90] In my view, Dean, it's simply not possible that Beasley, an outsider to the German rocket team, could so quickly pair the V-2 and an atomic weapon in his mind without Kammler, von Braun, Dornberger and others in Germany having thought the same. Surely that was the future Kammler envisioned for the V-2."

"Anything else?" I asked, almost afraid of the answer.

"Schumann and Diebner's work in Gottow was so close to the original rocket research program in Kummersdorf I think they had to be linked. From the beginning. Later they would transfer to Ilm, Thuringia, again alongside the relocated rocket research team." Later I would

confirm something I thought I had down correctly: the statement of
Hauptman Wagner, a German prisoner of war, that Schumann was
"frequently in consultation" with the V-1 and V-2 rocket programs,[91]
showing an undeniable link between Germany's known nuclear research
and the rocket program.

I also knew that physicist von Ardenne, his patron Dr. Wilhelm
Ohnesorge of the Reich Postal Ministry, and Kammler were as thick as
thieves. Himmler even recommended Kammler and Dornberger as board
members for the high frequency research being done at von Ardenne's
installation.[92] We also have documentary evidence linking von Ardenne
and his underground lab in Berlin Lichterfelde to experiments with von
Braun and the V-1 on the Baltic Coast.[93] In a document never before
published, conversations of German lieutenant general Heinrich Kittel
were secretly recorded while he was a prisoner of war. In one of those
conversations General Kittel emphatically discussed Germany's experiments with "the atom bomb," carried out on Bornholm Island in the
Baltic, very near the experiments to which we've linked von Ardenne.[94]
A second document Keith discovered shows remarkably high radioactivity levels on Bornholm, which could be explained by atomic research or
perhaps just as likely by rich uranium deposits.[95] Bornholm's role as an
atomic research site has been little understood, though it was the subject
of brief discussion in the British Houses of Parliament just two months
after Hiroshima, with a question posed to the prime minister about
contact with atomic research scientists on the island.

"Dean, don't forget that Carl Friedrich von Weizsacker, the nobleman who lived until 2007, the son of a German diplomat and himself
the father of 'die Lesart,' [the agreement the German scientists at Farm
Hall made to deny that they had been working toward an atom bomb]
was connected to the rocket team through von Braun's brother, Sigismund. Remember our speculation that Sigismund and Ernst von Weizsacker were involved in the Lisbon outreach by Dornberger and Wernher
von Braun." I began to wonder, were there any German nuclear scientists
not tied to the rocket scientists?

There was still more to link nuclear weapons to Kammler's rockets. The Manhattan Project's General Groves was told by Navy captain William Sterling Parsons that the "larger stations" located next to the German rocket launching sites for the V-1 and V-2 on the coast of France, the massive concrete fixed bunkers, were likely constructed to produce "radioactive poisons evolved from disintegration of products of a [nuclear] pile" to be placed into a missile's warhead. "It is unnecessary to picture the destructive possibilities,"[96] Parsons warned ominously. Parsons, no alarmist, was particularly well credentialed to form this opinion—he was associate director of the Manhattan Project and rode on the Enola Gay to Hiroshima, arming the nuclear weapon en route.

Separately, reconnaissance expert Colonel Roy Stanley II noted that some Allied researchers who inspected the fixed Vengeance Weapons launch facilities on the northern coast of France after the war found rooms designed for isolation, in his words "suggesting anticipation of nuclear or chemical weapons." He conceded that other researchers disputed the assessment, but he sided with those making the case in the affirmative, pointing out that "there is no indication that the nay-sayers have ever set foot in one of the destroyed V-2 bunkers."[97] Those who had seen the V-2 launch sites after they were captured agreed—those V-2 sites were nuke-ready.

"There is also an overlooked part of the post-war transcripts," Colm continued his presentation. "Dornberger, so central to the rocket team, in a secretly recorded post-war statement of his own, mentions Germany's nuclear research, trying to split the atom through 'disintegration' rather than the outright 'destruction' of the atom.[98] Why would Dornberger have access to this research information unless the rockets were directly involved? And remember Dornberger is on record as expecting to receive a report from Heisenberg himself on progress in Germany's nuclear research."

Dornberger even said, "I wanted Professor Braun to give us a lecture on the atom bomb, as the results of the research work could have materially influenced the development on the Vengeance Weapons." Dornberger and von Braun both believed that the research on atomic weapons "could have materially influenced the development of the Vengeance Weapons."[99]

Dornberger was not the only high-level German officer who believed Kammler was working to pair nuclear weaponry with the Vengeance Weapons. Himmler's chief adjutant, Werner Grothmann, known to be a friend of Kammler's, stated that Kammler was in charge of active nuclear tests.[100] "Dean," Colm told me, "it's just crazy to believe that Kammler headed both rockets and a nuclear testing project without trying to combine the two. That would have been Step One for him!"

Then I offered something up to Colm: "One commonsense argument is worth making. The V-2 had great range and a large payload, but we know it lacked a proximity fuse, so it exploded ten feet below ground. The V-2 was also vastly more expensive to produce than was the V-1, costing ten to twenty times as much to manufacture, making some question its value,[101] though its longer range did allow the Germans to continue to menace England after retreating, when ground launches of the V-1 would have fallen short. Maybe research on the V-2 continued only because Kammler and others were striving towards at least a dirty bomb payload, or a chemical or biological payload, which would have multiplied its destructive force exponentially. The V-2 makes altogether more sense as a delivery platform for a nuclear payload."

"So does another rocket under Kammler's domain, the Rheinbote. Take a look at it, too," Colm suggested.

I did. We are in good company in identifying the Rheinbote as a possible mode of delivery for a nuclear weapon. In 1945, a joint American, English, and Austrian technical commission struck upon the Rheinbote as a possible bearer of an atomic payload. The Rheinbote had gone into development in 1943, not long after Germany reportedly closed down its research into nuclear weaponization. Kammler was the driving force behind the Rheinbote's development, and he personally oversaw the firing of two hundred Rheinbotes during the Battle of the Bulge. A solid-fuel missile, it had superior dependability and stability on the launch pad and in flight—something that would be highly desirable when launching a nuclear weapon.

Author and German historian Heinrich Klein explained that a Lieutenant Colonel Troller, a member of the German Rheinbote firing unit, admitted to him that there had been discussions in August 1944 about the feasibility of outfitting the Rheinbote V-3 with an atomic warhead.[102] These discussions, it seems, were between Troller and Kammler. Armed with a small nuclear device, the Rheinbote could have destroyed the heart of a major city from a hundred miles away. It had nearly the same range as the V-2, but was much smaller and delivered a meager forty-five-pound payload of high explosives, compared to the V-2's twenty-two-hundred-pound payload, nearly fifty times the explosive force if conventional explosives were used. In fact, the Rheinbote made a lot more sense as a device for delivering nukes than conventional weapons; launching a four-stage thirty-seven-feet nearly two-ton rocket to deliver forty-five pounds of conventional explosives was akin to sending heavy bombers to drop a bee hive.[103]

After miles of work, I believe our team assembled a good case that German nuclear science went on longer and made greater strides than conventional history allows. This research could well have been part of the Kammler Deal. We make an even stronger case that the rocket team was in touch with the nuclear researchers, and a long-range missile with a nuclear payload (at least a dirty bomb) was contemplated. Kammler sat atop this structure and squarely behind the thinking.

CHAPTER NINE

Think Tank Kammler

*"In the last years of the war, central command for
the development and manufacturing of the most
secret weapons and equipment was in the hands of
SS Gruppenführer Dr. Kammler and his Special Staff.
It included secret weapons, equipment and proceedings, which were either in use or which were not yet in
use at that time, and as much as I know, this mainly
involved work in the area of atomic fragmentation,
the conversion of the elements, the atomic bomb and
nuclear energy, and additionally rockets, the latest airplane propulsion systems and remote control."*

—Dr. Wilhelm Voss, director of Skoda Armament Works,
Czechoslovakia[1]

It was time for another conference call. We needed all three of us on
this one.

"If any organization could have overseen and kept secret an
atomic bomb program, it was the SS. It was Kammler," I began, convinced of at least the possibility. "But where?"

Keith was first out of the gate. "The most likely locations would be
those never surveyed by ALSOS, and those that fell behind the Iron
Curtain after the war. Unless we want to claim ALSOS found it and
covered it up, it was someplace ALSOS overlooked, or never went, or
misread. The best bet is somewhere they never went."

"Not a short list," this was Colm's bailiwick, "but there are ways to
hone this more precisely. Kammler's oversight of a high-tech weapons
research cell at Skoda would make Czechoslovakia the likely location,

and his highly-specialized SS weapons research Think Tank would have been the perfect vehicle."

"Agoston, Blunder," Keith said.

"Tom Agoston, a British journalist of some renown, discussed this at length in his book *Blunder!* That was the 1980s." Colm clarified.[2] "But no one has since mentioned it, and no one has been able to provide any documentation supporting its existence." Colm had been down this avenue in the past. He had visited Czechoslovakia for the express purpose of touring Skoda, the massive munitions operation with facilities in Prague, Pilsen, Pribram, and elsewhere, still in existence, still thriving.

"I interviewed the current head of archives at the Skoda museum, a nice fellow. But he denies high-tech research took place at Skoda during the war."[3]

"Right," Keith acknowledged, of Dr. Vladislav Kratsky, the archivist, "but we don't think he is credible. There had to be research there. Agoston is very clear on this. He had Voss as a source." Wilhelm Voss was Skoda's director, the man who ran the facility, and a major source for Agoston when he wrote *Blunder!*[4]

"Would he even know?" I asked, referring to the archivist.

"Well, he'd have access to all surviving documents."

"But that's just it," Keith jumped in, "Agoston says the Think Tank documents were taken away." Keith and Colm both continued to insist that Kammler had established a special Think Tank, Working Staff Kammler, within Skoda known only to Hitler and Himmler. Göring and even Hitler's armaments minister, Albert Speer, were totally unaware of the think tank's existence, and it was not limited to rocket research. I'd read *Blunder!* and found it incredible—literally. Unfairly, I realized, Agoston's jacket photo on the book makes him look a little goofy. He also made sweeping statements about things like the ability of the Germans (apparently every single one of them) to remember the smallest details. But he was credentialed—a Cambridge graduate turned journalist—and he had access to key personnel on both sides after the war ended.[5] Agoston had an annoying habit of pretending to know more than he was able to disclose in his writing, but even so he might have been on the right track, for we do know Kammler was involved at Skoda. Checking the summary of my interview with Kammler's son Jörg, I saw I had remembered correctly: Jörg had told me his father had been "involved at Skoda." Not understanding the reference at the time, I had failed to ask any follow-up questions, but at least I could confirm Kammler's engagement there.

"In addition to everything else, that region was the greatest source of uranium at the time, with credible reports of several tons with a purity of 98–99 percent having been produced by the German Degussa company[6] out of the mine in Joachimsthal, just northwest of Prague near the German border. Not fissile material, but hugely valuable nevertheless." Colm was always at the ready with what sounded like esoterica, but was great information.

"Tell me more."

"Skoda," Colm resumed, "headquartered in Prague, consisted of several sites and production plants, with the main production facility in Pilsen, eastern Czechoslovakia, with eighty buildings. Skoda was, recall, the second largest munitions manufacturer on the Continent. In my humble view, possessing the Skoda conglomerate was itself reason enough to explain Germany's pre-war grab for the Sudentenland."[7]

When Walther Gerlach was appointed head of all physics research for Germany, replacing Abraham Esau, he ostensibly oversaw all nuclear research under the Reichsforschugsrat (RFR). The RFR was originally launched by Erich Schumann, a nuclear scientist we've already encountered, and charged with coordinating all nuclear research in Germany, save aeronautical research. It reported for some time to Göring, but Gerlach would regularly report to Himmler, at whose right hand Kammler sat. So the SS was demonstrably in charge of all the nuclear research.

I had to concede that Skoda, in the virtual center of Germany's occupied territory, was the perfect location for an undiscovered nuclear research project overseen by Kammler and guarded by his SS. ALSOS had never been there. As one of the final German holdouts, it was also the ideal place for Kammler's surrender, as it would have allowed him the maximum time to get his house in order. We also knew it was one of the last places Kammler dared to visit before the end of the war, when all was fire and smoke—perhaps to make certain the fruits of that secret project were removed, or at least securely stowed.

Keith and Colm now turned to Kammler's other reason for coming to Czechoslovakia: to secure secret research records from Working Staff Kammler. After the war, neither the U.S. representatives nor even the Czech officials were permitted to enter many of the German Skoda research sites taken over by the Soviets. Czech officials declared all weapons research and experimental information "State Secrets," not to be disclosed to anyone outside the state hierarchy.[8] Much of the equipment and technology was "tagged and sent to Russia."[9] Consequently, to this day the West doesn't know what research was going on in these facilities, including a mysterious underground facility at Podmokly, the subject of post-war correspondence directed to Colonel L. E. Seemans,[10] a Leslie Groves associate involved in the Manhattan Project. "No way Seemans would have been looped in on Top Secret documents that weren't linked to nuclear weapons research," Colm explained, "which makes me suspect it might have been a nuclear research laboratory, and so the Americans thought."

Elsewhere, massive centers of German armaments production— including, for example, a thirty-thousand-man I. G. Farben concern in eastern Czechoslovakia[11]—were never investigated by the Western Allies, even though that site was reportedly producing a "component of a new explosive."[12]

• • •

Colm and Jaro, his treasure-hunting guide, hadn't confined their adventures to the crossroads where Kammler supposedly committed suicide. They had also made a house call in Prague to confront the Czech archive officials about Kammler's diary. From there, they were all over

Czechoslovakia, including Skoda country, trying desperately to pin down details for our story.

"My absolute favorite locale was Rabštejn, right on the Czech-Germany border. We went there after Prague. About sixty or so miles north. A beautiful hilltop town. Picturesque. Enchanting. Very old Europe. It looks like a village one would build for a model train set. The sinister part lay below ground. It's not nearly their largest underground factory, but it's a big one there. Dug by hand, by slaves, like all the others."

"The WFG, Weser Flugzeugbau"—the German name flowed right out of Colm's mouth—"known by the shorthand Weser Werkes, was located within the tunnels, its original above-ground factory having been bombed. They made aircraft, both bombers and fighters. The rumors were this factory also manufactured cyclotrons for atomic research, shipping three out in the last eighteen months of the war. That's per *Time* magazine, November 1945."[13]

"So, was that rumor or fact?" I had Colm on speaker in my office. Keith was incommunicado. I could hear the TV in my family room, Taylor watching a YouTube video about physics. A dish clanged one room further away. That was Hannah making something gluten-free. I got up to close my office door. I still wasn't sure why Colm was telling me about this particular site, of all the ones he had visited.

"I'm not certain myself, but it was the most eerie place I've been in. Ever. Spooky, even." That was odd talk coming from Colm, the scientist. I didn't interrupt. "We had to walk to the site, the main tunnel opening, a broad, level path going straight to the mountain, like many of the other underground sites." I was picturing the architectural drawings bearing Kammler's signature, which Colm had found earlier. "The path had been a roadway or even railroad tracks during the war. We passed dilapidated machine gun nests along the way, and it didn't take much imagination to picture SS troops on high alert within them. I saw a guard post, too, where approaching vehicles would have been checked. We eventually came to a concrete wall built right into the granite mountain side. So odd looking—the rough, craggy granite giving way to smooth concrete. I could see the outlines of boards used as forms for the poured concrete, and the empty bolt holes that showed various apparatuses were once affixed to the face of the wall. The wall itself was maybe thirty feet across, twenty-five feet high. In the center were two large steel doors, I'd say twelve to fifteen feet high, hinged on the outside, thick steel. Big enough to drive a truck through. Oddly, about eight feet up on each door was a pair of wide, open grates—too high to see through, but maybe designed to allow for a little light and ventilation. The doors, massive, were spotted with rust. It was a damned imposing entrance."

"But everything the SS built underground was like that," I pushed a bit. "Blast doors. High security. SS troops everywhere."

"Yes, yes. True enough. I'm not saying this was different. There were other entrances, too, smaller but well-guarded. More purpose-built concrete machine gun nests guarding the approaches [like] other troops on foot patrols, inner check points. A blast of dank, cold, ghostly air belched out of the tunnel as the steel doors were first swung open. We had to use torches throughout. Inside was a perfectly shaped tunnel, a long cavern really. Perhaps thirty-five to forty feet wide, an arched ceiling that peaked at about twenty feet. And a perfectly level, smooth floor throughout. The whole place, Dean, couldn't have been made any better today. It was perfect."

I knew that behind those perfectly-poured concrete cavern walls was solid granite, chipped away a half-inch or so at a time, twenty by thirty feet, miles long, with pick axes and ten-pound sledge hammers swung by Kammler's slaves. Is that what Colm was getting at?

"As we walked into the mountain, in my head, I could hear the blasting, the machines working, fittings clanging, guards shouting orders, dogs barking. The clamor of machines working in the first five hundred feet of the tunnel, the cacophony of six thousand slaves further in still excavating. It was very real to me. The underground was accompanied by a massive industrial park, a main four-story building over a block long, several other buildings, tens of thousands of square feet. None of these have been maintained. Yellow, peeling paint, all the window glass broken. Just enormous, and mysterious." The research was getting to Colm, too, I thought. But that wasn't where he was headed.

"Dean, think about that," Colm said. "This was just one small site. I mean, it was large. But it was just one of so many. So many subterranean haunts. But this one could have been the place, *the* place, where Working Staff Kammler was moving ahead on nuclear research."

Sometime later, Keith pinged the Pentagon's Air Force Intelligence Division with a document request. The response is the first-ever documented proof that an operational cyclotron was removed from Czechoslovakia by the Russians at the end of the war—and not just a laboratory version, but an industrial grade "large cyclotron."[14] So, as we are the first to establish, courtesy of this Daily Activity Report of the Air Intelligence Division, the number of cyclotrons in Nazi control during the war, and therefore their ability to enrich uranium, has been underreported by history. This also fits well with our information from yet another newly discovered document that there was a nuclear research facility operational in Czechoslovakia, "the German 'URANMOTOR' project [to create a uranium-powered engine for propulsion]…in Czechoslovakia under Prof. Huettig."[15]

● ● ●

The documents were coming in fast and furiously. We were really building up a picture of Think Tank Kammler and its research. Clearly Working Staff Kammler was a highly organized, ultra-secret weapons research project, a tightly knit organization that Kammler staffed personally to develop off-book weapons projects. Kammler recruited engineers and designers freely from across the Reich, including other Skoda plants as well, but also more broadly from "universities and technical schools." Key staff included leaders and team members in physics, ballistics, chemical research, rockets, explosives, magnetics, and more, operating in six main buildings, making "prototypes of new products." That information is in the "BIOS Final Report" on the British Armament Design Department's 1945 investigation of Nazi research in Pribram, Czechoslovakia[16]—about which we'll see more below.

The complete activities of the Kammler Think Tank have never been established. But clearly it would have been the perfect vehicle for hidden nuclear research, in the perfect location, organized under the perfect man for the job. According to facility director Voss, Working Staff Kammler at Skoda was protected by a triple ring of SS counterintelligence specialists to prevent leaks or sabotage and internally was nicknamed "the Kammler Group."[17] Even for the Nazis and the SS, the security was heightened, everything redoubled. As at Nordhausen, security passes for personnel allowed entry into the facility, and then limited access to specified sectors only.[18]

● ● ●

We know that Kammler was in Prague at the end of the war, at a point when travel was incredibly risky there. What made the risk worth it? The presence of Kammler's Think Tank, or Working Staff Kammler, in Czechoslovakia. I believe Kammler's last-minute mission was to hide the most treasured Skoda research and the Working Staff documents in a bunker built for that purpose. The likelihood that Skoda was the location of a secret nuclear program under Working Staff Kammler also helps explain an unthinkable venture undertaken by U.S. forces, into that same area of Czechoslovakia. This part of our story takes place near a seemingly obscure town in western Czechoslovakia— Štěchovice. While Pilsen, the home of Skoda's main facility, is about forty-five minutes west of Prague, Štěchovice is some thirty-minutes' drive south of Prague (and just fifteen minutes from Jílové u Prahy, the location of Kammler's alleged suicide), so this action takes place in a compact triangular area of western Czechoslovakia. After the war ended, something of a divided government ruled in Czechoslovakia, which was not yet fully behind the Iron Curtain. The U.S. knew Nazi research documents were hidden everywhere, and not all had been found. And at that point, as we have established, Hans Kammler was still safely in custody of the U.S. Army, still subject to interrogation, still a possible source for information about that research. While records indicate that the Americans found out about the specially excavated cavern at Štěchovice from an informant to the French government,[19] no historian who has examined America's post-war venture there knew that Kammler had survived—and might well have directed or at least triggered America's brazen raid.

The Americans assembled a unique, if not outright odd, strike force of over a dozen men to go to Štěchovice, led by First Lieutenant William J. Owen and Captain Stephen M. Richards, an explosives expert. Their mission was to penetrate Czechoslovakia and recover documents buried at Štěchovice. We believe those were Kammler Think Tank documents buried on Kammler's orders. Adding to the intrigue, the insertion team also included an informant, a former SS colonel who had helped with the original excavation of the site, and a guard for the colonel. They were joined by two other explosives experts, several drivers, and a journalist named Lionel Shapiro, who would afterward write a story of the mission for the *New York Times*.[20] A final character, Major Charles Katek, was the very OSS asset running intelligence networks in Prague and Pilsen that Keith had identified as a possible facilitator of Kammler's surrender into American custody. At the time of this raid, Katek's cover was war crimes investigator.[21]

"Operation Hidden Documents," which took place fully nine months after the war ended, was an audacious plan, to say the least. In fact, the Americans were risking an international crisis. Despite the respect due to sovereign Czechoslovak territory, the American strike team drove right in, using five military vehicles, including two two-and-a-half-ton cargo trucks, all emblazoned with U.S. military insignia. Their cover story— that they were looking for the grave of an American pilot—was a brazen lie.[22] With the help of the SS colonel, they quickly located the site. After removing the surrounding underbrush and carefully digging through to the site's concealed wooden doorway, the demolition experts went to work. They gingerly removed the individual planks of the custom-made door, every one of them wired to an explosive booby trap—every one except, fortuitously, the one they removed first. It was perilous work, heart-stopping even, removing one booby-trapped plank after another. Personally, I can't even begin to put myself in the shoes of the men pulling one plank after another, feeling for booby trap wires, waiting for the whole area to explode. Inside the cave, the Americans found thirty-two heavy wooden crates, each four feet by three feet by two feet and weighing four hundred pounds. It was another nerve-racking task to remove all thirty-two crates, checking each for booby traps as they went, and then hauling them to the trucks. In all, the demolitions team removed over a ton of explosives and fuel oil set to kill interlopers and incinerate the contents of the underground site. Then after loading the cargo, the team split up. The trucks carrying the stolen crates left directly and made it safely back to the American Zone in Germany. The three explosives experts, exhausted, their nerves frayed, stayed behind and were captured before they could be extricated—exposing the operation.

After some international turmoil and the passage of several days' time, during which the Americans surely scoured the contents of every crate, the Americans apologized for the transgression and agreed to return the crates. They claimed the operation was the work of low-level operators, not sanctioned by the higher levels of the U.S. government. But at least one U.S. military document we have places blame at USFET headquarters, meaning the operation was sanctioned at the highest levels.[23] Reports vary as to what was in those crates—archives of Germany's wartime occupation and administration of western Czechoslovakia, Gestapo files, inventories of German treasure, documentation of Germany's weapons projects. Reports also vary as to whether the United States returned all files, switched out some files, or at least made microfilm copies of whatever interested them before returning them.[24] One thing is certain: what was in the boxes has never been disclosed to the public, despite recent efforts to pry them lose, which certainly makes me wonder. What still requires secrecy today, decades later? Operation

Hidden Documents bleeds over from the audacious to the foolish if the Americans didn't have very good reasons to believe that the Štěchovice vault held something extraordinary. This was no Geraldo Rivera expose on the Al Capone vault. Everything, including how the material was stored, pointed to the contents being extremely valuable. As Dennis Reece has pointed out in *Captains of Bomb Disposal 1942–1946*, "only papers of great sensitivity would merit putting them in a specially-constructed, booby-trapped facility hidden in the woods.... The involvement of a detachment from the elite SS [in hiding the materials] was another indication that something out of the ordinary was involved. This was in a different category than a castle with books and newspaper clippings thrown in the attic."[25] Do notice that the documents at Štěchovice were hidden by Kammler's SS in a cavern underground—Kammler's domain.

There is yet another layer to the story. Keith posed an unanswerable question: "Why had the Americans, decades later, immediately after the collapse of communism, returned to Štěchovice with a team of scientific experts—forty-four years later?" Officially, the team on this second mission hailed from the Jet Propulsion Laboratory in Pasadena, California. But it was much more likely, Colm's research showed, that they were really from Lawrence Livermore and Los Alamos, the Americans' leading nuclear labs.[26] The new American team went back not to the same Štěchovice cavern, which had already been emptied, but to a related location. Acting on the interrogation reports of the SS officer who had overseen construction at Štěchovice under Kammler, the research team identified a location—Mednik Hill—described as being "the key to what had been hidden at Štěchovice."[27] Working under a veil of secrecy, and in partnership with Czechoslovakian weapons exporter OMNIPOL and insurance giant FUJIYAMA, the team conducted an extensive two-month long excavation of the underground complex. What they recovered from the site has never been disclosed.[28]

Still later in 2004, Jeffrey E. Patterson, a geological engineer and geophysicist from the University of Calgary, conducted a private survey of Mednik Hill using Ground Penetrating Radar. The Patterson Survey concluded that an excavated tunnel complex, along with a large circular chamber some twenty yards in diameter deep underground, had been filled in with hundreds of tons of concrete. Could this have been a nuclear research facility, a circular nuclear pile? Otherwise, why fill in the entire complex with concrete? The Štěchovice raid, and the follow-up decades later, raise enough questions to fill a book, and they surely add fire to our theory that Kammler used the sites as his cache for the most important Working Staff Kammler research documents and hardware he could not move out of reach of the Russians.

The shenanigans at Štěchovice nine months after the war and again decades later betray at least the perceived value of documents and hardware buried there—most likely documents laying out research by Think Tank Kammler at Skoda.

● ● ●

Next, Keith asked that I take a closer look at Skoda director Wilhelm Voss, Agoston's most important source on the subject of Working Staff Kammler. Voss was the one who claimed that "the Kammler group" at Skoda was protected by a triple ring of SS counterintelligence specialists to prevent leaks or sabotage.[29] Voss had been removed as head of Skoda in January 1945 by Göring, but remained on its board of directors until March 1945.[30] Accounts of the reasons for Voss's removal differ, with one historian claiming he was fired because of his refusal to seat two nominees to the Skoda board, and a restricted OSS report stating that he was removed for failing to meet production quotas.[31]

But on May 10, 1945, four days after the Western Allies seized Skoda, Voss made the dangerous trek from Germany to Skoda—even though he was an automatic arrestee. Skoda was like Nordhausen in that the Americans had it but it was ultimately going to end up in Russian hands, per Yalta. According to the account he gave Agoston, Voss went to Skoda to implore the Americans to seize as much of the Skoda paperwork as possible before the handover to the Russians.[32] And while Voss never made this clear, I believe his mission back to Skoda was at the behest of Kammler. At Nordhausen, the Americans knew exactly what to do—removing hardware, rounding up scientists still in the area, and hunting down hidden documents. Their guiding hand on site was Hans Kammler himself, aided by his intelligence officer, Major von Ploetz. But Kammler could not be in two places at once. He urgently needed someone to represent him at Skoda—in just the same way that, as we have seen, he had left SS Obersturmführer Schürmann behind at Ebensee to make sure the surrender there went well.[33] Voss was left to steer the Americans to the most important documents at Skoda, including the unknown Working Staff Kammler documents.

One more bit of evidence from Skoda shows both the value of the Nazi research there and the determination of the U.S. to exploit that research after the war. Just as it had at Nordhausen, General Electric immediately sent its own representatives to Skoda as soon as the prized site was in American hands.[34]

Voss was given a cool reception at Skoda. No longer in charge, he held no official status. He was admitted but made to follow an escort. He lucked upon one of the members of the former SS security team that had guarded the work of the Working Staff Kammler and was delighted to learn that the SS man had already compiled the most precious of Working Staff Kammler documents, crated them, and loaded them into a truck, all with the idea of driving them into the American zone.[35]

Now Voss approached the American army officer in charge. He patiently, and repeatedly, explained who he was—and the singular value of the documents. Despite Voss's repeated appeals, the American officer could not be moved, insisting that U.S. intelligence units had already combed the site and removed what they deemed necessary, and his orders were to ready everything for handover to the Soviets.[36] In fact, we know that no Western Ally team with any expertise had so much as perused the records, given the geographic limitations of ALSOS. The Russians drove away with everything. Forever gone.

What precisely were the documents that Voss claimed to be protecting in his account to Agoston? What was the nature of the underlying
research? That, frustratingly, is information only hinted at in Agoston's
book.

If I was going to make a claim about that research, essentially putting
myself on the line, I wanted more information. As ever, Keith and Colm
would deliver.

Keith circled back to some of his old contacts. One of them, Bill
Cunliffe of the Interagency Working Group—a special commission
tasked by the U.S government with accelerating the declassification of
World War II–era documents over fifty years after the war—coughed
up a single post-war report on interrogation.

The subject of the interrogation report Cunliffe produced was Wilhelm Voss. Keith had shared the document with Colm before they were
able to reach me, and Colm had applied his expertise to verify that Keith's
interpretation of the report was correct. Colm called me from across the
ocean to break the news. I could hear the energy in his voice; it was as if
he were standing in the next room.

Colm laid out the findings as if he had rehearsed his presentation.
He was choosing his words carefully, not overstating his case. He told
me that during the interrogation, which took place while memories were
still fresh, Voss had described the work of Kammler's Think Tank in
spectacular detail—with many more specifics than Agoston had put in
his book. According to Voss, the Think Tank's work "included secret
weapons, equipment and proceedings, which were either in use or which
were being readied for deployment and, as much as I know, this mainly
involved work in the area of atomic disintegration and transformation
of elements, the atomic bomb, nuclear energy, and additionally—rockets,
the latest airplane propulsion systems and remote control."[37] Colm
waited for my response, but I had nothing. The silence hung between us
over the miles. I had heard him clearly. I just didn't have words—a highly
unusual condition for me, a lawyer, after all. Kammler's Think Tank,
working "in the area of atomic disintegration and transformation of

elements, the atomic bomb." Keith had unearthed a flat-out statement by the former head of one of Germany's largest weapons manufacturers listing a nuclear bomb among the projects of Working Staff Kammler!

That took a long minute to absorb.

"Damn!" was my eventual, thoughtful response.

"It's true," Colm assured me. "No doubt. The document is genuine. Keith's nailed it."

There was a pause as I tried to process. Then Colm hit me with the next logical jump. "Dean...?"

"Yes."

"Think about this. Kammler, building a nuke. Hans Kammler, in charge of the V-2, in charge of the Amerika Rocket," he reminded me, "trying to build a nuclear weapon." His voice was remarkably calm for someone pointing out to me that we had pried free evidence that a single Nazi general had with his left hand run a project to design a nuclear weapon, while with his right hand he was developing a missile that could reach New York, Washington, D.C.—name your target. "We also have a U.S. intelligence doc from the Strategic Vulnerability Branch of the Army Air Forces that recounts a German report of a planned transatlantic bomber, with detailed descriptions of an attack on New York City. Nobody else has this. No one has seen this document."[38]

"There's more," Colm advised. Why was I not surprised? With these two, no matter how rich the documents got, there was always more. I was sure that I had been to the greatest heights of the roller coaster and plummeted down the opposite side, racing this way and that, only to hear the click, click, click of Keith and Colm's chain pulling me to the heights once again.

Some of the Voss file Keith got was in German. His review concentrated on the sections of the report documenting Voss's flight from Pilsen, with the Russians just behind him, just after his exasperating encounter with the Americans at the Skoda facility at Pilsen. On his hasty departure he was accompanied by Kammler's right-hand man, Oberführer Erich Purucker, Skoda's general director at the time.[39] Kammler's son Jörg had said Kammler trusted Purucker. So it made sense that Purucker would have had Kammler's personal papers if Kammler didn't have them himself.[40]

Then Colm read from the next page of the file, a memorandum dated April 25, 1946, from the CIC Munich Regional Office and addressed to CIC Region IV, Dale Garvey's group. It reported on the interrogation of Voss: "Dr. Voss…claims that he has valuable information on atom bomb research in Germany."[41]

Further down, the document states, "On the 10 May 1945 VOSS and PURUCKER were in Schimelitz, fleeing in the direction of the American troops. PURUCKER was driving a large civilian car, which contained many of the plans on the atom bomb. This car plus material fell into the hands of the Russians, and VOSS was separated from PURUCKER."

Atom bomb?? This is no reference to nuclear power or propulsion *research*. It was a *weapon*. An atom bomb. This was astounding!

• • •

Purucker, we learned, was head of all research for the *Heereswaffenamt* (HWA), the Army Ordnance Office, which itself oversaw the Kurt Diebner and Erich Schumann nuclear research projects. With Schumann and Diebner working for Purucker, Kammler's deputy, Kammler had his hooks in even more of the Nazis' nuclear research than we had realized. Schumann had also served as von Braun's doctoral advisor.[42] Schumann, we know, would later disappear into Russia, where he reemerged as the lead researcher for the Soviets' atom bomb project, which would bear fruit within four short years.[43]

The report Keith received also mentioned that Director Alfred Baubin and a Director Engel, "manager of another research laboratory in [the nearby Czechoslovakian town of] Pibrams," both knew "more detailed plans on the atomic bomb and other secret weapons." Both of these men were closely connected to Kammler. These documents were bursting with proof the Nazis had a secret atomic weapons research project in Czechoslovakia—and that Kammler ran it. A likely site for their work was the facility at Pribram (sometimes spelled Pribam), a center of rocket research headed by Engel, who answered directly to Kammler.[44]

Still there are reasons to doubt Voss. At the time of this interrogation, he was actively seeking release from detention. In fact he had already, in August 1945, once escaped from a detention camp in Erlangen, just south of Nordhausen.[45] Perhaps Voss was outright lying, hoping the Americans might help him if he provided "crucial" material. But the Americans surely thought him credible: USFET Headquarters sent a high-level request to CIC Region IV (Dale Garvey again) asking for Voss to be transferred to DUSTBIN, interrogation central, P. M. Wilson's domain.[46] The Allies were convinced that something momentous had happened at Pribram and that Voss had the details, so he was whisked off to DUST-BIN. Shortly thereafter, by November 1945, the U.S. began diplomatic negotiations to allow an official visit to pierce the wall of secrecy surrounding Skoda, a mission that had "particular emphasis on the experimental station at Pribram."[47]

Colm was all over this angle. He told me that the Russians had sent paratroopers to try to secure the Pribram facility, that they stripped the equipment there and sent it east. If that wasn't enough evidence of the significance of the research at that site, Colm had a copy of a report that recorded the results of the exhaustive three-plus week visit to Pribram at the war's end by the British Intelligence Objectives Sub-Committee—BIOS Final Report 313. The seventy-four-page tome had been misfiled and lost to other researchers. Colm's personal connection to Stephen Walton, a diligent archivist at the Imperial War Museum in London, led to the discovery. The document reveals that the Pribram site came online in mid-1944, just as Kammler was reaching the pinnacle of his authority, in the immediate aftermath of the Hitler assassination attempt. The Pribram facility, the report noted, had helped satisfy the "anxious need" of the SS to possess a research center for "brilliant new designs of weapons" with "their own department of development and research."[48] The report described a super-secret high-tech weapons research and development facility operated by the SS.

Pribram had a distinct advantage as a site for secret programs—like Skoda HQ in Prague and the main facility at Pilsen, it was as far from enemy bombers as it could be. Unlike Prague and Pilsen, though, Pribram was unknown to the Allies during the war as a Nazi asset and thought to be strategically insignificant. Colm, of course, had made a journey to Pribram. He had sent photographs to me and Keith, photos of the facility that housed Working Staff Kammler. This red brick chunk of a building, next to the Pribram mining museum but so near the quaint Bohemian village, seemed out of place to me. The raw, imposing structure interfered with what would otherwise be a splendid view of the rolling hills in which it was situated.

Pribram housed parts of the V-1 and V-2 projects, but also the Rheinbote, the V-4, most likely the ramjet,[49] and the V-101, a gargantuan 140-ton rocket with a range of over 1,100 miles, being developed wholly independently of the von Braun team, under the tutelage of Rolf Engel,[50] in league with scientist Nils Werner Larsson.[51] I was fascinated by this massive rocket, with a range of over a thousand miles, being developed entirely outside von Braun's orbit. Colm also told me about something called the Rott, a truly exotic rocket-assisted aircraft that should be of real interest to weapons buffs, as it appears nowhere else in literature we've encountered.[52] The extensive handwritten BIOS report notes that "the most qualified technicians in the field of R-technique [also known as a rocket technique] were brought together"[53] at Pribram. This was not just an unknown nuclear bomb project; it was an unknown rocket project. Keith found further indications of a guided missile project at Pribram in an Army Air Forces intelligence document.[54]

Rolf Engel, second only to von Braun in terms of brain power on rockets, was a physicist and member of the SS, hailed as "a most able engineer and mathematician."[55] Born in Menz, Germany, in 1912, he was an early associate of von Braun, even described as "a friend,"[56] having joined the German Rocket Society with him in 1928 at the age of sixteen and later following him to Peenemünde.[57] He held a grudge against Dornberger and the entire German Army on account of having been excommunicated from rocket research from 1935 to 1942,[58] the period during which rocket research was consolidated under the control of the army. After the war, Engel would work in France, Egypt, Rome, and then once again in Germany.

Nils Larsson, a leader on Engel's team at Pribram, we can report for the first time, was an Allied spy.[59] A Swedish national, he had been working on weapons for private industry before the war, including a recoilless anti-tank gun, and he approached British and American officials with hopes of working for either one. In June 1943, the British and American secret services inserted him in Germany, where he became involved in the Rheinbote and V-2 projects at Peenemünde. Later at Pribram he also worked on the V-101. From Pribram, Larsson made his covert reports to the Allies through Berlin, and sometimes through private correspondence with his wife. At the end of the war he was able to use his position to preserve critical documentation of the development of Germany's rockets.[60] He might well have been a point of contact for Kammler's surrender.

Strangely, one notorious name was also associated with Pribram— Otto von Bolschwing, the author of the scurrilous 1937 report "The Jewish Problem," which urged emigration of Jews from Germany. Von Bolschwing, in the SS, "worked with Adolf Eichmann and helped devise programs to persecute and terrorize Germany's Jewish population.... he was the highest-ranking German prosecuted by the OSI."[61] That was the U.S. Department of Justice Office of Special Investigations, the American government's official Nazi-hunting organization. As with other Nazis we've learned about, von Bolschwing was recruited by the Army CIC, the Counter Intelligence Corps, in the spring of 1945. After the war he worked for the Reinhard Gehlen group, providing contacts to ethnic Germans in Romania. By 1949, von Bolschwing was working directly for the CIA, who employed him despite knowledge of his ugly past. In

1954, he emigrated to the U.S. with help from his CIA contacts, thereafter working in American private enterprises.[62]

Do not overlook the implications for a possible link between Kammler
and the CIA or the CIC. CIC chief Lieutenant Colonel Dale M. Garvey's
name keeps popping up everywhere. As we learned from a CIC document,
Garvey's job was not just recruiting intelligence assets, but German scientists, as well, under Operation Mesa. Mesa was a top-secret CIC venture
to track recruitment of scientists by America's former allies, "contrary to
instructions from the [U.S.] War Department that all scientific and technical personnel were to remain in the United States Zone."[63]

Mulling all this information, I returned to the "Fleming document,"
the one-page blockbuster Kammler interrogation report, recalling not
something it said but something it omitted—which made more sense
now that we could show Kammler was involved in atomic weapons
research. The Fleming document had noted that after the war Kammler
was preparing a written report for the Allies. It even listed subject matter
areas Kammler would report on. What piqued my curiosity now wasn't
the subjects listed, but the subject redacted:

> Kammler is preparing a detailed report (in German). This is
> to include the following:
>> Secret weapons developments
>> [redacted]
>> Underground research and production facilities
>> Security measures concerning the above

Also telling are two other redactions from the body of the
document:

> Dr. Ing. KAMMLER is a trained architect by profession and
> was head of all secret projects including the V-1 and V-2. He
> further claims to have been head of [redacted] project based
> at the [redacted].

It is axiomatic that anything redacted from government documents is more sensitive than the information left on the page. Whatever was redacted here had to be of greater importance than the V-2, and more secret than "all secret projects." That implies some very high-level, super-secret project. In my view, the redactions likely refer to Germany's nuclear weapons research supervised by Kammler.

The Fleming document is one of many, many redacted documents that we have received in response to our requests, but there is another government response that bears special mention. In 2008, well after the congressional mandate to declassify World War II documents and open the U.S. archives to researchers, Keith requested any and all files on Kammler from within the U.S. Department of Justice Criminal Division, which included the Office of Special Investigations (OSI). The official government response to his request did not even include heavily redacted documents. It included *no* documents—while acknowledging that the government did hold relevant documents, which it refused to provide. The rejection letter went on to briefly describe the documents the government was refusing to provide: a thirty-five-page document created in 1969, withheld in full, and an eighty-seven-page report, written in 1987, withheld in full. I was shocked at those dates—documents created in 1969 and 1987! Both documents were said to involve foreign governments. Might they shed light on the Kammler Working Group, Skoda in Czechoslovakia, Štěchovice, and the British extradition request for Kammler? Who knows?! Keith's appeal of the denial was itself denied, so this is yet another dead end.

• • •

We have made the best case we can that Germany had a previously unknown nuclear weapons research project. We do not claim the project succeeded in any large way, merely that the Nazis were working toward a nuclear weapon when conventional history tells us they were not, and that by the end of the war that effort was largely under the control of

Kammler. We do not claim to have unearthed all, or nearly all, relevant documents. We challenge others to provide documents confirming or undermining our claim.

And while Germany worked toward a nuclear weapon, its rocket team was perfecting the ideal delivery vehicle, which morphed into the modern-day ICBM. Research overseen by Kammler and carried out by his subordinates, including famed rocket scientist Wernher von Braun, was aimed at placing a nuclear bomb, a mini-tactical nuke, or a dirty bomb on one of Germany's rocket systems.

I do not want to overstate our case here. We are not claiming that the Nazis were on the cusp of putting a functioning nuclear warhead in the nosecone of a V-2, a Rheinbote, or an even longer-range Amerika Rocket. But we can make a sound circumstantial case that Kammler and Voss believed they were closer to realizing a nuclear weapon than previously acknowledged by historians. Certainly Kammler, Voss, and von Braun all thought they had both rocket and nuclear weapons science that would be of great interest to the Americans—and they were right.

CHAPTER TEN

A Parallel Case

"Justice delayed is justice denied."

—*Alan Ryan, author of the 1983 Klaus Barbie Department*
of Justice Report, quoting the well-known legal maxim

A t this point I was 100 percent on board our project, but I still found myself road-testing our material, really trying to make sure I wasn't professionally stepping off the gang plank. I had run it past my father, my brother, my sister, and countless others. To a person, they thought the story was riveting, more like a movie than a book. But today I was dining at Oceanaire, one of Washington's power lunch spots, with two well-respected non-fiction authors, a husband and wife team. Both were accomplished scholars, one a retired chaired history professor from Harvard. I could not ask for a better pair to give me a reality check on a developing angle of our story about Hans Kammler—the case of rocket scientist Wernher von Braun.

Even before we ordered our lunch, I began sputtering: "To an American like me, it does not sound possible, but the same scientist who led Germany's rocket program, raining down missiles on London, Antwerp, and other cities, killing more citizens than soldiers, headed the American rocket research project for decades after the war. Wernher von Braun, lead rocket expert for the Nazis and for NASA, is today revered by most. His life has been examined extensively, but typically with nothing more than a brief mention or complete blackout of his war record. After the war, America did whatever was necessary to build its arsenal of intercontinental missiles. It did whatever was necessary to put an American on the moon first. Von Braun was necessary, and the Americans hid his record, so they could utilize his talents freely. I get it. I see this as evidence they would do the same for Hans Kammler, who gave them von Braun and more. For that reason alone, von Braun's case is worth study. It's worth including in the book." Four elbows on the table told me I had my friends' attention.

One great piece of advice they gave me, near the end of our lunch, I took to heart. To paraphrase, *You always know what you have, and likely what it means. But you never know what you didn't discover; what document lies in the next box or folder that you didn't see that might completely change the meaning of the document you have in hand.*

I took them to mean, *Be careful. Always allow for the possibility that further research—the research you might have done just after your stopping point—could lead in a new direction.*

Still, even given those caveats, we pieced together quite a bit of information on Wernher von Braun. And it was not flattering.

Wernher Magnus Maximilian Freiherr von Braun was born on March 23, 1912, in the old German Empire in what is now Wirsitz, Poland, just 130 miles from Kammler's birthplace, to an old aristocratic Prussian family.[1] When Wernher was very young his father, a civil servant, moved the family to Berlin. Von Braun studied the cello as a youth and dreamed of composing music and making a mark on history. He veered from that course when he was presented with a telescope for his confirmation gift and became fascinated with space travel. Ultimately, though, Wernher von Braun did make a lasting mark on history—both in war and in peace.

From 1932 until 1945 he was employed by the German Army Ordnance Department, working continuously alongside Walter Dornberger.[2] For the final part of the war he worked for Hans Kammler. After the war von Braun was quietly brought to America, where he worked for decades, first for the U.S. Army and later for NASA, even earning a Top Secret clearance. By 1955, von Braun was a naturalized U.S. citizen and a popular figure in American culture, starring in Disney television films to promote space exploration. The irony was striking: in Nazi Germany von Braun strained to get the attention and earn the funding dollars of Adolf Hitler for his Vengeance Weapons; a mere decade later he was working with ultimate showman Walt Disney, striving to sway the American public to see the benefits of space travel and make funding a priority.

In a well-known photograph from 1970, a bearded and tanned von Braun sits at his desk at NASA with eleven of his rocket models arrayed behind him, shining like wet paint, arranged from left to right in chronological order of their production, culminating in the massive Saturn IB at the far right. I can't help but wonder whether just out of frame to the left side of the photograph, deliberately cropped from the picture, he had a model of the deadly V-2, but I suppose not. Once he arrived in the U.S., his wartime work on behalf of the Nazis seemed always just outside the frame. Von Braun died in northern Virginia in 1977, a veritable hero of American space exploration memorialized by President Jimmy Carter: "Not just the people of our nation, but all the people of the world have profited from his work. We will continue to profit from his example."[3] The *Washington Post* obituary mentioned the V-2, but spent most of its ink on unequivocal plaudits, as did the *New York Times*.[4]

Von Braun's record cries out for critical examination. Historians have largely handled it with kid gloves. Frederich Sharpe and Mitchell Ordway, for example, the authors of *The Rocket Team: From the V-2 to the Saturn Moon Rocket—the Inside Story of How a Small Group of Engineers Changed World History*, thanked von Braun for his "untiring aid, encouragement and guidance"[5] with the book, even including an approving forward by von Braun in which the former Nazi rocket researcher stated, "the authors have produced as complete and as accurate an account as we are likely to ever see." The book reads as if the authors were seeking von Braun's approval; you can almost see von Braun looking over their shoulders as they pecked away at their typewriters.

Of course von Braun made many peacetime contributions. As David DeVorkin lays out in *Science with a Vengeance*, "The space sciences in the United States would not have emerged in the way they did without the existence of the V-2"[6]—and without von Braun in the U.S. after the war. But while it would be convenient to believe that von Braun was only ever interested in space travel, not military applications for his rockets, in fact he spent World War II designing rockets for military payloads. He enabled the Nazis to project destructive power further and with greater speed and accuracy than ever before—upon a defenseless enemy, usually citizens living in cities. Von Braun is on record assuring the Führer his test rockets would make useful weapons,[7] and he even claimed in a post-war interview for the U.S. Seventh Army's *Beachhead News* that given two more years, his V-2 could have won the war for Germany.[8] A post-war interrogator reported that the "ambition" of the von Braun–led V-2 rocket team "was to develop a weapon with which to dominate the world."[9]

During the war Von Braun didn't limit his activities to designing rockets; he intervened on the production side numerous times, making sure facilities and labor were available to produce the V-2 in numbers adequate for launching on the enemy[10] and interceding to remove labor and production bottlenecks. As late as 1945, when the war was clearly lost, von Braun harangued the developers of a guidance system who were about to be overrun by the Soviets; rather than give up their work as they intended, von Braun enlisted the authority of Kammler to ensure their continued efforts. He even inveighed that refugees who had found their way to Nordhausen at the war's end be evicted from the rocket assembly spaces they clung to for shelter to increase V-2 research and production.[11]

• • •

Was von Braun an ardent Nazi?

Yes. He joined Hitler's National Socialist Party in November 1937. Party membership was not even open from 1933 to 1937, so this was his earliest opportunity after 1933. After the war, he inexplicably gave the wrong date for his SS membership, claiming 1939.[12] A mistake, or a lie?

First row, from left to right, General Dr. Walter Dornberger (partially hidden), General Friedrich Olbricht (with Knight's Cross), Major Heinz Brandt, and Werner von Braun (in civilian dress) at Peenemünde, in March 1941. Bundesarchiv, Bild 146-1978-Anh.024-03/CC-BY-SA 3.0

We have also learned that von Braun joined the SS-Reitersturm, an SS cavalry unit, the same SS calvary unit Kammler joined, and at the same time—1933.[13] Von Braun reportedly joined under duress,[14] a claim difficult to confirm or refute. But we do know that he has a low membership number, having been among the very earliest to join.[15] Remember, the Nazis did not come to power until 1933, and von Braun joined the party that very same year, just a year after Kammler. Both were ambitious men, and both would have been trying hard to develop contacts that could further those ambitions. Von Braun also admitted to joining a number of other Nazi organizations at later dates.[16]

We have already drawn a distinction between membership in the Nazi Party, a more common and less offensive thing than membership in the SS, the worst of the worst. Von Braun was a member of both. He paints himself as a reluctant SS member, explaining that he joined in May 1940 at the direct request of Himmler and on the advice of Dornberger.[17] Even if we accept this account, Von Braun's rationale—that his boss told him to join the notorious SS—has strong echoes of the roundly rejected Nuremberg Defense. In any case, the fact that Albert Speer, in contrast, refused to join the SS, even as an honorary member, and still had a successful career at the highest levels of the Nazi government, would seem to suggest that membership was a matter of some choice. In an affidavit that we discovered in a 1948 FBI report, von Braun tried to explain away a letter, apparently unknown to history, which he had written asking to be considered for membership in the SS.[18] That's truly damning—after all, there's a big difference between being pressured to join and seeking service in the SS.

● ● ●

Did von Braun know slave laborers were used to support his work? The answer is unequivocal—he did know.

Let's look at Peenemünde first. When the German rocket team moved from Kummersdorf to Peenemünde before the war, von Braun moved into an apartment close by, just "off-base."[19] Von Braun was at Peenemünde daily, and to reach the research buildings and launch sites he managed, he had to take the lone road onto the facility, passing the fenced worker camp where the slave laborers were housed. Von Braun's Peenemünde colleague Dieter Huzel describes the camp, called Trassenheide, in these bleak words: "To our right, chain-link fence seven or eight feet high swept into sight. Behind it the barracks were dark, dull structures lined up at fixed intervals."

Another one of von Braun's co-workers admits in his memoir that he and all others at Peenemünde were aware of the use of slave labor, "mostly laborers from the captured eastern areas."[20] And Karl Krüger, another German employee at Peenemünde, describes enslaved prisoners unloading cement sacks and moving them over great distances, urged on by threats from SS guards, who shot those who could not keep up the pace.[21] By 1943, Peenemünde's camp held three thousand laborers, a population of a size that would have been hard to miss. If you knew how to find the restaurants and shops at the enclave, you knew where the slave labor barracks were. It is simply not possible that von Braun was ignorant of the presence and use of slaves.

But there is more than circumstantial evidence for von Braun's knowledge that his rockets were built with slave labor. Colm dropped yet another startling new document into my lap. In a 1947 interrogation conducted by Edmund Tilley—the same Tilley we had already linked to P. M. Wilson, gatekeeper of DUSTBIN, by this time a lieutenant colonel in the British army[22]—von Braun himself noted that "Kammler...was entrusted with the new Peenemünde construction work for which he used chiefly inmates of concentration camps."[23]

If that's not enough evidence, von Braun actually let slip the term "forced laborers" when describing the Allied bombing of Peenemünde: "The full weight of the bombs fell on the Trassenheide forced laborers' camp, with disastrous results. Trapped behind barbed wire and lacking any shelters, six hundred workers were killed."[24] And he used very similar language about Dora-Nordhausen, describing the general working conditions at Nordhausen as "extremely primitive" and saying that in the early months at that facility "the prisoners were housed in the tunnels proper under the most primitive conditions." Von Braun also described Kammler's "construction organization" in general as having been "made up of prisoners from concentration camps."[25]

When Kammler moved the rocket team to Nordhausen, slaves were living within and then alongside the production facility, in conditions we have already taken note of, as described by the war crimes tribunal at the trial of Oswald Pohl: "clothing was insufficient, especially for cold weather; barracks were inadequate; the air was very bad from lack of ventilation. The inmates, approximately 1,500 to 2,000, were housed in the shafts of tunnels which were 8 to twelve meters high. The inmates slept on bunks, four on top of each other, and had insufficient covers.... The food was insufficient.... Medical care was also insufficient...inmates died probably as a result of exhaustion and cold."[26] Jean Michel, a Dora survivor admitted of no chance that von Braun was ignorant of the use of slaves there.[27] In fact, he wrote that von Braun was a regular visitor and noted that von Braun never expressed shame, guilt, or even regret for his role there.[28] Slaves were as much a part of the missile production programs at Dora-Nordhausen as were electronic components, or metal sheathing, liquid fuel, and rocket motors.[29]

Again, von Braun incriminates himself in writing. In a November 12, 1943, letter to Gerhard Degenkolb, the early administrative head of V-2 mass production, the rocket scientist endorsed the use of slave labor, helpfully suggesting a ratio of one German civilian for every two prisoners, to avoid mischief.[30] Von Braun also admitted to touring the tunnels and seeing the workers living within them.[31] He acknowledged at one point that he suspected what was happening in the concentration camps and even admitted that, given his authority, he could have found out for certain.[32]

The villa that von Braun lived in at Nordhausen had been confiscated by the SS from a Jewish businessman.[33] Is it possible that von Braun knew nothing of this? That he never saw the faded shadows of family portraits removed from the dining room walls?

Von Braun also participated in a conference with Dornberger and twenty-eight other engineers and SS officers on May 6, 1944—at the height of the struggles to bring the V-2 online—at which the addition of eighteen hundred slave laborers at Nordhausen was discussed. All agreed the ideal solution was more and better slave laborers; the plan they fixed on was to "take prisoner 1800 skilled workers in France," and house them in camp Dora.

Von Braun with Fritz Todt, Albert Speer's predecessor as Reich Minister for Arma-
ments and Ammunition until his death in 1942 (in uniform with back to camera),
who utilized forced labor for major works across occupied Europe. Bundesarchiv,
Bild 146-1978-Anh.023-02/CC-BY-SA 3.0

We even have documentary evidence that as the quality of the slave
labor dropped as they were worked to death, von Braun made a hurried
day trip to the Buchenwald concentration camp specifically, in his words,
"to seek out more qualified detainees. I have arranged their transfer to
the Mittelwerke"[34] at Dora-Nordhausen. Having repeatedly admitted to
the exploitation of slave labor, von Braun was a repeated, self-confessed
war criminal.[35]

It is also fair to judge von Braun for actions by his underlings, particularly
when it comes to war crimes for which a superior could be found guilty. Arthur
Rudolph was von Braun's right-hand man at Nordhausen. He came to
America after the war, worked alongside von Braun in the United States,
and like him became an American citizen. But Rudolph was run back to
Germany in 1984 by the U.S. Department of Justice OSI to stand trial when
his use of slave labor became known.[36] I like to believe that only von Braun's
death in 1977 saved him from the same belated confrontation with justice.[37]

• • •

But even knowing all this, I was nearly flattened by what Colm gave me next. My phone buzzed with a new email from him just as I got settled on my morning bus. We had been collaborating for so long now, we all knew each other's schedules, and Colm dropped this in my lap when he knew I'd have time to look it over. I had been up too late the night before and was actually planning to read the *Washington Post* until I dozed off. No rest for the weary. I hot-linked to my laptop and read Colm's incoming email.

"Keith has broken new ground," Colm proclaimed. "Several weeks ago he found documents related to something called 'Project Abstract.' He was, per usual, coursing through box after box of records at your National Archives. He spotted Kammler's name among these records and, as always, made copies and read them later at home. Dean, he was over the moon when he called me. I mean insane. He was 90 percent sure he was reading them right but sent them on to me to have a look. Neither one of us had heard of Project Abstract, but Keith was right. The documents are devastating, so much so that I made an immediate request for all related materials here and hit a vein of gold myself. I'm sending you my documents first, though I never would have found them without Keith's pointer."

I scrolled down but didn't find any documents.

I typed back, "NO ATTACHMENT!!"

A half minute later, "Oops. Here you go…."

I clicked the PDF to open and waited a bit while my laptop spooled, then the file popped open. I began to scan it, but was soon stopped in my tracks by what I read.

Page one was the familiar white page gone to grey. On further inspection I could tell it was the cover of a tabbed manila folder, mostly blank, save for the words "PROJECT ABSTRACT" in bold handwriting stretched across the top—inch-tall letters shouting out from the past that the folder's contents were important. Someone had used a grease pencil, or gone over and over the lettering with a regular pencil to achieve the effect. Beneath that, in lettering the same size but not as bold, was written "Operation Bad Sachsa/Oberjoch." The entire pack of documents Colm had sent me was from "Project Abstract," a special top-secret investigation that none of us had heard of—that nobody had heard of: a 1947 attempt to learn the true intentions of Dornberger and von Braun. This was an entirely new thread for our story.

The Project Abstract file contained two large documents. The first was a British overview Report on Abstract; the second was the report on interrogation of von Braun by Tilley and Marchant. I had seen dozens of these interrogation reports by now, but the date of this one was March 8, *1947*, late for post-war interviews of a German scientist. And this was not just *a* German scientist, this was *the* German scientist—Wernher von Braun.[38] *Why was von Braun being interrogated so long after the war?* At that point von Braun had long been been in the U.S. working for the American army on its highly secret military missiles programs.

The next page began the Project Abstract overview report: "These notes refer to a Joint Intelligence Investigation aimed at the recovery of research and development reports and equipment secreted under the direction of General Dornberger and Dr. von Braun, with the intention of rebuilding a Guided Weapon organization in Germany after the relaxation of Allied surveillance."

"God Almighty," I thought. Von Braun was planning for the Fourth Reich.

The overview report states that U.S. intelligence agents "have been the more active" in Project Abstract—more active than the Brits, that is, suggesting it was primarily the U.S. that suspected von Braun and Dornberger of duplicity, which makes sense, since the Americans were so heavily invested in von Braun. On the British side, Tilley was apparently alone in his enthusiasm for Project Abstract; British Chief of Intelligence General John Sydney Lethbridge saw little value in the project though he conceded, "It is fairly clear that U.S. Intelligence recognizes Operation 'ABSTRACT' as important and potentially valuable."

The report impugns the attempt to recover buried records and instruments as high drama, fanciful, describing "[s]ecret hiding places…[m]aps divided into two or three sections, each useless by itself. Code words, colored numbering and lettering, hollow trees, buried copper cylinders containing receipts, and so on." This does seem to be the stuff of conspiracy theorists, the aluminum-foil-hat crowd—but in the very next paragraph the report dutifully admits that nearly all these far-fetched things have been proven to exist, and the impossible becomes the factual: "sectioned maps and receipts…have been scrutinized here, with the colored number and code word 'Munchen' [Munich] all mentioned. And research reports from Peenemünde, so carefully protected in soldered zinc-lined boxes that they would be safe for years, were found only with the aid of those melodramatic clues." Later, when Tilley was set to leave active duty, none other than U.S. Air Force general Curtis LeMay intervened, explaining to his British counterparts that he "would welcome an extension of his services." The extension was granted, and Project Abstract continued.[39]

Fascinating. I wanted to read on through the second document, but I was out of time. I walked the last four blocks to my office and my workday began.

● ● ●

That afternoon, though, I walked to Farragut Park, near my office in D.C. It was an unexpectedly pleasant day, and others had flocked to the park with its towering, mature trees. There were no tables, just benches. This foray was unusual for me—on days like this one, when I didn't have a business lunch lined up, I usually ate at my desk, working through the lunch hour. Today, though, Colm's emails had gotten the better of me. I found a seat in the shade and opened Colm's second email.

The subject line of this second email was uninspired but accurate "Second K document." In the email body, Colm asked me to review it and let him know my thoughts. Then in all caps: "NO ONE ELSE HAS

THIS!" Colm certainly had my attention. This was a report on the interrogation of von Braun, just as revelatory. Not only had von Braun actively withheld documents, as it turns out, but he also had failed to be honest in other ways. In play now were documents beyond those we've already discussed. Perhaps the very cream of the German rocket program's research had been hidden by von Braun and Dornberger before the final leg of their arduous journey to the U.S.—and never revealed to the Americans, for whom the pair were now supposed to be working. The Americans suspected von Braun was withholding information on burial sites at Bad Sachsa, thirty minutes west of Nordhausen, and also at Oberjoch in the south. Getting information on these sites was the purpose of this von Braun interrogation.

The interrogation was conducted on March 8, 1947, at H.Q., USFET, by head FIAT interrogator Edmund Tilley and Dr. John H. Merchant of Brown University, who would become dean of Brown University's engineering department and the chairman of the Center for Scientific Computation.

Tilley and Marchant begin the interview knowing that in April 1945 someone had ordered boxes buried, including a small tin box that contained a master location map for other, larger buried boxes—one at Oberjoch in the south and several at Bad Sachsa, the headquarters of von Braun and Kammler. Oberjoch was in Bavaria, near the rocket team's surrender. The tin box had now been found, though not in its original spot, and it still contained several master location maps. The burial site of the lone box at Oberjoch in the south had been located, but that lone box had already been removed, though some of its documents remained scattered at the site, damaged to the point of uselessness. The burial sites in Bad Sachsa for the several other boxes were found, but those locations had also already been pilfered. This began to smell like a Tom Clancy novel.

In the interrogation, von Braun claimed he knew nothing about these caches. But it's clear he was lying. Von Braun's testimony is contradicted by the testimony of Dornberger, of others who buried documents at von

Braun's direction, and even of von Braun's own parents. Dornberger and others distinctly remember von Braun being present when the tin box with the master location map was buried, though von Braun denied it. Dornberger also testified that von Braun had shown him a location map just after their joint surrender to the Americans. This suggests that it was von Braun, or his agents, who had already returned to the burial site of the lone tin box, retrieved that box, copied the location maps, returned the tin box to its approximate but not precise location, and then pilfered the caches of hidden boxes.

Major General Walter Dornberger (left), commander of the Peenemünde missile base, with Lieutenant Colonel Herbert Axster, Wernher von Braun (with arm in a cast) after they surrendered to U.S. Seventh Army troops in Austria on May 3, 1945. National Aeronautics and Space Administration

It is clear that von Braun directed the burying of documents, records and instruments to make a post-war German rocket program possible. And once he was in American custody, he failed to disclose the cached records promptly. Of course, von Braun was in a tricky situation. If he had told the Americans about the buried records up front, he would have been giving up leverage, and also foreclosing the possibility of a fallback deal with the French or British. Then once he had formalized a deal with the Americans, he could not admit to the existence of the records or his part in keeping them from the Americans because he would be viewed as less than forthcoming. So von Braun had tried to finesse the situation by sending the master location sketch—the legend to the sites of the large stashes of buried documents—to colleagues in Germany who were bound for America. Once they arrived in America they would then present this gem to von Braun, who could in turn offer it up as new-found information.

In fact, Dornberger's wife in Germany admitted that she had received location maps from von Braun just a couple of months before this 1947 interrogation. And von Braun's own brother Sigismund confirmed that their parents had also received them in the same time frame, "sent through the regular mail channels from the United States by Werner von Braun." Von Braun had ensnared himself.

Hans Waas, the former general manager of Peenemünde West, made a statement concerning yet another set of buried records and instruments. Waas stated that in September 1946 he and Bernhard Hohmann, a Peenemünde West engineer, dug up "one of three copper tubes which contained (a) lists of instruments hidden on various farms near Weser-munde and (b) location sketches of the hiding places of three boxes of Peenemünde-West documents." This angle of inquiry was so important to the agents on Project Abstract that they went to the extraordinary step of tracking down, interrogating, and taking a signed statement from Hohmann's wife. Hohmann was supposed to take the purloined documents to America and turn them over to von Braun, who would triumphantly present them to the Americans.[40]

According to both Waas and Dornberger, von Braun was not a mere participant but "the directing genius" in this scheme.[41] Von Braun's withholding of documents and instruments from the rocket program was not a one-off. He also snuck at least two non-scientists into the U.S. under false pretenses.[42]

The March 1947 interrogation next jumped wildly to nuclear research in Germany. But why? *Why would Tilley and Marchant ask von Braun about nuclear research?* What did they know about Germany's nuclear program that led them to confront Germany's—now America's—number one rocket scientist on that subject? Of course, von Braun denied even contemplating mating a nuclear warhead with one of his rockets, much less taking concrete steps in that direction. I don't believe him. He did admit, for the first time ever, that he had been in contact with the German nuclear research team headed by Professor Werner Heisenberg, Dr. Weizsacker, and Manfred von Ardenne, but he claimed that was only about the possibility of using nuclear power to propel the V-2.

The interrogator asked von Braun whether he had ever disclosed this information to any superior in America. Von Braun, a highly intelligent man, knew the Americans had a keen interest in any information concerning German nuclear physics and research. But no—von Braun had not disclosed the contact between his rocket team and Germany's nuclear research project: "Nobody has ever asked me about this"[43]—an appallingly cagey response.

Von Braun then let drop that fellow rocket expert Helmut Gröttrup had recently visited him. Under Operation Osoaviakhim, a project under which the Russians forcibly recruited German scientists, Gröttrup had been recruited at gunpoint by and was working for the Russians. Gröttrup was inarguably the best German engineer the Russians had. Von Braun's mention of his contact with Gröttrup should have raised red flags. It is unthinkable the Russians would send their highest-ranking German recruit to visit with the Americans' highest-ranking German recruit without an ulterior motive—without trying to win von Braun over to the Russian cause. But this lead was left dangling.

Von Braun did his credibility further damage when he claimed that he had no rank in the SS in 1942.[44] His flat-out lies were becoming so obvious I was finding it difficult to believe anything he had said.

Still, von Braun did make some other disturbing admissions in this 1947 interrogation. For example, he admitted that in 1944 he had told German Army weapons research that the V-2 could be outfitted with the Roechling Geschosse shell—a chemical weapon, a bunker-buster shell, that could pierce armor or as much as six feet of concrete, and would be filled with "a new, highly concentrated acid smoke" that would blind everyone it touched.[45] The pairing of the V-2 and Roechling shell was ultimately vetoed by Hitler himself, who feared retaliation by the Allies. Unbelievably, Colm had uncovered proof that von Braun was prepared to do what even Hitler thought too extreme. Think about that for a moment.

When confronted about having not revealed this information before, von Braun repeated his earlier self-defense: "He did not tell any American experts of this project because he was never questioned on this topic."[46] Unbelievable! Naturally, the Allies had been unable to ask about a project they did not know existed. Given all this, I put no confidence in von Braun's denial that he had never contemplated delivering nuclear weapons with any of his missiles.

I spent a very long, hungry afternoon at work, having skipped lunch. I made sure to download Colm's final attachment to my laptop before I left the office. Once on the bus, I resumed my review while, as typically happened, my fellow passengers nodded off and began a snoring and snorting contest. I liked it when they slept, though, because when they were awake I got odd glances at my computer screen when I scrolled past "CONFIDENTIAL" or "TOP SECRET" stamps on documents I was reading. The glow of the screen, illuminating my face in the growing darkness, added to the scene. They probably thought I was with WikiLeaks.

This final batch of documents was quite the batch—the ones found by Keith weeks ago that had triggered Colm's targeted search. Keith and Colm had decided not to share them with me until Colm's half of the search had been concluded.

Keith's first document was an August 19, 1947, "Brief Operational Report on [REDACTED]" from the CIC. What wasn't redacted from the report's title was simply spectacular: "Transfer by SD from TUCHE-LER HEIDE to Italy of 4 Boxes Containing Documents, Research Data, Instruments and Substances Connected with Guided Missiles and Atomic Energy." Tucheler Heide, in northern Poland, near the town of Tuchola, became the V-1 and V-2 test launch site after the Russians got too close to Blizna. But Tucheler Heide was also an SS experimental research station. A fair amount of the rest of the report was redacted, but much was intact. Paragraph 4.a.: "Atomic research and development at Tucheler Heide was coupled with research on guided missiles." So many things I had to read twice—not from inattention, but from incredulity, even when I was expecting revelatory material. This was really something—missiles paired with atomic research. Then my eye caught "atomic research and development." Development meant production, at least of prototypes.

But to my surprise, even this mind-blowing information was not the most incredible part of this report. The CIC report documents the shipment of four important boxes from Tucheler Heide to Italy in March 1945. The manner of their shipment and the guards present "mean that the boxes were considered unusually precious." Indeed, they contained "research data on V-weapons and atomic research," and "40-50 small ampullae (phials) 'full of whitish liquid,' labeled U-234, U-235 and PLU." Enriched uranium! Plutonium! The atomic research had been conducted in 1943 and 1944. The boxes were buried near Verona, Italy. This part of Project Abstract, Operation Arrival, was out to recover the missing records and equipment, noting that the Russians were also in hot pursuit, so it was a race between the Americans and the Russians. The burial site had been discovered by the Americans, the CIC, but it had already been pilfered by parties unknown, with only bits of paper and one of the labeled phials left behind.

Then came a most bewildering mention in the report, a new name—Professor Dr. Niels, not otherwise identified, at Tucheler Heide, who "produced a number of atomic bombs, weighing from 1 to 5 kilograms. Niels should be traced and questioned in detail." Unbelievably, Keith unearthed a U.S. Army CIC report claiming that the Germans had created small atomic bombs. Oddly (and suspiciously), there is no further detail on this claim, which is so confounding it makes me question its seriousness. I have no doubt it was reported as true, but perhaps the author of the report, without saying so, found it not credible—otherwise, why slip this bombshell finding into paragraph twenty-five on page ten of a twelve-page report, without even repeating the finding in the report's conclusion section? Still, this was a spectacular find by Keith. Not just an atomic bomb—more than one. Our subsequent search on Niels and any other information on a small tactical nuke brought to fruition by the Germans failed to provide definitive confirmation, though it does dovetail with our other findings about Germany continuing nuclear weapons research well beyond the date conventional history records. Tucheler Heide was an SS post and V-2 research facility. A ten-pound payload would easily fit within any of Kammler's rockets. I recalled the links between von Ardenne and his underground lab in Berlin Lichterfelde and von Braun and the V-1 on the Baltic Coast, very close to Tucheler Heide. Von Ardenne, recall, claims he was inventing a "super weapon." These links between Kammler, von Braun, missiles, and atomic weapons are beyond fascinating, and Keith and Colm kept piling them up.

Yet another document Keith discovered under the Project Abstract rubric implicated von Braun in the case of yet more hidden documents. This on "Operation Oberjoch." Oberjoch is a small German village, southwest of Munich, quite near the border with Austria. The search for research documents there was in part directed by the location maps von Braun had sent from America to his family and Frau Dornberger in Germany. The report found that, while such documents had been stashed there, they had since been removed. As before, von Braun was the mastermind of hiding documents: "All evidence points to Von Braun and Axster as those chiefly responsible."[47]

● ● ●

In summary, the Project Abstract investigators concluded, "The evidence forces us to declare him [von Braun] deliberately untruthful unless we reject the testimony of Lt. Gen. Dornberger, Frau Dornberger and his brother Sigismund von Braun.... Statements made by many witnesses indicate that von Braun was the directing genius in a futile game of withholding information which was vital to us two years ago and perhaps may still be important in several respects."[48]

So the Americans knew in *1947* that von Braun was withholding important documents and instruments from Nazi research. Even worse, they also believed that in his work for the United States, he was "not reproducing freely all the latest phases of German development in guided missiles."[49] And of course from the very beginning of their relationship with him they were well aware that he was a Nazi war criminal who had used concentration camp inmates as slave laborers—in the production of rockets that terrorized civilian populations. The Americans knew all that in 1947. And yet they harbored von Braun *until 1977.* His value in the development of ICBMs, the U.S. space program, and the Cold War was just too great for the United States to allow him to face justice. They did the same for Kammler, I had no doubt.

CHAPTER ELEVEN

The Kammler Deal

"The end of the beginning...."

—*Winston Churchill*

B ut who actually did the deal? Who on the American side had the boldness to actively pursue a partner like Kammler and seal an agreement with him? And who had the clout to cover it up?

On this question, Keith had been pursuing two strains of research. His first idea was the Army Air Forces, and it had merit. The Army Air Forces (AAF), precursor of the U.S. Air Force, would have been keenly interested in Kammler. After all, nearly every weapon Kammler had overseen involved aerial warfare. And we had the General McDonald documents on underground research produced by the Maxwell and Wright-Patterson Air Force bases. We also knew Nordhausen general manager Rickhey and his documents had been sent to Wright-Patterson, home to Army Air Forces, by Colonel Beasley, so there was a Kammler connection. But we had little other concrete evidence, so I put the AAF on the back burner.

Keith next steered me in another direction to one name and one organization—Allen Dulles, the station chief of OSS in Bern, Switzerland. OSS was the forerunner of the CIA. I was dubious at first. It didn't get much bigger than the Dulles brothers. If Allen Dulles, subsequently the director of the CIA, brother of future secretary of state John Foster Dulles, had made the Kammler Deal, our Kammler story would reach seismic proportions.

But given the documents we have, we can make a solid but only circumstantial case that it could have been Dulles who made the deal. There is no doubt that Dulles was the type of man who would make such a pact. The motivation for such a deal is certainly there. And he had the opportunity. Dulles is proven to have been involved in extensive negotiations with other Nazis and, critically, though he lacked the explicit de jure authority, he had the de facto power to close the deal and cover it up.

We know the OSS, the Office of Strategic Services, very actively recruited well-placed, well-informed Nazis in support of its intelligence-gathering even before the war ended, and certainly after the war. Before heading the CIA, though, even before coming to OSS, Allen Dulles was an American diplomat and a partner in a white-shoe New York law firm, as was his brother John Foster, and before the war he had contact with Mussolini and Hitler, as well as with the leaders of what would become the mighty Allied countries.

OSS was a large and diverse secret agency. Its branches included R&A (Research and Analysis), SI (Secret Intelligence), SO (Special Operations), X-2 (Counter-intelligence), to mention just a few. The OSS did not impose military-style discipline, but instead, "rewarded unusual even frankly peculiar thought, and on occasion, action."[1] OSS was known for its ingenuity and creativity, demonstrated in one story from the Pacific Theater. During America's famous island-hopping conquest of Japanese-held territory in the Pacific, the American military was at a loss to estimate the number of enemy soldiers they might face on any given island. Using aerial photos and "intelligence" about Japanese toiletry standards, OSS counted the total number of latrines, multiplied by the Japanese standard of 'X number of latrines per soldier,' and arrived at a remarkably close estimate of the number of Japanese soldiers on the island,[2] which proved invaluable in planning invasions and keeping American loss of life as low as possible.

So unconventional thinking and the urgency created by dire, exigent circumstances can yield impressive results. But they can also lead to all sorts of problems. As clever as OSS operators were, the agency was neither infallible nor perfectly unified. Dissension in OSS, and between OSS and other intelligence agencies, led both to self-dealing and to situations in which the left hand often (often by design) did not know what the right hand was doing.

Dulles's position as President Roosevelt's personal representative in Switzerland during the war had, as he himself explained, "the result of bringing to my door purveyors of information, volunteers and adventurers of every sort, professional and amateur spies, good and bad."[3] And as head of OSS in Europe, Dulles received regular intelligence beginning in early 1943 on Germany's secret weapons.[4] Dulles would have seen Kammler as a high-value point of contact or target. By the end of the war Kammler was at the apex of all German weapons research and manufacturing. He was a fount of information, well worth Dulles's attention.

Unfortunately, scholars face a daunting task when researching OSS. There is the passage of time. There is the secrecy that was the agency's very reason for being. And on top of all that, there is the fact that *over five million pages* of OSS records were destroyed after the war.[5] One National Archives archivist told Keith that in the mid-1980s *two thousand feet* of records being kept by the CIA, most likely early records of the OSS, were "disposed of" because they were deemed to be of no historical value. Recognizing a serious problem across U.S. government record-keeping and disclosure, in 1999 the U.S. established a special commission, the Nazi War Crimes and Japanese Imperial Government Records Interagency Working Group (IWG), to review the agency document reviewers. The IWG was tasked with accelerating the release of war records more than five decades after the war ended. Unfortunately, as Keith discovered when he contacted those in charge of the IWG, the agencies holding documents only produced records for persons requested by the IWG. The IWG had requested no Kammler records, so none were received or reviewed.

The extraordinary career of Allen Dulles was characterized by bravado, a preoccupation with intrigue, and a readiness to break rules. He was "well-known for his tendency to behave recklessly" and had "a fascination with unconventional projects."[6] He was known for cutting people out of the loop, leaving his colleagues in Washington "in the dark about details of his talks with the emissaries of the German resistance," when he spearheaded negotiations for a partial peace, and a pattern of behavior of actively misinforming his superiors about his work.[7] An adventurer, he was reportedly always captivated by the clandestine operations side of OSS more than the pedestrian research and analysis.[8]

Keith first tried to convince me that Dulles had a single, overriding character flaw that made him Suspect Number One: he was a Robber Baron who would sacrifice the interests of America for his own benefit. Keith pointed to Dulles's clients, intertwined American and German businesses, banks, and industrialists, many of whom profited fantastically before and during the war. Many could also have made or lost substantial fortunes depending on how the war ended—not just who prevailed, but also the condition of the loser. Although there is no indication that he or his clients longed for a lasting Reich, Dulles ultimately did prevail over those who "wanted to pastoralize Germany so that it might never again be capable of significant industrial production."[9] The post–World War II Germany would be allowed to rebuild its industrial and commercial base, all inuring to the benefit of Dulles's clients.

In the inter-war years, American businesses and banks invested heavily in the German economy. As collateral, American investors often took back shares of stock in Swiss holding companies that themselves owned German bank stocks. Numerous U.S. companies had German sister companies or subsidiaries, and vice versa, with interlocking boards of directors. It was the beginning of the era of global companies, or at least international businesses. One such company was General Electric, which had a German counterpart, AEG, which did manufacture V-2 electronics. The two businesses produced many of the same goods and shared some board members and investors. And GE was a client of

Dulles's firm. If in his position in the OSS Allen Dulles made a deal with Hans Kammler and could offer up the German rocket industry to GE, lock, stock, and barrel, he would be saving one of his firm's clients a decade of work and perhaps untold sums of money.

But we don't need to prove that Dulles was mercenary or self-dealing to explain why he would have been willing to make a deal with Kammler. As a patriotic intelligence agent of the United States, he would have been motivated by an overarching commitment to American victory against the Soviet Union in the Cold War. The Nazis' rocket and nuclear technology was absolutely essential to that victory. And Hans Kammler was the man who could deliver it.

As the Bern, Switzerland, OSS station chief, the most controversial highlight of Dulles' OSS service was undoubtedly his role in Operation Sunrise, in which he helped negotiate the late-war surrender of German troops in northern Italy. Here we see him wheeling and dealing, interpreting orders and restrictions broadly, and perhaps even disregarding them altogether when he deemed it necessary—in the face of potentially dire international consequences. At least one respected author argued that when Operation Sunrise was shut down by his superiors in Washington, Dulles failed to suspend negotiations in defiance of direct orders that originated in the Oval Office.[10] Dulles claimed that he was careful to suspend all negotiations when ordered to do so, and that he resumed those negotiations only after given a clear go-ahead from Washington,[11] but he also said that "if a man tells too much or asks too often for instructions, he is likely to get some he doesn't relish, and what is worse, he may find headquarters trying to take over the whole conduct of the operation."[12] This seek-forgiveness-rather-than-permission attitude makes it easier to believe Dulles would have gone out of his way to deal with Kammler and shelter him after the war, too.

Kammler would not have been the only Nazi that Dulles shielded. According to some historians, for example, Dulles protected German general Wolff—his point of contact in the Operation Sunrise negotiations—and Wolff's aides after the war.[13] Wolff "was rewarded two years later with an unprecedented private meeting with the U.S. judges who declined to prosecute him thanks to his covert contacts with Dulles.... Evidence that Wolff had facilitated Jewish transports to Treblinka was ignored...."[14] Interestingly, there is good evidence that Wolff used Nazi treasure as a bargaining chip in these negotiations.[15] And Christopher Simpson, author of *The Splendid Blond Beast: Money, Law, and Genocide in the Twentieth Century,* reports that Dulles supported amnesty not just for the likes of Karl Wolff, but for "technical men...with brilliant industrial records."[16] That's a pretty good description of Hans Kammler.

Though Dulles was not a Nazi sympathizer, he was among those in the U.S. willing to join forces with Germany to fight Russia.[17] Dulles certainly knew, given the Allies' agreement requiring nothing short of Germany's unconditional surrender on all fronts, he was risking a crisis among the Allies by continuing his negotiations. Dulles even conceded that Operation Sunrise was nearly derailed when the Soviets got late news of the surrender negotiations. Secret letters of recriminations and responses between Roosevelt and Stalin ensued, but all seems to have been forgiven in the end.

Heinrich Himmler was aware of Operation Sunrise as it was unfolding, which establishes a clear but indirect link between Dulles and Kammler, since Kammler was so closely tied to Himmler. If Himmler could open secret talks with the Americans and at least get their ear, Kammler could have done the same. At this late point in the war, as we have seen, Kammler was almost as powerful, certainly just as mobile and connected.

Another Himmler negotiation is relevant to the Kammler Deal. The SS chief negotiated with Swiss politician Jean-Marie Musy, bargaining for a cash payment in return for the release of over twelve hundred concentration camp prisoners. History records that Musy and Himmler met for the first time on November 3, 1944, and then again on January 15, 1945. But we have discovered a connection that has never before been reported—a copy of Himmler's calendar that memorializes three meetings on October 25, 1944, between Himmler, Walter Schellenberg, and Musy—and Hans Kammler.[18] Kammler's participation in these meetings puts him, with Himmler, in secret negotiations with the enemy—again in direct defiance of Hitler's orders. A final point—the Musy negotiations were being monitored by OSS, which means Dulles had his fingers in this pie.

A closer look at Wild Bill Donovan, head of the OSS and Dulles's stateside boss, sheds some additional light. Donovan and Dulles were not only colleagues, but fast friends. And we know that on August 26, 1944, after Operation Anvil-Dragoon, the American Seventh Army's landing in southern France, Donovan met with Hitler's ambassador to the Vatican, Baron Ernst von Weizsacker. His son, as we have already seen, was the German atomic scientist who, in Allied custody after the war, would come up with the cover story that Nazi science was pursuing only nuclear energy, not weapons. Ernst Weizsacker, the diplomat, was himself a close friend of Himmler and a member of the SS, given an honorary rank by Himmler himself. Donovan cultivated Weizsacker as a source of information, establishing a "back channel" to Weizsacker through intermediaries for precisely that purpose. The relationship was formal enough that Weizsacker earned a code name from OSS: Jackpot II.[19] Donovan was sufficiently interested in peace overtures, even from Nazis, that in December 1944 he asked President Roosevelt for permission to make immunity offers to those coming forward.[20] Dulles, as Donovan's friend and man in Europe, would have known all of this. So, physicist Carl von Weizsacker and the German nuclear program were now at least indirectly connected, via Bill Donovan and the OSS, to Dulles.

Dulles was naturally interested in Germany's Vengeance Weapons.[21] Did Kammler know that? Under the general heading of "knowing your enemy," Kammler would surely have known about Dulles, his intelligence role, and his role as a liaison between U.S. and German businesses. The German industrial and financial leaders with whom Kammler routinely dealt had direct ties to Dulles.

• • •

While Allen Dulles and OSS are strong contenders for arranging the
Kammler Deal, I was seeing many documents pointing more convincingly to Dale M. Garvey and the U.S. Army CIC. Or perhaps the real
answer is the Murder-on-the-Orient-Express solution: Dulles, OSS,
Garvey, and the CIC could all have been involved in the Kammler Deal.
With so many destroyed, redacted, and otherwise missing documents,
it is impossible to reach a definitive conclusion. What we do know is that
despite his reported suicide, Kammler survived the war, was detained by
the Americans—who interrogated him about rocket scientists, underground facilities, secret weapons programs, and more—and was still in
U.S. custody months after his arrest, at which point he was being shielded
from war crimes investigators. During this period, CIC, in the form of
Dale Garvey, continued to carry Kammler on its wanted lists and continued to "search" for Kammler, apparently as a way to confuse allies
and enemies alike.

One significant piece of evidence for CIC's involvement in the Kammler Deal: von Braun and the rocket team surrendered in Oberjoch,
southern Germany, not just to the U.S. Army, but to Army CIC.[22] At
this time the CIC was tiny, with only three hundred officers and just
over a thousand agents.[23] The statistical chance of German scientists
surrendering to them, as opposed to the regular army, was minute.
Recall that Kammler had sent the rocket team to this location on his
personal train in what was an arduous trip, wending through treacherous territory for days. They could have been moved toward the center
of German-held territory more easily, more safely. Instead, in an orches-
trated movement, Kammler sent them to the American front lines—into
the arms of the CIC.

CIC had the free-wheeling "means justifies the ends" culture that
makes it a great candidate for the Kammler Deal. Moreover, as hostilities ended, the most experienced and consequently the most able
CIC agents were cycled out of Europe, taking with them the most

seasoned judgment. And apprehending Kammler was squarely within the mission of CIC—as the Allies advanced into Germany the role of CIC was expanded to explicitly include hunting and arresting Nazi leaders like Kammler. Ironically, CIC succeeded marvelously in one part of this mission—the identification of potential war criminals—but then often turned them into intelligence assets rather than prisoners.[24] One government report, authored comfortably thirty years after the war, noted frankly, "CIC employed many informants who had once served actively in the Nazi Party or SS or had collaborated with Germany during the war."[25]

CIC used notorious Nazis as informants after the war and then covered its tracks successfully, sometimes for decades. Examining known CIC recruitment cases in greater detail is useful in determining Kammler's ultimate fate. Was he brought to America? Did he stay in Europe? Did he live under an assumed name? Could he somehow have made it to South America, for so long the safe haven of so many other Nazi war criminals?

Scenario #1: Kammler Is Given Safe Haven in the U.S.

Our first scenario for Kammler's ultimate fate is that he came to America with help from the U.S. This is perhaps the most disturbing scenario of all, and it is possible, but it is also the scenario that we judge least likely.

Could this Nazi slavemaster war criminal really have been allowed to live out his days in safety and comfort in the United States? It seems incredible.

Yet we have the Operation Paperclip history answering "Yes" to this question for other war criminals. Many German experts were brought to the U.S. under Paperclip to continue their work. In some cases, their Nazi pasts were minimized, ignored, or even rewritten in official files.[26] Most of what has been written about Paperclip focuses on German scientists and technicians who came to America after the war. But a wholly different kind of Nazi was also sometimes brought to America under the same operation—not scientists, but intelligence experts, hard-line ideologues, Nazis involved in the daily persecution of innocent civilians. It can be difficult to separate the merely bad from the truly evil, but it is important to do so. Not enough attention has been paid to how and why America brought to its shores some of these worst-of-the-worst actors.

Take the case of Mykola Lebed. Although Army CIC knew by July 1947 that Lebed, a leading member of the most radical wing of the Ukrainian Nationalist Organization (OUN), was "a well-known sadist and [Nazi] collaborator"[27] who had energetically aided the Nazis during the war, CIC "utilized his services well into 1948." It did so because he was ostensibly able to provide information on Soviet activity in the U.S. Zone. By June 1949, the situation in Europe became too risky for Lebed and, rather than cutting him lose, the Americans brought him to the United States. Despite resistance from many quarters in the government chain of command, Lebed ultimately became a naturalized U.S. citizen. Allen Dulles actively intervened on his behalf at the time.[28] Interestingly, even forty years after the war and during the writing of a 1985 U.S. Government Accounting Office report, the CIA still actively shielded Lebed, who was still living comfortably in the U.S.—denying he was ever connected to the Nazis. He died in 1998 and is buried in New Jersey. He was never deported, never punished.[29]

Whether Dulles or Garvey (or some altogether different American agent) negotiated the Kammler Deal, the membrane that separated OSS and CIC was quite porous. Mykola Lebed began his intelligence career with the Americans as a CIC recruit. Later he crossed into the OSS and then the CIA, becoming an Allen Dulles acolyte. Crossing over from CIC recruitee to OSS-CIA operative like this was common.

It is certainly possible that a new life in America was one of Kammler's demands. That might seem a ridiculous condition, but let's not lose sight of Lebed and other characters like Georg Rickhey, Kammler's principal deputy at Nordhausen, who we know was shipped to America by the eager Colonel Beasley in 1945.

Late in our research, we came upon a tantalizing but ultimately unsupported story from John Richardson, the surviving son of Donald Richardson, a member of both OSS and CIC. John, the surviving son, explained to me that his father had told him that he had actually interviewed Kammler after the war. John Richardson also claimed his now-deceased brother had been told by their father that Kammler committed suicide in 1947. But during a ninety-minute interview with me, the 1947 suicide story was displaced by a claim that Kammler was murdered in 1947. John Richardson provided no supporting documentation for any of his claims, and I became reluctant to rely on a story that originated with a deceased father, told to a now-deceased son, then was related to a surviving son I had interviewed.

There was no name change involved for Lebed or Rickhey. Yet while we have plenty of information that very bad actors came to the U.S. with help from the Americans and we can prove Kammler survived the war and was in U.S. custody, we cannot prove he came to America and lived out his life in safety and comfort here.

Scenario #2: Kammler Stays in Europe

Our second scenario: Might Kammler have stayed in Europe with help from the Americans? Again, there are well-documented cases of similar Nazi war criminals being protected in just this way.

The list of U.S. government employees, contractors, and paid informants who had been high-ranking Nazis or collaborators includes Viktors Arājs, who had been head of Sonderkommando Arajs, a commando unit within Latvia that helped the German Einsatzgruppen to slaughter four thousand Jews and others.[30]

Another example is Robert Jan Verbelen. Verbelen was employed by the 430th CIC in Vienna from 1946 until 1955, arguably under an assumed name after having been convicted in absentia of war crimes and sentenced to death by a Belgian court in 1947.[31]

There is also the former Nazi Dr. Friedrich Buchardt, head of the murder squad Einsatzgruppen B. Buchardt had also headed yet another group in Lodz, Poland, where he supervised the deportation of eighty thousand to the Chełmno extermination camp. Buchardt was employed by the Brits, released, and then likely employed by the Americans. Guy Walters, the author of *Hunting Evil: The Nazi War Criminals Who Escaped and the Quest to Bring Them to Justice*, concludes that "Buchardt can be regarded as the most murderous Nazi employed by the Allies after the war"—though we could make the case that Kammler was responsible for even more carnage.

Nazi general Reinhard Gehlen, too, enjoyed a remarkably long and successful post-war career in West Germany under his own name—even becoming president of the BND (the Bundesnachrichtendienst), the primary intelligence agency of the West German government—in 1956. Gehlen retired from government service in 1968 with a pension at one of Germany's highest civil service grades (Ministrialdirektor), and a second pension from the CIA. During the war, Gehlen had been a German army general and the chief of German army intelligence in Eastern Europe. In that capacity he stood up a vast network of Nazi collaborators, agents, and informants. After the war, he was recruited by CIC to oversee and operate an intelligence network that consisted almost exclusively of his former Nazi and collaborator colleagues, all reporting to CIC. CIC bought Reinhard Gehlen and his Nazi intelligence network in toto,[32] and the Gehlen Organization was born. The U.S. secretly used and paid wanted war criminals as agents and informants, making it possible for their spymaster, lead war criminal Gehlen, to enjoy a long life unmolested in Europe.[33]

The CIA even today remains reluctant to divulge information about these cases. It was not until September 2000 that the recalcitrant CIA for the first time even admitted it had "connections" to Gehlen. This admission came over fifty-five years after the war and over twenty years after Gehlen stopped receiving his CIA pension, and only then at the insistence of a U.S government–appointed special commission. Unsurprisingly, the special Interagency Working Group (IWG) commission found that of all the U.S. agencies it contacted in its work, the CIA was least cooperative.[34] And no wonder. Documents released to the IWG showed that at least five known associates of SS officer Adolf Eichmann found gainful post-war employment with the CIA or one or more of its predecessor organizations. In addition, the CIA tried to recruit at least two dozen other war criminals and collaborators.[35] It's likely that even in the twenty-first century, a Kammler Deal would not be willingly disclosed by the CIA.[36] Of course until now, there has been no call for the U.S. to acknowledge its post-war connections with Kammler—because Kammler is "dead."

Scenario #3: Kammler Escapes to South America

Our third scenario is the one that Colm, Keith, and I deem most plausible: Kammler had American help in escaping to safety in South America after the CIC and OSS-CIA exhausted his usefulness in interrogation.

Consider the remarkably similar—and deeply disturbing—case of Klaus Barbie, the Butcher of Lyon. Klaus Barbie, like Mengele, is a name I knew before becoming involved in this project. His case tracks Kammler's closely. Barbie's case proves that American agents were willing to get into bed with a high-ranking Nazi war criminal, utilize him, and—this is critical—when *Allied* countries exerted pressure to bring him to justice, help him escape with a new identity and engage in a decades' long international cover-up that lasted until outsiders forced disclosure. Barbie did not die until late in 1991.

Barbie's moral compass was as compromised as Kammler's, though he never rose to the same heights and operated on a more limited scale. As a *New York Times* piece marking Barbie's death in 1991 noted, during the war in Lyon, France, Barbie "ran a campaign of torture and death against resistance leaders and caused uncounted other people, most of them Jews, to be sent to the gas chambers of Auschwitz."[37] Barbie was head of the Gestapo in Lyon. One of his main tasks was to combat the very active French resistance there, and he met with some "great successes," even arresting Jean Moulin, the head of the French resistance, and General Charles Delestraint, the commander of the Armée secrète, striking the greatest blows of the war against the resistance. For this work, Barbie built a web of informants and intelligence assets.[38] He is alleged to have tortured men, women, and children—using electroshock as a preferred method of terror, but also shattering limbs, using trained attack dogs on his victims, and even skinning some alive. Barbie was responsible for the deaths of as many as fourteen thousand innocent men, women, and children—almost five times as many as killed on 9/11. A post-war statement of charges issued by France against Barbie reads like a bad horror movie review: "murder and massacres, systematic terrorism, and execution of hostages." In short, Barbie would do anything necessary to extract the information he thought he needed to crush the resistance in Lyon. He was ruthless and uncompromising. And after the war, Klaus Barbie vanished.

Although it was not known at the time, the U.S. Army CIC had recruited Barbie as its own intelligence asset, hoping he had insights into America's new enemy, the Soviet Union, and the means to develop additional reliable information in the future.

Barbie's story tracks eerily with Kammler's. Both men had deplorable records, both disappeared after the war, and both, it turns out, fell in with the Americans because they had something valuable to offer. Eventually both men were formally pursued by American allies with extradition orders. The one difference: Kammler's faked death allowed him to escape. The lower-ranking Barbie was dragged back to face justice, albeit decades later.

We can demonstrate definitively that Army CIC knew it was dealing with a bad actor when it employed Barbie and then spirited him away, just as it did with Kammler. Decades after Barbie's enrollment in service

with CIC, Allan A. Ryan Jr., director of America's Nazi-hunting organization DOJ OSI, authored a report investigating the Barbie affair. As
that report found, agent Robert S. Taylor of CIC Region IV in Munich
had recruited Barbie in January 1947 through a mutual contact, Kurt
Merk, who was already working for CIC as an informant.[39] Ryan concluded that CIC had no knowledge of Barbie's atrocities until May 14,
1949, two years after Taylor recruited him, making the recruitment of a
known Nazi seem accidental. We believe the U.S. knew Barbie's past long
before this. But even the Ryan report concedes that the U.S. sheltered
Barbie and arranged his escape after they knew he was a war criminal.
Erhard Dabringhaus, the CIC agent who actually handled Klaus Barbie
for some time in the 1940s, pegged the date of CIC's guilty knowledge
as July of 1948[40]—years before they shipped Barbie to South America.
Dabringhaus told his CIC Region IV headquarters in Munich about
Barbie's record—but was ordered to carry on. But even Dabringhaus's
date of CIC's guilty knowledge is generously late. Already twice before
that date, Barbie had been tried in absentia by the French and twice
sentenced to death—first on May 16, 1947, and again in 1952.[41] How
on earth could CIC plausibly claim ignorance after the 1947 public trial
of Barbie? Pondering this damning evidence, I noticed something. It was
CIC *Region IV* that recruited Barbie? That was Dale Garvey's region—
the same Dale Garvey who signed Kammler papers, who knew Kammler
was in custody and likely oversaw his interrogation, shielding him from
extradition for his war crimes and hoping to profit from his extensive
knowledge of Nazi research and technology. When Barbie was recruited,
we know that Garvey was the commanding officer of CIC Region IV,
headquartered in Munich. So he was Taylor's supervisor at the time
Taylor recruited Barbie. Anything that Garvey and CIC were willing and
able to do for Klaus Barbie, they surely would have done for Hans Kammler. After all, Kammler was in possession of vastly more useful knowledge and connections than Barbie.

By January 1947, CIC Headquarters, located in Berlin, learned who
Barbie was and that he was wanted, but reportedly did not know Region

IV had recruited him as an informant. HQ shared its Barbie information with at least Region III, but not necessarily with other regions, for reasons not explained in Ryan's report. Information sharing to and from HQ from any particular region was admittedly imperfect, but it beggars belief that while CIC HQ and Region III, and soon Region I, all knew of Barbie's wartime record, Region IV—the region that had recruited and was running Barbie as an informant—did not know he was wanted. In February 1947, just weeks after Barbie was brought on by Region IV, HQ Berlin authorized Operation Selection Board, a CIC "swoop" designed to capture and shut down a group of former SS officers operating as a guerrilla organization in the American Zone, specifically including Barbie. Barbie very likely had unknown help in avoiding that sweep. By April of 1947, CIC HQ specifically instructed Region I to arrest Barbie and within a month Region I informed Region IV of the arrest order. So in the very worst-case scenario it was not later than May 1947, just three months after having recruited him, that Region IV and Dale Garvey knew Barbie was wanted. Dale Garvey and Region IV did nothing. Taylor, Barbie's handler, and CIC Region IV commander Garvey decided to continue to use Barbie as an informant in defiance of the arrest order.

CIC HQ was made aware later that Barbie was being used as an informant, yet nothing in the record indicates so much as a raised eyebrow.[42] Finally in December 1947, following orders from HQ and over the protests of the replacements of both Garvey (who had been promoted within CIC) and Taylor—Lieutenant Colonel Ellington Golden and CIC agent Camille Hajdu—Barbie was finally detained for questioning. Barbie's new handler, Hajdu, and new Region IV chief Golden objected to Barbie's interrogation. Garvey, from his new position as head of CIC for all of Europe, objected that the interrogation "would damage considerably the trust and faith which informants place in this organization," a sweeping claim that CIC's core mission of gathering intelligence with informants would suffer.[43]

Following that alarm, HQ gave assurances that Barbie would be permitted to return to life as an informant in Region IV after the interrogation, provided that he did not incriminate himself during it. With a wink and a nod, CIC HQ was providing Barbie with a road map to pass the interrogation, advising him to steer clear of any discussion of his wartime atrocities. Dabringhaus has it that when Barbie was interrogated,[44] CIC HQ, now home to Dale Garvey, even gave "interrogation instructions to ECIC [the interrogators] requesting that Barbie be interrogated only about his postwar activities,"[45] a stunning concession. Indeed, the 1983 DOJ report states CIC HQ "did not appear interested in Barbie's wartime activities," but only in former SS officers and others still at large about whom Barbie might have information.[46] Ironically, my inner voice screamed, the most significant former SS officer known to Barbie that the CIC should be ruthlessly hunting was Barbie himself!

In an internal report prepared for Region IV just after this kid-gloves interrogation, one CIC agent noted candidly, "Barbie is concerned about the French and realize[s] that if the French were ever to get control of him he would be executed." So it was clear to CIC that Barbie was not only wanted, but that he was wanted for capital offenses. But HQ concluded that Barbie's "knowledge of the mission of CIC, its agents, subagents, funds, etc." was "too great" for him to be turned over to outsiders. The report went on: if his detention was continued, he might escape; if he escaped, he might divulge CIC's secrets to the French or British intelligence services. War criminal Klaus Barbie was returned to service; he would not be turned over for prosecution.

In 1948 and again in 1949, while still being used as an informant, Barbie was finally questioned by the French, but only within the U.S. Zone—for the upcoming trial of French resistance leader René Hardy. Hardy was about to be tried by the French for betraying his own resistance organization to, of all people, Klaus Barbie. In May of 1949, news stories about the Hardy trial hit the front pages in France, and with its collective memory refreshed, the French citizenry began demanding the arrest and extradition of Barbie. The 1983 DOJ report cites this as "the date CIC officials were later to maintain was their first inkling that

Barbie may have been a war criminal"—a risible position. Paperwork indicates CIC HQ did finally order Barbie to be dropped as an informant at that time; but even then he was not really dropped. In fact, years later in January 1950 in a gambit that can only make sense in the surreal world of intelligence and counterintelligence, it was determined by CIC HQ, now under Dale Garvey's command, that Barbie should no longer be used as an asset, but that he should continue to be paid as an asset, CIC should continue to accept information from him as an asset, and he should not be told he was no longer being used as an asset. To suspend payments, HQ reasoned, would be to make Barbie aware of his reduced status. As the DOJ report notes, CIC would "continue to accept his services...and provide him with new and continuing assignments."[47] In other words, CIC continued to use Barbie as an asset while feebly pretending that it was not doing so.

Dale Garvey's involvement with Klaus Barbie and other wanted Nazis bolsters our suspicion that he was involved in the Kammler Deal. Included in the networks run by Garvey's Region IV in Munich was also one Dr. Emil Augsburg, a member of Barbie's network, a sub-informant who reported to CIC through Barbie. As an SS colonel, Augsburg had led a wartime murder squad, Einsatzgruppen B, in occupied territory in Russia.[48] He had also served in Germany's East Institute in Königsberg, responsible for developing a means to dispose of the conquered Russian population and obliterate its culture after Germany's anticipated military victory.

Augsburg was tried in absentia by Polish authorities even while he was part of the Garvey-Barbie network, but he never faced justice. Instead, he found his way into the Reinhard Gehlen organization, where he remained for over a decade. But Augsburg proved too unpredictable even for Gehlen; by the late 1950s, he had been bounced out as a suspected double agent.[49]

Garvey's name also shows up on paperwork for Karl Fiebinger, who, as we have seen, had built underground facilities for Kammler using slave labor. Despite negative reports on his background, Fiebinger made it into

America under Operation Paperclip, once again courtesy of Dale Garvey. Garvey appears yet again in the case of Kurt Debus, a V-2 rocket scientist who came to America under Paperclip. His success in America's rocket program is well documented. Less well-known is that he betrayed to the Gestapo one of his colleagues who had criticized the Nazis during the war. Garvey nevertheless supported his immigration to the U.S.[50] Time and time again, Garvey and the CIC used known Nazis and helped them escape. And Garvey and the CIC were all over Kammler's paperwork. I am making these connections not to judge the actions of CIC or Garvey, but to argue that they make it more likely Garvey and CIC did the same for Kammler.

When Hardy's trial began, the French made renewed requests of the Americans for Barbie to testify at the trial—requests that were denied, though Barbie's testimony was read for the court. The Americans were unwilling to let Barbie out of their control for even a moment; the decision to that effect was made at the highest levels. The surfacing of Barbie's name in the run-up to the Hardy trial caused a second wave of public outrage that had to be managed—the Butcher of Lyon not being returned to France to face justice.[51] This was an international scandal, and there is no chance the Barbie debacle happened without the State Department weighing in.

CIC had now essentially trapped itself. They had Barbie and they had been using him clandestinely for years. Charitably, they were not able to admit it because to do so would be to admit wrongdoing of various sorts. Beyond the obvious, some of the U.S. intelligence-gathering at the time included illicit operations in the French Zone,[52] and those activities, if revealed, would lead to a diplomatic firefight. It was at this point in December 1950 that the 66th CIC Detachment, the part of CIC now running Barbie, turned to the 430th CIC Detachment, its sister organization operating nearby in Austria, and its secret "Ratline," an underground network used to remove people surreptitiously from Europe, transplanting them under assumed names to Central and South American countries. The Ratline was used primarily for people from the

Russian Zone who were, in the eyes of its operators, being unjustly pursued as political enemies by Communist regimes. Though Russia, like the other Allied countries, was entitled to bring war criminals to trial, there was justified concern that the Soviets were using war crimes allegations to persecute political opponents. But the Ratline was also used by "hundreds of German, Austrian, French, Belgian, Dutch, Slovakian and Croatian war criminals and Nazi collaborators."[53] Some would say thousands.

The U.S. Army used the Ratline to move people like Barbie, who were too hot to bring to the States, to South America. The account of retired U.S. Army colonel James U. Milano, who was point man for the Ratline at the 430th CIC in Austria, may be relevant to the Kammler case. Milano said that he had used an escape route conceived of and constructed by Father Krunoslav Draganović, secretary of the Croatian Confraternity of San Girolamo. Draganović's goal was to move Croats being persecuted by Communists off the continent to safety. Father Draganović's line moved people over land from Eastern Europe, south through the Alps, to central Italy, where they received false ID papers via the International Red Cross, and then traveled by ship to South America.

And here is how American agents used the Ratline to get Nazi war criminals to South America: The Americans identified a subject they wished to evacuate: in this case, Barbie and his family. They paid a handling fee of between $1,000 and $1,400 per evacuee. CIC transferred Barbie to Genoa, Italy, after obtaining travel documents from the Combined Travel Board, a branch of the Allied High Commission for Germany, which allowed them to travel only as far as Italy. Barbie traveled under the name Klaus Altmann. The European end of the Ratline was operated by Father Draganović, who as we have seen had originally set it up to save Croats—particularly as many members of the now-persecuted Croatian Revolutionary Movement as possible. The ruthlessness of the Croatian revolutionaries had made them controversial after the war. Draganović used the International Committee of the Red Cross to obtain necessary documentation for the remainder of the trip, allowing the "Altmanns" to leave Genoa for Bolivia in March of 1951. According to the 1983 DOJ report, CIC HQ afterwards commended everyone involved for a job well done. Barbie lived quietly in South America for decades, was exposed in the early 1970s, but was not returned to France until 1983, when a change in the Bolivian government made his expulsion possible. He was tried in 1987 and sentenced to life in prison. He spent four years in prison until his death.

For years from his station in Austria, Milano used the line—admittedly illegally—to benefit intelligence assets after their value had been depleted. Milano viewed the higher-ups, including not just the army brass but especially the State Department, as meddlers, impediments to the successful completion of his intelligence-gathering mission. Milano's purview included "industrial sites in Eastern Europe and in the Soviet Union itself, that produced armaments or serviced weapons systems."[54] As I read the words of Milano's memoir, my thoughts turned to everything Kammler had ruled in Austria, Czechoslovakia, Poland, and elsewhere. Milano couldn't have constructed a sentence to better describe Kammler's remit, which must have been a high-priority item for Milano's mission.

By his own account, Milano didn't begin using the Ratline until 1947, but could he have misremembered or misreported his earliest use? That would be very difficult to double-check since, as it unbelievably turns out, a 1988 U.S. government report observes almost off-handedly, "records of the 430th CIC Detachment for the period 1945 to 1947 are no longer in existence."[55] That is suspiciously convenient.

Kammler could easily have been held until 1947 and then dropped into the Ratline. Milano makes it clear that the records of Nazis who went that illicit route were always deliberately destroyed—the CIC agents involved knew that their work needed special protection from discovery forever. Indeed, Milano's book includes a scene in which he and his colleagues, including Pentagon representatives, burn all Ratline-related files bonfire-style to get rid of all traces of the operation. So if

Kammler used the Ratline, we would expect to find a trail of ash, not paper.[56] Indeed, this would account perfectly for the dearth of Kammler files we found—CIC kicking off a search-and-destroy mission of Kammler files as he was sent abroad; that was CIC policy, according to Milano.

Milano insists that he never used the Ratline to evacuate a war criminal or a wanted man. He does, however, acknowledge knowing that Father Draganović was helping war criminals, former SS, Croatian ultra-nationalist Ustaše, and others evade justice. Milano even acknowledges misgivings that the fungible $1,500 per person he paid to evacuate his own defectors would subsidize Draganović's other illicit operations.[57] He makes a commendable and frank admission; though in the third person, these are his own words: "Milano and his colleagues closed their eyes to the deplorable fact that he [Milano] was helping war criminals to escape justice because he [Draganović] alone could supply a safe, efficient method of sending their Soviet defectors off to a new life."[58]

If not Milano, could some other American have seen Kammler's value, extracted all useful intelligence from him, and then dropped him into the Draganović Ratline? Or was there another Ratline? As Milano explained in his memoir, he was careful to tell very few people, especially possibly uncooperative higher-ups, about the Ratline; again, in his own words, though in the third person, "Milano believed that the less his superiors knew of his doings, the better."[59] What if Father Draganović had the same operational security concerns as Milano and took similar precautions? Was it possible that Draganović offered up his Ratline to other divisions of CIC, or other parts of the U.S. military, or to OSS, without Milano's knowledge? If Milano could keep his activities secret, someone within a different chain of command could have done the same. And that someone might have dropped Kammler into the Ratline from a different entry point, even if Milano didn't! We have no direct evidence of a Kammler escape along this route, but it certainly seems likely, given Garvey's involvement in the Kammler case, Barbie's, and several others.

Maybe Milano's story is only one sliver of the tale, and even if he didn't aid Kammler, others did.

● ● ●

Just how high did knowledge of the Barbie scheme and the Ratline run? Well, the CIC HQ operations officer in Berlin knew of the scheme—it was he who instructed Region IV to discontinue using Barbie, but to keep paying him and keep accepting information from him. We know the coverup went even higher: Brigadier General Robert K. Taylor (a different Robert Taylor), the chief military intelligence officer for the entire U.S. Zone of Occupation, knew about the scheme and covered it up. On June 15, 1950, Taylor told the State Department that use of Barbie by CIC had ended in late May of 1949. This was patently untrue, and we know Taylor knew it to be untrue as he wrote it because the previous month, May 1950, he had written to CIC's commanding officer that the Barbie case might prove "very embarrassing."[60] So long before Barbie was whisked out of Europe, CIC HQ and the Director of Intelligence for U.S. European Command knew exactly what was happening. As we have seen, unnamed representatives of the Pentagon did, too, participating in the burning of official records.

Furthermore, former agent Dabringhaus stated that when anyone was placed in the Ratline, CIC was required to notify the State Department of the real and cover names of the emigrants.[61] The State Department, then, knew of the Ratline and knew the assumed and true identity of every person transported through it by CIC. The Barbie affair and the Ratline were not run by some rogue cell, but were known and authorized by the highest civilian and military circles.

● ● ●

A 1985 investigation by the U.S. General Accounting Office (GAO) into the U.S. use of Nazis and Axis collaborators is damning.[62] It concluded that American intelligence would rather deal with known or suspected Nazis than forgo the information and expertise they had to offer: "U.S intelligence units knowingly employed alleged Nazis and Axis collaborators to obtain information about Soviet intentions and capabilities."[63] The bottom line: "if a person was a war criminal, the decision of whether or not to use him depended on what he could do for you."[64] The GAO report concluded that in a handful of instances U.S. agents helped war criminals escape Europe. It's not a stretch to think Kammler was among those who was provided with a new life.

Bizarrely, even though it admitted to having incomplete information on which to base its conclusion, the GAO report concluded that it "did not find evidence of any specific program to help such persons immigrate to the United States."[65] So although it discovered several instances of the use of war criminals by the U.S. and of Americans' help in their escape and immigration assistance, it discerned no "specific program" dedicated to that purpose.

Whether or not there was a specific program, we can prove Barbie and several other known and suspected Nazi war criminals were aided in their escape and post-war lives by the Americans. We know Kammler did not die as reported, but in fact surrendered to the U.S. Army; we have seen him, in the days leading up to that surrender, protecting resources he could have used to make a deal with the Americans, and even moving them toward American forces. And once in U.S. custody, Kammler has never been heard of since. That is as close as we can come to proving that Kammler was aided in his post-war life—admittedly circumstantial evidence, but very powerful nevertheless.

• • •

It was at this point that Keith and Colm fed me what they styled the pièce de résistance, the case most similar to Kammler's: senior Gestapo officer Rudolf Mildner.[66] Born on July 10, 1902, near what is now the Poland-Czech Republic border, Mildner was of Kammler's generation, just a year younger. He joined the German navy at age fourteen as World War I began and struggled to find employment after that war. He graduated from high school late but went on to earn a law degree in Innsbruck. After some bouncing around, he landed on the police force in Salzburg, Austria.[67] During the war, Mildner served above Eichmann and for Reinhard Heydrich, investigating Austrians to verify their loyalty to Germany. He also headed Denmark's Security Police when it deported Jewish prisoners and was involved, in his words, in "mass arrests."[68] Both Kammler and Mildner had served in the *Freikorps* calvary and later in the Reich Main Security Office. Mildner was lead man in the Gestapo in Katowice, Poland, and is best known for giving suspected Polish resistance members one-minute trials at Auschwitz— executing hundreds,[69] something he tried to explain away after the war rather than deny. Testimony by none other than Auschwitz commandant Rudolf Höss verified that Mildner toured the camp, visiting its gas chambers and crematoria, the ultimate destination of the Jews he deported from Katowice[70]—that is, he not only toured Auschwitz, but he knowingly supplied the camp with Jews to be murdered.

Like Kammler, Mildner was no stranger to the OSS during the war.[71] On May 30, 1945, Mildner was captured by the 80th CIC detachment in the Austrian Alps. Like Kammler, Mildner's guilt in the Holocaust, though never adjudicated, is indisputable—both were in the automatic arrest category. Mildner had a long resume as a faithful Nazi in the Gestapo, and the U.S. knew this, so both were known war criminals. Mildner, like Kammler, was interrogated at Nuremberg, having been turned over to the U.S. Chief of Counsel for War Crimes on October 1, 1945, but never tried.[72] Also as in the case of Kammler, there was a British request for Mildner's extradition while he was in American custody. Precisely as in Kammler's file, CIC noted in scribbled writing in Mildner's file that it had no further interest in him. Mildner's records include a notation eerily identical to the one in Kammler's file—hand-written note saying that he had been placed in the "Rogues Gallery." As is the case in Kammler's file, CIC lieutenant colonel Dale Garvey's name is everywhere to be found in Mildner's paperwork. The similarities were so striking that I joked we could almost do a search-and-replace for the name "Mildner" with "Kammler" and produce the Kammler dossier we had in hand.

We know Mildner was never extradited, despite the request and stated lack of opposition, as in Kammler's case. Instead, Mildner "escaped" from his internment in Nuremberg on August 11, 1946.[73] Then, "In 1949, like a number of other Nazi war criminals, Mildner went to Argentina."[74] The parallels between Mildner and Kammler are jarring, even down to the timing and, of course, the involvement of the CIC in both cases and the fact that the same man—CIC chief Dale Garvey—had signed off on both.

The identical handwritten reference to "Rogues Gallery" in both the Mildner and Kammler files is most intriguing. Was this a notation used by CIC to indicate the identified person, Mildner in this case, Kammler in ours, was being taken out of circulation by CIC and dropped into the Ratline? We have no concrete evidence this is what was meant, but we do know the handwritten reference appears in both files of men in CIC custody with open extradition requests, who shortly thereafter disappeared without being extradited. And we know that one of them—at least one of them—ended up in Argentina.

Both Kammler and Mildner were in U.S. custody as the war ended and for months afterward, and then both of them simply fell off the face of the earth. Finally, both Kammler and Mildner were declared dead by European courts, without a body, ending Allied manhunts even before they began. With Mildner having gone to Argentina, it seems logical to conclude that Kammler did, as well.

● ● ●

I needed a break and decided to go for a long run to get away from all the Nazi gruel I had been consuming, or that had been consuming me. "Too much Kammler," was a phrase I had developed in my internal monologue, and I was suffering the symptoms. Despite degrading knees and hips, forty-five minutes of jogging with my iPhone piping blood-pumping music was a great way to clear my head. Running just before summer sundown allowed me to enjoy the least hot part of the day and a great chance to see some wildlife. I passed some teenagers on bikes, their mouths working but their words lost to my earbuds, and then a woman pushing a double jogging stroller. The contraption was nearly as big as she was, and I admired her effort, thinking of my sister who, like me, was a bit of an exercise nut, working to maintain high school–level fitness. Then, because of the stroller, I thought again of the toddler in the Polish ghetto Joe Gringlas had told me about. Even with Led Zeppelin thumping in my head, Kammler and his SS contemporaries found a way in, uninvited. I gave up on the music and made the turn for home as my brain created its own soundtrack:

Our evidence is striking. As World War II ended, enough American agents with enough power were so intent on stopping Communism they would and did work with nearly any individual in either theater of operation. Barbie, Gehlen, hundreds brought to the U.S. under Operation Paperclip and other programs, all those in the IWG report, Japan's bio warfare director, and who knows who else. The people who made this possible included not just line-level agents and supervisors, but headquarters staff, generals, and Pentagon and State Department personnel. The Kammler Deal was never a rank-and-file operation.

At this point, my mind and body were both racing too fast, but I carried on, the trees gliding by. Be careful not to attack the work of CIC, the Army, the OSS, or other agencies that used former Nazis in their work, even helping them escape. I might have done the same. We need to acknowledge the United States was in a near panic as it swung around to oppose the Soviet Union. As pernicious as the Germans were, the Soviets were not simply military adversaries, but were also ideological enemies bent on worldwide Communist revolution. The Nazis, as atrocious as they were, didn't pose the same existential threat to America. Hitler envisioned the United States as one of the world powers after the war, a competitor but not an enemy. It was in this context that Barbie, Mildner, and the others were recruited to ply their trade against the Soviets. It was in this context that the Kammler Deal was made.

The Vengeance Weapons technology, Kammler's knowledge of German scientists, and his expertise at building underground installations were certainly highly sought by the Allies, and Kammler was the only route to obtaining all of it. We also know he had access to purloined treasures, including gold and bank accounts. We threw in what Kammler was offering in nuclear research. I am confident Working Staff Kammler was conducting such research and had made meaningful advances.

I had run myself out of air and stopped, doubled over, breathing heavily in the moist heat, legs burning, still a mile from home. The thoughts swirling in my head had caused me to completely blow my pacing. I found myself roiling with anger: The son of a bitch did not die at the end of the war. He surrendered to the U.S. Army and was held in custody for at least ten months. We know this. He was questioned about everything he knew—treasure, nuclear research, secret weapons, underground facilities. Records are so sparse it is fair to conclude that they were deliberately destroyed or misfiled. Everyone involved in the cover-up is long since dead, but the inertia to hide documents persists. Loads of documents that we received, even in the last five years, have been heavily redacted. The outright rejection of Keith's 2008 FOIA request is a prime example of the continuing government reticence to come clean.

I walked a few paces, looking skyward at the glowing clouds, then turned to see the sun touching the horizon in the west. My lungs were aching, my legs were still complaining. My phone buzzed with an incoming email. I glanced and saw Colm's name on my screen, cc'ing Keith. I opened the attachment without reading his message, still breathing hard. The document took a long time to open on my phone, so I knew it had some heft to it. As my phone worked, it buzzed again, and reverted to my email. Yet another Colm email, with another document. I tried opening it as well, still walking though I should have been jogging again.

The first document sprang to life on my screen. Something called Blue Book on Argentina, written by the U.S. government in February 1946, a date not lost on me: *The same month Great Britain was requesting Kammler's extradition.* Just a coincidence, more of Keith's synchronicity, but interesting. I began scanning, immediately impressed, when a few minutes later my phone abruptly switched itself to Colm's second document, now open and available. This second document was CIA, over sixty pages of post-war analysis of Argentina. Words and phrases from both documents leapt off the pages as I tortured myself over which to scan first: "shadow organizations," "hard core Nazis in Argentina," "Germandom," "Nazi controlled schools," "a clear channel for the transfer of funds between Germany and Argentina," "defensive strategy of camouflage," "Nazi economists and military experts," "German scientists are retained for research in nuclear physics, jet propulsion and guided missiles," "creation in this Hemisphere of a totalitarian state...." *Extraordinary. All happening in Argentina. These phrases read like tabloid headlines—impossible yet somehow true. The Fourth Reich.*

The documents made it clear that Argentina had a population of some twelve thousand Germans who had made the South American country their new home, moving their families, establishing communities, networks, civil organizations, businesses, even a German Chamber of Commerce.[75] It was nothing less than a German outpost within a friendly country. The reports agreed: after the war, Argentina became prime real estate for fleeing Nazis, and it welcomed not just Germans, not just Nazis, but "SS veterans," the worst of the worst—Kammler's peers. Kammler could have traveled there under his own name, but more likely he assumed a new identity, and his was among the "60,000 to 90,000 visas" Argentina granted "to desperate Nazis" after the war, including "Eichmann, Barbie and Mengele."[76] Kammler would be right at home with that unholy trinity. *Sixty to ninety thousand visas. A thriving, permanent presence in Argentina.*

Kammler would blend in perfectly in the German enclave within Argentina, and he would be enthusiastic about his fellow Germans' "intention to carry on Nazi activities," and their shared "belief in eventual resurgence of Nazism."[77] As the Blue Book states, "In Argentina the Germans have constructed a complete duplicate of the economic structure for war which they had in Germany...a base for the reconstitution of German aggressive power."[78] The protocols discussed at the August 1944, Strasbourg meeting planning a Fourth Reich were everywhere in these two U.S. documents. I was reading about the realization of that Strasbourg plan. It was all here: "The industries essential to warfare in which experimentation in the weapons of future wars may take place and in which prototypes may be developed exist in Argentina and are controlled by Germans."[79] This was a factual report—not 'what if' speculation.

Still sweating in the fading summer daylight, I was chilled to the bone.

Though we had turned over every rock we could, I had not been satisfied that we could know where Kammler had ended up. Now, all signs pointed to Argentina, where the foundation for the Fourth Reich had been laid. The Kammler Deal made a great deal more sense in that context—not only was Kammler saving his life in delivering the rocket technology, but he was buying his ideology, his disturbing world-view, a second life.

I got myself together and resumed the final leg home, the waning sun at my back. I couldn't help imagining Kammler's life after the war. I could picture him in Argentina, on a beach chair, in the same pose he struck for the photo in his SS uniform with the old campaigner's chevron during the war. But this image is in color, not black and white, and the backdrop is an Argentine seaside villa rather than a snow-covered European forest. Kammler is an old man in a swimsuit instead of his SS uniform and black leather jackboots. He is smirking knowingly, looking forward, never over his shoulder, having cheated history. His bare feet rest on the smooth white sand. Another small table is at his elbow, coffee service replaced by summer drinks.

Now knowing about the Nazi haven in Argentina, I picture Kammler in the evenings at his ease, strolling the small, quiet streets of the villa unmolested, checking the post for a letter from the princess, exchanging knowing nods with other Nazi insiders. Drinks in the cantina with Eichmann, Barbie, Mengele? Perhaps even the rakish Otto Skorzeny, who maintained profound influence in German politics after the war but was also an advisor to Juan Perón and bodyguard to Eva. Altogether, they are a government in exile. Kammler is a big wig. Perhaps by virtue of his final position in the Third Reich, he is even the de facto leader of the Fourth. He and his unrepentant Nazi colleagues hold regular meetings to take stock of their work toward realization of the Fourth Reich, always planning. They are eternally patient, playing the long game. *So many Nazis made it to South America. They savaged the world and were then left to enjoy the rest of their lives unpunished. They considered the end of the war an intermezzo, not a final defeat. Knowledge of supersonic missiles, revolutionary jet aircraft, heretofore unknown advances in nuclear weapons research—all at the fingertips of the surviving Nazis. Could it be true? Is the Fourth Reich merely lying dormant, biding its time?*

We can't possibly stop. We need to pry the rest of the records loose, even from recalcitrant governments.[80] *All the records. Someone has them. Someone knows more, not just about Kammler, but about stolen gold and other treasures. The Fourth Reich.*

Churchill's famous lines from late 1942 came thrumming into my mind out of the evening sky: "Now this is not the end. It is not even the beginning the end. But it is, perhaps, the end of the beginning." That describes our situation perfectly, I thought, "the end of the beginning."

I picked up my pace, nearing home, taking the last hill in a sprint as I realized I needed another conference call with Keith and Colm. This time I would be imploring them, not the other way around. I already had the opening line worked out in my head: *"Guys, there's still so much more to do...."*

Acknowledgments

Keith Chester would like to thank researcher-author Kenneth D. Alford, who graciously supplied material from his personal collection; William Cunliffe, archivist at the National Archives, College Park, Maryland, who helped locate important files; and especially his wife, Nancy, who has consistently stood behind him during this entire journey.

Colm Lowery would like to thank Professor Joerg Kammler, Professor Gerald Fleming, Dr. Tilmann Kammler, Kristian Knaack, and Heiko Petermann for years of communication, interviews, and discussions, and for kindly providing documents and photographs; Jaro Svěcený for your friendship and kind hospitality during my visits to the Czech Republic—your wealth of knowledge, documents, and contacts was priceless—Alexander vom Hofe (grandson of Heinrich Prinz zu Schaumburg-Lippe) for granting access to his family archive of letters relating to Hans Kammler; Max Williams for kindly providing some stunning photographs; Stephen Walton of the Imperial War Museum in London, who went above and beyond to help locate documents; research staff at Bundesarchiv (Federal Archives), Koblenz, Germany, at the National Archives,

Kew, U.K., and at the National Archives and Records Administration (NARA), Washington, D.C.; and Professor Friedwardt Winterberg, Professor Christopher Simpson, and Michael Neufeld for email communications.

Dean Reuter would like to thank his wife and children who, without complaint, spent countless hours watching him spend countless hours on this book. He would also like to express his gratitude to the many, many people who encouraged him along the way or offered counsel, but particularly those who read unending versions of chapters or the entire manuscript as it evolved, most especially his father, Roy Reuter. He appreciates the encouragement from John and Mary Lee Malcolm, David Masci, Joe DeSanctis, John and Chrissy Shu, Chris Hage, Arthur Herman, Abigail and Stephen Thernstrom, and Ron Coleman and the staff at the United States Holocaust Memorial Museum library.

We all acknowledge a debt of gratitude to our agents at Javelin, Keith Urbahn and Matt Latimer, and the fine people at Regnery History, including Elizabeth Kantor and Alex Novak.

Notes

Chapter One: "One of Himmler's Most Brutal and Most Ruthless Henchmen"

1. Albert Speer, *Infiltration: How Heinrich Himmler Schemed to Build an SS Industrial Empire* (Japan: Ishi Press, 1981), p. 12.
2. The black was a tribute to fallen leader Frederick William, Duke of Brunswick-Wolfenbüttel, nicknamed "the Black Duke," who was killed at the Battle of Quatre Bras in 1815.
3. Chris McNab, *The SS World War Two Data Book, 1923–1945* (London: Amber Books Ltd., 2009), p. 8.
4. Tilmann Kammler, email to the authors. Document in possession of the authors.
5. U.S. Department of War, Strategic Services Unit, *The Career of Heinrich Himmler*, undated, www.cia.gov/library/readingroom/

docs/The%20CAREER%20OF%20HEINRICH%20
HIMMLER_0001.pdf, pp. 1–2.

6. A few peaceful inter-war years passed during which Germany
largely complied with the terms of the Treaty of Versailles, though
internal resentment began to simmer. European industry was still
struggling to complete its reconversion to a peacetime economy,
while Germany had already reached its maximum pre-war
industrial output. Many Germans thought the treaty unfair
because it demanded outsized reparations. The German General
Staff, the body that headed the German army, disbanded by the
treaty, began a furtive "police" recruitment scheme that attracted
over three hundred thousand men who lived in army barracks, and
drilled openly in military uniforms.

7. "History," Gdańsk University of Technology, https://pg.edu.pl/
about/history?p_l_id=2601363&p_v_l_s_g_id=0&.

8. Nikolaus Wachsmann, *KL: A History of the Nazi Concentration
Camps* (New York: Farrar, Straus and Giroux, 2015), p. 5. See also
U.S. Department of War, "The Career of Heinrich Himmler," p.
51.

9. The world-wide depression that followed the 1929 crash on Wall
Street was the undoing of the German economy. Germany saw
wild unemployment, failing businesses everywhere, and rampant
inflation, with no relief in sight. As a new party, Hitler's Nazis
were positioned to blame the older political parties and deride them
as ham-handed. Hitler and the Nazi Party promised to unleash the
natural power of the German people. In the late 1920s and early
1930s, Hitler and the Nazis had had enough success at the ballot
box to gain real influence in the German parliament, the Reichstag.

10. Nazi Party Number 1 011 855.

11. William L. Shirer, *The Rise and Fall of the Third Reich* (New
York: Simon and Schuster, 1990), p. 5.

12. Adolf Hitler, *Mein Kampf* (Boston: Houghton Mifflin, 1998), p. 134.

13. During the Spanish Civil War (July 1936 to April 1939) the Luftwaffe experimented with new tactics and aircraft while helping Spanish dictator Francisco Franco defeat the Republican forces. A new generation of over twenty thousand German airmen and crews gained valuable combat experience that would give the Luftwaffe an important advantage going into the World War II.

14. A schism between the Nazis and Christian churches—both Catholic and Protestant—had erupted, driven primarily by the antagonism of Nazi Martin Bormann, who declared National Socialism and Christianity incompatible belief systems. Although the opposition to the churches was broadly supported by the Nazi hierarchy, there were differences in Nazi leadership over tactics—how overt should Nazi opposition to Christianity be, and when should it fully blossom?

15. Richard Steigmann-Gall, *The Holy Reich: Nazi Conceptions of Christianity, 1919–1945* (Cambridge: Cambridge University Press), pp. 218–22.

16. U.S. Department of War, "The Career of Heinrich Himmler," p. 17.

17. Request for Apprehension, Central Registry, U.S. Forces European Theater, Counter Intelligence Corps, October 26, 1945.

18. U.S. Department of War, *The Career of Heinrich Himmler*, pp. 20–21.

19. "Trial of Ulrich Greifelt and Others," U.S. Military Tribunal, Nuremberg, October 10, 1947–March 10, 1948, Case No. 73, p. 3, as cited in "Law Reports of Trials of War Criminals, Selected and Prepared by the United Nations War Crimes Commission, Vol. XIII," London, 1949, https://www.loc.gov/rr/frd/Military_Law/pdf/Law-Reports_Vol-13.pdf.

20. McNab, *The SS World War Two Data Book*, p. 177.

21. Jews were forced out of many professions, starting with civil service positions, then spreading like a bloodstain. From early

1937, Jews were ineligible to receive degrees from any German university in any subject. Their Aryan colleagues benefited from reduced competition and, in many instances, by taking over vacated positions directly. Jews began to flee Germany in droves, giving away their homes and property at fire-sale prices. A nationwide boycott of Jewish businesses was organized. Next, Germany forbade Jews from owning businesses and other Germans profited, buying the businesses at rock-bottom prices. The 1935 Nuremberg Laws also clarified who was and was not Jewish and, consequently, who was subject to what had become a legalized and increasingly organized pogrom of overt discrimination.

22. Michael Thad Allen, *The Business of Genocide* (Chapel Hill, North Carolina: University of North Carolina Press, 2003), p. 16.

23. McNab, *The SS World War Two Data Book*, p. 27.

24. Tilmann Kammler, email to Colm Lowery, January 6, 2018.

25. Albert Speer, *Der Sklavenstaat* (New York: Macmillan Publishers, 1982), pp. 28–29.

26. Albert Speer, *Infiltration: How Heinrich Himmler Schemed to Build an SS Industrial Empire* (Japan: Ishi Press, 1981), p. 12.

27. "Interrogation Report on Generalleutnant Richard John," Interrogation Report No. 37, Headquarters, Third U.S. Army, Interrogation Center (Provisional), September 5, 1945, p. 26.

28. The tactic was developed in Germany by an army officer named Hans Guderian, "the father of the Blitzkrieg," who had written a military pamphlet called "Achtung Panzer." Hitler was enthralled by Guderian's bold ideas, even more so when Guderian told him that, if he were given a free hand, once he set upon France he could sweep through the country and reach the coast in a matter of weeks.

29. German forces rolled over the outdated and ill-equipped Polish military. They smashed through fixed enemy lines, surrounded and crushed massed armies, and swept over the land. Before World War II, warfare was more static, with entrenched lines heavily defended.

Infantry soldiers would defeat the enemy before them, advance, and take their trench. The retreating forces would fall back to the next line of trenches. Vast amounts of territory rarely changed hands and casualties in this closely fought style of war could be astounding.

30. At the time, France had one of the largest (though outdated) armies on the continent and Britain had the world's strongest navy. France had invested heavily in immovable defenses along the Maginot Line, which separated France and Germany.

31. The French generals inexplicably relied on motorcycle couriers rather than telephone and radio to carry time-sensitive messages and orders to reposition what mobile forces they possessed.

32. In a massive purge, Stalin had not only decapitated the highest leadership of the Red Army, but he also had gone through the ranks, removing leadership down to the level of division commanders, taking a reported 80 percent of them. Russia had some 185 divisions, 150 without experienced leadership at the time of the German invasion. Hitler was convinced that they would be unable to contend with Germany's smaller but better-trained and highly disciplined forces. He took as proof Russia's lackluster performance against the much smaller Finnish forces in the winter of 1939–1940.

33. As was said after the war by infantry general Rohricht, "Even if the [German] army had a higher opinion of Russia's power than the Party did, it didn't estimate it nearly high enough." G.G. Report, Combined Services Detailed Interrogation Center (C.S.D.I.C.), G.R.G.G. 341, July 28–August 7, 1945, p. 12. This recording was made at a Combined Services Detailed Interrogation Center in Great Britain used specifically to house German officers. The officers were housed together and were permitted open communication, some of which was recorded.

34. Alan Clark, *Barbarossa: The Russian-German Conflict, 1941–1945* (New York: William Morrow and Company, 1965), p. 43.

35.   Initially, the Germans were extraordinarily effective against the
      Russians, sweeping east with the same rapid pace that they had
      poured through France. All went according to plan. Russian troops
      were captured by the tens of thousands. Stalin was seriously
      considering suing for peace and had even organized a getaway train
      to take him to safety as German guns started pounding Moscow.

36.   On May 29, 1941, Kammler was dismissed from active duty in the
      Ministry of Aviation and headed for other challenges within the
      rapidly expanding SS.

37.   Rudolf A. Haunschmied, Jan-Ruth Mills, and Siegi Witzany-
      Durda, *St. Georgen-Gusen-Mauthausen: Concentration Camp
      Mauthausen Reconsidered* (Norderstedt, Germany: Books on
      Demand GmbH, 2007), p. 80.

38.   The Schutzstaffel, or SS, grew out of the Sturmabteilung, or SA,
      which was founded in 1921 and known alternately as the Storm
      Detachment or the Brown Shirts. The SA played a key role in
      Hitler's rise to power in the 1920s. The SA's main assignments
      were providing protection for Nazi rallies and assemblies,
      disrupting the meetings of the opposing parties, fighting against
      the paramilitary units of the opposing parties, and intimidating
      Jewish citizens. The SA was the first Nazi paramilitary group to
      develop pseudo-military titles for its members. The SA titles were
      adopted by several other Nazi Party groups, including the SS.
      Brown-colored shirts were chosen as the SA uniform because a
      large batch of them was cheaply available after World War I,
      having originally been ordered during the war for colonial troops
      posted to Germany's former African colonies. I found accidents of
      history like these fascinating: the dreaded sartorial calling card of a
      vicious cadre of Nazis, "the Brown Shirts," was essentially a result
      of excess wardrobe.

39.   Martin Allen, *Himmler's Secret War: The Covert Peace
      Negotiations of Heinrich Himmler* (New York: Carroll & Graf
      Publishing Group, Avalon Publishers, 2006), p. 19.

40. In the words of their own propaganda, the mission of the SS was "protection of the Fuehrer" and "internal security for the Reich." International Military Tribunal Transcript, Vol. 4, Day 23, p. 161.

41. The SS was also home to the feared Einsatzgruppen mentioned above, the bands of marauding madmen who followed German ground troops as they invaded Eastern Europe. They formed death squads, rounding up and massacring civilians. As Adolf Eichmann said coldly at his eventual trial, "The purpose of the Einsantzgruppen was to murder Jews and deprive them of their property." McNab, *The SS World War Two Data Book*. Historians estimate that this concentrated group of SS thugs murdered as many as two million people.

42. *U.S.A. v. POHL*, et al., U.S. Military Tribunal Nuremberg, Judgment of November 3, 1947.

43. Jochen von Lang, *Top Nazi: SS General Karl Wolff, The Man Between Hitler and Himmler* (New York: Enigma Books, 2005), p. 21. The Allgemeine SS were the Hitler body guards and protectors, as well as concentration camp guards. When the need for front line soldiers expanded greatly, rather than lose his best men to the Wehrmacht, the German army, Himmler formed the Waffen SS, "an independent branch of the armed forces of the State, the self-professed racial and soldiery elite of the Nazi movement." U.S. Department of War, Strategic Services Unit, p. 45. See also Wachsmann, *KL*, p. 53.

44. Nicholas Rankin, *Ian Fleming's Commandos: The Story of the Legendary 30 Assault Unit* (Oxford: Oxford University Press, 2011), p. 300.

45. The ruthlessness of the SS was not exclusively projected outward. "[I]t was not in the least frowned upon to use one's elbows to move ahead" within the SS. Von Lang, *Top Nazi*, p. 199.

46. In a thoroughly researched study of a select group of concentration camps, authors Rudolf A. Haunschmied, Jan-Ruth Mills, and Siegi Witzany-Durda credit the successes of the business side of the SS to managers like Kammler, who were able to "incorporate

extermination and labor into a modern business structure."
Haunschmied, Mills, and Witzany-Durda, *St. Georgen-Gusen-Mauthausen*, pp. 49, 151.

47. "Plan for the Distribution of Work of Amstgruppe C," Berlin,
     January 1, 1943, translation of Document No. NO-1288, Office of
     the Chief Counsel for War Crimes, Harvard Law School Library,
     Nuremberg Trials Project Digital Document Collection.

48. Wachsmann, *KL*, p. 286.

49. Speer, *Infiltration*.

50. Heydrich, a true believer, was so notorious that he would be
     targeted and killed by partisans before the end of the war. But few
     know that it was Heydrich who hatched the plan of dressing
     German soldiers in Polish army uniforms, having them attack their
     own German border towns, and then using those attacks as a
     pretense for the military invasion of Poland in 1939.

51. Albert Speer, *Inside the Third Reich* (New York: Orion Books,
     1970), p. 478.

52. Ilse Christine Anna Wiegandt, "Final Interrogation Report," Berlin
     District Interrogation Center, October 13, 1945.

53. Walter Dornberger, *V-2*, (New York: Ballantine Books, 1954), pp.
     198–99.

54. *U.S. v. Kurt Andrae*, Case No. 000-50-37, Deputy Judge
     Advocate's Office, Review and Recommendations of the Deputy
     Judge Advocate for War Crimes, April 15, 1948, p. 17.

55. For Pohl, Kammler rises to the level of Nietzsche's superman, or
     Übermensch, the exact opposite of the racially inferior
     Untermensch.

56. Rudolf Höss, *Death Dealer: The Memoirs of the SS Kommandant
     at Auschwitz* (Cambridge: Da Capo Press, 1996), pp. 294–95.
     Höss's book, written from a cell after the war, must be viewed as
     the work of a guilty informant, a cornered man hoping to salvage
     some scrap of dignity as his legacy. Everything he says should be
     understood as self-serving and likely crafted to influence the

outcome of his trial or to earn him a pardon or commutation of his sentence.

57. Michael Neufeld, *Von Braun: Dreamer of Space, Engineer of War* (New York: Knopf Doubleday Publishing Group, 2007), p. 159.

58. Interrogation Report of von Braun, July 8, 1947, p. 18, paragraph 60.

59. Frederick Ordway and Mitchell Sharpe, *The Rocket Team: From the V-2 to the Saturn Moon Rocket—the Inside Story of How a Small Group of Engineers Changed World History* (Oxford: Oxford University Press, 1979), p. xiv.

60. Ibid, p. 81.

61. Ibid, p. 80.

62. Ibid, p. 199.

63. U.S. National Archives, Decimal File 1942–1945, Decimal 471.9 (45), Sections 1-3, Box 475, Loc. 190/1/10/5, CIOS Evaluation Reports, Reference: C.I.C. 75 Series, Evaluation Report 117, June 30, 1945. Document in possession of the authors.

Chapter Two: Evil Deeds

1. Gerald Fleming, *Hitler and the Final Solution* (Oakland, California: University of California Press, 1987), pp. 142–43, citing report of SS-Sturmbannführer Franke-Gricksch, Berlin Document Center.

2. The U.S. Holocaust Museum reports a figure of 1.1 million people murdered at Auschwitz. Others, including camp commandant Höss, report higher figures. See the Nuremberg testimony of Commandant Rudolf Höss, April 15, 1946, during which Höss cited a figured of 2.5 million dead at Auschwitz by his own account, and 2 million dead according to Adolf Eichmann.

3. Robert Jan van Pelt, *The Case for Auschwitz: Evidence from the Irving Trial* (Bloomington, Indiana: Indiana University Press, 2002), p. 4.

4. Raul Hilberg, "Auschwitz and the 'Final Solution,'" in Yisrael Gutman and Michael Berenbaum, eds., *Anatomy of the Auschwitz*

Death Camp (Washington, D.C.: U.S. Holocaust Research Institute, 1994), p. 82.

5.   Franciszek Piper, "Gas Chambers and Cematoria," in Yisrael Gutman and Michael Berenbaum, eds., *Anatomy of the Auschwitz Death Camp* (Washington, D.C.: U.S. Holocaust Research Institute, 1994), p. 164, citing a June 2, 1942, telegram from Kammler.

6.   Oswald Pohl's testimony, Nuremberg Military Tribunal, Vol. 5, pp. 1018–24, the section on Kammler deputy Franz Eirenschmalz, chief of Amstgruppe C VI.

7.   Hilberg, "Auschwitz," pp. 82–83.

8.   Nikolaus Wachsmann, *KL: A History of the Nazi Concentration Camps* (New York: Farrar, Straus and Giroux, 2015), pp. 279, 374.

9.   Oswald Pohl's testimony, p. 1021.

10.   Albert Speer, *Infiltration: How Heinrich Himmler Schemed to Build an SS Industrial Empire* (Japan: Ishi Press, 1981), 296.

11.   Rudolf Höss, *Death Dealer: The Memoirs of the SS Kommandant at Auschwitz* (Cambridge: Da Capo Press, 1996), p. 236.

12.   RG-11.001M.o3: 19 (502-1-13), Hans Kammler, "Bericht des Amtes II-Bauten uber die Arbeiten im Jarrett 1941, Auschwitz," August 1, 1942. See also Request for Apprehension, Central Registry, U.S. Forces European Theater, Counter Intelligence Corps, October 26, 1945.

13.   Robert-Jan van Pelt, "A Site in Search of a Mission," in Yisrael Gutman and Michael Berenbaum, eds., *Anatomy of the Auschwitz Death Camp* (Washington, D.C.: U.S. Holocaust Research Institute, 1994), pp. 127–29.

14.   Ibid, p. 124.

15.   Hilberg, "Auschwitz," p. 82.

16.   Wachsmann, *KL*, p. 285.

17.   Van Pelt, "A Site," p. 101.

18.   Jean-Claude Pressac with Robert-Jan van Pelt, "The Machinery of Mass Murder at Auschwitz" in Yisrael Gutman and Michael Berenbaum, eds., *Anatomy of the Auschwitz Death Camp*

(Washington, D.C.: U.S. Holocaust Research Institute, 1994), p. 201.

19. See Adolf Hitler, *Mein Kampf* (Boston: Houghton Mifflin, 1998), Book 1, Chapter 11.
20. Fleming, *Hitler and the Final Solution*, p. xxxvi.
21. Wachsmann, *KL*, p. 52.
22. Hilberg, "Auschwitz," p. 84.
23. Piper, "Gas Chambers," p. 164.
24. Wachsmann, *KL*, p. 342.
25. Ibid., citing a June 2, 1942, Kammler telegram, 1994, p. 164. See also Oswald Pohl's testimony, p. 446.
26. Hans Kammler, report to Richard Gluecks from March 10, 1942, Nuremberg Trials Project, Harvard Law School Library, http:// nuremberg.law.harvard.edu/documents/5806-report-to-richard-gluecks?q=kammler#p.2; and http://nuremberg.law.harvard.edu/ documents/3948-report-to-richard-gluecks?q=date:%2210+March +1942%22#p.5.
27. Blatman, *The Death Marches*, 40; Wachsmann, *KL*, p. 279.
28. Van Pelt, *The Case for Auschwitz*, p. 72.
29. Pressac with van Pelt, "The Machinery of Mass Murder," p. 212.
30. Bischoff to Wirtschafts-Verwaltungshauptamt CV, October 13, 1942, cited in Hilberg, "Auschwitz," p. 87.
31. Van Pelt, "A Site," 127–129; Pressac with van Pelt, "The Machinery of Mass Murder," p. 226.
32. Van Pelt, *The Case for Auschwitz*, p. 72.
33. Rudolf Höss, *Death Dealer: The Memoirs of the SS Kommandant at Auschwitz* (Boston: Da Capo Press, 1996), p. 286.
34. Request for Apprehension.
35. Höss, *Death Dealer*, p. 21.
36. Piper, "Gas Chambers," p. 164.
37. Pressac with van Pelt, "The Machinery of Mass Murder," p. 199.
38. Van Pelt, "A Site," pp. 139–40.
39. Blatman, *The Death Marches*, p. 40.

40. Nuremberg Testimony of Commandant Rudolf Höss, April 15, 1946, https://www.jewishvirtuallibrary.org/rudolf-h-ouml-ss.

41. Brigadier General Telford Taylor, "Prosecution Brief Concerning the Organization and Activities of the SS and the WVHA," p. 6, http://nuremberg.law.harvard.edu/documents/ 3924-brief-prosecution-brief-concerning?q=Karl+sommer#p.7.

42. Oswald Pohl's testimony, p. 2, affidavit of Wolfgang Grosch, Sturmbannführer.

43. Ibid, p. 58.

44. Martin Kitchen, *Speer: Hitler's Architect* (New Haven, Connecticut: Yale University Press, 2015), pp. 88, 633.

45. Jean Michel, *Dora: The Nazi Concentration Camp Where Modern Space Technology was Born and 30,000 Prisoners Died* (New York: Holt, Rinhart and Winston, 1975), p. 60.

46. Pressac with van Pelt, "The Machinery of Mass Murder," 199; see also Wachsmann, *KL*, p. 316.

47. Translation of interrogation by Captain Otto N. Nordon of Martin Gottfried Weiss, November 6, 1945, http://hydrastg.library.cornell.edu/fedora/objects/nur:00733/datastreams/pdf/content, p. 4.

48. "Basic Handbook, KLs (Konzentrationslager), Axis Concentration Camps and Detention Centres Reported as Such in Europe," Supreme Headquarters Allied Expeditionary Force, Evaluation and Dissemination, Section G-2, p. 15.

49. On the other hand, the Weiss interrogation indicates that the crematoria built under Kammler's command had "large disinfection unit[s]" within them, and some scholars contend that such a disinfection unit was used, at least experimentally, to gas prisoners at Dachau. Translation of interrogation by Captain Otto N. Nordon of Martin Gottfried Weiss.

50. "Dachau Concentration Camp, Dachau, Germany, May 1945," Jewish Virtual Library, https://www.jewishvirtuallibrary.org/ jsource/images/dachau2/Dachau7.jpg.

51. Ibid.

52.	In 1944, Kammler took charge of razing the Warsaw Ghetto, famous for the 1943 uprisings by resistance forces, which had been put down over a month-long battle and house-to-house fighting with German forces that burned down structures within the ghetto, killing thousands. Kammler headed the forces "to eliminate certain hiding places of the resistance movement." United Nations War Crimes Commission documents filed by the Poles charge Kammler with leveling the Warsaw Ghetto after the uprising. See also the judgment of the International Military Tribunal, citing the responsibility of WVHA and Kammler's Amstgruppe C for the "destruction of the Warsaw ghetto...." Oswald Pohl's testimony, pp. 446, 58.

53.	See, for example, Michael Thad Allen, *The Business of Genocide* (Chapel Hill, North Carolina: University of North Carolina Press, 2003), among the most thorough examinations.

54.	Max Hastings, *Inferno: The World at War, 1939–1945* (New York: Vintage Books, 2011), p. 488.

55.	Rudolf A. Haunschmied, Jan-Ruth Mills, and Siegi Witzany-Durda, *St. Georgen-Gusen-Mauthausen: Concentration Camp Mauthausen Reconsidered* (Norderstedt, Germany: Books on Demand GmbH, 2007), p. 49.

56.	Edgar Hotz and Hans Kammler, *Foundations of Price Calculation and Organization of Construction Firms for Dwelling and Settlement Construction in City and Country* (Berlin: Verlagsgesellschaft R. Muller, 1934). Document in possession of the authors.

57.	Ibid., p. 1.

58.	Wilhelm Fussl and Stefan Ittner, eds., *Biographies und Technikgeschicte* (Berlin: Springer-Verlag, 2013), p. 226.

59.	Hilberg, "Auschwitz," pp. 81–82.

60.	Peter Longerich, *Holocaust: The Nazi Persecution and Murder of the Jews* (Oxford: Oxford University Press), pp. 316–18.

61.	Allen, *The Business of Genocide*, p. 153.

62.	Speer, *Infiltration*.

63. Van Pelt, "A Site," p. 149.

64. On July 17, 1941, under Hitler's Decree for the Administration of the Newly Occupied Eastern Territories, Kammler's boss, Himmler, was selected to police all territory conquered in the east. Longerich, *Holocaust*, pp. 214–15.

65. Hans Kammler, "Haftlinge enisatz fur Zwecke der Luiftfartindustris," February 21, 1944, from Samuel A. Goudsmit's papers, Neils Bohr Library & Archives, American Institute of Physics, One Physics Ellipse, College Park, Maryland, Digital Collections, Box 26, Folder 21, Flossenburg: Caves, 1944.

66. *Basic Handbook KLs (Konzentrationslager)*, p. 8.

67. Wachsmann, *KL*, pp. 451–53.

68. See, generally, Oswald Pohl's testimony.

69. Karl Sommer, an SS member and WVHA's Deputy Chief of Prisoner Labor Allocation, provided a small list of Kammler slave labor assignments: Ohrdruf, 10,000 prisoners; Halberstadt, 3,600 prisoners; Giessen, 100 men; Woebbelin-Ludwigslust, 1,000 prisoners for construction of POW camps; Arlen near Hannover, approximately 900 prisoners; Lerbeck near Porta Westfalica, 2,000 prisoners; construction brigade Hamburg, 2,000 prisoners; Osnabrueck, 1,000 prisoners; Bremen, 1,000 prisoners; Alderney, 700 prisoners; Hydro-Works Poelitz, 2,500 prisoners. *U.S. v. Kurt Andrae*, Case No. 000-50-37, Deputy Judge Advocate's Office, Review and Recommendations of the Deputy Judge Advocate for War Crimes, April 15, 1948, p. 4.

70. Frederick Ordway and Mitchell Sharpe, *The Rocket Team: From the V-2 to the Saturn Moon Rocket—the Inside Story of How a Small Group of Engineers Changed World History* (Oxford: Oxford University Press, 1979), p. 255.

71. Heinrich Himmler, letter to Albert Speer, BAB, NW 19/2055, published in Albert Speer, *Der Sklavenstaat* (New York: McMillian Publishing, 1982), p. 293.

72. Jean Michel, *Dora: The Nazi Concentration Camp Where Modern Space Technology Was Born and 30,000 Prisoners Died*, in

association with Louis Nucera, Louis, trans. by Jennifer Kidd (New York: Holt, Rinehart and Winston, 1975), p. 66.

73. Ibid.

74. Quoted in Wayne Biddle, *Dark Side of the Moon: Wernher von Braun, the Third Reich, and the Space Race* (New York: W.W. Norton, 2009), p. 122.

75. Oswald Pohl's testimony, p. 1012.

76. Egon W. Eleck and Edward A. Tenenbaum, *Buchenwald, A Preliminary Report*, Headquarters of the 12th Army Group, Publicity and Psychological Warfare, April 24, 1945, pp. 7, 17. See also *U.S. v. Andrae*, p. 21.

77. Dennis Piszkiewicz, *The Nazi Rocketeers: Dreams of Space and Crimes of War*, (Mechanicsburg, Pennsylvania: Stackpole Books, 2007), p. 173

78. NMT Vol. 2, Case No. 2, The "Milch Case," *United States against Erhard Milch* (formerly a Field Marshal in the German Air Force) http://www.mazal.org/NMT-HOME.htm.

79. *U.S. v. Andrae*, p. 11.

80. Michel, *Dora*, p. 64. See also *U.S. v. Andrae*, p. 20.

81. Piszkiewicz, *The Nazi Rocketeer*, p. 135.

82. Wachsmann, *KL*, p. 452.

83. Affidavit of Heinrich W. Courte, June 20, 1947, p. 12 of original, http://nuremberg.law.harvard.edu/documents/4207-affidavit-concerning-ss-construction?q=author:%22Heinrich+W.+Courte%22#p.1.

84. 1945 Prisoner Report, Material Otto Halle, in: Harald Rockstuhl (ed.), Günter Fromm: Die Weimar-Rastenberger Eisenbahn–Die Buchenwaldbahn, Bad Langensalza 1993, p. 85, http://learning-from-history.de/sites/default/files/attach/8515/b008t01e.pdf.

85. *Report on the Work of the SS Construction Brigades, SS Sturmbannführer Weigel*, July 29, 1944, http://nuremberg.law.harvard.edu/documents/4278-report-on-the-work?q=evidence:no*#p.2.

86. Wachsmann, *KL*, p. 283.

87. Kammler, as Chief of Amstgruppe C, WVHA, to Gluecks, the inspector of concentration camps, March 10, 1942; Oswald Pohl's testimony; U.S. Military Tribunal Nuremberg, Judgment of November 3, 1947, pp. 1048–49.

88. Affidavit of Karl Sommer, October 4, 1946, pp. 1–12 of original, http://nuremberg.law.harvard.edu/ documents/5281-affidavit-concerning-factories-and-other?q=Karl+sommer#p.6.

89. See, generally, Oswald Pohl's testimony.

90. Höss, *Death Dealer*, p. 294.

91. International Military Tribunal, Vol. XXIX, p. 1919; Himmler's speech in Poznan, Poland, October 4, 1943.

92. Daniel Goldhagen, "How Auschwitz is Misunderstood," *New York Times*, January 25, 2015, http://www.nytimes. com/2015/01/25/sunday-review/how-auschwitz-is-misunderstood. html?_r=0.

Chapter Three: Vengeance

1. Interrogation report of Wernher von Braun, July 8, 1947, p. 18, paragraph 58.

2. G.G. Report, C.S.D.I.C. (Combined Services Detailed Interrogation Center), G.R.G.G. 341, July 28–August 7, 1945, p. 11.

3. George E. Riddlebarger, Special Agent, Fourth Army, Security Survey, Res. and Dev. Sv., Fort Bliss, Texas, "Memorandum for the Officer in Charge," May 17, 1947, p. 1. Document in possession of the authors.

4. Wolfgang W. E. Samuel, *American Raiders, The Race to Capture the Luftwaffe's Secrets* (University Press of Mississippi, 2004), p. 5.

5. G.G. Report, C.S.D.I.C., p. 12.

6. Norman Longmate, *Hitler's Rocket: The Story of the V2s* (New York: Skyhorse Publishing, Inc., 2010), p. 112.

7. Wernher von Braun was born in 1912 in the German Empire, in what is now Poland, just 130 miles from Kammler's birthplace. He died in 1977 in Alexandria, Virginia, and is buried in a cemetery he shares with Lord Fairfax, Confederate spy Benjamin Stringfellow, and other notables.

8. S. R. Report, Interrogation of Oberleutnant Schroder, C.S.D.I.C., July 28, 1945, pp. 2, 6.

9. The Organization of Research in Germany, Report by U.S. Naval Technical Mission in Europe, Headquarters Air Technical Service Command, Wright Field, Dayton, Ohio, October 1945.

10. James McGovern, *Crossbow and Overcast* (New York: William Morrow and Company, 1964), p. 94.

11. Ibid, pp. 94–95.

12. U.S. National Archives, Interrogation of Albert Speer, Report No. 12, June 11, 1945, RG 331, Entry 18A, Box 158.

13. U.S. National Archives, Decimal File 1942–1945, Decimal 471.9 (45), Sections 1–3, Box 475, Loc. 190/1/10/5, CIOS Evaluation Reports, Reference: C.I.C. 75 Series, Evaluation Report 117, June 30, 1945. Document in possession of the authors.

14. Peenemünde also had cafes, bakeries, book stores, a beauty salon, a school, four theaters, and much more. There were several restaurants, including a fine dining establishment where "the waiters wore white tie and tails," and tables were decked in white linens. Dieter Huzel, *From Peenemünde to Canaveral* (Pickle Partners Publishing, 2014), p. 130. The scientists at Peenemünde were undoubtedly "coddled," von Braun would say. Frederick Ordway and Mitchell Sharpe, *The Rocket Team: From the V-2 to the Saturn Moon Rocket—the Inside Story of How a Small Group of Engineers Changed World History* (Oxford: Oxford University Press, 1954), p. 352. The cuisine and service were not quite so elaborate at Peenemünde's thirty slave labor barracks.

15. David H. DeVorkin, *Science with a Vengeance: How the Military Created the U.S. Space Sciences After World War Two* (New York: Springer Verlag, Smithsonian Institution, 1994), p. 36.

16. Wayne Biddle, *Dark Side of the Moon: Wernher von Braun, the Third Reich, and the Space Race* (New York: W.W. Norton, 2009), p. 113.

17. Huzel, *From Peenemünde to Canaveral*, p. 75.

18. Dennis Piszkiewicz, *The Nazi Rocketeers: Dreams of Space and Crimes of War* (Mechanicsburg, Pennsylvania: Stackpole Books, 2006), p. 24.

19. Toward the end of the war the V-1 was adapted so that it could even be launched from below the wing of a modified Heinkel He III, a medium-sized German bomber aircraft, greatly increasing its range, as Germany's targets became more distant.

20. "If used suddenly on a large scale the effect is expected to be devastating," predicted one navy captain. U.S. Navy captain Forrest B. Royal, Memorandum for the Secretary, Joint Committee on New Weapons and Equipment, January 3, 1944, "Implications of Recent Intelligence Regarding Alleged German Secret Weapon," U.S. National Archives, RG 165, Entry 489, Box 177.

21. U.S. National Archives, "Enemy Long Range Weapons— Intelligence and Counter-Measures, Report by the Deputy Chief of the Air Staff for Four Weeks Ending 0600 Hours," March 17, 1945, RG 165, Entry 487, Box 151, March 20, 1945. Eventually in July 1944, the jet-powered Gloster Meteor, the first operational British jet, was pressed into service specifically to thwart the V-1 onslaught. The Meteor had the speed to match that of a V-1 in flight, and although only credited with having shot down thirteen V-1s, this is the first recorded air-combat encounter between two jet-powered aircraft in the history of aviation. Mustangs, Mosquitos, and Meteors were all drawn away from combat duty to hinder the V-1 attacks. Eugen Walter, untitled, undated report on the performance of the V-1 and V-2, RFI# 12-24486, p. 53. Note that Walter was Chief of Staff of Germany's Corps Hq LXV Inf Corps (the Vengeance Weapons Corps) and Commander of the V-1 Division.

22.   U.S. National Archives, "Long Range Rocket Projectiles,
      Experiments at Peenemünde," received in response to FOIA request
      from Keith Chester to Steven D. Tilley, chief, Special Access, May
      8, 2003.

23.   Roy M. Stanley II, *V Weapons Hunt: Defeating German Secret
      Weapons* (South Yorkshire, England: Pen and Sword Books, Ltd.,
      2010), p. 236.

24.   Ordway and Sharpe, *The Rocket Team*, p. 42.

25.   Interrogation report of Major General Dornberger, p. 27.

26.   Fixed bunkers could also serve as a protected place to stockpile
      ready-to-fire V-2s and the required large quantities of liquid
      oxygen, which was expensive and difficult to transport. But none
      of the hardened bunker sites launched a single V-2 against
      England—largely due to the fact that the V-2 was not ready for
      deployment before the facilities were abandoned to advancing
      Allied forces.

27.   Stanley, *Weapons Hunt*, 214; U.S. National Archives, Decimal File
      1942–1945, Decimal 471.9 (45), Sections 1–3, Box 475, Loc.
      190/1/10/5, CIOS Evaluation Reports, Reference: C.I.C. 75 Series,
      Evaluation Report 117, June 30, 1945. Document in possession of
      the authors.

28.   Watten, near Calais, France, was the first such bunker site, just
      across the channel from England. Hitler ordered construction of a
      second V-2 launch facility at Wizernes-Helfaut beginning in July
      1943. The entire facility was protected beneath an enormous
      dome-shaped concrete roof measuring seventy-one meters in
      diameter and five meters thick, large enough to stockpile rockets
      and liquid oxygen. The rockets were to be launched outside on two
      launching pads (called Gustav and Gretchen). Only when they were
      needed for launch would the missiles be rolled out through bomb-
      proof, iron-clad doors.

29.   Ordway and Sharpe, *The Rocket Team*, p. 41.

30.   Dornberger argued that the V-2 would have been perfected and
      operational much earlier in the war if it had been made a priority

from the outset. Interrogation Report of Major General Dornberger, formerly head of all German Army Rocket Development, June 30, 1948, p. 2.

31. Huzel, *From Peenemünde to Canaveral*, p. 27.

32. Prisoner of War Interrogation Report, Major von Ploetz, April 29–30, 1945, p. 1.

33. Jean Michel, *Dora: The Nazi Concentration Camp Where Modern Space Technology Was Born and 30,000 Prisoners Died*, in association with Louis Nucera, trans. by Jennifer Kidd (New York: Holt, Rinehart and Winston, 1975), p. 15.

34. McGovern, *Crossbow and Overcast*, p. 21.

35. Interrogation Report of Major General Dornberger, p. 1.

36. The raid, code-named Operation Hydra, was part of a larger plan named Operation Crossbow that sought to destroy Germany's secret weapons facilities.

37. Within walking distance, Peenemünde West, home of the V-1, was unmolested. Why was the V-2 alone targeted? Was it fear of the long-range, supersonic V-2 with some special atomic, chemical, or biological warhead?

38. A small group of aircraft set down parachute marker flares, colored target indicators highlighting three aiming points. Many of them were mislaid, and so the first wave of bombers was largely off-target. Tragically, eighteen of the thirty slave-worker barracks were destroyed and hundreds of workers killed or injured by the mistake. Before the second wave of bombers came in, the misdirected fire was corrected, and the subsequent bombing runs did better at reaching their targets. The third and final wave was not as efficient as the second, but still caused significant intended damage and little collateral damage. It also suffered the greatest losses of Allied aircraft as, by this time, some German fighters over Berlin had seen the bombing activity to their north and were at last dispatched to defend Peenemünde.

39. Two points support an affirmative conclusion. First, the ruse of Berlin was a smashing success and even an embarrassment for the

Germans. They had launched every plane they had in defense of
their capital city, against a force of just eight small aircraft,
bringing only one of them down. Meanwhile, the real target of the
attack force lay almost completely undefended. Allied losses were
not insignificant, but they were far lower than they could have
been. Second, damage on the ground at Peenemünde was at least
significant enough to cause the German leadership to relocate
rocket research and rocket manufacturing.

40.   Interrogation of Bernhard Zaenker, U.S. National Archives, CIOS,
      Speer Ministry and Secret Weapons, Target No. 028/5.66, June 18,
      1945, U.S. National Archives, RG 165, Entry 79, Box 577, Loc.
      390-33-32-33-6-1.

41.   G.G. Report, C.S.D.I.C., p. 12.

42.   Interrogation Report of Major General Walter Dornberger, p. 168.

43.   Ibid.

44.   Interrogation of Georg Rickhey, director general, Mittelwerke,
      G.m.b.H, Germany, by Colonel Peter Beasley, June 6, 1945, p. 2.
      Document in possession of the authors.

45.   Albert Speer, *Der Sklavenstaat* (New York: McMillian Publishing,
      1982), p. 217. Speer disagreed with Hitler on this plan. One year
      later, the continuing dispute would intensify, ultimately resulting in
      Speer's dismissal.

46.   Rudolf Höss, *Death Dealer: The Memoirs of the SS Kommandant
      at Auschwitz* (Cambridge: Da Capo Press, 1996), p. 173.

47.   Huzel, *From Peenemünde to Canaveral*, p. 133. Von Braun himself
      lacked the authority to order a relocation. See also McGovern,
      Crossbow and Overcast, p. 90.

48.   The Germans designed a purpose-built railway vehicle to transport
      the liquid oxygen needed to power the V-2. The V-2 itself traveled
      by rail on a distinctive combination of flat cars that could be
      readily detected by reconnaissance aircraft. In the spring of 1945,
      when the V-2 was operational and after the general launch area
      became known, the oxygen tankers and V-2 railway cars in transit

were traced from those forward areas back to Nordhausen—the only way the Allies learned about Nordhausen.

49. Interrogation Report of Wernher von Braun, July 8, 1947, p. 7, paragraphs 20 and 21.

50. Höss, *Death Dealer*, p. 21.

51. Michael Brian Petersen, *Engineering Consent: Peenemünde, National Socialism, and the V-2 Missile, 1924–1945* (Ph.D. dissertation, University of Maryland, 2005), p. 255. Document in possession of the authors.

52. Interrogation Report, von Braun, paragraph 58.

53. FBI Report, Wernher Magnus Maximillian Frieherr von Braun, Special Inquiry, Department of Justice, German Scientists under the Protective Custody and Control of the Joint Intelligence Objectives Agency, September 25, 1948, incorporating Affidavit of Membership in NSDAP of Professor Dr. Wernher von Braun, June 18, 1947, p. 4.

54. Interrogation Report of Major General Walter Dornberger, p. 222.

55. Frederick Ordway and Mitchell Sharpe detail the arrest and release of von Braun, which supports this thinking. Michael Neufeld, in his biography of von Braun, has it differently, concluding that Dornberger actually sought Himmler's involvement in the rocket project. Ordway and Sharpe, *The Rocket Team*.

56. The Organization of Research in Germany, Report by U.S. Naval Technical Mission in Europe, Headquarters Air Technical Service Command, Wright Field, Dayton, Ohio, October 1945.

57. Interrogation Report on Generalleutnant Richard John, Interrogation Report No. 37, Headquarters, Third U.S. Army, Interrogation Center (Provisional), September 5, 1945, p. 24

58. Interrogation Report of Major General Dornberger, formerly head of all German Army Rocket Development, June 30, 1948, p. 3.

59. Otto Skorzeny, *My Commando Operations: The Memoirs of Hitler's Most Daring Commando* (Atglen, Pennsylvania: Schiffer Military History, 1995), p. 169.

60. Major P. M. Wilson to G-2 War Department, May 25, 1945, Exploitation of German Scientific Personnel, transmitting the report of Dr. Hermann Oberth, Plan for a Trans-Atlantic Rocket. Oberth went on at length about his calculations for and work on the German missile, designed to travel over 3,700 miles, with a one-and-a-half-ton payload.

61. The Peenemünde rocket assembly building was large enough for assembling the Amerika Rocket.

62. Headquarters, Army Air Forces, Daily Activity Report, Washington, D.C., March 27, 1947, p. 1.

63. *U.S. v. Kurt Andrae*, Case No. 000-50-37, Deputy Judge Advocate's Office, Review and Recommendations of the Deputy Judge Advocate for War Crimes, April 15, 1948, p. 4.

64. U.S. National Archives, War Department Report, Enemy Preparations for Attack Against England by Long Range Projectiles Launched from Channel Coast of France, RG 107, Entry 85, Box 278, Loc. 390-9-03-02/3, May 20, 1945.

65. News of the V-2 rocket's development was reported by civilian workers who had escaped Peenemünde and found their way to freedom. See, for example, Prisoner of War Report on Rocket Research at Peenemünde, KO-26168, September 1, 1944.

66. U.S. National Archives, Decimal File 1942–1945, Decimal 471.9 (45), Sections 1–3, Box 475, Loc. 190/1/10/5, CIOS Evaluation Reports, Reference: C.I.C. 75 Series, Evaluation Report 117, June 30, 1945. Document in possession of the authors.

67. Piszkiewicz, *The Nazi Rocketeers*, p. 113.

68. Oswald Pohl's testimony, Nuremberg Military Tribunal, Vol. V, p. 446, opening statement by Mr. Robbins.

69. Rudolf A. Haunschmied, Jan-Ruth Mills, Siegi Witzany-Durda, *St. Georgen-Gusen-Mauthausen: Concentration Camp Mauthausen Reconsidered* (Norderstedt, Germany: Books on Demand GmbH, 2007), 128.

70. Within a week, Kammler was planning a huge, technologically advanced underground factory, code-named Rock Crystal

(Bergkristall) for the production of Me 262 jet fighters. Kammler estimated that when fully operational Bergkristall would manufacture 1,250 Me 262s per month. He drew upon the unending stream of sickly forced labor from the Mauthausen-Gusen concentration camp complex, a group of forty-nine Nazi concentration camps in Upper Austria, about twelve miles east of Linz. The work and death rates there were among the worst of all those associated with Kammler's construction projects; the conditions were so horrendous that it was known to its inmates as the "Hell of Hells." The "only water, pumped in from the nearby River Danube, was suicidal to drink." People died by the thousands. SS guards tortured and killed inmates for entertainment, using a variety of bizarrely cruel measures that included dragging inmates along the stone roads and throwing them off the high cliff faces into the quarries below. One prison guard, SS-Hauptscharführer Heinz Jentzsch, earned the nickname "The Bath Attendant" (Der Bademeister); his habit was to force as many as two hundred inmates into cold showers, exposing them to the frigid water until they died.

Chapter Four: On the Battlefield

1. U.S. National Archives, Special Report on Air Force Operations from USSTAF, No. UAX-68301, April 30, 1945, RG 18, Entry 6—General Arnold's Messages, May 1945, Box 28, Loc. 190/61/09/07.

2. In the Battle of Britain, four years ago by this time, RAF fighters were shot down over the London area and many managed to eject to safety and return to the air in a fresh plane, sometimes the same day. But Allied bombing runs over enemy-occupied territory meant that the pilots shot down, and their crews, if not killed, were lost for the duration as prisoners of war.

3. U.S. National Archives, Enemy Long Range Weapons—Intelligence and Counter-Measures, Report by the Deputy Chief of the Air Staff for four weeks ending 0600 hours 17th March 1945, RG 165, Entry 487, Box 151, March 20, 1945.

4.   Terry Charman, "The V Weapons Campaign Against Britain, 1944–1945," Historian Research and Information Department, Imperial War Museum.

5.   The day after 9/11 in Washington, we were all concerned about the next attack. The sense of dread lessened over time, but never fully abated, and everyone felt like targets on Thanksgiving Day, Christmas, New Year's Eve in Times Square, and the Super Bowl. Every occasion felt less like a celebration and more like the date a diabolical enemy might attack.

6.   U.S. National Archives, Long Range Rocket Projectiles, Experiments at Peenemünde, received in response to FOIA request from Keith Chester to Steven D. Tilley, chief, special access, May 8, 2003.

7.   Chris Hastings and Fiona Govan, "MI6 Urged Churchill to Nuke Berlin," *Telegraph*, December 1, 2002, https://www.telegraph. co.uk/news/uknews/1414878/MI6-urged-Churchill-to-nuke-Berlin. html.

8.   Martin Allen, *Himmler's Secret War: The Covert Peace Negotiations of Heinrich Himmler* (New York: Carroll & Graf Publishing Group, Avalon Publishers, 2006).

9.   Amidst the turmoil, a dutiful Kammler took the time to make a trip to the southernmost part of Germany, Schliersee, to speak at the funeral of SS Gruppenführer Wilhelm Grimm, who had been killed in an accident unrelated to the assassination attempt. Request for Apprehension, Central Registry, U.S. Forces European Theater, Counter Intelligence Corps, October 26, 1945.

10.   Rudolf A. Haunschmied, Jan-Ruth Mills, Siegi Witzany-Durda, *St. Georgen-Gusen-Mauthausen: Concentration Camp Mauthausen Reconsidered* (Norderstedt, Germany: Books on Demand GmbH, 2007), p. 155.

11.   Begun in 1938 but never completed, the line stretched almost four hundred miles from the Dutch border south to Switzerland. The Germans used its shelters and pill boxes as rallying points to reorganize and rebuild their strength.

12.   Continued refinement of the V-2, continued attempts to iron out
       significant bugs, led to continued design changes that were not
       always perfectly communicated to the parts manufacturers or the
       assembly staff. At times, newly modified parts would not work
       with the existing parts, or production crews had no idea how to
       work the newer parts into the assembly process.

13.   Walter Dornberger, *V-2* (New York: Ballantine Books, 1954), pp.
       236–38.

14.   Michael Thad Allen, *The Business of Genocide* (University of
       North Carolina Press, 2002), p. 224, quoting Jagerstabbesprechung
       [Jager Staff Meeting], May 2, 1944, BA MA RL3/6.

15.   There was great Allied concern that either rocket could
       accommodate a larger payload when reconfigured for shorter
       ranges needed in the war on the continent as Germany retreated.
       U.S. National Archives, A.W.A.S. Comments on Memorandum
       CICS/1, RG 331, Entry 98, Box 1, November 15, 1945.

16.   SS Officer Personnel Files, Microfilm Publication A3343, Series
       SSO, RG 242, National Archives Collection of Foreign Records
       Seized, Microfilmed records received from Berlin Document
       Center, received in response to a February 1, 2008, FOIA request
       to the U.S. Department of Justice Criminal Division, Office of
       Special Investigations. Document in possession of the authors.

17.   Lieutenant Colonel M. D. Helfers, "The Employment of Vengeance
       Weapons by the Germans During World War II," Draft
       Monograph, Office of the Chief of Military History, Department
       of the Army, September 8, 1954, p. 73.

18.   SS Officer Personnel Files, Microfilm Publication A3343, Series
       SSO, RG 242, National Archives Collection of Foreign Records
       Seized, Microfilmed Records Received from Berlin Document
       Center. Received in response to a February 1, 2008, FOIA request
       to the U.S. Department of Justice Criminal Division, Office of
       Special Investigations. Document in possession of the authors.

19.   Dornberger, *V-2*, p. 251.

20. Eugen Walther, untitled, undated report on the performance of the V-1 and V-2, RFI# 12-24486, NARA. Walther was chief of staff of Germany's Corps Hq LXV Inf Corps (the Vengeance Weapons Corps) and commander of the V-1 Division.

21. Other Kammler construction kommandos were deployed to "Berlin and all the major cities in western Germany" by "special trains carrying specialized equipment," making "remarkable achievements," repairing and rebuilding bomb-ravaged buildings and infrastructure. Rudolf Höss, *Death Dealer: The Memoirs of the SS Kommandant at Auschwitz* (Da Capo Press, 1996), p. 295.

22. Pohl, et al., U.S. Military Tribunal Nuremberg, Judgment of November 3, 1947, p. 445.

23. Helfers, "The Employment of Vengeance Weapons," p. 84.

24. Hugh M. Cole, *U.S. Army in World War Two, European Theatre of Operations, The Ardennes: Battle of the Bulge* (Washington, D.C.: Office of the Chief of Military History, Department of the Army, Washington, 1965).

25. Interrogation Report on Generalleutnant Richard John, Interrogation Report No. 37, headquarters, Third U.S. Army, Interrogation Center (Provisional), September 5, 1945, p. 23.

26. A revolutionary beam guidance system was dependent on an onboard radio receiver device wired into the missiles' autopilot system. A pair of signals emitted from a ground radio station and received by the V-2 provided precise directional data for the missile, which made continuous fine-tuned adjustments to its rudders along its flight path; also incorporated into the improved missile design was a Buchhold electrolytic integrating accelerometer, which measured the missiles' velocity and initiated engine shut-off more accurately—all giving the V-2 a theoretical target radius of just one mile, an astonishing figure for that era. To this point in time, the legendary Paris Gun had been the most highly developed piece of artillery in history. It could lob a 230-pound shell about eighty miles, but only half its munitions could be expected to fall within a four-mile radius of the target area. Given

its size and weight of over 250 tons, it was not readily moved about. The V-2 was more mobile and more accurate, and it delivered a payload nearly ten times as large.

27. One American analyst concluded that "the V-weapons campaign against Antwerp severely retarded the clearing of the port and the unloading of supplies." "Army and Navy: City of Sudden Death," *Time*, March 26, 1945.

28. Ibid.

29. Ibid.

30. Dornberger was a key figure in the Nazi's rocket program, as evidenced by his post-war career. Not only did he become vice president at Bell Aircraft, but he worked on NASA's X-15 series rocket, which set altitude and speed records. He also worked on the Boeing Dyna-Soar project, a rocket-powered long-range bomber. It's important to realize that Kammler's ability to deliver Dornberger alone would be significant to the Americans.

31. C.S.D.I.C., G.G. Report on Information Obtained from Senior Officer PW on August 2–7, 1945, PRO file WO.208/4178, p. 11.

32. Ibid.

33. Ibid.

34. Ibid.

35. Charles S. Chestson, "Memorandum of Information for the Joint Chiefs of Staff," January 24, 1945, p. 7.

36. Ibid.

37. Acting Director Charles S. Cheston, Office of Strategic Services, Washington, D.C., "Memorandum of Information for the Joint Chiefs of Staff," January 24, 1945, p. 7.

38. At this point in the war, peace proposals were not uncommon, not coordinated, and often not authorized. For example, the German ambassador to Portugal, von Halem, was working through his own contacts in Lisbon toward some end, the details of which are not known. Report, Major Paul Kubala, commanding, Seventh Army Interrogation Center, German and Russian Separate Peace Offers, June 30, 1945, p. 1.

39. Michael Neufeld, *Von Braun: Dreamer of Space, Engineer of War* (New York: Knopf Doubleday Publishing Group, 2007), p. 206.

40. Michael Neufeld, *The Rocket and the Reich: Peenemünde and the Coming of the Ballistic Missile Era* (Cambridge, Massachusetts: Harvard University Press, 1996) pp. 258–59. See Colonel Henry M. Zeller, chief, Intelligence Section, Air Division, Headquarters United States Air Forces in Austria, "Underground Industrial Installations of Air Interest in Austria," June 20, 1946. Document in possession of the authors. See also *Hitler's Miracle Weapons: From the 'America Rocket' to an Orbital Station*, Vol. 3. (West Midlands, England: Helion & Company Limited, 2009) p. 7.

41. Brief Interrogation Report on Professor Dr. Wernher von Braun, Special Investigations, Field Information Agency, Technical, T-Force, 69 HQ, July 8, 1947, paragraph 60; Dennis Piszkiewicz, *Wernher von Braun: The Man Who Sold the Moon* (Westport, Connecticut: Praeger Publishers, 1998), p. 40.

42. Von Braun Report on Interrogation, paragraph 42.

43. Under the contract, GE would operate at the White Sands Proving Grounds in New Mexico, now known as the White Sands Missile Range, the largest military testing site in the U.S., studying, reassembling and launching captured German V-2 rockets. Ultimately GE was able to build the Hermes rocket, a V-2 imitator, in the end one of the great American military success stories of the twentieth century. Having the German rocket team would save years, and millions of dollars.

44. The rocket team at Peenemünde alone included ten thousand people.

45. David H. DeVorkin, *Science with a Vengeance: How the Military Created the U.S. Space Sciences after World War Two* (New York: Springer Verlag, Smithsonian Institution, 1994), p. 47.

46. Memorandum to the Joint Chiefs of Staff for Their Information, USAF Report on Project "Paperclip," October 20, 1947, p. 7.

47. Interesting to note, during the war Kammler ran in the same circles as board members and leaders of Allgemeine Elekrizitats

Gesellschaft (AEG), partly owned by General Electric. Many of the board members of AEG also served on boards of directors of other German industrial and financial giants, including overt supporters of Hitler—even in the earlier years when Hitler was heir apparent to nothing. Some researchers claim this early support—coupled with affiliations with American companies, including overlapping boards, joint stock ownership, and shared investors—meant that the German companies enjoyed immunity from Allied campaigns.

48. James P. O'Donnell, *The Bunker* (Cambridge, Massachusetts: Da Capo Press, 1978), p. 23.

49. Frederick Ordway and Mitchell Sharpe, *The Rocket Team: From the V-2 to the Saturn Moon Rocket—the Inside Story of How a Small Group of Engineers Changed World History* (Oxford: Oxford University Press, 1979), p. 255.

50. Hugh L. Dryden, Consultant for Guided Missiles AAF Scientific Advisory Group, Status of Development of Special Missions in Germany as of February 6, 1945, U.S. National Archives, RG 227, Entry 179, Box 290, Loc. 130/22/27/02.

51. Allen, *Himmler's Secret War*, p. 270.

52. By this time, "with the assumption of command in combat action by SS Gruppenführer Kammler the entire V-2 project had, to all intents and purposes, been wrested from the Army and transferred exclusively to the SS." Walter, untitled, undated report, pp. 81–86.

53. D. D. Schience, "V.2. Attacks on Bridges," SORS/1/88, March 19, 1945, http://www.v2rocket.com/start/deployment/v2s-on-remagen. html.

54. Ken Hechler, *The Bridge at Remagen: A Story of World War II* (New York: Random House Publishing Group, 2009), p. 232.

55. Ibid, pp. 205–12.

56. Thomas Jentz, "Bertha's Big Brother: Karl-Geraet (60 cm & 54 cm)," Panzer Tract, 2001.

57. Charles Foley, "Otto Skorzeny Comes to Life," *Sunday Express* (London), April 18, 1952, p. 2.

58. Interrogation Report on Generalleutnant Richard John, p. 23.

59. The Allies calculated the odds of a direct hit on the bridge as one in one hundred thousand, or one in fifteen thousand for V-2s with radio control. See D. D. Schience.

60. U.S. National Archives, RG 165, Entry 194, Box 3, Kammler War Department File.

61. The loss of the bridge was by then no longer hugely strategically significant. The Americans had already marched critical equipment and eight thousand troops across the Rhine and placed pontoon bridges. Hitler would be haunted by the failure to destroy the bridge sooner. Joseph Goebbels, who kept a diary of his own private thoughts, which tended to mirror Hitler's, mentioned Remagen no less than thirty-five times in his entries from March 7 to April 9, 1945.

62. Winston S. Churchill, *Triumph and Tragedy: The Second World War* (Cambridge, Massachusetts: Houghton Mifflin Co., 1951), p. 52.

63. Max Hastings, *Inferno: The World at War, 1939–1945* (New York: Vintage Books, 2011), pp. 455–59.

64. Ordway and Sharpe, *The Rocket Team*, p. 266.

65. Speer favored "burying or hiding key components…because recovery would be quicker when the Germans got their territory back." Nicholas Rankin, *Ian Fleming's Commandos: The Story of the Legendary 30 Assault Unit* (Oxford: Oxford University Press, 2011), p. 301.

66. Alan S. Milward, *The German Economy at War* (University of London, Athlone Press, 1965), p. 185.

67. Haunschmied, Mills, and Witzany-Durda, *St. Georgen-Gusen-Mauthausen*, p. 221.

Chapter Five: Saving the Technology for the Americans

1.   U.S. National Archives, Oral History Interview with Herbert Axster, RG-50.702*0001, Accession Number 2003.44.2.1, U.S. Holocaust Memorial Museum.

2.   Interrogation Report of von Braun, July 8, 1947, p. 13, paragraph 42. See also Dornberger, p. 271.

3.   David H. DeVorkin, *Science with a Vengeance: How the Military Created the U.S. Space Sciences After World War Two* (New York: Springer Verlag, Smithsonian Institution, 1994), p. 37.

4.   James McGovern, *Crossbow and Overcast* (New York: William Morrow and Company, 1964), p. 4.

5.   Interrogation Report of von Braun, July 8, 1947, p. 8, paragraph 25.

6.   Dieter Huzel, *From Peenemünde to Canaveral* (Pickle Partners Publishing, 2014), pp. 151–65.

7.   Ibid., p. 151.

8.   Ibid., p. 162.

9.   Ibid., p. 196.

10.   McGovern, *Crossbow and Overcast*, p. 130.

11.   A Prisoner of War Interrogation Report also indicates that the prisoner heard Dornberger tell a German general the location of the documents, further proof that Dornberger was also in the loop. H. P. Robertson, expert consultant, Scientific Intelligence, Advisory Section, G-2, GBI/Scientific/314.4, Location of Peenemünde Documents, information obtained from Major V. Ploetz, May 15, 1945.

12.   Yalta also included an agreement between the Allies to accept nothing less than the complete, unconditional surrender of Germany on all fronts. To do otherwise would unfairly shift the burden of the war between the Allies.

13.   Historian Max Hasting concludes that the Russians regarded Berlin as a high priority target not just for its political value and the glory of capturing the German capital, but because it was home to the Kaiser Wilhelm Institute for Physics in Dahlem. Max Hastings, *Inferno: The World at War, 1939–1945* (New York: Vintage Books, 2011), pp. 589–90. German nuclear research certainly played a part in Russia's rush to Berlin, and helps account for the

loss of life the Russians were willing to endure. Anthony Beevor, *The Fall of Berlin 1945* (New York: Penguin Books, 2003), p. 430.

14. Oscar W. Koch and Robert G. Hays, *G-2: Intelligence for Patton*, (Atglen, Pennsylvania: Schiffer Publishing), p. 117.

15. At that point, the French sat outside the V-2-sharing arrangement. U.S. National Archives, Decimal File 1942–1945, Decimal 471.9 (45), Sections 1–3, Box 475, Loc. 190/1/10/5, Memorandum from SHAEF Forward Rheims, France, May 1, 1945. Document in possession of the authors.

16. Michael Neufeld, *Von Braun: Dreamer of Space, Engineer of War* (New York: Knopf Doubleday Publishing Group, 2007), p. 209.

17. Lieutenant Robert B. Staver, letter to Colonel S. B. Ritchie, Office Chief of Ordnance, SPOT, the Pentagon, "Transmitting an Account of the Location and Recovery of the Scientific Documents Belonging to the German Army Rocket Research Station of Peenemünde," May 23, 1946, pp. 3–7.

18. A memorandum memorializes an Ordnance request for one hundred missiles. Memorandum for Record, Lieutenant Colonel Stace to Colonel Trichel, May 11, 1945.

19. Norman Beasley, "The Capture of the German Rocket Secrets," *American Legion Magazine*, October 1963.

20. Colonel Peter Beasley, memorandum to Commander S. P. Johnston, USNR, "Report on Examination of Mittelwerke Target," June 5, 1945, pp. 2–3.

21. Lieutenant Colonel K. Pepple, Memorandum to Colonel H. D. Sheldon, Competent Scientific Interrogators, April 23, 1945.

22. Staver was in favor of utilizing all German scientists to the fullest extent possible without regard for their war records. He even wrote a letter to his boss in Paris suggesting that all German scientists be sent to the U.S. for "utilization in the war against Japan." U.S. National Archives, memo from General Omar Bradley to commanding generals of the First, Third, Ninth, and Fifteenth U.S. Armies, 211 (AG-P), April 16, 1945, Combined Intelligence

Objective Sub-Committee and Other Investigators, RG 33, Entry 18A, Box 159.

Chapter Six: The Reveal

1. *U.S. v. Kurt Andrae*, Case No. 000-50-37, Deputy Judge Advocate's Office, Review and Recommendations of the Deputy Judge Advocate for War Crimes, April 15, 1948, p. 20.

2. John Patrick Finnegan and Romana Danysh, *Army Lineage Series: Military Intelligence* (Washington, D.C.: Center for Military History, U.S. Army, 1998).

3. Ian Sayer and Douglas Botting, *America's Secret Army: The Untold Story of the Counter Intelligence Corps* (London: Grafton Books, 1989), p. 157.

4. N. Ervin, SS Section, SOI, USFET, Hans Kammler, 2494, November 10, 1946. Document received from U.S. Holocaust Memorial Museum Library and Archives in possession of the authors.

5. Cover Sheet, Dr. Hans Kammler, D-6797. Document in possession of the authors, received from U.S. Holocaust Memorial Museum Library and Archives.

6. February 26, 1946, letter from Deputy Theater Judge Advocate's Office, War Crimes Branch, United States Forces, European Theater, to Central Registry, Counter-Intelligence Branch, G-2 Division, U.S. Forces, European Theater, APO 757, U.S. Army.

7. Report of the Deputy Judge Advocate for War Crimes European Command, June 1944 to July 1948, p. 1.

8. Those accused at the International Military Tribunal included Hermann Göring, Rudolf Hess, Joachim von Ribbentrop, Ernst Kaltenbrunner, Albert Speer, and many others.

9. "The President Announces the Plan to Try Nazi War Criminals," in Public Papers of the Presidents of the United States: F. D. Roosevelt, 1942, Vol. 11, Best Books, 1950, p. 410

10. Lieutenant Colonel Dale M. Garvey, Central Registry, Counter Intelligence Corps, Summary of Information re: Dr. Hans Kammler, CIC/S-3/CR, March 7, 1946.

11. Jörg Kammler, letter to Colm Lowery, February 20, 2003. Document in possession of the authors.

12. CIOS, Establishment of Special Detention Centres for Suspects and Important German Personages, U.S. National Archives, RG 165, Entry 79, Box 583, June 19, 1945.

13. Major P. M. Wilson, Memorandum to Maunsell, Brigadier General R. J., Detention of German Scientific and Industrial Technological Personnel, U.S. National Archives, RG 331, Entry 18A, Box 160, June 7, 1945.

14. Annie Jacobsen, *Operation Paperclip, The Secret Intelligence Program that Brought Nazi Scientists to America* (New York: Little, Brown and Company, 2014), p. 3.

15. Ibid.

16. U.S. National Archives, Minutes of Working Group Held in G-2 Conference Room Supreme Headquarters, RG 331, Entry 18A, Box 164, Loc. 290-7-9-5, May 10, 1945.

17. Stephen Tyas and Peter Witte, *Himmler's Diary 1945: A Calendar of Events Leading to Suicide* (Stroud, England: Fonthill Media), p. 433.

18. The wives of Himmler, Bormann, and Göring were also in the Tyrol at the time. See Gerald Steinacher, *"The Cape of Last Hope": The Postwar Flight of Nazi War Criminals through South Tyrol/Italy to South America*, Faculty Publications, University of Nebraska, Lincoln, Department of History, Paper 115, 2006, p. 207.

19. Major General K. M. D. Strong, Digest 311, Supreme Headquarters, Allied Expeditionary Force, Office of Assistant Chief of Staff, April 13, 1945, p. 5.

20. Melissa Eddy, "Hidden Treasures of Nazis' Art Dealer Finally Go on Display," *New York Times*, November 1, 2017, https://www.nytimes.com/2017/11/01/arts/design/gurlitt-nazi-art.html.

21.   Plan for the Distribution of Work of Amstgruppe C, Berlin,
       January 1, 1943, Translation of Document No. NO-1288, Office
       of the Chief Counsel for War Crimes, Harvard Law School
       Library, Nuremberg Trials Project Digital Document Collection.

22.   "Nazi Gold: Information from the British Archives, Foreign and
       Commonwealth Office, General Services Command, No. 11,"
       Second Ed., January 1997, p. 3.

23.   Ibid, p. 27.

24.   German Nationalist and Neo-Nazi Activities in Argentina,
       Prepared by [REDACTED] for the Western Hemisphere Division,
       CIA, Case number K-10046, July 8, 1953, p. 11. Document in
       possession of the authors.

25.   Paul Manning, "Martin Bormann and the Future of Germany,"
       New York Times, March 13, 1973. See also Secret Reports Re:
       Nazi Post War Plans—Director, Federal Bureau of Investigation,
       DOJ, to American Embassy, November 16, 1945, document in the
       possession of the authors; and Simon Wiesenthal, *The Murderers
       Among Us*, (London: William Heinemann, 1967) p. 86.

26.   Henry Morgenthau Jr., *Germany is Our Problem: The
       "Morganthau Plan"* (New York: Harper and Brothers Publishers,
       1945).

27.   For example, Laudenberger's claims about a flush secret German
       account in a Swiss bank are difficult to square with the fact that
       high-ranking Nazis apprehended years after the war were living in
       relative poverty, and his explanation that the resources were
       controlled by a tiny group of surviving Nazi elites is thin.

28.   CIOS Evaluation Report 112, Speer Ministry and Secret Weapons,
       June 10, 1945; CIOS Evaluation Report 112, Speer Ministry and
       Secret Weapons, June 10, 1945. Michael Brian Petersen,
       *Engineering Consent: Peenemünde, National Socialism, and the
       V-2 Missile, 1924–1945* (Ph.D. dissertation, University of
       Maryland, 2005), p. 255. pp. 302–4. Document in possession of
       the authors.

29. Kenneth D. Alford, *Nazi Plunder: Great Treasure Stories of World War II* (New York: Hachette Books, 2003), pp. 101–103.

30. CIOS Objectives Sub-Committee, Evaluation Report 58, Messerschmitt Production Plans with Special Reference to the 262 Program, Target No. C-25/410, May 11, 1945.

31. Oliver P. Hodge, G-2 Section, SHAEF, Economic Section, CIOS, Messerschmitt Production Plans with Special Reference to the 262 Program, Target No. C-25/410, May 11, 1945, p. 5.

Chapter Seven: The Final Days

1. U.S. National Archives, New German Aircraft, Report No. 2263, Wing Commander, RG 165, Entry 79, Box 45, September 5, 1944.

2. William Green, *Warplanes of the Third Reich*, (London: MacDonald and Jane's Publishers, 1970) p. 519; Kössler Karl and Günther Ott, *Die großen Dessauer: Junkers Ju 89, Ju 90, Ju 290, Ju 390 Die Geschichte einer Flugzeugfamilie* (in German) (Berlin: Aviatik-Verlag, 1993).

3. Igor Witkowski, *The Truth About the Wunderwaffe* (New York: RVP Press); Igor Witkowski, *Odessa i Hitler w Argentynie* (Warsaw: Wis-2, 2016), pp. 221–25.

4. Intelligence Report No. EW-Te 4, Teutsch, Kurt, CIOS USSTAF, April 26, 1945, p. 3.

5. Hans Kammler, telegram, April 23, 1945. Document in possession of the authors.

6. Hodge, Messerschmitt Production Plans, p. 5.

7. James P. O'Donnell, *The Bunker* (Cambridge, Massachusetts: Da Capo Press, 1978), p. 91.

8. Monika Renneberg and Mark Walker, *Science, Technology, and National Socialism* (Cambridge: Cambridge University Press, 1999), p. 115.

9. Adolf Hitler, *Hitlers Tischgesprche Im Fuhrerhauptquartier, 1941–1944*, 1st ed. (Athenum Verlag, 1951), p. 493.

10. Captain George Davis, Memorandum to Major H. K. Calvert, Report of Interview with P/W Hauptman Wagner, December 11, 1944, p. 2.

11. There is also evidence that Nazis modified the V-1 at a factory in Breslau. The new version, known as the D-1, was designed to carry a special nerve agent as its payload. Though a prototype was made, it was never mass produced. See, for example, OSS Report A-44 316, report 5985, November 7, 1944; Donald Nijboer, *Meteor I vs V1 Flying Bomb: 1944* (London: Bloomsbury Publishing, 2012), p. 35; Mantelli, Brown, Kittel, and Graf (no author first names), *Wunderwaffen: The Secret Weapons of World War II* (Milan: Edizioni REI, 2017), p. 39.

12. "Speer on the Last Days of the Third Reich," USSBS Special Document, Copy, Cornell University Law Library, Ithaca, New York, Vol. 104; Transcripts of Albert Speer Interrogations and Intelligence Reports, http://lawcollections.library.cornell.edu/nuremberg/catalog/nur:01456, p. 8.

13. Special Interrogation Report of SS Ogruf Oswald Pohl, NARA, RG165 E179 Box 657, 390-35-7-05, p. 6.

14. O'Donnell, *The Bunker*, p. 139.

15. Ibid, p. 177.

16. Interrogation Report, Oberst G. F. Geist, ALSOS Mission, July 28, 1945, p. 11.

17. G.G. Report, CSDIC, p. 13.

18. Ibid.

19. Television interview of Heinz Schurmann by Heiko Petermann, 2003. Recording in possession of the authors.

20. "Speer on the Last Days of the German Reich."

21. Ben Tufft, "Secret Nazi Nuclear Bunker Discovered in Austria by Filmmaker," *Independent*, December 29, 2014, https://www.independent.co.uk/news/world/europe/secret-nazi-nuclear-bunker-discovered-in-austria-9948647.html.

22. U.S. National Archives, German Intelligence and Investigation Records Pertaining to German External Assets, compiled 1948–1950, documenting the period 1945–1950.

23. Ingeborg Alix Prinzessin zu Schaumburg-Lippe, Letter to Jutta Kammler, April 29, 1951. A second letter from the princess, written to Kammler's son Jörg on March 31, 1955, confirms the account. Documents in possession of the authors.

24. The District Court of Berlin-Charlottenburg on September 7, 1948, at the request of Kammler's wife, Jutta, officially declared Kammler dead as of May 9, 1945.

25. The German War-Grave Association searched for the grave without success. See Tom Agoston, *Blunder! How the U.S. Gave Away Nazi Supersecrets to Russia*, (London: William Kimber & Co., 1985) p. 116.

26. Ibid., p. 110.

27. Bernd Ruland, *Wernher von Braun: Mein Legen fur die Raumfahrt*, (Rome: Arnoldo Mondadori Editore, 1970) p. 292.

28. Agoston, *Blunder!*, p. 112.

29. William Donovan, Job Description in the Case of Charles Katek, June 10, 1943.

30. See, e.g., Max Hastings, *Inferno: The World at War, 1939–1945* (New York: Vintage Books, 2011), p. 609.

31. Sean Longden, *T-Force: The Forgotten Heroes of 1945* (London: Constable & Robinson Ltd, 2009), pp. 169–209.

32. Colonel K. J. Foord, G-2, to Colonel H.G. Sheen, G-2, October 18, 1944.

33. Lieutenant Colonel Peter G. S. Mero, Signal Corps, Communications Branch, OSS (Prov.), to Captain Robert Newell, Prague City Team, memorandum, April 18, 1945.

34. Igor Lukes, *On the Edge of the Cold War: American Diplomats and Spies in Postwar Prague* (Oxford and New York: Oxford University Press, 2012), pp. 46–51.

35. Louis D. Caplane and William G. Magee, memorandum, Source of certain funds held for Sammelkonto Accounts by the Austrian

National Bank at Linz, Upper Austria. Document in possession of the authors.

36. Memorandum, Twelfth Army Group TAC, Ref: [illegible]—005, May 21, 1945. Document in possession of the authors.

37. Albert S. Callan, to HQ Twelfth Army Group Thru G-2 Duty Room Third Army, Army CIC IRR Files, NARA, undated document.

38. Captain Albert S. Callan Jr., CIC Operations Section, to HQ Twelfth Army Group, date illegible. Documents referred to are part of Kammler's U.S. Army CIC Dossier, variously numbered D001767, FNU XE001765 (mislabeled as "Hammler"), and D001765, all received in response to an author FOIA request of U.S. National Archives, Case Number NW43577. Documents in possession of the authors. Gerl is notable for having treated Rudolf Hess's wife for thyroidism, and for his extensive wartime contacts with government officials in Great Britain, which might have included peace overtures, perhaps even as an intermediary for Kammler. Gerhard L. Weinberg, *Hitler's Foreign Policy 1933–1939: The Road to World War Two* (New York: Enigma Books, 2010), p. 568.

39. Kammler's U.S. Army CIC Dossier, variously numbered D001767, FNU XE001765 (mislabeled as "Hammler"), and D001765, all received in response to an author FOIA request of U.S. National Archives, Case Number NW43577.

40. Request for Apprehension, Central Registry, U.S. Forces European Theater, Counter Intelligence Corps, October 26, 1945.

41. Lieutenant Colonel Dale Garvey, Summary of Information, to Commanding Officer, 303 Counter Intelligence Corps, Dahmen, October 20, 1945.

42. James McGovern, *Crossbow and Overcast* (New York: William Morrow and Company, 1964), p. 210.

43. Brigadier General George C. McDonald, Memorandum to Commanding General, U.S. Air Forces in Europe, August 26, 1945. Document in possession of the authors.

44. McDonald took time to note that the facilities were built with slave labor. Ibid., p. 2.

45. Brigadier General George C. McDonald, Memorandum to Major Ernst Englander, headquarters, USAFE, November 2, 1945.

46. James Lucas, *Das Reich: The Military Role of the 2nd SS Division* (Arms & Armour, 1992), pp. 195–99.

47. R. M. Thorouchman, memorandum, "The Tucheler Heide Proving Grounds for the A-4 Weapon (V-2)," Ref. Brief #2, OPS Br, ORDI December 12, 1947, and September 14, 1948.

Chapter Eight: Nuclear Secrets

1. Jeremy Bernstein, *Hitler's Uranium Club*, 2nd ed. (New York: Copernicus Books, 2000), p. 132, citing a conference of German scientists in September 1939.

2. Samuel A. Goudsmit, Memorandum to Major R. R. Furman, ALSOS Mission, (quoting Harteck and Groth proposal to the German War Ministry of April 24, 1939), May 25, 1945, Evaluation of TA Information Obtained at Heidelberg and Frankfurt, ALSOS Mission, April 5, 1945. See also David M. Hiebert, Public Law 81-415: The Unitary Wind Tunnel Plan Act of 1949 and the Air Engineering Development Center Act of 1949, Address presented January 15, 2002, Reno, Nevada, p. 5.

3. Samuel A. Goudsmit, Memorandum, Preliminary Report on TA Information, April 18, 1945, p. 2.

4. Goudsmit, Memorandum to Major R. R. Furman, p. 2.

5. Bernstein, *Hitler's Uranium Club*, p. 46.

6. He earned Hitler's respect when, very early on, he struck upon the scheme of issuing a Hitler postage stamp, requiring a royalty for each printed stamp be paid directly to Hitler, making Hitler a wealthy man. Carter P. Hydrick, *Critical Mass: How Nazi Germany Surrendered Enriched Uranium for the United States' Atomic Bomb*, 3rd ed. (Waterville, Oregon: Trine Day, 2016), p. 170.

7. Ibid., p. 70.

8.   Ibid., pp. 6 and 64, citing *Hitler's Table Talk*: Adolf Hitler, *Hitlers Tischgesprche Im Fuhrerhauptquartier, 1941–1944*, 1st ed. (Athenum Verlag, 1951).

9.   Ibid., pp. 42, 493.

10.   Hitler, *Hitlers Tischgesprche*.

11.   Walter Jessel, Acting Chief, Steering Division, Brief Number 79, July 15, 1946, paragraph 10, p. 3.

12.   Bernstein, *Hitler's Uranium Club*, p. 46.

13.   Interrogation Report on Generalleutnant Richard John, Interrogation Report No. 37, Headquarters, Third U.S. Army, Interrogation Center (Provisional), September 5, 1945, p. 8.

14.   Schumann and Diebner held several post-war patents on ignition of thermonuclear reactions, thermonuclear fuels, fusion processes shock waves, and more.

15.   Notes on German Weapons Development, Seventh Army Interrogation Center, Ref. No. SAIC/38, June 3, 1945, p. 4.

16.   Some even argued that Diebner was not worth detaining for further research purposes. See Captain Bosquet N. Wev to CIC, European Command, Director of Intelligence, Memorandum, Detention of German Scientific Personnel, March 12, 1948.

17.   Captain David S. Temple, "Report: Information Obtained by the German Intelligence Service Relative to Allied Atomic Research," October 23, 1945, p. 5.

18.   Transcript of surreptitiously taped conversations among German Nuclear Physicists at Farm Hall, August 6–7, 1945, Vol. 7, p. 3, http://germanhistorydocs.ghi-dc.org/pdf/eng/English101.pdf.

19.   Samuel A. Goudsmit, Heisenberg et. al., memorandum, "War Research by Physicists," September 9, 1944.

20.   OSS Report: German Scientists and Materials in the Soviet Union for the Construction of the Atomic Bomb, Berlin, Germany, November 6, 1945, p. 11, paragraph IV, 1.

21.   Major R. R. Furman, Alsos Mission, "Report: New Information From OSS Switzerland Which May or May Not Have Been Previously Reported," November 10, 1944.

22. Leipzig was identified as an "experimental" site related to atomic energy as early as May 1944 by the U.S., which asked for help from the Russians in investigating the site under Operation FRANTIC. The Kaiser Wilhelm Institute was slated for Allied bombing as early as August 1943. "Arnold Concerned Over German Atomic Bomb," L/C Box 231, REEL 43811, p. 1078.

23. Bernstein, *Hitler's Uranium Club*, p. 133.

24. Goudsmit, Memorandum, Preliminary Report, p. 2.

25. Goudsmit, Memorandum to Major R. R. Furman, p. 3.

26. Author Jeremy Bernstein describes the need for twenty-two thousand centrifuges for a viable bomb-making project using this method. Bernstein, *Hitler's Uranium Club*, p. 119.

27. Walter Gerlach, Letter to Dr. Albert Vogler, president, Kaiser Wilhelm Society, June 10, 1944. See also Lieutenant F. J. Bierman, Memorandum to Chief FIAT (U.S.), August 2, 1946, p. 1.

28. Memorandum, Ultra-centrifuge installation in Celle, Headquarters, European Theater of Operations, U.S. Army, ALSOS Mission, April 21, 1945.

29. Exploitation of German Scientists and Technicians, Joint Intelligence Committee, January 5, 1946, JIC Reference 317/9/D, p. 2.

30. Lester C. Houck, Memorandum to Lieutenant Colonel Selby Skinner, December 24, 1945.

31. Major Francis J. Smith, Corps of Engineers, Memorandum to Lieutenant Colonel H. K. Calvert, Cable Information re: Russia, October 12, 1945.

32. P. Morrison, Metallurgic Laboratory, Chicago, Illinois, Memorandum to R. R. Furman, August 1, 1944.

33. AAF Asks for Soviet Assistance in "Investigation of German Experimental Stations," Spaatz Box 15, 7-81, IRIS #1103009, Reel #43811.

34. Daily Activity Report, Assistant Chief Air Staff, Call 122.25, IRIS-00111330, USAF Collection, AFRA, Maxwell Air Force Base, June 26, 1947.

35.   Interrogation of Oberleutnant Dr. Helmut Arntz, Headquarters
       Twelfth Army Group, Office of the Assistant Chief of Staff, G-2,
       APO 655, March 29, 1945, p.2.

36.   Daily Activity Report, Assistant Chief Air Staff, June 26, 1947. See
       also Allan Hall, "Nazi Nuclear Waste from Hitler's Secret A-bomb
       Programme Found in Mine," *Daily Mail*, July 13, 2011, https://
       www.dailymail.co.uk/news/article-2014146/Nazi-nuclear-waste-
       Hitlers-secret-A-bomb-programme-mine.html.

37.   Ibid. See also report entitled "Befragung von Buergern zu
       Ereignissen zue oertlichen Geschichte," Property of Arnstadt Town
       Hall, 1989. Document in possession of the authors.

38.   Transcripts, Nuremberg Trial Proceedings, Vol. 16, testimony of
       defendant Albert Speer, June 21, 1946, p. 528.

39.   Oscar W. Koch and Robert G. Hays, *G-2 Intelligence for Patton*
       (Philadelphia: Whitmore Publishing Company, 1971), p. 117.

40.   Himmler's Diary, p. 286.

41.   William J. Broad, "Experts Wonder About Fate of Nazi Uranium,"
       New York Times, December 31, 1995, https://www.sun-sentinel.
       com/news/fl-xpm-1995-12-31-9512300284-story.html.

42.   Secretary David B. Langmuir, Guided Missiles Committee, Joint
       Chiefs of Staff, memorandum to Brigadier General J. F. Phillips,
       "Notes on Submarine U-234," May 23, 1945.

43.   Hydrick, *Critical Mass*, p. 2.

44.   William J. Broad, "Captured Cargo, Captivating Mystery," *New
       York Times*, December 31, 1995, https://www.nytimes.
       com/1995/12/31/us/captured-cargo-captivating-mystery.html.

45.   Hydrick, *Critical Mass*. Chapters 5 and 6, generally.

46.   Wolfgang W. E. Samuel, *American Raiders, The Race to Capture
       the Luftwaffe's Secrets* (Jackson, Mississippi: University Press of
       Mississippi, 2004), p. 10.

47.   "DC Mil Attaché AmEmbassy Memorandum to War Department
       for Chamberlain," March 28, 1947. See also Colonel Shuler,
       memorandum to Major General Groves, "Sir Charles Hambro on
       Joachimsthal," November 15, 1945; and H. S. Lowenhaupt,

"Russian Mining Operations in the German-Czech Border Region," December 5, 1946.

48. Annie Jacobsen, *Operation Paperclip, The Secret Intelligence Program that Brought Nazi Scientists to America* (New York: Little, Brown and Company, 2014), p. 103.

49. Ute Deichmann, *Biologists under Hitler* (Cambridge, Massachusetts: Harvard University Press, 1999), pp. 278, 287. See also memorandum to commanding general, Fifth Army, "Interview of Dr. Andrew C. Ivy re: German Biological Warfare," MID File No. 000.71, February 18, 1947.

50. Major General Leslie R. Groves, memorandum to the chief of staff, War Department, Office of the Chief of Engineers, March 22, 1944, cited in Leslie Groves, *Now it Can Be Told: the Story of the Manhattan Project* (Da Capo Press, June 16, 2009), p. 201.

51. Roy M. Stanley II, *V Weapons Hunt: Defeating German Secret Weapons* (South Yorkshire: Pen and Sword Books, 2010), p. 227.

52. The remaining quantities of heavy water, interestingly, were controlled at least in part by I.G. Farben. See Office of Strategic Services Official Dispatch, #4319, Bern, Switzerland to Office of Strategic Services, August 2, 1944, stating that Farben turned down the request of a scientist for heavy water.

53. See generally, Boris T. Pash, *The ALSOS Mission* (New York: Award House Books, 1969).

54. Ibid, p. 11.

55. Ibid, p. 157.

56. Vincent C. Jones, *Manhattan: The Army and the Atomic Bomb* (Washington, D.C.: Center of Military History, United States Army, 1985), p. 287.

57. Samuel A. Goudsmit, Scientific Chief, ALSOS Mission, memorandum, "Strasburg Intelligence on German Nuclear Physics and TA," December 17, 1944, p. 1.

58. For example, see Koch and Hays, *G-2 Intelligence for Patton*, p. 79.

59. See, for example, Goudsmit, memorandum, Preliminary Report, noting that "all secret files were removed." See also Intelligence Report No. EW-Te 4, Teutsch, Kurt, CIOS USSTAF, April 26, 1945, p. 2.

60. Lieutenant Colonel George R. Eckman to Major Francis Smith, Transmittal Memorandum of Hechingen Area Operation, ALSOS Mission, April 30, 1945. See also Interrogation Report of Professor Walther Bothe, ALSOS Mission, April 4, 1945, paragraph 16, p. 3.

61. Jacobsen, *Operation Paperclip*, p. 38; Colonel Peter Beasley, Preliminary Report, USSBS, June 7, 1945, pp. 1–2. See also Leslie E. Simon, *German Research in World War II* (Chapman & Hall, 1947), pp. 5–8.

62. CIOS Evaluation Report, Cyclotron Investigation at Heidelberg, Interview with Prof. Walter [sic] Bothe, July 17, 1945, p. 1.

63. Bernstein, *Hitler's Uranium Club*, p. 47.

64. Goudsmit, Memorandum, Preliminary Report, p. 3.

65. "Special Section set up for investigating German secret processes," T Force Orientation Talk, March 5, 1945, U.S. National Archives, RG 331, Entry 18, Box 157, Subject File 44–45.

66. While ALSOS remained "the only intelligence team authorized to investigate for the United States and British interests the German progress on the Atom Bomb," that was no longer its sole mission. U.S. National Archives, Report by the Scientific Chief of the ALSOS Mission, RG 200, Box 6, December 7, 1945, pp. 15–16.

67. Ibid.

68. Jones, *Manhattan*, p. 286.

69. U.S. National Archives, Report by the Scientific Chief of the ALSOS Mission, RG 200, Box 6, December 7, 1945, pp. 1–2.

70. Ibid., pp. 15–16.

71. Ibid, p. 16.

72. Ibid, p. 18.

73. David H. DeVorkin, *Science with a Vengeance: How the Military Created the U.S. Space Sciences After World War Two* (New York:

Springer Verlag, Smithsonian Institution, 1994), pp. 36, p. 50, footnote 3, citing Kuiper to F. E. Terman, March 13, 1945, ALSOS folder Kuiper Papers, University of Arizona Special Collections.

74. Vincent C. Jones, *Manhattan: The Army and the Atomic Bomb*, (Center for Military History, United States Army, Washington, D.C., 1985), p. 288.

75. Interestingly, decades later Pash would face the Congressional Church Committee, which investigated intelligence agency overreach and abuses.

76. Sheldon H. Harris, *Factories of Death: Japanese Biological Warfare, 1932– 1945, and the American Cover-up* (Abingdon, U.K.: Routledge Company), p. 289.

77. E. V. Hill, In Botulism: Summary Report on B.W. Investigations, Memorandum to General Alden C. Waitt, Chief, Chemical Corps, Department of the Army, December 12, 1947. Archived at U.S. Library of Congress.

78. Ibid.

79. Harris, *Factories of Death*, p. 302.

80. Frederick I. Sharpe III and Mitchell Ordway, *The Rocket Team: From the V-2 to the Saturn Moon Rocket—the Inside Story of How a Small Group of Engineers Changed World History* (Oxford: Oxford University Press, 1979), p. 58.

81. Jochen von Lang, *Top Nazi: SS General Karl Wolff, The Man Between Hitler and Himmler* (New York: Enigma Books, 2005), p. 268.

82. Koch and Hays, *G-2 Intelligence for Patton*, p. 79.

83. Dr. F. Zwicky, "Short Interview of General Dornberger," CIOS 183, conducted at Garmisch-Partenkirchen, May 16, 1945, p. 7. Document in possession of the authors.

84. Report on the Investigation of I.G. Farbenindistrie A.G., prepared by Division of Investigation of Cartels and External Assets, OMGUS, November 1945, p. 73.

85. Koch and Hays, G-2 Intelligence for Patton, p. 79.

86. Albert Speer, *The Slave State: Heinrich Himmler's Masterplan for SS Supremacy* (London: Weidenfeld and Nicolson, 1981).

87. CIOS Evaluation Report 112, Speer Ministry and Secret Weapons, June 10, 1945.

88. Bernstein, *Hitler's Uranium Club*, p. 28.

89. Beasley, Preliminary Report, pp. 1–2.

90. Colonel Peter Beasley, "Draft of Suggested Comments to be Included in General Aurnold's Report," undated document in possession of the authors.

91. Captain George Davis, "Memorandum to Major H. K. Calvert, Report of Interview with P/W Hauptman Wagner," December 11, 1944, p. 2.

92. Brigadegeneral Keilhaus, Memorandum to von Herf, Obergruppenführer, February 13, 1945.

93. Von Ardenne's group also held a contract with the Peenemünde rocket team to study nuclear propulsion for missiles and nuclear power for rocket propulsion. Claus Reuter, *The V2 and the German, Russian and American Rocket Program*, (London: S.R. Research and Publishing, 2000), p. 40.

94. Top Secret CSDIC (U.K.), S.R.G.G. Report 1118, 10 January 1945, Great Britain/Combined Services Detailed Interrogation Center, Call # 512.619C-6C, IRIS# 00212013, USAF Collection, AFHRA, Maxwell Air Force Base. This recording was made at Trent Park detention center, North London. Captured German officers were housed together and were permitted open communication, some of which was recorded. G.G. Report, CSDIC, p. 10.

95. Lieutenant Colonel S. H. Kirkland, acting chief, Strategic Vulnerability Branch, Air Intelligence Division, Headquarters Army Air Forces, Daily Activity Report, March 31, 1948, p. 2.

96. Captain W. S. Parsons, memorandum to Major General L.R. Groves, "Possible Use of Radioactive Poison in Rocket Propelled, Unmanned Aircraft," April 20, 1944.

97. Stanley, *V Weapons Hunt*, p. 230.

98.   G.G. Report, CSDIC, p. 9.

99.   Ibid., p. 10.

100. Werner Grothmann, Interview by Wolf Krotzky, August 3, 2000.

101. In addition to including a proximity fuse which triggered the explosion of its warhead at an ideal height over its target in the final moment of its descent, the V-1's warhead housed a special high explosive, Amatol, approximately four times more powerful than any Allied explosive. The V-2, however, could not be outfitted with the relatively unstable Amatol, as the heat generated by supersonic speed would cause mid-air detonation.

102. Heinrich Klein, *Vom GescHöss zum Feuerpfeil* (Vowinkel Motorbuch Verlag, 1977).

103. Some military specialists theorize that the Rheinbote did have usefulness as rapid-fire long-range artillery support even with conventional explosives. Traditionally, the problem with heavy artillery had been the difficulty of rapid movement, something even more problematic with Germany's innovative Blitzkrieg style of war, in which German ground troops advanced so quickly. As the troops and artillery advanced, they got further and further from fixed ammo dumps and manufacturing sites and supply lines become an issue. A longer-range form of artillery like the Rheinbote, with its hundred-mile range, could support rapidly advancing troops over greater distances without itself having to move. Rheinbote missile launchers could theoretically support the advance of ground troops in any direction for over a hundred miles without the artillery emplacement and ammo moving an inch and without the supply lines lengthening a millimeter. Yet the Rheinbote did not begin development until 1943. By then, the era of the Blitzkrieg was over. Germany was not experiencing rapid gains in territory. Absent an especially lethal warhead, the Rheinbote wasn't much better than spending millions of Reichsmarks to develop an enormously complicated weapon to lob a conventional hand grenade a hundred miles. The Rheinbote really only makes sense with biological, chemical, or nuclear

weapons in its smaller warhead. The Joint Commission's report concluduing that the Rheinbote was intended to be paired with an atomic payload, then, makes perfect sense.

Chapter Nine: Think Tank Kammler

1. Wilhelm Voss file, RG 319, Army CIC IRR (Investigative Repository Records), provided to Keith Chester in 2007 by William Cunliffe, director, IWG Staff, NARA.
2. Tom Agoston, *Blunder! How the U.S. Gave Away Nazi Supersecrets to Russia* (New York: Dodd, Mead, 1985).
3. Author interview of Vladislav Kratky, head archivist, SKODA Museum, September 2, 2004.
4. Agoston, *Blunder!*, generally.
5. Ibid., pp. xiii–xv.
6. F. A. C. Wardenburg, memorandum, Interrogation of Dr. Baerwind, Technical Director—DEGUSSA, ALSOS Mission, April 5, 1945.
7. As a bonus of its first move into Czechoslovakia, Germany gained control of Europe's largest uranium mine. No one has ever determined whether it was this reservoir of material necessary for production of a nuclear weapon, or the presence of the munitions manufacturer Skoda that weighed more heavily in Hitler's determination to annex the area. But with this move, Germany's capacity to make war increased dramatically, including nuclear warfare. As Martin Allen stresses, in Germany's negotiated takeover of the Sudetenland via the Munich Conference in 1938, attended by Hitler, Chamberlain, and French prime minister Daladier, Germany got one of the crown jewels in armaments manufacturing and technology: "the all-important Skoda armaments factory." Martin Allen, *Himmler's Secret War: The Covert Peace Negotiations of Heinrich Himmler* (New York: Carroll & Graf Publishing Group, Avalon Publishers, 2006), p. 46.

8. Military Attaché Report, Czechoslovakia, Report No. R-32-45, "Russian Demand for German Scientific Secrets," September 30, 1945, p. 1.

9. Czechoslovakia—Scientific and Technical Institution Reestablishment, Intelligence Division, Office of Chief of Naval Operations, Navy Department, December 9, 1946.

10. LaVerne Baldwin, acting chief, Dist. Div., Office of Collection and Dissemination, Memorandum to Colonel Seemans, November 22, 1946.

11. Office of Strategic Services Official Dispatch, #54484, USTRAVIC, London, to Office of Strategic Services, June 20, 1944.

12. Office of Strategic Services Official Dispatch, #332, MacFarland Istanbul to Office of Strategic Services, May 4, 1944.

13. "The Puzzle of Podokly," *Time*, November 12, 1945.

14. Colonel Baskin R. Lawrence, chief, Strategic Vulnerability Branch, Air Intelligence Division, Headquarters Army Air Forces, Daily Activity Report, June 4, 1947.

15. R. U. Hyde, acting secretary, Joint Intelligence Committee, Exploitation of German Scientists and Technicians, J.I.C. 317/9/D, January 5, 1946.

16. BIOS Final Report No. 313, "Report on Visit to Czechoslovakia by Armament Design Department," November 16–December 9, 1945, Colonel R. V. Shepherd, pp. 30–42.

17. Agoston, *Blunder!*, p. 13.

18. Report No. 1/1945, A.D.I. (K), Armament Industry–Czechoslovakia, Skoda-Waffenfarbrik Brunn, Felkin, S.D., July 1944, pp. 7–8. Document in possession of the authors.

19. T. Dennis Reece, "Mission to Štěchovice: How Americans Took Nazi Documents from Czechoslovakia—and Created a Diplomatic Crisis" *Prologue Magazine*, winter 2007, p. 2, https://www. archives.gov/publications/prologue/2007/winter/stechovice.html.

20. Lionel Shapiro, "Bohemia Raiders Gambled Lives to Recover German Documents, *New York Times*, February 26, 1946, p. 2.

21.   William Donovan, Job Description in the Case of Charles Katek, June 10, 1943.

22.   Commander Frank G. Wisner, memorandum to Major General W. J. Donovan, "The Establishment of a Status for Major Charles Katek and His Prague Mission," July 8, 1945.

23.   Major Gordon M. Stewart, memorandum to Whitney H. Shepardson, et. al., February 20, 1946, stating in part "USFET organized a raid," paragraph 12, p. 3.

24.   Reece, "Mission to Štěchovice," p. 5.

25.   Dennis T. Reece, *Captains of Bomb Disposal 1942–1946* (Bloomington, Indiana: Xlibris Corporation, 2005), p. 117.

26.   Jaro Svěcený, *The Search for Nazi Treasures III*, proposal for an exploration project and documentary television series, 2005, pp. 12–14. Document in possession of the authors.

27.   Ibid.

28.   Ibid.

29.   Agoston, *Blunder!*, p. 13.

30.   BIOS Final Report No. 313, p. 17.

31.   Agoston, *Blunder!*, pp. 11, 98.

32.   Ibid., pp. 79–80.

33.   Speer on the Last Days of the German Reich, USSBS Special Document, International Military Tribunal.

34.   Keith Chester Field Report.

35.   Agoston, *Blunder!*, p. 84.

36.   Ibid., pp. 85–86.

37.   Wilhelm Voss Interrogation Report, U.S. Army CIC IRR (Investigative Repository Records), provided to Keith Chester by William Cunliffe, Director, IWG Staff, NARA RG 319. Document in possession of the authors.

38.   Colonel Baskin R. Lawrence, chief, Strategic Vulnerability Branch, Air Intelligence Division, Headquarters Army Air Forces, Daily Activity Report, June 26, 1947. Document in possession of the authors.

39. Wilhelm Voss, Written Statement at Dustbin, September 18, 1946, p. 4.

40. Author interview of Jörg Kammler, July 3, 2008. Transcription in possession of the authors, July 3, 2008.

41. Memorandum to commanding officer, CIC Region IV, APO 205, U.S. Army, April 25, 1946, p. 1.

42. Michael J. Neufeld, "Rolf Engel vs. the German Army: A Nazi Career in Rocketry and Repression," *History and Technology: An International Journal* 13:1 (1996), p. 61.

43. Paul Rosbaud, letter to Samuel A. Goudsmit, September 9, 1945, Samuel A. Goudsmit papers, Neils Bohr Library & Archives, American Institute of Physics, One Physics Ellipse, College Park, Maryland, Digital Collections, Box 26, Folder 20, Flossenburg: Caves, 1944.

44. LaVerne Baldwin, Acting Chief, Dist. Div., Office of Collection and Dissemination, memorandum to Colonel Seemans, November 22, 1946.

45. AB000 For AB030, Amzon, Memorandum to AB011, Erlangen, August 27, 1945. Voss Dossier received in response to author FOIA.

46. Telex, USFET HQ, to Chief, Counter Intelligence Corps Region IV, June 22, 1946.

47. BIOS Final Report No. 313, p. 4.

48. Ibid., p. 54.

49. Colonel Richard P. Klocko, Chief, Foreign Branch, Memorandum to Military Attaché, American Embassy, Prague, German Vengeance Weapons in Czechoslovakia, August 7, 1946.

50. Notes on German Weapons Developments, Report Ref. No. SAIC/12, Interrogation of Nils Larsson, May 17, 1945. See also Survey of German Activities in the Field of Guided Missiles, Technical Report No. 237-45, U.S. Naval Technical Mission in Europe, NND760139, August 1945, p. 190. Document in possession of the authors.

51.   Ibid., p. 8. See also Survey of German Activities in the Field of
       Guided Missiles, Technical Report No. 237-45, U.S. Naval
       Technical Mission in Europe, NND760139, NARA Date 8-25-08,
       August 1945, p. 130. Document in possession of the authors.

52.   Dr. Edgar Ruppelt, "Interrogations of German Prisoners and
       Witnesses," International Military Tribunal, Cornell University
       Library, Vol. 099, June 3, 1945.

53.   Document in possession of the authors.

54.   Colonel Baskin R. Lawrence, chief, Strategic Vulnerability Branch,
       Air Intelligence Division, Headquarters Army Air Forces, Daily
       Activity Report, May 13, 1947.

55.   BIOS Final Report No. 313, p. 69.

56.   Neufeld, "Rolf Engel vs. The German Army," p. 54.

57.   Smithsonian National Air and Space Museum, at https://
       airandspace.si.edu/collection-objects/
       rolf-engel-collection-1935-1936.

58.   Neufeld, "Rolf Engel vs. The German Army," p. 59.

59.   Nils Larsson, engineer, Stockholm, Interrogation of German
       Technicians, June 8, 1945, accessed from the Maxwell Air Force
       Base. Document in possession of the authors.

60.   Report: Interrogation of German Technicians, Nils Larsson,
       Engineer, Stockholm, Augsburg, June 8, 1945, Call Number
       570.6191—IRIS Number 00241180, USAF Collection, Air Force
       Historical Research Agency, Maxwell Air Force Base. See also
       Report Ref. No. SAIC/12, May 17, 1945.

61.   Judy Feigin, "The Office of Special Investigations: Striving for
       Accountability in the Aftermath of the Holocaust," U.S.
       Department of Justice, December 2006, p. 259.

62.   Ibid., p. 261.

63.   Vernon W. Nickerson, CIC Operations, Periodic Report of Theater
       Directed CIC Operations, Report No. 9, HQ, Counter Intelligence
       Corps Detachment, December 27, 1946, approved by Lieutenant
       Colonel Dale M. Garvey.

Chapter Ten: A Parallel Case

1. FBI Report, Wernher Magnus Maximillian Frieherr von Braun, May 17, 1961, p. 7.
2. Ibid., p. 2.
3. J. Y. Smith, "Dr. Wernher von Braun, 65, Dies," *Washington Post*, June 18, 1977.
4. Ibid. Also John Noble Wilford, "Wernher von Braun, Rocket Pioneer, Dies," *New York Times*, June 18, 1977.
5. Frederick I. Sharpe III and Mitchell Ordway, *The Rocket Team: From the V-2 to the Saturn Moon Rocket—the Inside Story of How a Small Group of Engineers Changed World History* (Oxford: Oxford University Press, 1954), p. xiv.
6. David H. DeVorkin, *Science with a Vengeance: How the Military Created the U.S. Space Sciences after World War Two* (New York: Springer Verlag, Smithsonian Institution, 1994), p. 36, 341.
7. Michael J. Neufeld, *Von Braun: Dreamer of Space, Engineer of War* (New York: Knopf Doubleday Publishing Group, 2007), p. 112.
8. Ibid., p. 201.
9. Walter Jessel, *A Travelogue Though a Twentieth Century Live: The Memoirs of Walter Jessel* (self-published, 1996), p. 141.
10. Michael Brian Petersen, *Engineering Consent: Peenemünde, National Socialism, and the V-2 Missile, 1924–1945* (Ph.D. dissertation, University of Maryland, 2005), p. 255., pp. 367–77. Document in possession of the authors.
11. Ibid, pp. 403–6.
12. Wernher Magnus Maximillian Frieherr von Braun FBI Report, p. 3.
13. FBI Report, Wernher Magnus Maximilian Freiherr von Braun, Special Inquiry, Department of Justice, German Scientists Under the Protective Custody and Control of the Joint Intelligence Objectives Agency, September 25, 1948, incorporating Affidavit of Membership in NSDAP of Professor Wernher von Braun, June 18, 1947, p. 3.

14. Ibid., stating he was "officially demanded to join the National Socialist Party," p. 3.

15. SS 113 619, Personalnachweis, Dr. Hans Kammler, p. 1. Document in possession of the authors.

16. Ibid., p. 5.

17. Ibid, pp. 3–4.

18. Ibid.

19. Neufeld, *Von Braun*, p. 90.

20. See Deiter Huzel, *From Peenemünde to Canaveral* (Pickle Partners Publishing, 2014).

21. During von Braun's entire tenure at Peenemünde, the facility was under continuous construction—all by slave laborers.

22. Jacobsen, *Operation Paperclip*, p. 39.

23. Brief Interrogation Report on Professor Dr. Wernher von Braun, Special Investigations, Field Information Agency, Technical, T-Force, 69 HQ, July 8, 1947, p. 18, paragraph 60.

24. Michael J. Neufeld, *The Rocket and the Reich: Peenemünde and the Coming of the Ballistic Missile Era* (New York: Free Press, 1995), p. 154; of the 732 killed during the bombing raid, "only 120 were of the regular German staff, while the rest consisted of Russians, Poles, etc." Interview with General Dornberger, Garmisch-Partenkerchen, May 21, 1945, within *The Story of Peenemünde*, p. 306.

25. Dennis Piszkiewicz, *Wernher von Braun: The Man Who Sold the Moon* (Westport, Connecticut: Praeger Publishers, 1998), pp. 51–52.

26. *U.S.A. v. POHL, et. al.*, U.S. Military Tribunal Nuremberg, Judgment of 3 November 1947, p. 1012.

27. Jean Michel, *Dora: The Nazi Concentration Camp Where Modern Space Technology was Born and 30,000 Prisoners Died*, in association with Nucera, Louis, trans. Jennifer Kidd (New York: Holt, Rinehart and Winston, 1975), p. 92.

28. Ibid., pp. 89, 204. Von Braun visited Nordhausen at least a dozen times to supervise and oversee the work there.

29. As Pulitzer Prize–winning author Wayne Biddle observed, the Nordhausen facility was constructed in a way that knowledge of the entire camp culture and existence of the Dora camp must be imputed to any visitor or regular worker—it was all one thing. Wayne Biddle, *Dark Side of the Moon: Wernher von Braun, The Third Reich, and the Space Race* (New York: W.W. Norton, 2009).

30. Von Braun to Degenkolb, November 12, 1943, FE 732, NASM, cited in Petersen, *Engineering Consent*, p. 366.

31. Biddle catalogued fifteen visits by von Braun to Nordhausen. During his October 8–9, 1943, visit, nearly four thousand slave laborers were being exploited, sleeping on bare rock or a scattering of straw before the wooden-slab bunk beds were constructed within the tunnels. By the time von Braun returned for his next visit some eight weeks later, some ten thousand forced laborers were living in these squalid conditions. Biddle, *Dark Side of the Moon*.

32. Neufeld, *Von Braun*, p. 145.

33. Annie Jacobsen, *Operation Paperclip: The Secret Intelligence Program that Brought Nazi Scientists to America* (New York: Little, Brown and Company, 2014), p. 102.

34. Neufeld, *The Rocket and the Reich*, p. 229.

35. There are no records of any objections to the use of slave labor by von Braun. To show that objections, per se, were not verboten, numerous records show that von Braun was comfortable enough saying no to his boss's boss—SS chief Heinrich Himmler—when it came to recognizing Degenkolb's authority.

36. Ralph Blumenthal, "German-Born NASA Expert Quits U.S. to Avoid a War Crimes Suit," *New York Times*, October 18, 1984, p. A1.

37. In an interesting side note, Rudolph's case resurfaced in 2014 when it was revealed that he and other former Nazis who had worked in the U.S., only to be deported or otherwise forced out, had been receiving Social Security payments for decades afterward.

38. Special Agent George E. Riddlebarger, Fourth Army, Memorandum for the Officer in Charge, Security Survey, Res. and Dev. Sv., Fort Bliss, Texas, May 17, 1947. Document in possession of the authors.

39. Cypher Telegram, British Ministry of Supply London, to ACC, for information of Major-General Lethbridge, June 7, 1947.

40. Transcript of Interrogation, May 5, 1947, Irmgard Hohmann, Landshut, Germany; Signed Statement of Irmgard Hohmann, May 5, 1947, Landshut, Germany, PRO, Kew.

41. Interrogation Report of von Braun, July 8, 1947, p. 23, paragraph 91.

42. William D. Gunn, special agent, CIC headquarters, Sub-region, Counter Intelligence Corps Region III, April 30, 1942.

43. Interrogation Report of von Braun, July 8, 1947, p. 20, paragraph 73.

44. Ibid., p. 18, paragraph 61.

45. Ibid., pp. 19-20, paragraph 62–69.

46. Ibid, p. 20, paragraph 69.

47. Ibid., p. 23, paragraph 91.

48. Ibid., p. 22, paragraph 84.

49. Ibid., p. 3, paragraph 3.

Chapter Eleven: The Kammler Deal

1. Robin W. Winks, *Cloak and Gown: Scholars in the Secret War, 1939 - 1961* (New York: William Morrow and Company, 1987), p. 24.

2. Ibid., p. 113.

3. Allen Dulles, *The Secret Surrender* (New York: Harper and Row, 1966), p. 15.

4. See generally Neal H. Petersen, ed., *From Hitler's Doorstep: The Wartime Intelligence Reports of Allen Dulles, 1942–1945* (University Park, Pennsylvania: Pennsylvania State University Press, 1996); and John McKinney Tucker, "Technologies of Intelligence and Their Relation to National Security Policy: A Case Study of the

U.S. and the V-2 Rocket," dissertation submitted to the faculty of the Virginia Polytechnic Institute and State University, May 2013.

5. A 1999 newsletter report of the World War Two Studies Association concluded that of nine thousand cubic feet of records, two thousand, or over 20 percent, were ordered destroyed after the war as "they had no historical value." Lawrence McDonald, U.S. National Archives, "OSS Textual Records at the National Archives: An Outline for Researchers, World War Two Studies Association," newsletter, ISSN 0885-5668, No. 61 (spring 1999), pp. 7–8.

6. Christof Mauch, *The Shadow War Against Hitler: The Covert Operations of America's Wartime Secret Intelligence Service* (New York: Columbia University Press, 1999), pp. 199, 214.

7. Ibid., p. 118.

8. Winks, *Cloak and Gown*, p. 123.

9. Ibid., p. 94.

10. Martin Allen, *Himmler's Secret War: The Covert Peace Negotiations of Heinrich Himmler* (New York: Carroll & Graf Publishing Group, Avalon Publishers, 2006), p. 256.

11. See Dulles, *The Secret Surrender*.

12. Hersh, p. 116.

13. Christopher Simpson, *The Splendid Blond Beast: Money, Law, and Genocide in the Twentieth Century* (New York: Grove Press, 1993), p. 13.

14. Richard Breitman, et al., *U.S. Intelligence and the Nazis* (Cambridge: Cambridge University Press, 2005), p. 448.

15. Kersten Von Lingen, *Allen Dulles, the OSS, and Nazi War Criminals: The Dynamics of Selective Prosecution* (Cambridge: Cambridge University Press), 2013.

16. Simpson, *The Splendid Blond Beast*, p. 189, citing OSS, Bern, Switzerland to OSS headquarters and division chiefs, December 26, 1944 (Secret): OSS, Bern November 1, 1944–January 31, 1945, Wash Sect R & C 78, U.S. National Archives, RG 22, Box 278, Entry 134, folder 19.

17. High-ranking Nazis including Hitler himself hoped that they could make peace with the Anglo-Americans and then turn their combined might on the Communists.

18. Termine des Reichsführer, October 25, 1944, Bundesarchiv, Folder N-104.

19. Douglas Waller, *Wild Bill Donovan: The Spymaster Who Created the OSS and Modern American Espionage* (New York: Free Press, 2011), pp. 265–66.

20. Papers of Edward R Stettinius Jr., Box 733, Special Collections, University of Virginia Library, Charlottesville, Virginia, Memos for the Secretary, undated.

21. Dulles, *The Secret Surrender*, p. 23.

22. John Noble Wilford, "Wernher von Braun, Rocket Pioneer, Dies," *New York Times*, June 18, 1977.

23. Sayer, pp. 272–73, 275.

24. In addition, although hundreds of thousands of Nazis were removed from their government positions after the war, by 1950 the vast majority had found their way back. Ian Sayer and Douglas Botting, *America's Secret Army* (London: Grafton Books, 1989), p. 300.

25. Director Neal M. Sher, "Robert Jan Verbelen and the United States Government," Office of Special Investigations, U.S. Department of Justice, Report to the Assistant Attorney General, Criminal Division, June 16, 1988, p. 83.

26. For a thorough discussion of Operation Paperclip, see Annie Jacobsen, *Operation Paperclip: The Secret Intelligence Program that Brought Nazi Scientists to America* (New York: Little, Brown and Company, 2014).

27. Richard Breitman and Norman J. W. Richard, *Hitler's Shadow: Nazi War Criminals, U.S. Intelligence, and the Cold War* (U.S. National Archives, 2005), p. 86.

28. Richard Breitman, et al., *U.S. Intelligence and the Nazis* (New York: Cambridge University Press, 2005), pp. 249–54.

29. Breitman and Richard, *Hitler's Shadow*, p. 91.

30. Guy Walters, *Hunting Evil: The Nazi War Criminals Who Escaped and the Quest to Bring Them to Justice* (New York: Broadway Books, Random House Group Ltd., 2009), pp. 225–31.

31. Ibid.; see also Sher, "Robert Jan Verbelen."

32. Gehlen and his principal Nazi officers had decided as early as mid-1944, fully a year before the war ended, to make his intelligence network available to the Western Allies. Major General W. A. Burress, G-2, to Lieutenant Hoyt S. Vandenberg, Director of Central Intelligence, "Operation RUSTY—Use of the Eastern Branch of the former German Intelligence Service," with attachments, October 1, 1946, http://www2.gwu.edu/~nsarchiv/NSAEBB/NSAEBB146/doc19.pdf.

33. Walters, *Hunting Evil*, p. 17.

34. The Interagency Working Group (IWG) was established by an act of the U.S. Congress and concluded its work with a hundred-plus-page report issued in 2007. It included representatives from U.S. agencies such as the National Archives, the Department of Defense, the CIA, the FBI, and others and was charged with facilitating disclosure of classified records related to Nazi war criminals, and particularly those war criminals and collaborators utilized by any part of the American government. The IWG was never satisfied with the production of documents by one particular entity, the CIA. Do note, though, that the mandate giving the IWG access to documents included exceptions for documents whose release might compromise some aspect of national security.

35. Douglas Jehl, "C.I.A. Said to Rebuff Congress on Nazi Files," *New York Times*, January 30, 2005, https://www.nytimes.com/2005/01/30/world/europe/cia-said-to-rebuff-congress-on-nazi-files.html. In 2005, before the IWG even concluded its work, Jehl noted that there existed "a closer relationship between the United States government and Nazi war criminals than had been previously understood."

36. Naturally, it is possible that if records were destroyed, knowledge of the Kammler Deal died with the original deal-makers.

37.   Wolfgang Saxon, "Klaus Barbie, 77, Lyons Gestapo Chief," *New York Times*, September 26, 1991, https://www.nytimes. com/1991/09/26/world/klaus-barbie-77-lyons-gestapo-chief.html.

38.   Breitman and Richard, *Hitler's Shadow*, p. 40.

39.   Merk had been recruited in 1946; he was not SS, but was in the regular German army. He had known Barbie during the war and recommended him to Taylor as an informant. Erhard Dabringhaus, *Klaus Barbie: The Shocking Story of How the U.S. Used this Nazi War Criminal as an Intelligence Agent* (Washington, D.C.: Acropolis Books, Ltd., 1984), pp. 51–52. Allan A. Ryan, "Klaus Barbie and the United States Government, A Report to the Attorney General of the United States, Submitted by Special Assistant to the Assistant Attorney General," Criminal Division, United States Department of Justice, August 1983.

40.   Ibid. See also Dabringhaus, *Klaus Barbie*, pp. 51–52.

41.   Ibid, p. 102. Ryan, *Klaus Barbie*. p. 78.

42.   Christopher Simpson, *Blowback: The First Full Account of America's Recruitment of Nazis and its Disastrous Effect on the Cold War, Our Domestic and Foreign Policy* (New York: Collier Books, 1989), p. 39.

43.   "Week in Death: Earl Browning, the Moral Spy," *Telegraph*, November 10, 2013, http://www.thedailybeast.com/ week-in-death-earl-browning-the-moral-spy.

44.   The interrogation took place at the European Command Intelligence Center (ECIC) near Frankfurt.

45.   Dabringhaus, *Klaus Barbie*, p. 53.

46.   Ryan, *Klaus Barbie*, p. 42.

47.   Special Assistant to the Assistant Attorney General Allan A. Ryan, Klaus Barbie and the United States Government, p. 78.

48.   Simpson, *Blowback*, p. 49.

49.   Dabringhaus, *Klaus Barbie*, p. 290.

50.   Lieutenant Colonel Dale M. Garvey, Headquarters CIC, USFET, to Chief, CIC Region III, Dossier No. 35246, April 1, 1946. Document in possession of the authors.

51. It has been suggested, correctly I think, that Barbie had a great deal
     of mud to sling at French officials who had collaborated with the
     Nazis during the war. Putting him on the witness stand would
     amount to giving him a platform from which to slander—or
     accurately impugn—French government officials. Thus the French
     efforts to have Barbie extradited to testify were not necessarily
     full-throated.

52. Documents authored by CIC special agents memorialize missions
     and activities of CIC agents, sub-agents, and informants in the
     French zone. CIC special agent Camille Hadju, memorandum, to
     the officer in charge, "Subj. BARBIE, Klaus, alias Becker,
     Behrendts, Mertens, Spehr and Holzer," November 21, 1947.
     Dabringhaus noted that "Four of the [Petersen] network's sub-
     sources lived in the French Zone of Occupation and had good
     connections with French intelligence." They helped "keep tabs on
     all French activities." Dabringhaus, *Klaus Barbie*, p. 79. The
     French did not know this, and CIC did not want the French finding
     it out from a discarded Klaus Barbie.

53. Uki Goni, *The Real Odessa: How Peron Brought the Nazi War
     Criminals to Argentina*, revised ed. (London: Granta Books,
     2002), p. 63.

54. James U. Milano and Patrick Brogan, *Soldiers, Spies, and the Rat
     Line: America's Undeclared War against the Soviets* (Washington,
     D.C.: Brassey's, 2000), p. 44.

55. Sher, "Robert Jan Verbelen," p. 80.

56. In another interesting bit of side discussion, Milano tells his reader
     that his "visitors" traveled solo or in pairs. And always, always, the
     visitors were made to believe that the Ratline was used only for
     them. This enhanced operational security, as any "visitor"
     apprehended along the route would be unable to report on an
     ongoing evacuation route.

57. Milano and Brogan, *Soldiers, Spies, and the Rat Line*, p. 44.

58. Ibid., p. 53.

59. Ibid., p. 63.

60. Ryan, *Klaus Barbie,* p. 110.

61. Dabringhaus, *Klaus Barbie*, p. 179.

62. "Nazis and Axis Collaborators Were Used to Further U.S. Anti-Communist Objectives in Europe—Some Immigrated to the United States," report by the Comptroller General of the United States, GAO/GGD-85-66, June 28, 1985.

63. Ibid., p. ii.

64. Ibid., p. 19.

65. Ibid., p. ii.

66. Breitman and Richard, *Hitler's Shadow.*

67. Leon Goldensohn, *The Nuremberg Interviews* (New York: Knopf Doubleday Publishing, 2007), pp. 368–69.

68. Ibid, p. 375.

69. Ibid, p. 298.

70. Breitman, *Hitler's Shadow*, pp. 36–38.

71. Ibid., p. 38.

72. Ibid., p. 37.

73. Ibid., p. 39.

74. Ibid., pp. 39–40.

75. "German Nationalist and Neo-Nazi Activities in Argentina, Prepared by [REDACTED] for the Western Hemisphere Division, CIA," Case number K-10046, July 8, 1953, pp. 1, 7. Document in possession of the authors.

76. Blue Book on Argentina, "Consultation Among the American Republics with Respect to the Argentine Situation," memorandum of the United States Government, New York, Greenberg, February 1946.

77. German Nationalist and Neo-Nazi Activities in Argentina, p. 1.

78. Blue Book on Argentina, p. 37.

79. Ibid.

80. Ann Louise Bardach, "Argentina Evades Its Nazi Past," *New York Times*, March 22, 1997, https://www.nytimes.com/1997/03/22/opinion/argentina-evades-its-nazi-past.html.

Index

About the Authors

Dean Reuter is general counsel of the Federalist Society for Law and Public Policy and a fellow at the National Security Institute at George Mason University's Antonin Scalia Law School. He was the editor of *Liberty's Nemesis: The Unchecked Expansion of the State* and *Confronting Terror: 9/11 and the Future of American National Security.*

Colm Lowery is an award-winning lecturer in biomedical science at the University of Ulster in Northern Ireland, where he lectures in molecular biology and its application to biowarfare and bioterrorism. He has published over forty peer-reviewed scientific papers, book chapters, and review articles.

Keith Chester is an investigative researcher and author. In 1999, he began researching aerial phenomena reported by Allied military pilots during the Second World War, an effort that culminated in the publication of *Strange Company* in 2007, the same year his focus turned to the mystery surrounding SS general Hans Kammler.